Manchester United

POCKET ANNUAL
1995-96

Phil Bradley
Andy Bradley

Manchester United Pocket Annual 1995-96

Copyright © Phil Bradley – 1995

ISBN: 1-898351-31-7

Typeset by Bruce Smith Books Ltd
Cover Photo: Brian McClair
Photo Credits: European Agencies

First published in 1995 by
Words on Sport

Words on Sport Ltd
PO Box 382
St. Albans
Herts, AL2 3JD

Registration Number: 2917013

Registered Office:
Worplesdon Chase, Worplesdon,
Guildford, Surrey, GU33LA

Printed and bound in the UK by
Bell & Bain, Glasgow

United player, Lou Macari, who is sacked as manager of Celtic after less than eight months in charge of the Glasgow outfit.

18th   Roy Keane and Denis Irwin star in the Republic of Ireland's shock 1-0 World Cup victory over eventual finalists, Italy.

20th   Phelan and West Bromwich Albion resolve their differences and the player leaves Old Trafford on a free transfer.

July

11th   Bryan Robson appoints former United player Gordon McQueen as first team Coach at Middlesbrough and extends his 'United' backroom team still further with Viv Anderson.

12th   United announce that they are not interested in joining in an auction to get Norwich City striker Chris Sutton. He signs later in the month for Blackburn Rovers in a deal rumoured to set back Jack Walker £5m.

13th   Eric Cantona is held in handcuffs in Los Angeles after an alleged press Box punch up moments before the World Cup semi–final between Brazil and Sweden on which he was supposed to be co–commentating for French TV. He is released by the police after the intervention of World Cup Press Officer, Guido Tognini.

16th   United are rocked by the news that their jinxed second choice 'keeper, Gary Walsh, has had to undergo an emergency operation to remove his appendix which means he is likely to miss the start of the season.

19th   United are drawn in the same group as Barcelona in the European Cup. Incredibly, they also face a trip back to Turkey to face Galatasary if the Turks overcome Luxembourg club, Avenir.

20th   Former United hero, Bryan Robson, celebrates his first game in charge at Middlesbrough by scoring in a 2-0 victory at Torquay.

23rd   United, fielding a young Reserve team, go down 3-2 to Rochdale in the first Group match of the 1994/95 Lancashire Cup. David Beckham scores both United goals.

24th   United starlet, Terry Cooke, scores twice for England Under 18s but they are held to a 3-3 draw by Norway.

26th   New signing, David May, captains a young Reds side on his United debut as the Old Trafford side beat Burnley 3-2 in the next Lancashire Cup group match. His first game, however, is marred by a booking, a fate reserved also for Chris Casper, son of former Burnley manager, Frank Casper. United's scorers are Simon Davies, Paul Scholes and Lee Sharpe.

30th United, with a full strength line up, surprisingly go two goals down to Irish part–timers, Dundalk, before recovering to win 4-2 despite Cantona missing a penalty in the Reds first full scale pre–season match.

31st United stumble out of the Lancashire Cup when whipped by four first half goals by Bury's former non–league striker, Mark Carter. The Bury side included former Manchester City boss, Peter Reid. The game witnessed the opening of Bury's superb new South Stand.

August

1st United's first team continue their Irish tour with a 3-0 win over Shelbourne. David May came in for the injured Paul Parker. Ferguson used the game to give youngsters Keith Gillespie and Chris Casper some senior experience and Gillespie, in particular, has an impressive game.

3rd United's new kit goes on sale with the expectation that it will net sales of £1m in the first week.

4th United set a new ground record attendance of 28,500 for the revamped Molineux ground with receipts of £227,962 for their friendly arranged with Wolves as part of the deal that took manager's Darren Ferguson to Wolves in 1993/94 season. After falling behind to an early Steve Bull goal, United come back to win 2-1 with goals from Ince and an own goal. Ferguson says "Gillespie was brilliant".

5th Paul Ince is told that United will not break their payment structure for him and that he should either sign the contract that has been on offer for almost twelve months or go. United draw 1-1 with Newcastle United in the Glasgow Rangers four team competition but lose 6-5 on penalties with Cantona again missing a spot kick.

6th United, with a weakened side, lose 1-0 to Rangers in the match for third place. Cantona, introduced as a half time substitute is sent off after receiving two bookings within a couple of minutes.

9th United scramble a 1-1 draw with Cambridge United when Lee Sharpe recovers from hitting his spot kick straight at the Cambridge 'keeper to hit home the rebound. Manager, Alex Ferguson, misses the game as he is in Czechoslovakia for the Preliminary Round European cup–tie between Prague and Gothenburg, the winners of which will be in United's group. Ince, meanwhile, states his side of the contract wrangle. He says he wants a guarantee that if new stars are signed on better terms than himself in future, he will be able to have his contract reviewed. He says "The contract being offered is for six years and a lot can change in that period of time. All I want is some sort of protection. I want to stay at Old Trafford". Meanwhile, former United midfielder, Micky Thomas, is back in European action as he makes his debut for Inter–Cardiff in the UEFA Cup but his side go down 2-0.

10th   Galatasary look to have booked their place against United by winning their away leg against Avenir Beggan 5-1.

12th   Cantona receives a three match ban for his Ibrox sending off which means he will miss the first three League fixtures but leaves him clear to play in the Charity Shield.

13th   Bryan Robson's League debut as a manager ends in success as Middlesbrough beat Burnley 2-0.

14th   United land the FA Charity Shield beating Blackburn Rovers 2-0 as Cantona signs off with his third successful Wembley spot kick in as many months.

15th   United's latest target, 16 year old Graham Cox, keeps the Old Trafford management waiting for his signature as he wins a three way sudden death play–off to win a place in the PGA Junior Golf Championships to take place in Florida in October. The talented youngster has already visited Manchester City, Crewe, Stoke City and Chester for training.

16th   United beat Middlesbrough 3-0 in Clayton Blackmore's Testimonial match at Ayresome Park. A crowd of 19,658 contributed approximately £150,000 to the Welsh international's bank account but Bryan Robson missed the game as he had been over in Lytham St Annes for a tribunal hearing. United's goals came from two Hughes' strikes supplemented by a header from Sharpe. United give goalkeeper Kevin Pilkington his first taste of senior action. The Reds also send a team including Ryan Giggs, Denis Irwin and Roy Keane to Wales to play Cwmbran Town in a memorial game for Frank Martin, a Football League linesman who passed away earlier in the year. United win 3-1 with goals from Dublin, McKee and Cooke.

17th	Galatasary, who gave United and their travelling fans such an ordeal in 1993, are ordered by UEFA to play their next home European tie against Avenir at least 250kms from Istanbul after both linesmen in the away leg in Luxembourg were hit by objects thrown by Turkish fans.
18th	United announce that after months of wrangling, Paul Ince, has finally signed a new contract. Norwich City make a £100,000 bid for Reserve centre–half Neil Whitworth who United bought from Wigan Athletic in 1990 for £95,000. Whitworth has had loan spells at both Preston and Barnsley but has never broken in to United's first team squad.
20th	United commence the defence of their title with a 2-0 home victory over QPR but substitute Paul Parker is sent off.
23rd	United fine Ince £1,000 for his Wembley dance of delight. The FA had told the Old Trafford hierarchy that if United did not discipline the player for leaving the field in the Charity Shield after his fabulous strike to celebrate with the fans behind the goal then they would step in themselves.
24th	United announce a ticket ban for all their European Cup games for anybody other than supporters prepared to go with groups officially organised by the club. Supporters condemn the move as "another rip–off" but United defend their action by saying they will be held responsible by the authorities for the actions of their fans and therefore they want to be in control of the situation. To make matters worse, Galatasary clinch their spot in United's group by beating Avenir 4-0 in the their second leg tie to win 9-1 on aggregate.
26th	It is revealed that Galatasary have claimed their two Yugoslav players are in fact now Turkish nationals and eligible to play as nationals rather than foreigners in European Cup games. The FA are understood to be taking the matter up with UEFA.
27th	United receive orders from UEFA to remove all advertising from their stadium for European matches. The ban extends to the sponsors names on their shirts as Sharp are a major rival to the major European Cup sponsors, Phillips. Sharp were given the opportunity by UEFA to pay 300,000 Swiss francs per game but it would have cost the United sponsors a further £1m for the group games and £2m if the Reds reached the Final.
30th	Latest club to show interest in Neil Whitworth are Kilmarnock.

1st　United pull Mark Hughes out of the Welsh World Cup squad in order to ensure his fitness for the Leeds United game following the failure of his injured hip to respond to treatment.

6th　Kilmarnock complete their move for Neil Whitworth but the big surprise is that Colin McKee, who made his FA Premier debut at the end of 93/94, joins him in a combined deal said to be worth £530,000 to United.

7th　United youngster Keith Gillespie makes his International debut for Northern Ireland who lose 2-1 to Portugal. Another Old Trafford youngster Joe Kirovski just fails to make his International debut as the USA leave him on the bench as the only outfield sub not used against England at Wembley.

8th　Former United striker Joe Jordan resigns as manager at Stoke City after just ten months at the helm. The departure is said to be "by mutual consent".

9th　Dion Dublin joins Coventry City in a £2m deal that looks to be good business by Ferguson. Dublin had played just twelve league games, scoring two goals, since signing for the Reds in a £1m deal two years previously.

10th　Dublin scores on his debut for Coventry to save them a point against QPR but former Red, Brian Carey, is sent off playing for Leicester City in another FA Premiership match.

11th　United lose a competitive game for the first time since April when Leeds beat them 2-1 at Elland Road. It was also the first time that Leeds had beaten United in thirteen attempts.

16th　Old Trafford is chosen by the FA to host the Press Conference that announces big sponsorship from Umbro for the FA Trophy, the non–league game's equivalent of the FA Cup.

17th　Coventry boss Phil Neal makes Dion Dublin captain on his home debut and the former Red obliges with his second goal in two games since his move to Highfield Road as Coventry beat Leeds United 2-1. United reveal that school teacher David Bushell will become their Youth Development Officer from January. He has been manager of the England Schoolboys side for the past eight seasons.

18th　For the first time in two years, United lose their place as the bookie's favourites to win the title. Newcastle United replace the Reds as 13-8 favourites following a 3-2 victory at Highbury. United are close behind at 7-4 with Blackburn on 4-1.

19th   Johnny Berry, who played over 250 games for United in the 1950s until he was seriously injured in the Munich Air Crash, dies in a Hampshire hospital after a short illness.

27th   Former United central defender Graeme Hogg is suspended for ten matches by the Scottish FA after being sent off for fighting with a team–mate!

October

1st   United teenager Phil Neville, a highly rated prospect like his brother Gary, undergoes a cartilage operation. He had been earmarked for promotion along with his brother and the other members of the club's 1992/93 youth team.

4th   Dion Dublin scores a brace to help Coventry to a 5-3 aggregate Coca Cola victory over Wrexham and that makes it six goals in six outings since his move!

8th   United lose at Sheffield Wednesday, it is their third successive way defeat in the FA Premiership.

11th   Former United star, Gordon Strachan, now with Leeds United, announces that he is to retire at the end of the 1994/95 season. In the event, he announced his retirement in January.

13th   Keith Gillespie scores in only his second International as Northern Ireland surprise Austria in Vienna with a 2-1 success in their European Championship qualifier. The goal, a tremendous volley from just outside the area is described by Austrian boss Herbert Prohaska as "The goal of the year".

15th   Dion Dublin makes it seven goals in seven outings since his move to Coventry when he helps the *Sky Blues* to a win at Goodison Park. Bryan Robson's Middlesbrough are blasted from the top of Division One with a 5-1 thrashing at Luton. Newcastle keep top spot in the FAPL with a last second goal at Crystal Palace as United beat West Ham to stay in the top four. The Spanish FA bring forward Barcelona's league game with Valencia by 24 hours to give the Spanish champions more time to recover for their tussle at Old Trafford.

19th   United's Old Trafford confrontation with Barcelona is beamed to no fewer than 107 countries. It is estimated that 80 million people worldwide tune in, an unprecedented number for a club game at such an early stage of the competition.

23rd The Football League back off from their threat to fine United £50,000 for fielding under strength teams in the Coca–Cola Cup. Indeed, they go further and suggest they are to look at the possibility of teams participating in the European Cup being given exemption until the 3rd Round in future. United take advantage of the dismissal of Henning Berg to hammer Blackburn 4-2.

26th United relinquish their grip on the Coca Cola Cup as their young team run out of steam in the final ten minutes against Newcastle United who continue their unbeaten start to the campaign.

29th United take their revenge on Newcastle, beating the Geordies 2-0 in the FAPL to close the gap on the leaders to four points. Dion Dublin scores the only goal of the game as Coventry beat Man City. Up in Scotland, former Red Junior, Colin McKee is on target for Kilmarnock at Motherwell.

November

2nd United crash 4-0 in Barcelona but there is more bad news with Gothenburg beating Galatasary whilst on the domestic front Blackburn go above United when Alan Shearer scores the only goal of the game at Hillsborough. Dion Dublin makes it nine goals in twelve games since his move to Coventry when he nets against Crystal Palace.

4th Former United goalkeeper Gary Bailey, back in England on holiday from his native South Africa, visits Old Trafford saying "I can't believe it, everything is so much bigger and better than when I was here" adding after a pause, "And that includes the 'keeper"!

5th Another full house at Old Trafford but this time it is for a Rugby League international. There are no Bonfire Night crackers, however, as Great Britain are humbled by Australia.

6th United beat Villa and Dion Dublin makes it ten in thirteen at Coventry!

9th It is announced that United have doubled up in the Carling Awards for October as Alex Ferguson takes the Manager's prize and Paul Ince picks up the Player of the Month title.

10th The Reds hammer City 5-0 to take a 45-33 lead in the 'derby' matches. As well as a record win for United, Kanchelskis becomes the

17

first United player to register a hat–trick in a league game since Hughes grabbed three against Millwall in September 1989. He also became the first player on either side to notch a treble in a 'derby' since Franny Lee at Old Trafford in December 1970 and the first United player since Alex Dawson in United's 1960 New Year's Eve 5-1 demolition of City.

11th   Former United boss Ron Atkinson is stunned by the news that he is sacked by Villa just days after the Old Trafford side had won at Villa Park.

15th   Nicky Butt turns out in England Under 21's 1-0 victory over The Republic of Ireland.

16th   Roy Keane scores his first ever international goal for the Republic of Ireland as they swamp a Northern Ireland team including Keith Gillespie 4-0. Another United player on the wrong end of a big scoreline is Mark Hughes as Wales suffer their biggest defeat in over forty years when hammered 5-0 by Georgia. It is announced that the FA have fined John Fashanu £6,000 for criticising Eric Cantona in a newspaper column. It is understood that the Villa striker was reported by United.

19th   United have a 35 year old substitute to thank for going top of the Premiership. Whilst the Reds are disposing of Crystal Palace, Wimbledon bring on the veteran Mick Harford who scores the winner in a 3-2 success over previous leaders Newcastle.

23rd   United lose to Gothenburg 3-1 and are all but out of the European Cup as Paul Ince is sent off.

24th   A crowd of 4,872 turn out at Prenton Park to watch United Reserves play Tranmere Rovers Reserves in a Pontins League game for the first time ever. The game ends 1-1.

26th   United are knocked off top spot when they are held to a draw at Arsenal. Finishing off a bad week for the Reds, Mark Hughes is sent off. Chairman Martin Edwards is also in trouble for visiting the referee's dressing room after the game. Blackburn have a good day to go top – whilst they are hammering QPR 4-0 not one of the other top five can manage a win.

27th   Former United player Jimmy Nicholl masterminds the biggest shock in decades of Scottish football as his Raith Rovers side lift the Scottish League Cup by beating Celtic on penalties, the same way they had beaten Aberdeen in the semi-final. He says after the game

"It would bring a tear to a glass eye". This makes a hat–trick of successes over the weekend for former Reds in management. Bryan Robson's Middlesbrough returned to the top of the Endsleigh League Division One and Sammy McIlroy's Macclesfield Town consolidated their lead at the top of the GM Vauxhall Conference.

28th   United are hit by the news that Peter Schmeichel will be out of action for at least a month with a back injury. He has torn muscles around his spinal discs.

29th   The referee of the Arsenal match, Kelvin Morton, confirms he has included a reference to Edwards' visit to see him in the dressing rooms after the Arsenal game in his report to the FA's Disciplinary Committee.

December

2nd   Martin Edwards learns he is to be let off with a warning over his intrusion into the referee's dressing room at Highbury following the recent drawn game against Arsenal.

8th   United Reserves pull in a crowd of 4,500 at Bury FC for their Pontins League match with Leeds United. This compares with the attendance of 2,700 at Gigg Lane the previous Saturday for Bury's home Endsleigh League game against Exeter City.

17th   United lose at home to Nottingham Forest but there is uproar at England player Stuart Pearce's alleged racial remarks directed at Paul Ince.

20th   Paul Ince says he is prepared to accept Pearce's offered apology. Ince says "I knew he would be on the phone soon because he is not the sort of player who would want to carry on this type of thing".

21st   United's Youth team need an injury time goal to grab a replay against Charlton Athletic in the 3rd Round of the FA Youth Cup at Old Trafford. United's hero is John Hudson whose last gasp effort cancelled out a goal as early as the seventh minute from Charlton hot shot Keith Dowson who was scoring his sixteenth goal of the campaign.

22nd   United's Mark Hughes is flattened with one punch by a club bouncer. The incident happened as Hughes was leaving Manchester's Hacienda Club with team mate Paul Ince. Hughes passed a flippant comment about Ince's colour whereupon the bouncer hit the Welshman.

Hughes said afterwards "It was just a joke, there is no problem between me and Paul, in fact we are the best of mates". Considering the fuss Ince made only days earlier about remarks made by Stuart Pearce, Hughes' comments would appear to have been ill advised to say the least.

26th   United win 3-2 at Stamford Bridge after Chelsea had pulled level from two down.

28th   The Reds slip up at home drawing 1-1 with next to bottom Leicester City.

31st   The year ends on a personal high note for Manager Alex Ferguson. Not only is it his birthday but he receives a CBE in the New Year's Honours. The team, however, fail to celebrate as they stumble to a 2-2 draw at Southampton in a lack–lustre display. Blackburn win 1-0 at Crystal Palace to end 1994 three points clear of the Reds with a game in hand. Twelve months earlier United had gone into 1994 and their pursuit of the double with a 14 point lead.

January

2nd   Blackburn Rovers come from behind to beat West Ham and increase their lead over United to six points.

3rd   Andrei Kanchelskis is presented with the Football Club Directory Good News Award for individuals who have made a significant contribution to promote the good side of football. The ceremony takes place prior to the kick off against Coventry City which sees the 'good news' continue with a 2-0 win that reduces Blackburn's lead at the top of the table by half.

7th   Lee Sharpe begins his come back by scoring the only goal of the game in the 'A' team's victory over Burnley 'A'.

8th   United are drawn at home against Wrexham in the Fourth Round of the FA Cup if the Reds can overcome Sheffield United at Bramall Lane. Wrexham qualified for the Fourth Round by doing something United couldn't earlier in the season – they beat Ipswich Town in the Third Round. On foreign fields, United's European conquerors Barcelona are in crisis. Their latest failing is a 5-0 defeat at the hands of Real Madrid with Stoichkov sent off for the eleventh time and facing a long ban which means that the Spanish club who took United to the cleaners could be without both strikers who did the damage. There are strong rumours that Romario wants to return to Brazil where he has written in his contract he will only cost a Brazilian club £3.5m although it will be difficult for a Brazilian outfit to raise that sort of cash.

9th   United beat Sheffield United 2-0 in awful conditions as the game goes ahead with the elements blowing a gale and pouring rain. Sharpe makes his first team return as substitute and Newcastle United manager Kevin Keegan is spotted in the stand.

10th   United stun the football world when they break the British record transfer fee by paying £6m plus the promising services of Keith Gillespie to land the signature of Newcastle United's free scoring Andy Cole all of which explains the appearance of Kevin Keegan at the previous evening's game.

11th   United's Reserves virtually relinquish all hope of retaining their Pontins Central League title when they crash 0-3 at Everton. They have now lost half of their sixteen fixtures to date after losing only five times in the whole of 93/94.

12th   United's Youth team make a sensational come back in their FA Youth Cup replay with Charlton Athletic. Trailing by two goals at the interval they score five times in a thirteen minute spell to win 5-2.

13th   Friday the thirteenth. Nicky Butt has his £15,000 Renault Clio pinched from outside the Cotton Tree pub in his home suburb of Gorton and the car is involved in a serious hit and run accident in which a man and his daughter are lucky to escape death. The thieves then set fire to the stolen vehicle. Paul Ince is told he will serve a three match European ban for his sending off against Gothenburg.

14th   Blackburn Rovers take a six point lead at the top of the Premiership when they dispose of Nottingham Forest.

15th   Neither Andy Cole or Keith Gillespie play in the United game against Newcastle as part of the agreement reached five days earlier. The man under most threat from the move, Mark Hughes, is injured and carried off as he scores the opening goal but Newcastle later equalise and Blackburn's lead is beginning to assume ominous proportions as they go five points clear with a game in hand. Nicky Butt completes a miserable 48 hours by being substituted at half time suffering from concussion but, there again, perhaps he wanted to forget things anyway!

16th   Former United player Gordon Strachan announces his retirement three weeks short of his 38th birthday. He was signed by United from

Aberdeen in August 1984 for £500,000 and left for Leeds in March 1989 in return for £300,000. The former midfielder, who has been plagued by back injury in recent months, is to stay at Elland Road in a coaching capacity.

18th   Blackburn Rovers are knocked out of the FA Cup by Newcastle United leaving United's main rivals with just the Championship to concentrate on.

19th   Paul Ince begins his come back from injury with a run out in the reserves against Stoke City at Gigg Lane.

20th   Blackburn boss Kenny Dalglish unashamedly tries to influence the referee for the weekend confrontation with the Reds by calling for the officials "to refuse to be intimidated by Old Trafford. It is a partisan stadium and hard for any referee. Decisions must be based on what happens not what the crowd think happened. I just hope the officials are up to it".

22nd   Dalglish's plan backfires on him as United win 1-0 and the referee controversially disallows a last gasp effort from Sherwood that would have given Rovers a draw.

25th   Former United player Mark Robins scores the only goal of the game following his £1m move to Leicester City from Norwich as the bottom club beat Manchester City and Wrexham warm up for their trip to Old Trafford in the FA Cup by drawing 2-2 with Bangor City in the Welsh Cup. But the sensational news comes from over 200 miles away as Eric Cantona is sent off at Crystal Palace and then leaps over hoardings to assault a spectator as he is led off the pitch.

26th   The FA announce that Cantona has 14 days in which to answer the charge of damaging the integrity of the game. It seems certain that the Police will also bring criminal charges. It is revealed that the spectator involved ran down eleven steps of terracing to hurl abuse at Cantona as he left the field and that he had a conviction in 1992 for attempted robbery at a petrol station. Allegations are also now made that Paul Ince assaulted a Palace fan.

27th   United suspend Cantona from all first team action until the end of the season and fine him the maximum £20,000 possible under the terms of his contract. The FA do not appear to be happy with the fact that United's ban leaves Cantona free to play in Reserve team football. Crystal Palace announce that they have banned the fan involved in the Cantona incident from their stadium for the rest of the campaign. The

Police also indicate that he may well be charged along with Cantona and, possibly, Ince whom they say they wish to interview at a later date.

28th United go a goal down to Wrexham in the fourth Round FA Cup tie but recover to win 5-2. Blackburn, however, beat Ipswich 4-1 with Alan Shearer netting a treble to go four points clear in the league with a game in hand.

February

1st Blackburn Rovers lose their 'keeper Tim Flowers after just two minutes when he is sent off against Leeds United. But a Shearer penalty looks to have given them a seven point lead over the Reds until a late penalty for Leeds reduces the gaps back to five points. United's Youth team beat the holders, Arsenal, 2-1 to progress into the last eight of the FA Youth Cup.

3rd The Police state they are taking the accusations against Eric Cantona and Paul Ince very seriously and will be interviewing them shortly to determine whether to bring charges against them.

4th United enjoy a good day. They beat Villa to reduce Blackburn's lead to two points whilst nearest challengers Newcastle lose 3-0 at QPR and Forest draw with Liverpool. Bryan Robson's Middlesbrough are knocked off the top of Division One when they are beaten at home by Reading and drop to third as both Tranmere and Bolton win to go above them.

5th A good weekend for the Reds is complete when Blackburn lose 3-1 at Spurs. This leaves Rovers just two points in front on level games played.

8th The Police interview Paul Ince regarding his alleged assault on spectator at Crystal Palace but is allowed home pending further enquiries. The Police express annoyance at Eric Cantona not turning up as he is on holiday in the Carribean.

9th United hit back at the Police saying no appointment had been made for Cantona and that the club had sent him away because of the TV crews and posse of photographers camped outside his house.

10th Kenny Dalglish takes a cheap jibe at United saying "It took them 26 years to win the title, it won't take us as long". Obviously, Kenny is not too hot at Maths – the last time Blackburn won the title was in 1914 – some 81 years ago!

11th	United beat City in the 122nd League 'Derby' game and go top of the League as Blackburn do not play until the following day. The 'A' team beat Crewe Alexandra 4-2 with American international Jovan Kirovski slamming a hat–trick. The win gives the youngsters the Lancashire League Division One title. But more trouble for Eric Cantona who is reported to have now karate kicked an ITN news reporter in the Caribbean.

13th   There is unexpected support for Eric Cantona from FA Chairman, Bert Millichip, who says Cantona's latest episode is totally "unrelated to football or this country" and will not play a part in any action the FA may take against him for his earlier misdemeanour. Support, too, from Alex Ferguson who says "The news reporter got off lightly. Anyone taking photographs of a man's wife six months pregnant in her swimwear on a private beach deserves what he got and more. Any husband worth his salt would have reacted like Eric did".

14th   Former United boss Ron Atkinson is installed as manager of Coventry City.

15th   United players Paul Ince, Gary Pallister and Denis Irwin are playing in the Republic of Ireland v England international that is abandoned in Dublin due to rioting. Mark Hughes begins his comeback with a goal for the reserves against Tranmere Rovers' second string in the Pontins League.

18th   The 'B' team lose at Preston. It is their third defeat on the trot and, after looking to have their Championship wrapped up in the middle of January, will now struggle to win it after taking just one point from the last twelve.

19th   United beat Leeds in the FA Cup and are then given a home draw against QPR. Up at Newcastle, former Red, Keith Gillespie scores twice for the "Magpies" who knock Man City out 3-1.

21st   Eric Cantona is formally charged by the Police for his karate style kick at the Crystal Palace game. Former United player George Graham is sacked as manager of Arsenal for "actions not in the best interest of the club" after allegations of taking a "bung" in the transfer deal involving John Jensen.

22nd   A busy day for the diary. United win at Norwich but stay two points behind Blackburn who win 2-1 at home to Wimbledon. Stewart Houston, who played in United's losing FA Cup Final side of 1976, is named as manager of Arsenal until the end of the 1994/95 season whilst up in Scotland, former United goalkeeper Jim Leighton is called into Scotland's squad for a European qualifier. Even further afield, United's arch European enemies, Galatasary creep into the Turkish Cup Final after winning a penalty shoot out against Fenerbache.

24th   Eric Cantona is suspended from all football until 1st October 1995 and fined a further £10,000 by the Football Association for his assault on the Crystal Palace agitator.

25th   United put on a poor display to lose 0-1 at Everton where Andrei Kanchelskis is amazingly relegated to the subs bench. Fortunately, the damage is limited as Blackburn Rovers are surprisingly held at home by Norwich and only increase their lead to three points.

28th   Ian Rush scores as Liverpool knock Wimbledon out of the FA Cup. The strike sees the Welsh international equal the English FA Cup record of 41 goals held by United's former Scottish international Denis Law. United's Youth team reach the semi finals of the FA Youth Cup by beating Aston Villa 3-2 in a thriller at Villa Park. But United's strike force takes another blow when young Paul Scholes tears his ankle ligaments in training to sideline himself for at least a month.

March

1st   Andrei Kanchelskis, upset at being dropped at Everton says he wants a transfer. Ferguson responds by saying he is going nowhere.

4th   United create FA Premiership history when they smash nine past Ipswich Town. It is the club's biggest win since beating Anderlecht 10-0 in 1956 and their biggest league victory in 103 years. Cole is the first player to score five in a FAPL game and the first to score five for United in either the Football League or the FAPL. It is Alex Ferguson's biggest win as a manager but it isn't, however, Ipswich's record league defeat – that was 10-1 against Fulham in a First Division game on 26 December 1963. Having started the day with a goal difference six worse than rivals Blackburn Rovers, United end it with a goal difference two better! But there is a 44th Birthday present for Rovers manager Kenny Dalglish as they win 1-0 at Villa Park where the home side are denied a blatant penalty in the last minute. Over at Preston, on loan David Beckham scores direct from a corner in the 2-2 draw against Doncaster.

6th   Andrei Kanchelskis drops a bombshell by opting to use his right to play for Russia in a meaningless midweek friendly and flies out leaving United to face Wimbledon the following night without the Russian. Even worse news for the Reds is that the Police have now decided to charge Paul Ince with assault for his part in the Crystal Palace fracas.

7th   Both United and the FA say they are not to act on the Paul Ince matter until the result of his Court hearing is known. Ironically, Selhurst Park, the scene of the Cantona/ Ince trouble, is once again the setting for indiscipline when United beat Wimbledon 1-0. The Dons have four players booked and one sent off whilst their manager Joe Kinnear is also shown the red card. Kinnear later lands himself in further trouble when he describes the referee, Robbie Hart of Darlington, as using "his usual Hitler fashion" in making his decision to "send off" the Wimbledon boss.

9th   Kanchelskis returns from Russia and says "United want me out. Nobody tried to stop me going to Russia until it was too late. That shows they don't want me".

10th   Ferguson says he cannot even begin to fathom what is going on in the mind of his Russian speed merchant. "But nothing will be done until after our FA Cup tie with QPR. We must concentrate all our energies on winning that one and then perhaps we can get down to sorting the problem out. But, for the record, we did apply to the Russians for the release of Kanchelskis two weeks prior to the game". The United boss was also quoted as saying he was of the opinion that "outside forces are getting to work on Andrei to destabilise his position with United. But he signed a three year contract with us only last summer and I expect him to honour it just as he would expect us to honour it".

11th   United old boy, Dion Dublin, does the Reds a big favour by giving Coventry a surprise lead against Blackburn. But Shearer scores a controversial equaliser two minutes from time to give Rovers a four point lead from a game more than United. Spurs knock Liverpool out of the FA Cup and the significance of that is Denis Law's FA Cup goalscoring record stands for another year as Ian Rush fails to find the scoresheet against the London side. On loan David Beckham scores what proves to be the winner in a 3-2 victory for Preston against Fulham.

12th   United reach the semi final of the FA Cup when they beat QPR 2-0 with Lee Sharpe notching his first ever FA Cup goal for the Reds. They are then paired with the winners of Crystal Palace or Wolverhampton Wanderers who drew 1-1.

14th	Liverpool's remote chance of getting into the title race is extinguished when they lose at home to Coventry City for whom Peter Ndlovu scores a hat–trick. He becomes the first visiting player to notch a treble at Anfield since Norwich City's Terry Allcock performed the feat in 1962 when Liverpool were still in the Second Division! It is the Anfield club's second successive home defeat in four days and they have not lost three home games on the trot for well over thirty years. Could United feel the backlash when they visit the famous stadium in five days time? The answer is an emphatic "Yes".
15th	United fail to close the gap significantly on Blackburn when they are held to a goalless draw at home to Spurs. It is the first time they have failed to score at Old Trafford in 94/95. In Europe, both United's Group conquerors, Gothenburg and Barcelona, go out at the quarter final stage. Gothenburg draw 2-2 at home with Bayern Munich but lose out on the away goals rule whilst Barcelona go down 2-1 at Paris St Germain to lose 3-2 on aggregate.
17th	United unveil plans for a new £28m development which will give the club the biggest cantilever stand in Europe. It will increase capacity to over 55,000 but whilst it is being built attendances will reduce to 31,000.
18th	Alan Shearer scores his 100th league goal as Blackburn beat Chelsea 2-1 at Ewood Park to go six points clear of United at the top of the FAPL.
19th	The Reds go down 2-0 at Liverpool after a lack lustre display. With eight games left they are now six points adrift and are now also back to having an inferior goal difference. They appear to have a mountain to climb. Further bad news is that Bruce is booked and will miss the semi final after topping the 40 point mark. By comparison, his central defensive partner, Gary Pallister, is without a single booking all season!
20th	More bad news for Paul Ince. He is omitted from the England squad to play Uruguay by Terry Venables who cites the reason as being Ince's pending Court Hearing.
21st	Gary Neville and Nicky Butt are named in the England Under 21 squad to play the Republic of Ireland. Former United player Gordon Strachan joins former United boss Ron Atkinson at Coventry City. Strachan will be Atkinson's number two with a guarantee of moving into the hot seat when Atkinson finishes in two year's time.

27

22nd   United beat Arsenal 3-0 to move to within three points of Blackburn but with a game more played. Crystal Palace win their FA Cup replay and will be United's opponents in the semi-final. Given the Eric Cantona situation that began against Palace, the game could make an interesting confrontation.

23rd   Eric Cantona is punished for the third time when he is incredibly sentenced to two week's imprisonment for his assault on the Crystal Palace fan. The player requests bail in order that he can lodge an appeal against the outrageous sentence but is refused it by the woman magistrate who appears intent on grabbing the headlines herself. This follows the fines of £20,000 and £10,000 already imposed on him by United and the FA in addition to his ban from playing football. He was later released from the cells after his legal team secured bail from a Judge in the High Court pending an appeal against the savage sentence. Paul Ince's case was adjourned to May as he pleaded not guilty. Paradoxically, Alex Ferguson, almost unnoticed in the furore, received his CBE at Buckingham Palace and Andy Cole is called up into the England squad to replace the injured Alan Shearer.

24th   The originator of the trouble at Selhurst Park pleads not guilty to two charges of foul and abusive behaviour. He alleges he only said "Off, Off, Off, Go off for an early bath". The case against him is adjourned until May. Lee Sharpe is the latest United player to be called up to the England squad for the game against Uruguay but he has to cry off due to undergoing treatment for an injury.

25th   United's Youth team outplay Wimbledon in the FA Youth Cup FA but only have a 2-1 first leg lead to show for it. as they miss chance after chance at Old Trafford in front of a crowd of 6,167 which is a higher attendance than the Don's first team average home gate! Phil Neville and Terry Cooke get the all important goals.

26th   Former United skipper Bryan Robson scores his first competitive goal for Middlesbrough as they beat Port Vale 3-0 to go four points clear at the top of Division One. It maintains Robson's incredible record of having scored at least one goal in the Football League or FA Premiership in each of the last twenty-two seasons! A Scottish Sunday paper states that Kanchelskis has let it be known that he would very interested in a move to Glasgow Rangers.

27th   Nicky Butt and Gary Neville play in the England Under 21 side that defeats the Republic of Ireland 2-0 in a European qualifier. Inter-Milan make a £5.5m offer for Eric Cantona which Martin Edwards says will simply lay on the table until Cantona's appeal against his jail sentence is heard. The money is hardly important to the Reds who announce on the same day record profits of £11.2m for the first *six* months of the season. Turnover was £36.4m for the period ended 31st January with merchandising contributing £14.7m. Playing in the European Champions League saw television income lifted from just under £2m to almost £5m.

28th A poll conducted for the magazine *Four Four Two* with a panel including the likes of Michel Platini, David Platt, Gordon Taylor, Graham Kelly, Sepp Blatter and several top referees, places George Best third in an all time list of The Greatest Players. United have no fewer than thirteen players in the top one hundred of the list which is headed by Pele in front of Johan Cruyff. In addition to Best, they are Bobby Charlton (ninth), Duncan Edwards, Bryan Robson, Ryan Giggs, Albert Quixall, Gordon Strachan, Jesper Olsen, Denis Law, Mark Hughes, Eric Cantona, Arnold Muhren, and Andrei Kanchelskis.

29th Former United 'keeper, the much maligned Jim Leighton, makes an incredible international come back five years after he last played for Scotland and plays a stormer to keep a blank sheet against a Russian side that includes Andrei Kanchelskis. Another Ex–Red, Keith Gillespie lays on Northern Ireland's goal for Dowie in a 1-1 draw against the Republic of Ireland team that includes Roy Keane and Denis Irwin. It is Northern Ireland's first ever goal in the Republic. Andy Cole comes on as a 72nd minute substitute at Wembley to earn his first ever cap and hits the bar with a header in a 0-0 draw. Other United players in action for their countries are Gary Pallister, Ryan Giggs and Peter Schmeichel but France, without Eric Cantona, are held to a goalless draw by Israel.

30th Steve Bruce, expecting a four match ban, gets off with two and a fine of £750 for topping the forty point mark in bookings when he is hauled before the FA. But he still misses United's FA Cup Semi Final against Crystal Palace and the league game against Leeds United.

31st Eric Cantona's prison sentence is squashed and the obvious sentence of community service applied. So the lady magistrate who seized her chance to grab a moment of fame finishes up looking rather silly.

April

1st   Everton, without five players including Duncan Ferguson through suspension, go two down in six minutes to Blackburn Rovers but then give the League leaders a torrid time only to narrowly fail to haul back the deficit. Blackburn go six points clear leaving United having to beat Leeds the following day to stay in the hunt.

2nd   Leeds mount a ten men defence to thwart United in a goalless draw that leaves United's title dreams looking just that – a dream.

3rd   Former United captain, Martin Buchan, the first player to lift both the FA Cup and the Scottish Cup, is fined £100 with £25 costs after pleading guilty at Bury Magistrates Court to driving without due care and attention. The Court heard that Buchan was now a Promotions manager with the football boot company Puma and was on business for them when he caused a minor accident on the M62 in November.

4th   Blackburn edge nearer the title when they beat QPR thanks to a Chris Sutton goal. The win puts them eight points clear. The Reserves play out a predictable draw with Sheffield United – it is their fourth consecutive drawn game whilst the 'Blades' second string have finished level in their last five! Hopes of an all Manchester FA Youth Cup Final disappear when Spurs beat City Youth 5-0 at Maine Road in the First Leg of their semi final tie.

6th   Former United manager Ron Atkinson is a surprise winner of the Carling Manager of the Month Award. His latest side, Coventry City, had won just one of their five games in March, scoring four goals and conceding six, and finished in exactly the same position, 12th, that they had started the month. A Carling spokesman said "We don't decide on statistics alone". A good job for Big Ron they don't!

7th   Former United 'keeper Jim Leighton continues his resurgent form with a penalty save for Hibernian in the Scottish FA Cup semi–final against Celtic. The game remains goalless. Nearer home Oldham Athletic are furious with United after the Reds sign 16 year old Bolton based striker David Brown. The *Latics* ask the Football League to conduct an inquiry into the circumstances of the signing. They had had the youngster at their School of Excellence for five years and had offered him a contract that met his family's requirements.

8th   United's Youth team make it to the Final of the FA Youth Cup with a double strike from Terry Cooke and a third from Phil Mulryne as the young Reds beat Wimbledon 3-0 at Selhurst Park to make it 5-1 on aggregate.

9th Tragedy in Walsall as a Crystal Palace fan dies in a brawl outside a pub when United and Crystal Palace fans meet up prior to the FA Cup semi final. United twice come from behind to earn a replay. A sign of the swing towards Blackburn comes at the PFA Awards. United have only two players in the 'best' Premiership side with Blackburn six! Paul Ince and Gary Pallister are United's two representatives with Blackburn contributing Tim Flowers, Graeme Le Saux, Colin Hendry, Tim Sherwood, Alan Shearer and Chris Sutton.

12th United beat Palace at Villa Park in the replay to reach the FA Cup Final. The gate of just under 18,000 is the smallest for a semi final since the Second World War. But there is bad news for the Reds as Roy Keane loses his temper and is sent off for stamping.

13th The FA announce that Roy Keane and the Crystal Palace player Darren Patterson, who was sent off with him, will face additional charges of bringing the game into disrepute. An FA spokesman said "They clearly ignored the requests of their respective managers for everybody to be on their best behaviour following the death of the Crystal Palace supporter on Sunday. It would seem they couldn't have done anything but bring the game into disrepute with their actions and they will be called upon to explain themselves".

14th Keane apologises for his part in the Villa Park incident and United threaten to take the matter to Court if the FA carry out their threat to bring disrepute charges, an action that would keep Keane in their Cup Final plans. The latest blow to United's season is confirmation that Kanchelskis is out for the rest of 94/95 and is to undergo a hernia operation.

15th United beat the already relegated Leicester City 4-0 and are given fleeting hope of retaining their title when Blackburn drop two points to an injury time goal at Leeds. Former United central defender Billy Garton and George Switzer, a member of the 'Class of '92' that won the FA Youth Cup, are denied a Wembley appearance when their non-league side, Hyde United of the UniBond League, are narrowly beaten 2-1 on aggregate by Kidderminster Harriers in the semi final of the FA 'Umbro' Trophy.

17th United throw away another chance of closing the gap on Blackburn when they only draw at home to Chelsea. A win would have put everything back in the melting pot as Manchester City, of all clubs, do

United the favour of beating Blackburn at Ewood Park. The gap, however, is only reduced to five points.

18th　A goal three minutes from time by Ben Thornley gives United victory over Lugano in the Final of the 55th Swiss International Youth Tournament. The Swiss side had earlier equalised a Jovan Kirovski opener. The young Reds therefore went one better than the previous season when they were beaten by Barcelona in the Final. The 1995 competition included teams from Benfica, Napoli, Kaiserslautern, Barcelona and PSV Eindhoven amongst others.

20th　Former United player Stewart Houston, now managing Arsenal, sees his side reach the Final of the European Cup–Winners Cup in a penalty shoot out against Sampdoria. Chelsea, beaten by the Reds in the 1994 FA Cup Final but able to take their place in the Cup–Winners Cup courtesy of United's double success beat Real Zaragoza 3-1 in the other semi but fail to make it an all English Final as they lost the first leg 3-0. Blackburn appear to all but wrap up the title when they beat Crystal Palace 2-1.

22nd　A Graeme Tomlinson goal against Everton gives United Reserves their first win in over two months.

26th　An old foe of United's, Galatasary's Mr Hakan, turns up with a goal that helps Turkey to a surprise European Qualifier away victory over the Swiss. Denis Irwin and Peter Schmeichel play as their respective countries grab 1-0 wins over Portugal and Macedonia but Mark Hughes returns from Germany the happiest of the lot as Wales hold Klinsmann and Co to a one all draw. An 86th minute goal from United junior John Curtis gives England Under 16s a 2-1 win over Slovakia as his side all but qualify for the quarter finals of the UEFA Youth Championships in Belgium.

27th　In the Groundsman of the Year awards, Manchester United's Keith Kent takes the prize for best FA Premiership playing surface and receives a Wilkinson ceremonial sword. The overall winner, however, is Charlie Hasler of Leyton Orient. Former United player David McCreery resigns as manager of Hartlepool United. He had been appointed boss in September after John MacPhail's sacking but is told after the club's best win of the campaign against Third Division Champions Carlisle United that his contract, which expires at the end of the season, will not be renewed. He decides to resign rather than play out time.

28th	At an Old Trafford Press Conference, United end speculation over Eric Cantona's future by announcing that he has signed a new contract. Inter Milan are said to be stunned.
29th	United announce they are to offer Denis Irwin a new three year contract that will take him up to the age of 33. Irwin still had a year of his present contract to run.
30th	Blackburn are beaten 2-0 by West Ham United to give the Reds a slender lifeline.

May

1st	United beat Coventry City to reduce the points deficit on Blackburn to five with a game in hand. Coventry play former United star Gordon Strachan and have further Old Trafford old boys Ron Atkinson and Dion Dublin pitting their wits against United in a tremendous game that sees the Reds just get the best of a five goal thriller. The Youth team are beaten 2-0 by Manchester City in the semi-final of the Lancashire Youth Cup at Maine Road. United's Youth international David Johnson is sent off after an incident that saw City defender Ged Tarpey stretchered off.
2nd	Alex Ferguson answers the charges of poaching youngsters by saying "I cannot understand what the fuss is all about. The boys have a free choice before committing themselves as professionals. Its swings and roundabouts. For example we lost Nicky Barmby to Spurs after coaching him for years but it's no use bleating about it. Of the three complaints, one asked to join us because his club's previous manager had left and the club had been relegated, the second had not been contacted by his club for a year which left him disillusioned and the third approached us. He is a good player so are we just expected to say go away?" The players involved in the poaching in addition to Oldham's David Brown mentioned earlier were Andrew Wright of Leeds United and Arsenal's Matthew Wicks.
3rd	Bryan Robson's Middlesbrough capture the First Division Championship when their nearest challengers, Bolton Wanderers, are held to a draw by Stoke City. Sammy McIlroy's Macclesfield Town are also confirmed as GM Vauxhall Conference Champions.
5th	Former United player Lou Macari, now manager of Stoke City, takes the Carling Manager of the Month award for April in the Endsleigh

League First Division. United announce Season Ticket prices for 95/96 as follows; South Stand £342, East, West Upper £304, Family Stand £304 (children £152), East Lower £209 (£104.50), West Lower Lower £228 (£114).

7th   United beat Sheffield Wednesday to narrow Blackburn's lead to two points.

8th   Blackburn Rovers beat Newcastle United with an Alan Shearer goal to leave United five points adrift again. Former United goalkeeper Dave Gaskell, now 54 and living in Wrexham, is discharged from hospital following a triple heart by-pass operation.

9th   Keane discovers he will not be called before a FA Disciplinary Committee prior to the FA Cup Final leaving him free to play in the showpiece. Tony Hopley, who played for United in the 1986 FA Youth Cup Final against Manchester City, scores for The Joiners pub team as they beat Southern Hotel 2-1 in the Final of the North West Champions Cup.

10th   United beat Southampton with the aid of a late penalty from Denis Irwin to take the Championship to a last day decider. If United can beat West Ham United at Upton Park and Blackburn fail to defeat Liverpool at Anfield, the title is United's. In Paris, former United player Stewart Houston sees his Arsenal side cruelly beaten twenty seconds from the end of extra time by Real Zaragoza in the European Cup-winners Cup Final.

11th   United's Youth team lose 2-1 to Spurs in the First Leg of the FA Youth Cup Final at White Hart Lane. But it could have been much worse as United 'keeper Paul Gibson made a fine save to prevent the London side, with five Irish players in it, going three up before Terry Cooke got one back for the young Reds six minutes from time.

12th   Everton's Duncan Ferguson is found guilty of headbutting John McStay of Raith Rovers by a Scottish court. The Scottish FA had originally banned Ferguson for twelve games for the incident but suspended it until after the outcome of the Court case was known. Ferguson, however, was freed to take part in the FA Cup Final as the Court withheld sentence pending reports. Gary Neville, who also faced missing the Cup Final after collecting 41 disciplinary points, will be at Wembley after the FA fined him £1,000 rather than impose a ban which would have prevented the youngster from playing. Stockport County announce they are giving a free transfer to former United forward Deniol Graham.

34

14th	Blackburn lose at Liverpool but the Reds are frustrated at West Ham in a 1-1 draw that sees Rovers lift the Championship. The winning margin of one point is easily the closest in the three year history of the FAPL following United's triumphs by ten and eight points respectively. Blackburn also fail to equal United's record number of 92 points set in 1993/94.
15th	United's Youth team win the FA Youth Cup after their third appearance in the last four Finals. But it's a close thing as Terry Cooke only equalises a 2-1 First Leg deficit in the final seconds of normal time. A crowd of 20,190 don't see any more goals in extra time leaving the trophy to be decided on penalties. Cooke is again the hero with the last spot kick after Spurs captain Kevin Maher converts his side's final kick to level the scores at 3-3 with just one kick remaining for the Reds before sudden death. Earlier, captain Phil Neville had hit the crossbar with the first kick but Neil Mustoe, Ronnie Wallwork and Des Baker all successfully converted their efforts.
20th	United's season ends in defeat at Wembley where Everton beat the Reds for the second time in three months by the only goal of the game to bring the curtain down on a disappointing week.
23rd	Gary Neville is the surprise choice in a 22 man squad named by Terry Venables for Umbro Cup Tournament to be held in June against Japan, Sweden, and Brazil. Also included in the squad are team-mates Paul Ince, Andy Cole and Gary Pallister.
24th	Paul Ince is found not guilty at Croydon Magistrates Court of assaulting a 48 year old father of two on the night of the Eric Cantona affair. In court it was revealed that the man who had lodged the complaint had run thirteen rows to hurl abuse at Ince, had been arrested for shouting 'Gestapo' at police on a previous occasion, had been banned by the Surrey FA for abusing a referee when acting as a manager of a Sunday league team and was so renowned for causing trouble that Millwall hooligans had put up 'Wanted' notices of him near their ground!
25th	Paul Ince withdraws from the England squad for the Umbro Cup saying he wants to spend some time with his family to get over the court case.

PREMIERSHIP GOALS

United's Goals Scored by Time Period

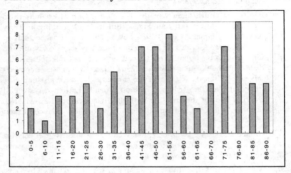

United's Goals Conceded by Time Period

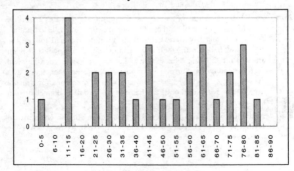

The Season
Match by Match

Results Summary

Date	Type	Opposition	Ven	Score	Scorers	Att
30/07/94	Friendly	Dundalk	(a)	4-2	Hughes 2, Ince, Giggs	12,000
1/08/94	Friendly	Shelbourne	(a)	3-0	Ince, Cantona (Pen), McClair	12,000
3/08/94	Friendly	Wolves	(a)	2-1	Ince, Blades og	28,500
5/08/94	Friendly	Newcastle Utd	(n)	1-1	Cantona	27,000
6/08/94	Friendly	Glasgow Rangers	(a)	0-1		29,000
9/08/94	Friendly	Cambridge Utd	(a)	1-1	Sharpe (Pen)	9,194
14/08/94	Char Shield	Blackburn Rovs	(n)	2-0	Hughes, Ince	60,402
16/08/94	Friendly	Middlesbrough	(a)	3-0	Hughes 2, Sharpe	19,673
20/08/94	FAPL	QPR	(h)	2-0	Hughes, McClair	43,214
22/08/94	FAPL	Notts Forest	(a)	1-1	Kanchelskis	22,072
27/08/94	FAPL	Tottenham H.	(a)	1-0	Bruce	24,502
31/08/94	FAPL	Wimbledon	(h)	3-0	Cantona, McClair, Giggs	43,440
11/09/94	FAPL	Leeds United	(a)	1-2	Cantona (Pen)	39,396
14/09/94	EC	IFK Gothenburg	(h)	4-2	Giggs 2, Kanchelskis, Sharpe	33,625
17/09/94	FAPL	Liverpool	(h)	2-0	Kanchelskis, McClair	43,740
21/09/94	CCC 2R1L	Port Vale	(a)	2-1	Scholes 2	18,605
24/09/94	FAPL	Ipswich Town	(a)	2-3	Cantona, Scholes	22,559
28/09/94	EC	Galatasary	(a)	0-0		30,000
1/10/94	FAPL	Everton	(h)	2-0	Kanchelskis, Sharpe	43,803
5/10/94	CCC 2R2L	Port Vale	(h)	2-0	McClair, May	31,615
8/10/94	FAPL	Sheffield Wed.	(a)	0-1		33,441
15/10/94	FAPL	West Ham Utd	(h)	1-0	Cantona	43,795
19/10/94	EC	Barcelona	(h)	2-2	Hughes, Sharpe	40,064
23/10/94	FAPL	Blackburn Rovs	(a)	4-2	Cantona (Pen), Kanchelskis 2, Hughes	30,260
27/10/94	CCC 3R	Newcastle Utd	(a)	0-2		34,178
29/10/94	FAPL	Newcastle Utd	(h)	2-0	Pallister, Gillespie	43,795
2/11/94	EC	Barcelona	(a)	0-4		115,000
6/11/94	FAPL	Aston Villa	(a)	2-1	Ince, Kanchelskis	32,136
10/11/94	FAPL	Manchester City	(h)	5-0	Kanchelskis 3, Cantona, Hughes	43,738
19/11/94	FAPL	Crystal Palace	(h)	3-0	Irwin, Cantona, Kanchelskis	43,788
23/11/94	EC	IFK Gothenburg	(a)	1-3	Hughes	36,350
26/11/94	FAPL	Arsenal	(a)	0-0		38,301
3/12/94	FAPL	Norwich City	(h)	1-0	Cantona	43,789

Date	Type	Opposition	Ven	Score	Scorers	Att
7/12/94	EC	Galatasary	(h)	4-0	Davies, Beckham, Keane, Bulents og.	39,350
10/12/94	FAPL	QPR	(a)	3-2	Scholes 2, Keane	18,948
17/12/94	FAPL	Notts Forest	(h)	1-2	Cantona	43,744
26/12/94	FAPL	Chelsea	(a)	3-2	Hughes, Cantona (Pen), McClair	31,161
28/12/94	FAPL	Leicester City	(h)	1-1	Kanchelskis	43,789
31/12/94	FAPL	Southampton	(a)	2-2	Butt, Pallister	15,204
3/01/95	FAPL	Coventry City	(h)	2-0	Scholes, Cantona (Pen)	43,130
9/01/95	FAC3	Sheffield Utd	(a)	2-0	Hughes, Cantona	22,322
14/01/95	FAPL	Newcastle Utd	(a)	1-1	Hughes	34,471
22/01/95	FAPL	Blackburn Rovs	(h)	1-0	Cantona	43,742
25/01/95	FAPL	Crystal Palace	(a)	1-1	May	18,224
28/01/95	FAC4	Wrexham	(h)	5-2	Irwin 2, Giggs, McClair, Humes og.	43,222
4/02/95	FAPL	Aston Villa	(h)	1-0	Cole	43,795
11/02/95	FAPL	Manchester City	(a)	3-0	Ince, Kanchelskis, Cole	26,368
19/02/95	FAC5	Leeds United	(h)	3-1	Bruce, McClair, Hughes	42,744
22/02/95	FAPL	Norwich City	(a)	2-0	Ince, Kanchelskis	21,824
25/02/95	FAPL	Everton	(a)	0-1		40,011
4/03/95	FAPL	Ipswich Town	(h)	9-0	Cole 5, Hughes 2, Ince, Keane	43,804
7/03/95	FAPL	Wimbledon	(a)	1-0	Bruce	18,224
12/03/95	FAC6	QPR	(h)	2-0	Sharpe, Irwin	42,830
15/03/95	FAPL	Tottenham H	(h)	0-0		43,802
19/03/95	FAPL	Liverpool	(a)	0-2		38,906
22/03/95	FAPL	Arsenal	(h)	3-0	Hughes, Sharpe, Kanchelskis	43,623
2/04/95	FAPL	Leeds United	(h)	0-0		43,712
9/04/95	FAC S/F	Crystal Palace	(n)	2-2	Irwin, Pallister	38,256
12/04/95	FAC S/F	Replay Crystal Palace	(n)	2-0	Bruce, Pallister	17,987
15/04/95	FAPL	Leicester City	(a)	4-0	Sharpe, Cole 2, Ince	21,281
17/04/95	FAPL	Chelsea	(h)	0-0		43,728
1/05/95	FAPL	Coventry City	(a)	3-2	Scholes, Cole 2	21,885
7/05/95	FAPL	Sheffield Wed	(h)	1-0	May	43,868
10/05/95	FAPL	Southampton	(h)	2-1	Cole, Irwin pen.	43,479
14/05/95	FAPL	West Ham United	(a)	1-1	McClair	24,783
20/05/95	FAC Final	Everton	(n)	0-1		79,592

The Pre-season Friendlies

United began their preparation for the defence of their Championship and FA Cup successes with a short tour of Ireland and promptly received the shock of their lives when they fell two goals down to the part-timers of Dundalk inside the first eighteen minutes. The Irish took the lead after fifteen minutes when ex-Lincoln City forward, Tony Loughlin chipped over Schmeichel. Three minutes later, the Reds were left bemused when former Northampton Town player Warren Patmore stroked a second goal past the giant Dane after being put through by Celtic guest player Paul Byrne. Hughes pulled the Reds back in contention from a Kanchelskis cross and five minutes in to the second period, Ince levelled after being set up by Sharpe. Cantona then missed a penalty after Ince had been brought down but made amends by putting Hughes through to give United the lead which was then increased when Giggs raced clear to shoot under the 'keeper.

Shelbourne held no such frights for United with Cantona having an outstanding game. Ince opened the scoring five minutes before the interval when he headed home a Ryan Giggs corner kick. Two minutes later, Cantona set Hughes free but the Welshman was bundled over leaving the Frenchman to atone for his miss against Dundalk by sending the 'keeper the wrong way. Cantona then crossed perfectly for McClair to head home the final goal some eight minutes from the end.

United's next stop was Molyneux where they attracted a record attendance of 28,500 for the revamped ground. Schmeichel denied the former England manager, Graham Taylor's outfit with a series of outstanding saves after United had fallen behind to an early Steve Bull goal. The equaliser came from Paul Ince who dived to head home a Giggs cross eight minutes after the break and in the 63rd minute the Reds went in front. Again it was Giggs who caused the problems with a left wing run that saw him cut in and fire a stinging shot at Stowell who couldn't hold it. Team mate Blades ran back to help out but only succeeded in hacking the ball in to his own net.

Then came the Ibrox tournament which proved to be a disaster as United lost 6-5 on penalties after Cantona had levelled a Raul Fox goal for Newcastle United. Rangers had lost to Sampdoria which meant United faced the Scottish hosts for third and fourth place. In a meaningless game, both teams contained many fringe players and United lost 1-0 with Simon Davies being booked. Worse still, however, was the sight of Eric Cantona being sent off for the fourth time in a turbulent ten months for a second bookable offence. He would miss the first three league games as a result.

The final trip was to Cambridge United where again United put out a team containing many fringe players. Again the Reds fell behind to lesser opposition when Canadian international Carlo Corazzin finished off a superb three man move. The equaliser came when Kanchelskis was brought down by Barrick for Sharpe to take the resultant penalty. Although his kick was straight at Australian 'keeper John Filan, it was powerful enough to force the 'keeper to drop it and Sharpe followed up to scramble the ball home.

Following their Charity Shield success, which is reported more fully elsewhere, United had their last warm up game at Ayresome Park where a crowd approaching 20,000 swelled Clayton Blackmore's Testimonial coffers by some £150,000. Missing from the home team's line up was former United captain, Bryan Robson, who had spent the day at the Football League's headquarters at Lytham St Annes attending a tribunal. Hughes opened the scoring after 25 minutes with a delicate chip shot, a feat he repeated in the last minute. In between, Sharpe had also netted with a diving header from a McClair cross as goalkeeper, Kevin Pilkington kept a clean sheet on his first team debut.

Manchester United
Blackburn Rovers

(1) 2
(0) 0

Sunday, 14th August 1994, Wembley   Att: 60,402

Manchester United

1	Peter	SCHMEICHEL
12	David	MAY
4	Steve	BRUCE – *Booked*
6	Gary	PALLISTER
5	Lee	SHARPE – *Booked*
14	Andrei	KANCHELSKIS
9	Brian	McCLAIR
8	Paul	INCE
11	Ryan	GIGGS – *Booked*
7	Eric	CANTONA
10	Mark	HUGHES

Subs

20	Dion	DUBLIN
19	Nicky	BUTT
21	Keith	GILLESPIE
22	Chris	CASPER

Blackburn Rovers

1	Tim	FLOWERS
20	Henning	BERG
2	Tony	GALE
5	Colin	HENDRY – *Booked*
6	Graeme	LE SAUX – *Booked*
17	Robbie	SLATER
4	Tim	SHERWOOD – *Booked*
22	Mark	ATKINS (*64)
11	Jason	WILCOX – *Booked*
25	Ian	PEARCE
7	Stuart	RIPLEY

19	Peter	THORNE *
13	Bobby	MIMMS (G)
18	Andy	MORRISON
26	Mick	HARFORD
3	Alan	WRIGHT

Match Facts

- United's twelfth post–war FA Charity Shield appearance, Blackburn's first since 1928.
- Cantona's third successful Wembley spot–kick in as many months following his double in the FA Cup Final in May.
- United's second successive FA Charity Shield victory, a feat they had not achieved since 1957 when they beat Aston Villa 4–0 after defeating Manchester City 1–0 a year earlier.

Score Sheet

E. CANTONA 21 min pen – 1–0

P. INCE 80 min – 2–0

Referee
Mr P. Don (Middlesex)

No Charity for Blackburn

United began this game not only without Irwin and Keane, who were still on extended holiday after their World Cup exertions, but also minus Parker and a substitute goalkeeper! Parker was still out injured whilst if anything happened to Schmeichel during the game, Ince was earmarked for going in goal. Reserve custodian, Gary Walsh was still sidelined following an appendix operation and third choice, Kevin Pilkington, was in Holland for a pre-season competition with the Reserve team. But Blackburn were no better off – indeed their missing players comprised an even more impressive list with Alan Shearer, new £5m signing Chris Sutton, David Batty, Mike Newall and Kevin Gallacher all missing from their line up. Kenny Dalglish dismissed his side's chances before the kick off saying "It is more important to take part than to win as it means you have achieved something. It will be a nice stroll".

It was anything but a stroll as both sides clearly saw it as an opportunity to impose themselves on the other before the season began in earnest. The scene was set with two Rovers players going in to the referee's book within the first 12 minutes and five others following suit. Amidst all this war-mongering, Cantona, playing his last game prior to starting a three match suspension, strutted around Wembley in what was arguably his best performance there for the Reds.

The first yellow card quickly came when Sherwood felled Ince in the centre circle and Le Saux soon followed when he disputed a free kick. United nearly took the lead when Bruce, Pallister, May and Kanchelskis linked up for the Russian to cross on the run from the right. In typical fashion, Hughes unleashed a tremendous volley which Flowers did well to save. The Blackburn 'keeper was quickly in action again when his former team mate, May, drifted a long ball over for Hughes to chest down and hit a strong shot on the turn which the 'keeper somehow got round his left hand post for a corner. Cantona then came into the action with a long, elegant run from the halfway line only to be tripped outside the area by Hendry which earned Blackburn's third booking. But there was to be no escape as, from the free kick, Cantona fought for the ball which broke to Ince who went for goal only to be upended by Hendry. Cantona converted the spot kick by caressing the ball to the right of Flowers as the 'keeper went left. The half ended on an unusual note with the sight of Giggs being cautioned for a tackle on Slater.

The second period began with probably the move of the game as Cantona took three men out on a mazy run before setting Giggs free to feed Kanchelskis but the Russian blazed harmlessly over. Rovers nearly equalised when Ripley turned Bruce and his cross ricocheted to the unmarked Pearce who shot wide from eight yards with only Schmeichel to beat. The same player was soon through again but was once more denied when the big Dane flung himself at the forward's feet before needing a slice of luck to grab the rebound from Sherwood to complete the save. The destination of the Shield was decided irretrievably ten minutes from time when Ince scored. A Giggs corner was backheaded by Cantona to Ince who had his back to goal as he unleashed a powerful right foot overhead scissor kick from eight yards that gave Flowers no chance.

FA Charity Shield Record

P	W	D	L	F	A
16	8	5	3	36	24

Manchester United (0) 2
Queens Park Rangers (0) 0

Match Two

Saturday, 20th August 1994, Old Trafford   Att: 43,214

Manchester United

1	Peter	SCHMEICHEL
12	David	MAY (*70)
3	Denis	IRWIN
4	Steve	BRUCE
5	Lee	SHARPE
6	Gary	PALLISTER
8	Paul	INCE
9	Brian	McCLAIR
10	Mark	HUGHES
11	Ryan	GIGGS
14	Andrei	KANCHELSKIS

Subs

25	Kevin	PILKINGTON (G)
2	Paul	PARKER * *Sent Off*
16	Roy	KEANE

Queens Park Rangers

1	Tony	ROBERTS
2	David	BARDSLEY
3	Clive	WILSON – *Sent Off*
4	Steve	YATES
14	Simon	BARKER
6	Alan	MCDONALD
7	Andrew	IMPEY
8	Ian	HOLLOWAY
9	Les	FERDINAND (*82)
20	Kevin	GALLEN (+88)
11	Trevor	SINCLAIR

12	Gary	PENRICE *
16	Danny	MADDIX +
13	Sieb	DYKSTRA (G)

Match Facts

- David May's League debut for United.
- Full debut for QPR's 18 year old Kevin Gallen who had scored 153 goals in 110 Reserve and Youth team matches for the London team.
- Parker becomes the eighth United dismissal in thirteen months.
- The result left the Londoners still looking for their first success over United in the FAPL.
- Second successive 2-0 opening day win for the Reds following the previous season's victory at Norwich City by the same scoreline.

Score Sheet

M. HUGHES 47 min – 1-0
B. McCLAIR 68 min – 2-0

Referee:
Mr. D. Gallagher (Banbury)

On the Right Track

United set off on the right track in pursuit of their third successive Premiership as they convincingly defeated QPR in their opening game at Old Trafford. Denis Irwin made his first senior appearance of the campaign following his World Cup exertions but not his international team mate and record United signing, Roy Keane, who found himself on the substitute's bench. David May came in at right back to leave Paul Parker alongside Keane.

Prior to the kick off, Alex Ferguson was presented with the 1993/94 Carling Manager of the Year award and the crowd were in carnival mood as they passed a gigantic flag celebrating the previous season's double around the ground over the heads of the fans. It wasn't long before the players began to reciprocate the supporters' mood with Roberts having to race out of his goal to deny Giggs. But QPR's teenage sensation Kevin Gallen, who was making his debut after scoring a mountain of goals for the Londoner's junior teams, beat both the offside flag and Pallister to look as though he might just make a quite extraordinary introduction to the FA Premiership. However, he was not able to get any power in his shot and the ball rolled to safety. It was certainly a lively opening and with Kanchelskis in his turbo boost format, Wilson was having a torrid time of it trying to keep the Russian under control. In the seventh minute, Kanchelskis again left Wilson standing as he moved to a Giggs ball and after the former Manchester City full-back had resorted to tripping the winger, the referee had little option under the FA's newly instituted clamp-down but to dismiss him.

Down to ten men, Rangers produced some neat football as Impey was switched to full back to mark Kanchelskis. Despite their man disadvantage Rangers were the first to have the ball in the net when Gallen, who was causing considerably more problems than England international Les Ferdinand, broke through to slot the ball home only to be adjudged to have handled the ball on his way. But, as half time approached, United began to exert themselves with Hughes, Ince, Giggs and McClair all going close.

United's domination of the period just prior to half-time continued after the break and brought almost immediate reward as May's pass allowed Kanchelskis to roll the ball in to the path of Hughes who gave Roberts no chance from the edge of the area. The Londoner's gamely tried to work their way back in to the match but McClair put the game beyond recall with a header from a rebound after Ince's first effort had crashed against the bar.

Ferguson replaced May with Parker but must have wished he hadn't when, five minutes later Parker was off after a late tackle on Ferdinand resulted in the referee brandishing the red card. Ferdinand himself never recovered from the knock and minutes later was substituted as the game drew to its obvious conclusion.

League Record

	Home						Away				
	P	W	D	L	F	A	W	D	L	F	A
FAPL 94/95	1	1	0	0	2	0	0	0	0	0	0
All Time FAPL	85	29	11	3	80	27	23	12	7	69	42
FL/FAPL	3641	1065	421	335	3630	1811	555	424	791	2475	3099

	Home	Away	Total
FAPL Attendances	43,214	-	43,214

Nottingham Forest (1) 1
Manchester United (1) 1

Monday, 22nd August 1994, The City Ground   Att: 22,072

Nottingham Forest			**Manchester United**		
1	Mark	CROSSLEY	1	Peter	SCHMEICHEL
2	Des	LYTTLE – *Booked*	12	David	MAY
3	Stuart	PEARCE	3	Denis	IRWIN
4	Colin	COOPER	4	Steve	BRUCE
5	Steve	CHETTLE	5	Lee	SHARPE
7	David	PHILLIPS	6	Gary	PALLISTER
8	Scott	GEMMILL	8	Paul	INCE
11	Steve	STONE	9	Brian	McCLAIR
14	Ian	WOAN – *Booked*	10	Mark	HUGHES
10	Stan	COLLYMORE	11	Ryan	GIGGS (*55)
22	Bryan	ROY – *Booked* (*80)	14	Andrei	KANCHELSKIS

Subs

13	Mark	RIGBY (G)	25	Kevin	PILKINGTON (G)
12	Jonathon	LEE	16	Roy	KEANE – *Booked* *
9	Lars	BOHINEN *	2	Paul	PARKER

Match Facts

- Collymore's goal is the first to be scored by a Forest player against United in the FAPL.
- The point that Forest take is their first in the FAPL against the Reds.
- Keane's first game at the City Ground since his departure for United fourteen months earlier.

Score Sheet

A. KANCHELSKIS 22 min – 0-1
S. COLLYMORE 26 min – 1-1

Referee:
Mr A. Wilkie (Chester-le-Street)

Champions Meet Their Match

United were unchanged for their visit to the City Ground for a game that proved to be hugely entertaining despite a crop of yellow cards. Forest were parading new foreign imports Brian Roy and Lars Bohinen for the first time in a home game and their flair certainly matched that of United who were playing in their all black-strip. Having secured an opening day victory at Ipswich Town, Forest manager Frank Clark was anxious to see how his team would cope against the best. After the game he would have been a happy man as his side matched United in every department.

Not that Ferguson's men had an off day, indeed they contributed much to the occasion and nothing was better than the strike by Kanchelskis that gave United the lead. Although only the second league game of the campaign, it was generally agreed that the goal would already be a serious contender for goal of the season. The first period was approaching its half way stage when Sharpe received the ball wide on the left about fifteen yards outside the Forest area. He slung over a cross of some forty yards that the Russian, out on the right edge of the area and at an acute angle to the goal, simply smashed on the volley across and past a bemused Crossley. But Forest, having counter attacked as attractively as United in the early stages matched the Kanchelskis effort within minutes with a superb strike of their own. Collymore headed the ball to his right some 35 yards out, went away from Ince who was obviously conscious of the new rules on tackling from behind, and then went round the outside of Pallister. Before the giant United central defender could get a tackle in, the he unleashed a venomous, swerving drive that escaped Schmeichel's left hand by an inch and the inside of the post for a classic equaliser.

Despite the constant threat of both Collymore and Roy to the United rearguard and the constant probing of Kanchelskis and Giggs, somewhat surprisingly there were no further goals before half time gave everybody, including the fans, time to get their breath back. The second half could have seen either team score but somehow they didn't. Keane was introduced in the 55th minute to chants of "Judas" from the Forest fans and the home supporters savoured his booking for a late tackle but in the yellow card stakes it was three to Forest with Roy, Lyttle and Woan all going in the book. United began to get on top and Ince hit the woodwork for the second consecutive game whilst Hughes had a typical effort well saved by Crossley. But Forest refused to lie down and gave Schmeichel as tough a time as the United forwards gave Crossley. Woan ran 70 yards unchallenged before letting loose with a thunderbolt. Fortunately it was straight at the Dane but he couldn't hold on to it. Roy closed in on the rebound but Schmeichel was equal to the follow up effort with a great block. He couldn't, however, keep out a header from Cooper but Irwin came to the rescue by clearing off the line.

League Record

	Home						Away				
	P	W	D	L	F	A	W	D	L	F	A
FAPL 94/95	2	1	0	0	2	0	0	1	0	1	1
All time FAPL	86	29	11	3	80	27	23	13	7	70	43
FAPL/FL	3642	1065	421	335	3630	1811	555	425	791	2476	3100

	Home	Away	Total
FAPL Attendances	43,214	22,072	65,286

Tottenham Hotspur (0) 0
Manchester United (0) 1

Match Four

Saturday, 27th August 1994, White Hart Lane   Att: 24,502

Tottenham Hotspur

13	Ian	WALKER
3	Justin	EDINBURGH
5	Colin	CALDERWOOD (*57)
7	Nicky	BARMBY
9	Darren	ANDERTON – *Booked*
8	Ilie	DUMITRESCU
10	Teddy	SHERINGHAM
14	Stuart	NETHERCOTT
18	Jurgen	KLINSMANN
22	David	KERSLAKE
23	Sol	CAMPBELL

Subs

30	Chris	DAY (G)
6	Gary	MABBUTT
16	Micky	HAZARD *

Manchester United

1	Peter	SCHMEICHEL
12	David	MAY
3	Denis	IRWIN
4	Steve	BRUCE
6	Gary	PALLISTER
5	Lee	SHARPE
8	Paul	INCE
9	Brian	McCLAIR
10	Mark	HUGHES
11	Ryan	GIGGS – *Booked*
14	Andrei	KANCHELSKIS

25	Kevin	PILKINGTON (G)
19	Nicky	BUTT
20	Dion	DUBLIN

Match Facts

- Spurs were looking to win their three opening games for the first time since their double season of 1960/61.
- Smallest attendance for a Spurs v Man Utd game since 20,085 watched a goalless midweek Second Division match between the two teams on 5/2/36.

Score Sheet

S. BRUCE 49 min – 1-0

Referee:
Mr K. Burge (Glamorgan)

FA Carling Premiership

		P	W	D	L	F	A	Pts
1	Newcastle United	3	3	0	0	12	2	9
2	Blackburn Rovers	3	2	1	0	8	1	7
3	**Manchester United**	**3**	**2**	**1**	**0**	**4**	**1**	**7**
4	Nottingham Forest	3	2	1	0	3	1	7
5	Manchester City	3	2	0	1	7	3	6

Bitter Sugar

Tottenham Hotspur paraded Alan Sugar's summer signings Jurgen Klinsmann and Ilie Dumitrescu but it was United's 1991 summer signing, Peter Schmeichel, that must have left Sugar feeling bitter at his team losing a game they dominated as far as shots on target were concerned. Indeed, Spurs forced the pace from the kick off and after only two minutes Teddy Sheringham fired in a shot from what appeared to be an impossible acute angle on the left wing. However, it was so accurate and powerful that Schmeichel was glad to tip it over for a corner. It heralded an impressive opening from the London side that saw Barmby just wide with a header, Sheringham having a shot blocked and Klinsmann just over with a another header. Irwin produced a strong long range shot that Walker had to dive full length to grab at the foot of the right hand post but it was an isolated Red attack. The two young internationals on show, Anderton and Giggs, then got themselves booked.

United were still being subjected to strong pressure from Spurs and Schmeichel had to dive headlong into the path of Klinsmann to deny the German. United replied with a right wing raid by Kanchelskis but his cross eluded everybody. Then, on the stroke of half-time, it appeared that Klinsmann had broken the deadlock when he burst through to snap a shot past Schmeichel's flailing left hand and in to the roof of the net. But the linesman was flagging for the tightest of offsides and the Reds left the field much in need of a pep talk.

Whatever was said certainly seemed to work as United came out looking much more organised and after four minutes of the second period they went into the lead, although they needed a bit of luck to do so. Hughes was embroiled in a struggle for possession with Campbell that resulted in United winning a corner on the right wing. Giggs came across to take it and planted a teasing cross to the far post swinging away from Walker. Coming in from the far side like an express train was Steve Bruce but, as Walker tried to make ground to his back post, he collided with Edinburgh to leave Bruce with a free header into the unguarded net. It was against the run of play but two minutes later it could have been game, set and match when a Kanchelskis cross found Hughes in front of goal. He didn't do anything wrong as he blasted the ball towards the net but Walker redeemed himself for his earlier clanger by making a superb save.

United again fell under pressure with Pallister and Bruce playing magnificently until the latter felled Dumitrescu inside the area. Sheringham had missed a spot kick in Spurs' previous game but he still stepped up to take this one which he blasted to Schmeichel's right only to see the Dane make a great save with less then fifteen minutes left to earn United the points.

League Record

	Home						Away				
	P	W	D	L	F	A	W	D	L	F	A
94/95 FAPL	3	1	0	0	2	0	1	1	0	2	1
All time FAPL	87	29	11	3	80	27	24	13	7	71	43
FAPL/FL	3643	1065	421	335	3630	1811	556	425	791	2477	3100

	Home	Away	Total
FAPL Attendances	43,214	46,574	89,788

Manchester United (1) 3
Wimbledon (0) 0

Match Five

Wednesday, 31st August 1994, Old Trafford   Att: 43,440

Manchester United

1.	Peter	SCHMEICHEL
12	David	MAY
4	Steve	BRUCE
6	Gary	PALLISTER
3	Denis	IRWIN
5	Lee	SHARPE
7	Eric	CANTONA
9	Brian	McCLAIR
10	Mark	HUGHES
11	Ryan	GIGGS
14	Andrei	KANCHELSKIS

Subs

25	Kevin	PILKINGTON (G)
19	Nicky	BUTT
20	Dion	DUBLIN

Wimbledon

1	Hans	SEGERS
2	Warren	BARTON
6	Scott	FITZGERALD
12	Gary	ELKINS
16	Alan	KIMBLE
26	Neal	ARDLEY
18	Steven	TALBOYS
19	Stewart	CASTLEDINE (*64)
4	Vinny	JONES
20	Marcus	GAYLE
30	Mick	HARFORD

23	Neil	SULLIVAN (G)
7	Andy	CLARKE *
21	Chris	PERRY

Match Facts

- United's third clean sheet in four games.
- Identical start to the campaign as in 93/94 with three wins and a draw.
- Already six different players had appeared on the scoresheet in just four FAPL games.

Score Sheet

E. CANTONA 40 min – 1-0
B. McCLAIR 81 min – 2-0
R. GIGGS 84 min – 3-0

Referee:
Mr T. Holbrook (Walsall)

FA Carling Premiership

		P	W	D	L	F	A	Pts
1	Newcastle United	4	4	0	0	15	3	12
2	**Manchester United**	4	3	1	0	7	1	10
3	Nottingham Forest	4	3	1	0	5	2	10
4	Liverpool	3	3	0	0	11	1	9
5	Chelsea	3	3	0	0	8	2	9

Cantona Back with a Bang

United were hit by the late withdrawal of Paul Ince with a knee injury but the better news was that Cantona was back for his first league outing of the campaign after serving his three match suspension for being sent off at Glasgow Rangers. And how he celebrated with a classic header to give United the lead just before half time after his team mates had been somewhat profligate with several other chances. Love him or hate him, he can't be kept out of the headlines and the Reds looked a far better outfit than they had in their opening three games.

Wimbledon themselves were down to the bones with team selection for, having sold Holdsworth and Fashanu, they were now suffering from a severe injury crisis and it was soon obvious that their sole objective was to simply contain the Reds and hopefully pinch a point from a goalless game. Their sole effort in the ninety minutes came towards the end of the first quarter of the game but it took young Marcus Gayle by as much surprise as everybody else and he headed badly wide from only ten yards out with the goal beckoning. Not that United's strikes were much more capable as Giggs, McClair and Hughes all missed good opportunities as Cantona pulled the strings that unhinged the Londoner's defence.

Then, five minutes before the interval, Cantona, as though fed up with creating chances only for them to be missed, floated in between two Dons to rifle home a header from a left wing cross that Giggs got in after a jinking run down the left caused Wimbledon all sorts of problems. The young Welshman had picked the ball up some five yards inside his own half before setting off to beat no fewer than three defenders before sending over an inch perfect cross. Indeed, no doubt inspired by the return of the Frenchman, this was the Giggs of old.

The second period merely confirmed the vast superiority of the Champions but they had to wait until the last ten minutes before turning their territorial advantage in to goals. Allied to United's lack of finishing power, Segers was in fine form for the Dons with nothing better than a double save from first of all Cantona and then Giggs for which he was rewarded by McClair blasting well off target from the second rebound.

But Wimbledon were undoubtedly at full stretch to contain the Reds and their stamina began to wane. McClair reacted quickly to pick the loose ball up when Vinny Jones stumbled some 35 yards out and rammed home a shot from the edge of the area that probably ranked as hard as anything he had ever hit in all his years at Old Trafford. The evening's entertainment was rounded off by Giggs with five minutes left when he raced on to a short through ball from Hughes to score as he pleased. His goal gave the scoreline that United's domination of the game deserved.

League Record

| | Home | | | | | Away | | | | |
	P	W	D	L	F	A	W	D	L	F	A
94/95 FAPL	4	2	0	0	5	0	1	1	0	2	1
All time FAPL	88	30	11	3	83	27	24	13	7	71	43
FAPL/FL	3644	1066	421	335	3633	1811	556	425	791	2477	3100

	Home	Away	Total
FAPL Attendances	86,654	46,574	133,228

51

Leeds United (1) 2
Manchester United (0) 1

Sunday, 11th September 1994, Elland Road   Attendance: 39,396

Leeds United			**Manchester United**		
1	John	LUKIC	1	Peter	SCHMEICHEL
2	Gary	KELLY – *Booked*	12	David	MAY – *Booked*
4	Carlton	PALMER – *Booked*	3	Denis	IRWIN
6	David	WETHERALL	4	Steve	BRUCE
10	Gary	McALLISTER	6	Gary	PALLISTER
11	Gary	SPEED – *Booked*	9	Brian	McCLAIR (+63)
14	David	WHITE (*30)	8	Paul	INCE
15	Nigel	WORTHINGTON	14	Andrei	KANCHELSKIS
8	Rod	WALLACE	7	Eric	CANTONA
19	Noel	WHELAN – *Booked*	10	Mark	HUGHES
26	Phil	MASINGA – *Booked* (+87)	11	Ryan	GIGGS (*63)

Subs

13	Mark	BEENEY (G)	25	Kevin	PILKINGTON (G)
9	Brian	DEANE * – *Booked*	5	Lee	SHARPE *
5	Chris	FAIRCLOUGH +	19	Nicky	BUTT +

Match Facts

- First time in thirteen games that Leeds had beaten United.
- First time in fifteen competitive games that United had conceded two goals in a game. The last occasion was against Oldham Athletic at Old Trafford on 4/4/94.
- Six Leeds players booked.

Score Sheet

D. WETHERALL 13 min 1-0
B. DEANE 49 min 2-0
E. CANTONA 74 min Pen – 2-1

Referee:
Mr D. Elleray (Harrow)

FA Carling Premiership

		P	W	D	L	F	A	Pts
1	Newcastle United	5	5	0	0	19	5	15
2	Nottingham Forest	5	4	1	0	9	3	13
3	Blackburn Rovers	5	3	2	0	11	1	11
4	Liverpool	4	3	1	0	11	1	10
5	**Manchester United**	**5**	**3**	**1**	**1**	**8**	**3**	**10**
6	Leeds United	5	3	1	1	7	5	10

Unlucky Thirteen

United, after a run of twelve games against Leeds without defeat, came a clear second to a Yorkshire outfit that started the better, scored twice and then nearly fell victim to a smash and grab raid as the Reds converted a controversial penalty before Steve Bruce came within inches of an equaliser in the dying moments. The early Leeds pressure was quickly rewarded when United's defence, which had a decidedly off-day in comparison to having only conceded one goal in 450 minutes since kicking off in the FA Charity Shield, failed to clear a corner. The ball bounced to Wetherall whose shot, from ten yards, gave away the fact that he was a central defender, not a goal poaching predator. However, the mishit deceived everybody as the ball bobbled into the net for a goal.

United hit back with Cantona releasing Giggs but Lukic quickly narrowed the angle and made a good save to deny the Welshman. A rash tackle by May on Whelan produced the first booking of the game but this was only the prelude to no fewer than six Leeds players being cautioned, a figure which gave a good indication of how wound up the Yorkshire side were for this match. They played with a vigour that the Reds couldn't equal and Ferguson's men were always a yard off the pace and the Reds were nearly another goal down when Schmeichel dropped a Whelan effort only to be saved further blushes by Pallister who cleared off the line. Palmer was lucky to escape with only a booking when he brought down Ince from behind when the United player looked to be in on goal but Giggs hit the resulting free-kick straight at Lukic. Cantona then showed that the game isn't all about running when he produced the most memorable moment of the match as he flicked the ball left-footed over Carlton Palmer's head before flicking it back over his head the other way with his right foot to leave the Leeds player giving an impression of a six foot odd corkscrew. Shortly after Dean contrived to miss two real sitters for the hosts.

The second half continued in much the same vein with United unable to free themselves from the shackles that Leeds had placed on them and it was no real surprise when Deane, after missing those two excellent first half chances, put Howard Wilkinson's men two up. Whelan did the spade work down the left with a mazy run that took him past both May and Pallister before crossing to the near post where Deane just beat Schmeichel to the ball. Ferguson tried to shake things up with a double substitution and just when there seemed no way back for United, they had a slice of luck when Ince was tripped by Deane, with the tackle clearly outside the area but both referee and linesman agreeing that the incident merited a penalty. Lukic dived left, Cantona stroked the ball right and a grandstand finish was in prospect. Given this unexpected lifeline, the Reds fought bravely in the final fifteen minutes. Lukic kept his side's lead intact with saves from Cantona and Butt before Bruce went inches wide at the death with a header.

League Record

| | Home | | | | | | Away | | | | |
	P	W	D	L	F	A	W	D	L	F	A
94/95 FAPL	5	2	0	0	5	0	1	1	1	3	3
All time FAPL	89	30	11	3	83	27	24	13	8	72	45
FAPL/FL	3645	1066	421	335	3633	1811	556	425	792	2478	3102

	Home	Away	Total
FAPL Attendances	86,654	85,970	172,624

Manchester United (1) 4
IFK Gothenburg (1) 2

Wednesday, 14th September 1994, Old Trafford   Att: 33,625

Manchester United

1	Peter	SCHMEICHEL
2	David	MAY
3	Denis	IRWIN
4	Steve	BRUCE
5	Lee	SHARPE
6	Gary	PALLISTER
7	Andrei	KANCHELSKIS
8	Paul	INCE
9	Nicky	BUTT
10	Mark	HUGHES
11	Ryan	GIGGS

Subs

12	Gary	NEVILLE
13	Kevin	PILKINGTON (G)
14	Paul	SCHOLES
15	David	BECKHAM
16	Simon	DAVIES

IFK Gothenburg

1	RAVELLI
2	KAMARK
3	JOHANSSON
4	OLSSON (*44)
5	BJORKLUND
6	NILSSON
7	MARTINSSON
8	LINDQVIST
9	ERLINGMARK
10	BLOMQVIST
11	PETTERSSON

12	LAST (G)
13	ANEGRUND
14	REHN *
15	BENGTSSON
16	GUSTAVSSON

Match Facts

- A first full start for Nicky Butt.
- First goals in Europe for both Giggs and Kanchelskis.
- The Gothenburg side contained seven of the Swedish side that reached the semi-finals of the World Cup.

Score Sheet

PETTERSSON 27 min – 0-1

R. GIGGS 33 min – 1-1

A. KANCHELSKIS 48 min – 2-1

REHN 50 min – 2-2

R. GIGGS 65 min – 3-2

L. SHARPE 70 min – 4 -2

Referee:

Mr G. Goethals (Belgium)

UEFA Champions' League – Group A

	P	W	D	L	F	A	Pts
Manchester United	1	1	0	0	4	2	2
Barcelona	1	1	0	0	2	1	2
Galatasary	1	0	0	1	1	2	0
IFK Gothenburg	1	0	0	1	2	4	0

On a Wing and a Prayer

United entered their first Champions' League game of the season without Eric Cantona, suspended for four European matches, and anxious to avoid last year's embarrassment at the hands of Galatasary. They eventually succeeded with a prayer said after they went a goal down and answered by three goals from wingers Giggs and Kanchelskis along with a fourth from Sharpe for good measure.

United dominated the early exchanges with Swedish international 'keeper, Thomas Ravelli making great saves to deny piercing efforts from Ince (twice) and Kanchelskis. Giggs missed a one on one with the 'keeper and then Ince thundered a shot against the bar whilst lying prone on the ground. The Swedes showed them the way to the net though with virtually their first attack of the night. Mikael Martinsson skipped down the right wing before playing a teasing ball into the area. Three United defenders stood still and watched as Pettersson rushed in with an outstretched foot to stab the ball past Schmeichel. But, if a question had to be asked about Schmeichel for his part in that goal, then the Dane almost certainly kept the Reds in the game minutes later with a smart left handed tip away when he should have had no chance against the onrushing Blomqvist. The United fans regained their voices just past the half-hour mark when Bruce found Hughes on the right wing. The Welshman looked well offside at first as everybody had moved up apart from one defender who was so far back that nobody saw him. With the flag thus staying down, Hughes made the byeline before pulling the ball into the centre where Sharpe's first effort was blocked but only as far as Giggs who gleefully thumped the ball home from twelve yards.

United made a great start to the second half when Giggs' corner was only partially cleared to Kanchelskis who hit a daisy cutter through a sea of legs from twenty yards to beat the unsighted 'keeper. The action, however, was not over by a long way and United were hit with a second sucker punch of the evening almost immediately. A free-kick some thirty yards out appeared harmless as Schmeichel moved to his right and looked to have it covered. Then former Everton player substitute Stefan Rehn applied a deft back heel flick which propelled the ball in the opposite direction to leave the Dane stranded and the Swedes level.

The Reds, however, kept up the pressure and some brilliant football saw Ince hit a tremendous thirty yarder which Ravelli dealt with equally as well. The 'keeper, having got a hand on it, deserved better than to see the ball rebound from the woodwork into the path of Giggs who had the easiest of chances to restore United's lead. The Red's momentum didn't slacken and a fourth goal came when Kanchelskis surprised the Swede's defence by playing a ball in very early from the right. Whilst Ravelli and his defenders hesitated as to who should deal with the cross, Sharpe made their minds up for them from all of six yards.

European Record

	Home						Away				
	P	W	D	L	F	A	W	D	L	F	A
Champions' Cup	46	21	2	0	73	19	8	7	8	39	34
All European Comps	106	39	13	0	136	36	17	16	21	77	76

	Home	Away	Total
European Attendances	33,625	-	33,625

Manchester United (0) 2
Liverpool (0) 0

Match Eight

Saturday, 17th September 1994, Old Trafford   Att: 43,740

Manchester United

1	Peter	SCHMEICHEL
12	David	MAY – *Booked*
3	Denis	IRWIN
4	Steve	BRUCE – *Booked*
5	Lee	SHARPE
6	Gary	PALLISTER
7	Eric	CANTONA – *Booked*
8	Paul	INCE
10	Mark	HUGHES (*59)
11	Ryan	GIGGS
14	Andrei	KANCHELSKIS

Liverpool

1	David	JAMES
2	Rob	JONES – *Booked*
20	Stig	BJORNEBYE
12	John	SCALES
25	Neil	RUDDOCK – *Booked*
14	Jan	MOLBY
15	Jamie	REDKNAPP
17	Steve	McMANAMAN
9	Ian	RUSH
10	John	BARNES
23	Robbie	FOWLER

Subs

25	Kevin	PILKINGTON (G)
9	Brian	McCLAIR *
19	Nicky	BUTT

6	Phil	BABB
7	Nigel	CLOUGH
13	Michael	STENSDGAARD (G)

Match Facts

- £3.6m Liverpool signing, Phil Babb, makes his debut.
- First defeat of 1994/95 for the Anfield side.
- United's Old Trafford superiority over Liverpool is extended. United have only been beaten by the Merseysiders once at Old Trafford since 1982.

Score Sheet

A. KANCHELSKIS 71 min – 1-0
B. McCLAIR 73 min – 2-0

Referee:
Mr K. Morton (Bury St Edmunds)

FA Carling Premiership

		P	W	D	L	F	A	Pts
1	Newcastle United	5	5	0	0	19	5	15
2	Nottingham Forest	6	4	2	0	10	4	14
3	**Manchester United**	**6**	**4**	**1**	**1**	**10**	**3**	**13**
4	Blackburn Rovers	5	3	2	0	11	1	11
5	Liverpool	5	3	1	1	11	3	10

Torpedoed

The only surprise about this game was that it took so long for a goal to be scored. Certainly by half time the scoreline could easily have equalled the amazing 3-3 draw played out by the two sides at Anfield the previous season. But after all the skillful attacking that had been on show, it took a crass error by Liverpool's £3m summer signing, John Scales, to disable the Merseysiders' ship which was then immediately torpedoed by Ferguson's sub, McClair.

United immediately tested James in the Liverpool goal when Kanchelskis hit a fierce angled shot which the 'keeper did well to bundle round for a corner. But Liverpool had their own attacking ideas and Redknapp's cross from the right found Ruddock completely unmarked at the far post only for Schmeichel to bring off the first of a string of good saves. Next McManaman tried his luck from twenty yards only to find the huge Dane hurling himself to his left to push the ball for a corner. Then a long ball from Cantona was headed on by Giggs into the path of Sharpe who really should have done better than scrape the bar from eighteen yards.

Liverpool almost opened the scoring from a free-kick. Redknapp was put clean through but found Schmeichel diving bravely at his feet to deny him. At the other end Hughes sent Kanchelskis scampering down the wing and his cross was right into the path of Cantona. The Frenchman didn't bother to control the ball but just hit it and James did well to parry the effort and then followed up by recovering to slide at the feet of Giggs as the ball broke loose.

The crowd had certainly had great value in the first half and the second period began with more of the same as Liverpool went even closer to scoring. Redknapp beat Schmeichel all ends up from 20 yards only to see the ball clip the crossbar. Jones was booked for pulling Giggs to the ground by his shirt. United were beginning to play some of their best football around this period and a cross from Cantona was inch perfect for Giggs to surely head home but, as everybody knows, heading is not the Welsh youngster's strongest point and he didn't hit the target. Cantona then tested James himself with a twenty yarder and then Ferguson sent on McClair for Hughes. Almost immediately, the Scot put over a great cross from the right that found Cantona who could only head directly at James. It was all United now but a long ball from inside his own half by Ince looked harmless enough until Scales decided to back head it to his 'keeper. Kanchelskis guessed the move and pounced to toe poke the ball over James to give the Reds the lead.

Two minutes later, the Merseysiders were sunk without trace. Ince won a midfield tussle to pass to McClair who then played double one-twos with Kanchelskis and Cantona respectively before firing home from close range. The game was now beyond Liverpool's recall but that didn't stop Cantona getting himself a needless booking with three minutes left. C'est la vie.

League Record

| | Home | | | | | | Away | | | | |
	P	W	D	L	F	A	W	D	L	F	A
94/95 FAPL	6	3	0	0	7	0	1	1	1	3	3
All Time FAPL	90	31	11	3	85	27	24	13	8	72	45
FAPL/FL	3646	1067	421	335	3635	1811	556	425	792	2478	3102

	Home	Away	Total
FAPL Attendances	130,394	85,970	216,364

Port Vale (1) 1
Manchester United (1) 2

2 Rnd 1 Leg

Match Nine

Wednesday, 21st September 1994, Vale Park   Att: 18,605

Port Vale			**Manchester United**		
1	Paul	MUSSELWHITE	1	Gary	WALSH
2	Bradley	SANDEMAN	2	Gary	NEVILLE – *Booked* (*75)
3	Gareth	GRIFFITHS	3	Denis	IRWIN
4	Dean	GLOVER	5	David	MAY
5	Allen	TANKARD	6	Roy	KEANE
6	Andy	PORTER	8	David	BECKHAM
7	Kevin	KENT	7	Keith	GILLESPIE
8	Robin	VAN DER LAAN	4	Nicky	BUTT (+84)
9	Martin	FOYLE	9	Brian	McCLAIR
10	Lee	GLOVER	10	Paul	SCHOLES
11	Tony	NAYLOR (*70)	11	Simon	DAVIES

Subs

12	Arjen	VAN HEUSDEN (G)	12	Lee	SHARPE +
13	Mark	BURKE *	13	Kevin	PILKINGTON (G)
14	Ray	WALKER	14	John	O'KANE *

Match Facts

- Debuts for O'Kane, Davies and Scholes who scored twice on his first appearance. The last home grown player to achieve this feat was Bobby Charlton in 1956.
- First start for David Beckham.
- The win maintained United's 100% record against Vale in Cup matches having won all eight games with a goal difference of 19 for, five against.
- Vale striker Martin Foyle scored the first of more than a century of goals at Old Trafford eleven years ago when a Southampton teenager.

Score Sheet

B. GLOVER 7 min – 1-0

P. SCHOLES 36 min – 1-1

P. SCHOLES 53 min – 1-2

Referee:
Mr J. Lloyd (Wrexham)

58

Full Graduates

They called them the 'Class of 92' and this was the night that United's FA Youth Cup winning side of that year graduated. There were debuts for Paul Scholes, Simon Davies and John O'Kane (who came on as substitute) and, along with a first start for David Beckham whilst Keith Gillespie and Gary Neville made their second starts, it left Nicky Butt with a handful of appearances looking positively experienced. Add in Giggs from that side along with the injured, but highly talented, Ben Thornley, substitute goalkeeper Kevin Pilkington, Colin McKee who reaped United over £250,000 when transferred to Kilmarnock, and Chris Casper, who has been substitute in European matches, it leaves just George Switzer, now playing for Hyde United in the Northern Premier League, as the odd man out.

With only David May and Denis Irwin retaining their places from the starting line up from the previous league match, Brian McClair was made captain as he led one of the least experienced United teams to ever take to the field. Port Vale, lost no time in showing they intended adding the *new* United to the *old* scalp just taken and after seven minutes were one up. A corner from the right was headed out by Beckham but only as far as full back Sandeman who let fly from some 20 yards. The shot was going wide until Lee Glover stuck his head in the way and the ball deflected just inside the post. Sandeman immediately tried his luck again but this time there was nobody on hand to prevent it going wide. Then a dreadful mistake let in the Reds for the equaliser.

Musselwhite threw the ball out to the edge of the area where Griffiths turned and passed square to Tankard. The pass was short and Scholes intercepted to skip into the area and advance on Musselwhite before calmly chipping over the 'keeper's despairing dive for a debut goal. Just before half time it looked like Vale were back in front with that man Sandeman again in the thick of the action. His cross was not cleared and eventually found its way to Porter whose fierce shot was only parried by Walsh leaving Sandeman to pounce and score from close range with United fortunate to be saved by a linesman's flag. It was very close.

The second period was end to end with the decisive 53rd minute strike coming in typical United style. Beckham, Butt and McClair linked up well in midfield before the captain's header found Davies on the left wing. The debutant jinked to go outside, came inside, twisted and went outside to leave Sandeman floundering before delivering an inviting ball to the near post area where Scholes scored with a quicksilver header that bore all the hallmarks of a great striker. Vale should have equalised when Van der Laan found himself with only Walsh to beat from six yards but the Dutchman proceeded to clear the bar by the same distance, something that couldn't be said for Beckham when he got down to the other end. His twenty yarder scraped the bar as United finished the game going forward looking for a third goal that would have killed off the second leg tie at Old Trafford.

League Cup Record

	Home						Away				
P	W	D	L	F	A	W	D	L	F	A	
122	44	11	8	134	53	23	14	22	81	75	

	Home	Away	Total
CCC Attendances	-	18,605	18,605

Ipswich Town (2) 3
Manchester United (0) 2

Saturday, 24th September 1994, Portman Road   Att: 22,559

Ipswich Town

1	Craig	FORREST
6	David	LINIGHAN
19	Frank	YALLOP
5	John	WARK (+88)
12	Claus	THOMSEN
4	Paul	MASON
7	Geraint	WILLIAMS
14	Steve	SEDGELEY – *Booked* (80)
8	Gavin	JOHNSON
18	Steve	PALMER – *Booked*
26	Adrian	PAZ (*77)

Subs

17	Simon	MILTON +
9	Bontcho	GUENTCHEV *
13	Clive	BAKER (13)

Manchester United

13	Gary	WALSH
3	Denis	IRWIN – *Booked*
4	Steve	BRUCE
6	Gary	PALLISTER
5	Lee	SHARPE (*62)
8	Andrei	KANCHELSKIS
4	Paul	INCE
16	Roy	KEANE – *Booked*
9	Brian	McCLAIR
7	Eric	CANTONA
11	Ryan	GIGGS

25	Kevin	PILKINGTON (G)
19	Nicky	BUTT
24	Paul	SCHOLES *

Match Facts

• First win in 12 home games dating back to 22nd February 1994 for Ipswich, a club record.
• A goal within eleven minutes of his FA Premiership debut for Paul Scholes.
• Debut for Town's Uruguayan Adrian Paz.
• The result continued United's poor FAPL form against Ipswich – only one win in five meetings for the Reds.

Score Sheet

P. MASON 15 min – 1-0
P. MASON 43 min – 2-0
E. CANTONA 71 min – 2-1
P. SCHOLES 73 min – 2-2
S. SEDGELEY 80 min – 3-2

Referee:
Mr P. Jones (Loughborough)

FA Carling Premiership

		P	W	D	L	F	A	Pts
1	Newcastle United	7	6	1	0	23	8	19
2	Blackburn Rovers	7	5	2	0	16	3	17
3	Nottingham Forest	7	5	2	0	14	5	17
4	**Manchester United**	**7**	**4**	**1**	**2**	**12**	**6**	**13**
5	Chelsea	6	4	0	2	12	8	12

United Destroyed by Mason

Despite the success of their youngsters at Port Vale in the Coca Cola Cup tie just days before, United left all of them out of the starting line up at Portman Road although Nicky Butt and Paul Scholes were on the bench. Ferguson, however, was forced to leave out Schmeichel, May and Hughes with injuries which gave first league starts of the season to Roy Keane and Gary Walsh whilst Ipswich gave their £900,000 Uruguayan signing Adrian Paz a debut as the East Anglians took to the field in the knowledge that they had not won at home in 11 games.

United swept straight into the attack from the kick-off and in a stream of one way traffic, Giggs shot over after Cantona had fashioned an opening for the Welshman who was again off target with a header from another Kanchelskis centre. Ince went even closer with a header in the next attack but continued his frustrating habit of hitting the woodwork. Having survived this bombardment Ipswich then proceeded to grab the lead with virtually their first attack. The move was started by new boy Paz who put in a cross to the edge of the six yard box and, as Sharpe was occupied watching Thomsen, Mason came in and beat both of them to the ball to stab it at Walsh who could only turn it on to his left hand post and in to the net.

Keane was booked for a fierce challenge on Palmer before United hit back only for Forrest to make a great save from a point blank Cantona header as the Reds stepped up their attacks. But again Ipswich came back off the ropes to score with only their third excursion into the United penalty area. A long ball from the halfway line saw Pallister in an aerial duel with Linighan and, although Pallister got his head to it, the ball just dropped to Mason out on the left angle of United's area where Sharpe was patrolling. Unfortunately for the Reds, when Mason began to advance, Sharpe slipped to give Mason the space he required to hit a powerful, angled effort past Walsh and give the East Anglians a two goal cushion.

United continued their domination after the break with both Giggs and Cantona having shots blocked before Ferguson sent on Scholes for Sharpe. Irwin set Giggs on a run which ended when he tried a one-two with Bruce. The captain's ball instead found Keane on the right and his low cross eluded everybody to give Cantona an easy tap home at the far post. Two minutes later and United were level with Scholes rounding off a dream few days with his first Premiership goal when he clipped in Keane's near post cross.

But there was still to be a sting in the tail as Ipswich regained the lead with just seven minutes left. Yallop slung over a long cross to the far post. Sedgeley met it but failed to get a great amount of power in his effort. Unfortunately, the ball struck Keane which diverted it past Walsh. A travesty of a result but one in keeping with United's poor form against the East Anglians in the FAPL.

League Record

| | Home | | | | | | Away | | | | |
	P	W	D	L	F	A	W	D	L	F	A
94/95 FAPL	7	3	0	0	7	0	1	1	2	5	6
All time FAPL	91	31	11	3	85	27	24	13	9	74	48
FAPL/FL	3647	1067	421	335	3635	1811	556	425	793	2480	3104

	Home	Away	Total
FAPL Attendances	130,394	108,529	238,923

Galatasary (0) 0
Manchester United (0) 0

Wednesday, 28th September 1994, Ali Sami Yen Stadium   Att: 30,000

Galatasary		Manchester United		
1	STAUCE	1	Peter	SCHMEICHEL
2	KORKMAZ	2	David	MAY – *Booked*
3	SEDAT	3	Lee	SHARPE – *Booked*
4	KORKMAZ	4	Steve	BRUCE
5	ALTINTAS	5	Nicky	BUTT
6	KERIMOGLU (*45)	6	Gary	PALLISTER
7	MAPEZA	7	Andrei	KANCHELSKIS –
8	HAMZAOGLU			*Booked*
9	SUKUR	8	Paul	INCE
10	SAFFET +	9	Roy	KEANE
11	TURKYILMAZ	10	Mark	HUGHES – *Booked*
		11	Ryan	GIGGS (*65)
Subs				
12	NEZIHI (G)	12	Paul	PARKER *
13	CIHAT	13	Gary	WALSH (G)
14	ARIF * – *Booked*	14	Paul	SCHOLES
15	OKAN	15	David	BECKHAM
16	OSMAN +	16	Gary	NEVILLE

Match Facts

- Galatasary fielded ten internationals.
- Fourth time in last five away legs that United had failed to score in Europe since winning the Cup-winners Cup in Rotterdam.

Score Sheet

Referee:
Mr M. Van der Ende (Holland)

UEFA Champions' League – Group A

	P	W	D	L	F	A	Pts
Manchester United	2	1	1	0	4	2	3
Barcelona	2	1	0	1	3	2	2
IFK Gothenburg	2	1	0	1	4	5	2
Galatasary	2	0	1	1	1	2	1

Turkish Delight

The banners again said "Welcome to Hell" but after the flares died down and the pall of smoke disappeared there was not much left to resemble the devil's lair, leaving the Reds to return home with smiles of Turkish delight following their traumatic experience at the hands of Galatasary twelve months earlier. Indeed, UEFA had done a magnificent job in ensuring that the Turks were well aware of the consequences should United, or their fans, be subjected to the harassment they had endured on the previous visit to Istanbul and Galatasary had over 5,000 police on duty to guard the United entourage and the 148 fans who made the trip.

Without Cantona, who was serving the second of his four match European ban imposed for the Frenchman's part in the 1993 fracas at the same ground, United again relied on young Nicky Butt. When the game got under way, United fans were soon biting their lips when Ince got up after committing a foul and immediately left the pitch clutching his arm as if it was broken. However, he soon returned to the fray but looked in some discomfort. Whilst United were sorting out Ince's problem, Schmeichel dived bravely at Saffet's feet to keep the sides level. Young Nicky Butt was barely putting a pass to a Red shirt and seemed overcome by the atmosphere, a remark which also applied to Giggs who had one of his least effective outings.

Mapeza had the Reds' defence at full stretch and it was fortunate that his shot was deflected for a corner after which it was Hakan's turn to test Schmeichel with a shot from outside the area but the Dane was more than equal to the task. Keane and Kubilay were involved in an incident which saw them squaring up to one another with the Turk afterwards alleging that Keane had spat at him but, fortunately for both players, the officials did not see the trouble.

Tugay, who had been one of the Turk's best players, was injured on the stroke of half-time and didn't reappear for the second period but it didn't stop Galatasary almost taking the lead in the 61st minute when Tugay's replacement, Arif was thwarted by Schmeichel who made a great close range block with his long right arm and then grabbed the ball just before Arif's outstretched boot could force it over the line. May, Hughes and Sharpe all picked up needless bookings in a fifteen minute spell as United began to lose just a little of their composure and Ferguson decided it was time to shake things up. Parker was introduced for Giggs which was not the defensive move it appears on paper for the substitute went to full back which released Sharpe to try to improve on Giggs' ineffectual marauding. And the move almost paid off when the Turk's Lithuanian international 'keeper dropped a Sharpe cross which allowed Kanchelskis to lob the ball over the stranded Stauce only for a defender to hack it away to safety off the line after which both sides decided to hold on to what they already had and the game became a stalemate in the last ten minutes.

European Record

		Home					Away				
	P	W	D	L	F	A	W	D	L	F	A
Champions' Cup	47	21	2	0	73	19	8	8	8	39	34
All European Comps	107	39	13	0	136	36	17	17	21	77	76

	Home	Away	Total
European Attendances	33,625	30,000	63,625

Manchester United (1) 2
Everton (0) 0

 CARLING

Match 12

Saturday, 1st October 1994, Old Trafford   Att: 43,803

Manchester United

1	Peter	SCHMEICHEL
12	David	MAY
3	Denis	IRWIN
4	Steve	BRUCE – *Booked*
5	Lee	SHARPE – *Booked*
6	Gary	PALLISTER
7	Eric	CANTONA
8	Paul	INCE
10	Mark	HUGHES (*75)
16	Roy	KEANE
14	Andrei	KANCHELSKIS

Everton

1	Neville	SOUTHALL
21	Gary	ROWETT
3	Andy	HINCHCLIFFE
4	Ian	SNODIN – *Booked*
5	Dave	WATSON
16	David	BURROWS – *Booked*
7	Vinny	SAMWAYS
8	Graham	STUART (*86)
26	David	UNSWORTH
18	Joe	PARKINSON – *Booked*
11	Daniel	AMOKACHI – *Booked*

Subs

13	Gary	WALSH (G)
24	Paul	SCHOLES
9	Brian	McCLAIR *

13	Jason	KEARTON (G)
2	Matthew	JACKSON
19	Stuart	BARLOW *

Match Facts

- First League goal of the season for Sharpe.
- Fifth successive victory over Everton.
- Everton failed to score against United in last five meetings.

Score Sheet

A. KANCHELSKIS 41 min –1-0

L. SHARPE 88 min – 2-0

Referee:
Mr G. Poll (Tilehurst, Berks)

FA Carling Premiership

		P	W	D	L	F	A	Pts
1	Newcastle United	8	7	1	0	25	8	22
2	Blackburn Rovers	8	5	2	1	17	5	17
3	Nottingham Forest	7	5	2	0	14	5	17
4	**Manchester United**	**8**	**5**	**1**	**2**	**14**	**6**	**16**
5	Liverpool	7	4	2	1	16	5	14

Handy Andy

Having lost a night's sleep through travelling home straight after the Galatasary European game on the previous Wednesday, United looked definitely on the jaded side as they took on bottom of the table Everton and they were grateful to Andrei Kanchelskis for scoring at a very handy time just before the interval. Cantona returned for United and the Reds also welcomed back Denis Irwin, left out in Istanbul because of the "foreigner" ruling. Making way were Nicky Butt and Ryan Giggs whose form had been patchy this season. For their part, the Merseysiders opted for a safety first formation which saw Joe Parkinson providing extra defensive cover just in front of the back four leaving Nigerian international Amokachi to plough a lone furrow up front.

Nevertheless, the Nigerian proved to be a handful for Bruce and he hustled the the United skipper into an early booking in the sixth minute. There was further hope for Everton in the 12th minute when a header from Parkinson fell in to the path of Gary Rowett only for Pallister to save the day with a tremendous goal saving tackle just as the youngster was poised to shoot from only twelve yards out. United got on top but Cantona mistimed his effort and then Kanchelskis tried his luck from an acute angle when a cross to either Cantona or Hughes would surely have brought a better dividend. Everton were now restricted to long range efforts but one of them, from a curling 25 yard free kick by Hinchcliffe, had Schmeichel making a save right out of the top drawer. The bookings were now coming thick and fast; Sharpe, Amokachi and Parkinson all had their names taken. With the interval beckoning, United took the lead with a rare Kanchelskis headed goal. It was Sharpe who delivered a looping cross towards the far post where the little Russian came running in to meet the ball, which by now had bounced and was nicely head high for Kanchelskis to meet with his head without breaking his stride.

Immediately after the interval Everton came as close to scoring as they had been all afternoon. A scramble in the Red's area ended with Rowett stabbing the ball towards goal only to find Schmeichel making a superb reflex save. At the other end, Kanchelskis tested Southall with a powerful long range shot after the Welsh international had earlier thwarted him by dashing out of goal to just nick the ball away from the onrushing Russian. Mike Walker's team, however, refused to lie down and Hinchcliffe again tried to beat Schmeichel with a thundering long range free-kick which the Dane had to be at the top of his form to deal with.

With the game still in the balance, United made it safe two minutes from time when Sharpe, put through into the penalty area by Ince, shot low to Southall's left giving the 'keeper no chance from ten yards. It was another three points but it was still not the fluent United of the previous season.

League Record

| | Home | | | | | | Away | | | | |
	P	W	D	L	F	A	W	D	L	F	A
94/95 FAPL	8	4	0	0	9	0	1	1	2	5	6
All Time FAPL	92	32	11	3	87	27	24	13	9	74	48
FAPL/FL	3648	1068	421	335	3637	1811	556	425	793	2480	3104

	Home	Away	Total
FAPL Attendances	174,197	108,529	282,726

Manchester United (1) 2
Port Vale (0) 0

2 Rd 2 Leg Match 13

Att: 31,615

Manchester United

1	Gary	WALSH
2	Chris	CASPER
5	David	MAY
6	Gary	PALLISTER
3	John	O'KANE
7	Keith	GILLESPIE (*65)
4	Nicky	BUTT
8	David	BECKHAM
9	Brian	McCLAIR
10	Paul	SCHOLES
11	Simon	DAVIES (+76)

Port Vale

1	Paul	MUSSELWHITE
2	Bradley	SANDEMAN
5	Neil	ASPIN
6	Dean	GLOVER – Booked
3	Allen	TANKARD
11	Mark	BURKE +
4	Andy	PORTER – Booked
7	Tony	KELLY
8	Kevin	KENT (*72)
9	Martin	FOYLE
10	Lee	GLOVER

Subs

12	Graham	TOMLINSON *
13	Kevin	PILKINGTON (G)
14	Gary	NEVILLE +

12	Robin	VAN DER LAAN +
13	Arjen	VAN HEUSEN (G)
14	Joe	ALLON *

Match Facts

- First full start for John O'Kane, Chris Casper (son of former Burnley player and manager, Frank).
- First appearance for Graham Tomlinson.
- First goal for David May since joining the club from Blackburn.
- The club's leading goalscorer in the League Cup, Brian McClair, increased his tally to 19.
- United make it nine wins out of nine in Cup football against Port Vale with a goal tally of 21 for and only five against.

Score Sheet

B. McCLAIR 34 min – 1-0

D. MAY 61 min – 2-0

Referee:

Mr A. Wilkie (Chester-le-Street)

Aggregate

United win 4-1

May Day for the Kids

United fielded an even more inexperienced team for this second leg Coca Cola cup tie against Port Vale than they had for the first game a fortnight earlier. Of the fourteen man squad, no fewer than eight had played in United's 1992 FA Youth Cup winning side whilst a ninth, Simon Davies, had captained the Youth team a year previous to that success. But despite this influx of youth, the four older members of the team all made their presence felt with Walsh having to make two superb early saves as May and Pallister defended brilliantly whilst McClair added to his tally of League Cup goals before May completed a memorable night with his first senior goal for the club.

Both managers had problems of different natures before the game with Ferguson being warned that the Football League would not consider the two legs as one match but rather as two separate incidents when considering what action to take against United for fielding under-strength teams. John Rudge, the Port Vale manager, had the more difficult problem of trying to motivate his high flying First Division side to play well against a virtual Youth team that had already beaten them well at Vale Park. Whatever Rudge said, however, had worked because Vale were the likeliest of the two sides in the early exchanges and Walsh had to be at his best to tip a Lee Glover header over his bar and then to deal with a 20 yard piledriver from Allen Tankard. United also needed Pallister and May at their best during this opening period and, if the summer signing from Blackburn had looked shaky in previous games at full back, then it has to be said that back in his proper role of central defender he gave an accomplished performance.

Having weathered the storm, United bounced back in the 25th minute to earn themselves a penalty kick down the left when Gillespie's cross to the near post was handled by Aspin. Butt, however, smacked the resulting spot kick against the angle of the crossbar and post to the keeper's left and could only watch in horror as the ball flew high in the air and came down behind the goal. Nine minutes later, the miss was forgotten as United sealed the result of the tie with a simple strike from McClair. O'Kane and Davies linked up down the left before Davies took on three defenders near the corner flag. His cross was to the near post where O'Kane beat two defenders to flick the ball over their heads. McClair, standing unmarked some eight yards out, simply stooped and placed a soft header into the corner of the net to Musselwhite's right with the 'keeper off balance.

United's youngsters were now putting on a stunning show of quick interpassing helped, no doubt, by years of playing together and it was one of these moves that led to the second goal. Vale actually managed to parry a slick Red attack down the right but only at the expense of a corner. When the kick came over, David May rose above the defence to deliver a powerful header into the net from ten yards out.

Shortly afterwards, United gave their other summer signing Graham Tomlinson, his first senior game whilst Nicky Butt showed just what a prospect he is with an all round display that, penalty miss apart, was quite outstanding.

League Cup Record

	Home						Away				
P	W	D	L	F	A	W	D	L	F	A
123	45	11	8	136	53	23	14	22	81	75

	Home	Away	Total
CCC Attendances	31,615	18,605	50,220

Sheffield Wednesday (1) 1
Manchester United (0) 0

8th October 1994, Hillsborough   Att: 33,441

Sheffield Wednesday

13	Kevin	PRESSMAN
2	Peter	ATHERTON
3	Ian	NOLAN
9	David	HIRST
10	Mark	BRIGHT (+88)
12	Andy	PEARCE – *Booked*
14	Chris	BART-WILLIAMS (*65)
11	John	SHERIDAN
16	Graham	HYDE
17	Des	WALKER
29	Les	BRISCOE

Subs

4	Ian	TAYLOR *
20	Gordon	WATSON +
23	Lance	KEY (G)

Manchester United

1	Peter	SCHMEICHEL
2	Paul	PARKER (*60)
3	Denis	IRWIN
4	Steve	BRUCE – *Booked*
5	Lee	SHARPE – *Booked*
6	Gary	PALLISTER
8	Paul	INCE
9	Brian	McCLAIR
10	Mark	HUGHES – *Booked*
16	Roy	KEANE
31	Keith	GILLESPIE (+76)

12	David	MAY *
13	Gary	WALSH (G)
24	Paul	SCHOLES +

Match Facts

- FAPL debut for Keith Gillespie.
- First full FAPL start of the season for Paul Parker.
- Second consecutive Saturday that both Bruce and Sharpe had been booked and third consecutive game in which he had played that Sharpe had been cautioned.

Score Sheet

D. HIRST 44 min – 1-0

Referee:
Mr P. Danson (Leicester)

FA Carling Premiership

		P	W	D	L	F	A	Pts
1	Newcastle United	8	7	1	0	25	8	22
2	Nottingham Forest	9	6	3	0	20	10	21
3	Liverpool	8	5	2	1	19	7	17
4	Blackburn Rovers	8	5	2	1	17	5	17
5	**Manchester United**	9	5	1	3	14	7	16

On the Slide

Forced to take to the field without Kanchelskis and Cantona on international duty for their respective countries and minus the injured Giggs, United boss Alex Ferguson opted to gamble on the fitness of both Parker and Keane rather than put in his youngsters on a wholesale basis. There was, however, still room for Northern Ireland international Keith Gillespie to make his first Premiership appearance. Sheffield Wednesday had almost as many injury problems as United but not as many points and the Reds went in to the game with the knowledge that they had defeated the Owls four times in the previous campaign.

Gillespie was quickly in to the action on his Premiership debut to win a corner that saw Hughes whip in one of his stunning volleys which Pressman was glad to see straight at him. It then appeared that the Reds had taken the lead with a brilliant decisive attack which Bruce started with an interception in his own area. He brought the ball away before feeding McClair who, in turn, found Keane on the right. McClair continued his run in to space down the right wing and was put clear by Keane's ball for the Scot to slide the ball in to the path of the onrushing Gillespie. The youngster's debut seemed to be a dream come true when he shot nonchalantly past a helpless Pressman but a linesman's flag ruled the effort out.

Despite the pressure Wednesday took a shock lead on half-time when the ball fell to Bart-Williams who cleared to Sheridan and then made ground in to the United half for the return ball. Williams spotted Hirst pulling away to the left and played the ball to him leaving both Bruce and Parker stranded. Hirst moved quickly in on Schmeichel and steered the ball past the advancing Dane from the edge of the penalty area. It was Hirst's first goal since the opening day of the season.

The second period saw chances galore as United went in search of the equaliser and, by so doing, left themselves exposed at the back. Straight from the kick off, Keane fired in a blockbuster that Pressman could only just grab at the second attempt and then Hughes and McClair combined well to set up a great opportunity for Sharpe only to see him fire well over. The Reds were fortunate not to go further behind when Pallister casually lost the ball at the edge of United's penalty area and was grateful to see Hyde fluff the chance with a powder-puff effort. Gillespie went close but back at the United end, Schmeichel had to save from Sheridan.

The Dane then had to be both quick and brave to thwart Hirst by diving at his feet as the striker bore down on goal. United, looking to avoid failing to score in the FAPL for the first time in 94/95 put together a brilliant late link up involving Sharpe, Irwin, Ince, Hughes and McClair resulting in Hughes getting a chance of the equaliser but his powerful shot was again straight at Pressman. So United lost for the third time on the trot away from home in the FAPL to give the suggestion of their being on the slide.

League Record

	Home						Away				
	P	W	D	L	F	A	W	D	L	F	A
94/95 FAPL	9	4	0	0	9	0	1	1	3	5	7
All time FAPL	93	32	11	3	87	27	24	13	10	74	49
FAPL/FL	3649	1068	421	335	3637	1811	556	425	794	2480	3105

FAPL Attendances	Home	Away	Total
	174,197	141,970	316,167

Manchester United   (1) 1
West Ham United   (0) 0

Saturday, 15th October 1994, Old Trafford   Att: 43,795

Manchester United

1	Peter	SCHMEICHEL
12	David	MAY (*45)
3	Denis	IRWIN
4	Steve	BRUCE
5	Lee	SHARPE – *Booked*
6	Gary	PALLISTER
7	Eric	CANTONA
8	Paul	INCE
10	Mark	HUGHES
11	Ryan	GIGGS
14	Andrei	KANCHELSKIS

West Ham United

1	Ludek	MIKLOSKO
2	Tim	BREACKER
12	Keith	ROWLAND
4	Steve	POTTS
5	Alvin	MARTIN
6	Martin	ALLEN
19	Mike	MARSH
26	Don	HUTCHINSON
14	Matthew	RUSH
10	John	MONCUR
27	Tony	COTTEE

Subs

9	Brian	McCLAIR
13	Gary	WALSH (G)
19	Nicky	BUTT * – *Booked*

7	Ian	BISHOP
21	Tony	FEUER (G)
22	Adam	WHITBREAD

Match Facts

● West Ham not won at Old Trafford since August 1986.
● Sharpe booked for third consecutive Saturday.
● United have not conceded a goal at Old Trafford in five FAPL games.

Score Sheet

E. CANTONA 44 min – 1-0

Referee:
Mr RB Gifford (Llanbadrach)

Alvin's Blues Suits Reds

In a lack lustre display, United were saved the dropping of two home points by the gifting of a goal right on the half time whistle. In an error of schoolboy proportions, Alvin Martin was left looking as blue as the colour of his shirt as he made a complete mess of dealing with a Kanchelskis cross to the near post. There appeared to be no danger with both Martin and Miklosko on duty by the goalpost but, somehow or other, Martin's attempted clearance ballooned up in the air. Miklosko clearly hesitated as he considered whether the referee would deem the ball to have been passed back whilst Martin simply didn't seem to have a clue as to where the ball had gone. Whilst these two were considering their respective options, Giggs made their minds up for them by nipping in and squaring the ball for Cantona to knock in to the empty net from five yards. The fact that such an error was the difference between the two sides just about summed up the game.

Ferguson had brought back Cantona, Kanchelskis, Giggs and May to strengthen the side but had the Hammers made the most of their second half chances they could well have grabbed a point. Indeed, West Ham started the game stronger and dominated the opening fifteen minutes without ever looking likely to become the first side to score in the league at Old Trafford in 94/95. Then the Reds began to get in the game with Ince rifling in a long range effort. This was followed by one of Hughes's stunning volleys performed as he was horizontal with the ground but the effort was straight at Miklosko. Cantona tried to set up both Hughes and Giggs but the former lost control whilst the intended ball to Giggs was just cut out in the nick of time. But over confidence crept in and Schmeichel saved the day after Bruce let in Cottee. The diminutive striker looked all set to put the Londoners in front but the Great Dane smothered the ball at the player's feet. A couple of minutes later, the Hammers paid dearly for the miss when they gifted the lead to the Reds.

United returned after the interval without May, who had suffered a groin strain and had been replaced by Nicky Butt. West Ham forced the pace and Sharpe, who had dropped to full back in the absence of May, was having a torrid time against the pace and trickery of Matthew Rush. Sharpe had earlier been booked for fouling Rush but it wasn't all one way and United did have their moments, particularly when Giggs clipped a post. But in the last two minutes West Ham had two great opportunities to level and fluffed them both as Schmeichel denied both Rush and Allen in the last minutes of play.

This was not vintage United as they headed into a period of five games in fifteen days against teams made of sterner stuff than West Ham. The Reds would have to step up a gear if the meetings with Barcelona (twice), Newcastle (twice) and Blackburn Rovers were going to reap a rich harvest.

League Record

| | Home | | | | | | Away | | | | |
	P	W	D	L	F	A	W	D	L	F	A
94/95 FAPL	10	5	0	0	10	0	1	1	3	5	7
All time FAPL	94	33	11	3	88	27	24	13	10	74	49
FAPL/FL	3650	1069	421	335	3638	1811	556	425	794	2480	3105

	Home	Away	Total
FAPL Attendances	217,992	141,970	359,962

Manchester United
Barcelona

(1) 2
(1) 2

Wednesday, 19th October 1994, Old Trafford   Att: 40,064

Manchester United

1	Peter	SCHMEICHEL
2	David	MAY – *Booked* (+69)
3	Denis	IRWIN
4	Paul	PARKER
5	Nicky	BUTT (*67)
6	Gary	PALLISTER
7	Andrei	KANCHELSKIS
8	Paul	INCE
9	Roy	KEANE
10	Mark	HUGHES
11	Lee	SHARPE

Barcelona

1	BUSQUETS
2	LUIS (*45)
3	SERGI
4	KOEMAN
5	ABELARDO
6	NADAL – *Booked*
7	GUARDIOLA
8	BAKERO
9	BEGUINSTAIN (+67)
10	STOICHKOV
11	ROMARIO

Subs

12	Steve	BRUCE +
13	Gary	WALSH (G)
14	Paul	SCHOLES *
15	Gary	NEVILLE
16	Simon	DAVIES

12	EUSEBIO *
13	LOPETEGUI (G)
14	CRUYFF +
15	JARA
16	AMOR

Match Facts

• United's 53rd home European match without defeat.

• Only five defeats in thirteen meetings with Spanish sides.

• First goal for Hughes since opening day of the FAPL season.

Score Sheet

M. HUGHES 18 min – 1-0
ROMARIO 34 min – 1-1
BAKERO 49 min – 1-2
L. SHARPE 80 min – 2-2

Referee:
Mr I. Craciunescu (Romania)

UEFA Champions' League – Group A

	P	W	D	L	F	A	Pts
Manchester United	3	1	2	0	6	4	4
IFK Gothenburg	3	2	0	1	5	5	4
Barcelona	3	1	1	1	5	5	3
Galatasary	3	0	1	2	1	3	1

Three Phase Brilliance

It lived up to its billing as Old Trafford's match of the season with United at last producing something more akin to their 1993/94 form. United's speed down the wings with Kanchelskis and Sharpe devastated the Spaniards time and again before Johan Cruyff's side got to grips with the situation around the thirty minute mark. They then controlled the game for forty minutes or so with their brand of cultured, slow build up football before the Reds came storming back in a frantic last twenty minutes. A marvellous game without any doubt prior to which United boss Alex Ferguson had dropped not only a bombshell but also his captain Steve Bruce. In his place came Parker, ostensibly to deal with the pace of Romario but the Reds paid a heavy penalty for the switch when Parker's lack of height gifted Barcelona their second goal just after the break.

Kanchelskis and Sharpe put on a display of wing wizardry not seen in Britain for a long time. Both clearly had the beating of their respective markers and caused mayhem. Barcelona came to Old Trafford on the back of four successive Spanish Championships but the 1994 European Cup finalists were being taken apart. Again the problem for the defence was initiated down the wing with Sharpe's pace taking him past two defenders before delivering the perfect cross to the far post. As the 'keeper desperately scrambled back across his line, Hughes put his header back into the space the 'keeper had just vacated for a super goal. The Spaniards retaliated by pushing Ronald Koeman forward some thirty yards from the entirely defensive position he had thus far been occupied in. His incredible passing skills now began to hurt United rather than just clear his own lines and it was his through ball to Bakero that set up the equaliser. United's defence moved out as Bakero went forward to slip the ball to Romario. The ace Brazilian beat the offside trap as May, on the far side, had not moved out quickly enough. The World Cup star did the rest.

After the break, the Reds suddenly looked up against it when a long ball from Koeman exposed Parker's lack of inches to fall right into the path of Bakero. The Spanish captain took aim, pulled the trigger and fired unerringly into Schmeichel's net. United tried to impose themselves once more with Sharpe skimming the bar and Kanchelskis the post as Ferguson's men lifted their pace. Stoichkov took his own retaliation following some hard tackling with a vicious, off the ball, kick at the May which went unwitnessed by the officials but put the defender on a stretcher.

United sent on Scholes for Butt in a last desperate throw of the dice and then came the goal that United deserved. Ince piled into his fifty something tackle of the night, beat two men and slipped Keane into the clear. His cross left Sharpe with a lot to do under pressure from a defender and the 'keeper but a back heel flick of sheer brilliance deceived them both to put the Reds level. Scholes nearly produced a late winner but if, in the end, a draw was the right result, one thing was for sure – it had been a magical night of football.

European Record

		Home					Away				
	P	W	D	L	F	A	W	D	L	F	A
European Cup	48	21	3	0	75	21	8	8	8	39	34
All Euro Comps	108	39	14	0	138	38	17	17	21	77	78

	Home	Away	Total
European Attendances	73,689	30,000	103,689

Blackburn Rovers (1) 2
Manchester United (1) 4

Sunday, 23rd October 1994, Ewood Park   Att: 30,260

Blackburn Rovers

1	Tim	FLOWERS
2	Tony	GAYLE (+85)
5	Colin	HENDRY
6	Graham	LE SAUX
20	Henning	BERG – *Booked/Sent Off*
22	Mark	ATKINS (*85)
7	Stuart	RIPLEY
16	Chris	SUTTON – *Booked*
24	Paul	WARHURST
11	Jason	WILCOX
9	Alan	SHEARER

Manchester United

1	Peter	SCHMEICHEL
16	Roy	KEANE
3	Denis	IRWIN
4	Steve	BRUCE –ß Booked
6	Gary	PALLISTER
5	Lee	SHARPE
19	Nicky	BUTT (*82)
8	Paul	INCE
14	Andrei	KANCHELSKIS
10	Mark	HUGHES
7	Eric	CANTONA

Subs

17	Robbie	SLATER *
25	Ian	PIERCE +
13	Bobby	MIMMS (G)

13	Gary	WALSH (G)
9	Brian	McCLAIR *
31	Keith	GILLESPIE

Match Facts

- First goals scored at Ewood Park by United since 1966.
- First double strike in FAPL for Kanchelskis.
- First Blackburn goal was the 50th conceded away from home by United in the FAPL.
- The win spoiled Blackburn's 100% 1994/95 home record.

Score Sheet

P. WARHURST 18 min – 1-0
E. CANTONA 45 min Pen 1-1
C. HENDRY 51 min – 2-1
A. KANCHELSKIS 52 min – 2-2
M. HUGHES 67 min – 2-3
A. KANCHELSKIS 82 min – 2-4

Referee:

Mr G. Ashby (Worcester)

FA Carling Premiership

		P	W	D	L	F	A	Pts
1	Newcastle United	11	9	2	0	29	10	29
2	Nottingham Forest	11	8	3	0	25	11	27
3	**Manchester United**	**11**	**7**	**1**	**3**	**19**	**9**	**22**
4	Blackburn Rovers	11	6	3	2	23	12	21

Blackburn Blitzed

On the day that the clocks went back, everything else moved forward with both United and Rovers committed to all out attack. United travelled to Ewood Park with history and current form against them for, not only had United failed to score at Ewood Park in the FAPL, Blackburn also enjoyed a 100% home record. The Reds quickly showed they were intent on consigning both those facts to history as Keane twice clattered Le Saux in the opening minutes without, much to the annoyance of the Rovers fans, either incident bringing a booking. When Sutton retaliated on Ince, though, he was booked. It was, however, Rovers who took the lead after 13 minutes whilst Keane was off the field for stitches to a head injury. Le Saux made the opening with a left wing cross which saw Schmeichel commit himself to a punch at the edge of the 18 yard box but the ball fell straight to Warhurst who, from 35 yards, chipped into the unguarded net.

As United hit back Berg was fortunate to only be booked when he brought down Sharpe but, on the stroke of half-time, his luck ran out when the referee judged he had not only brought down Sharpe in the penalty area but had done so to prevent a goal scoring opportunity. With the crowd in a frenzy following Berg's dismissal, the calmest man on the field was Cantona as he slotted the ball to Flowers' right.

After the break Blackburn's ten men took the game to United and six minutes into the half re-took the lead. Le Saux was again the provider with his left-wing corner picking out the unmarked Hendry who dispatched an accurate header past a despairing Schmeichel. United's response was immediate and equally devastating. Kanchelskis broke down the right only to find his hard driven cross blocked by Hendry. The Russian, however, was first to the rebound and having had his initial option closed he now chose an alternative route by blasting the ball past a bemused Flowers from an acute angle.

United began to make their extra man tell but the goal that put them in the lead for the first time came from an error of schoolboy proportions. There was absolutely no danger to the Rovers goal with the ball at Le Saux's feet in the left back position. In an amazing blunder, the England defender, some 30 yards out, rolled the ball square to Mark Hughes. Flowers, clearly not anticipating such a crass move, was stood at the edge of the 18 yard box from where he was completely helpless as the Welsh striker chipped the simplest of goals.

With time running out Rovers had little option but to throw men forward looking for the equaliser. Thus, they left acres of space and eight minutes from the end paid the penalty as one of their own attacks broke down. Sharpe picked the ball up just outside his own penalty area and found Cantona in the centre circle. The Frenchman simply helped the ball on to Kanchelskis who ran half the length of the field before rounding Flowers to put the ball into the net.

League Record

	Home						Away				
	P	W	D	L	F	A	W	D	L	F	A
94/95 FAPL	11	5	0		10	0	2	1	3	9	9
All time FAPL	95	33	11	3	88	27	25	13	10	78	51
FAPL/FL	3651	1069	421	335	3638	1811	557	425	794	2484	3107

	Home	Away	Total
FAPL Attendances	217,992	172,230	390,222

Newcastle United (0) 2
Manchester United (0) 0

3rd Rnd

Wednesday, 26th October 1994, St James' Park   Att: 34,178

Newcastle United

1	Pavel	SRNICEK
12	Marc	HOTTIGER
6	Steve	HOWEY
15	Darren	PEACOCK
3	John	BERESFORD
27	Philippe	ALBERT
19	Steve	WATSON
8	Peter	BEARDSLEY
11	Scott	SELLARS
9	Andy	COLE
28	Paul	KITSON

Manchester United

1	Gary	WALSH
2	Gary	NEVILLE
3	Denis	IRWIN (*52)
4	Steve	BRUCE
5	Nicky	BUTT – *Booked*
6	Gary	PALLISTER
7	Keith	GILLESPIE
8	David	BECKHAM
9	Brian	McCLAIR
10	Paul	SCHOLES – *Booked*
11	Simon	DAVIES

Subs

30	Mike	HOOPER (G)
18	Steve	GUPPY
10	Lee	CLARKE

12	Lee	SHARPE (*+72)
13	Kevin	PILKINGTON (G)
14	Graham	TOMLINSON +

Match Facts

• First ever win for Newcastle over the Reds in any knock-out competition.
• The win created a club record for Newcastle of 18 games undefeated at the start of a season.
• First goals for Newcastle for both of their scorers, Paul Kitson and Philippe Albert.
• First time United had not scored in a Coca Cola tie in thirteen games.

Score Sheet

P. ALBERT 82 min – 1-0
P. KITSON 87 min – 2-0

Referee:
Mr T. Holbrook (Walsall)

Out of Steam

Manager Alex Ferguson surprised everybody by keeping faith with his Coca Cola youngsters after the draw paired the Old Trafford outfit with the new FAPL leaders, Newcastle United. But the youngsters put on a spirited performance and looked like coming away with a replay until they ran out of steam in the final ten minutes.

The Reds were first on the attack but Nicky Butt's header from a Gillespie cross lacked power after which the home side began to apply plenty of pressure without actually getting much on target. They then re-adjusted their sights and Walsh had to finger tip a Kitson effort for a corner. His finger tips were again put to good use to thwart Albert before United at last broke away only for Gillespie's efforts in setting up McClair to be wasted. But the game was being played mainly at the United end and it seemed as if the Geordies had at last broken the deadlock when Howey, on his 23rd birthday, beat Walsh all ends up from 22 yards only to see the ball crash back into play off the post. Sellars was next to try his luck and the Reds were on the ropes. Kitson went close but, amazingly, it was United who almost took the lead as the interval beckoned. Bruce powered in a tremendous header from a Gillespie corner only for Hottiger to clear off the line with the 'keeper nowhere. Walsh was quickly into action again at the start of the second period when Kitson came in to meet a Beardsley cross with his head and then Watson was narrowly wide as Newcastle piled on the pressure. Ferguson introduced Sharpe into the fray for Irwin and the move was to eventually prove disastrous for the Reds. Walsh did brilliantly to foil Cole with Bruce completing the save by clearing off the line as the loose ball threatened to roll into the empty net and that proved to be Cole's only chance of the night as he was immediately substituted. Sharpe then tackled Watson on the halfway line only to fall in a heap after appearing to catch his studs on the ground and it later transpired that he had torn knee ligaments that were to sideline him for a considerable period.

Then to make matters worse, from the space that Sharpe had been occupying, came the goal that was to put Newcastle in the lead. Beardsley was the creator, feeding Hottiger down the Geordie's right flank. The Swiss international's cross was excellent and Philippe Albert came rushing in to head home from point blank range. Within minutes the game was beyond recall when Beardsley released Kitson to run through on Walsh and slip the ball past the United 'keeper's left hand. It had been a spirited showing by the youngsters but now the Reds could look forward to exacting quick revenge as the two teams were scheduled to meet again in the FAPL just 72 hours later.

League Cup Record

	Home						Away				
	P	W	D	L	F	A	W	D	L	F	A
	124	45	11	8	136	53	23	14	23	81	77

	Home	Away	Total
CCC Attendances	31,615	52,783	84,398

Manchester United   (1) 2
Newcastle United   (0) 0

Saturday, 29th October 1994, Old Trafford   Att: 43,795

Manchester United			**Newcastle United**		
1	Peter	SCHMEICHEL	1	Pavel	SRNICEK
16	Roy	KEANE	12	Marc	HOTTIGER
3	Denis	IRWIN	3	John	BERESFORD
4	Steve	BRUCE – *Booked*	27	Philipe	ALBERT
6	Gary	PALLISTER	15	Darren	PEACOCK
14	Andrei	KANCHELSKIS	6	Steve	HOWEY
7	Eric	CANTONA	19	Steve	WATSON
8	Paul	INCE	8	Peter	BEARDSLEY
9	Brian	McCLAIR	7	Robert	LEE
10	Mark	HUGHES	5	Ruel	FOX
11	Ryan	GIGGS (*65)	11	Scott	SELLARS

Subs

13	Gary	WALSH (G)	10	Lee	CLARK
31	Keith	GILLESPIE *	30	Mike	HOOPER (G)
19	Nicky	BUTT	14	Alex	MATHIE

Match Facts

- Newcastle United's first defeat of the season.
- First FAPL goal for Keith Gillespie who was to later join Newcastle.
- First goal of the season for Gary Pallister.
- United have not conceded a goal at home in the FAPL for 830 minutes.
- First Utd victory over Newcastle in four games since Geordies returned to the top flight.

Score Sheet

G. PALLISTER 11 min – 1-0
K. GILLESPIE 77 min – 2-0

Referee:
Mr J. Worrall (Warrington)

Coca Cola is for the Kids

Manager Alex Ferguson decided that the FAPL is the 'real thing' and that the Coca Cola Cup is for the kids when he named just four of the side that lost to Newcastle the previous Wednesday in his starting line-up for the second confrontation between the two sides in the space of 72 hours. Paul Ince went even further by saying "Okay, they've beaten the youngsters, now let's see them take on the big boys". It was another full house at Old Trafford with a further five figure crowd at St James' Park watching a live screening of the match.

And what a match. Right from the moment United kicked off it was end to end stuff with both goalkeeper's seeing plenty of action. United's first attack of note came to grief when a Kanchelskis rocket was blocked only for Newcastle to hit straight back as Lee and Fox led a counter attack that saw continental import Albert shoot wide. United took the lead after twelve minutes when Watson felled Ince just outside the box on the Newcastle side. Giggs floated over a perfect free-kick which saw Pallister outjump Peacock and leave Beresford rooted to the spot. His neck muscles jerked and from six yards his powerful downward header gave Srnicek no chance. Pallister may have earned himself the reputation of being a goal a season man but what a time to produce the goods.

The Geordies, however, hit back with a likely looking raid of their own and United were fortunate to see a shot from Sellars loop over their crossbar after taking a ricochet from Bruce. Play switched again back to the Newcastle end where a Kanchelskis cross found Cantona at the far post but his point blank header was somehow kept out by Srnicek. The 'keeper was quickly in action again, saving a Hughes volley to his left and then making an even better save from the same player as United began to get on top as the half drew to a close.

Newcastle began the second period on the offensive and Sellars should have at least hit the target but the Reds replied through a strong left foot shot from Giggs that Srnicek did well to hold onto. A tremendous run by Ince was only halted at the expense of a corner from which it looked as if United had increased their lead. The corner was headed home by an unmarked Hughes but Newcastle were saved by a linesman's flag indicating that the ball had gone out of play from the corner kick before swinging back in.

United were now getting on top and Ferguson removed Giggs and introduced in his place was young Keith Gillespie and he was to play a crucial role in sealing the game. Picking the ball up some forty yards out on the United left, Gillespie jinked past two defenders before cutting into the area and blasting a drive across Srnicek and into the far corner for a goal of some class. If United had a point to make after the Coca Cola Cup defeat then they had certainly done so in style.

League Record

| | Home | | | | | | Away | | | | |
	P	W	D	L	F	A	W	D	L	F	A
94/95 FAPL	12	6	0	0	12	0	2	1	3	9	9
All Time FAPL	96	34	11	3	90	27	25	13	10	78	51
FAPL/FL	3652	1070	421	335	3640	1811	557	425	794	2484	3107

	Home	Away	Total
FAPL Attendances	261,787	172,230	434,017

Barcelona
Manchester United

(2) 4
(0) 0

2nd November 1994, Nou Camp Stadium

Att: 115,000

Barcelona		**Manchester United**		
1	BUSQUETS	1	Gary	WALSH
4	KOEMAN – *Booked*	2	Paul	PARKER – *Booked*
6	ABELARDO	3	Denis	IRWIN
2	FERRER	4	Steve	BRUCE
5	GUARDIOLA	5	Roy	KEANE
3	SERGI	6	Gary	PALLISTER
7	AMOR	7	Andrei	KANCHELSKIS
8	BAKERO (+76)	8	Paul	INCE – *Booked*
9	ROMARIO	9	Nicky	BUTT
10	JORDI (*62)	10	Mark	HUGHES
11	STOICHKOV	11	Ryan	GIGGS (*79)
Subs				
12	IVAN *	12	Gary	NEVILLE
13	ANGOY (G)	13	Kevin	PILKINGTON (G)
14	SANCHEZ-JARA +	14	Paul	SCHOLES *
15	LUIS	15	David	BECKHAM
16	BEGUIRISTAIN	16	Simon	DAVIES

Match Facts

● Happy Families – Barcelona Manager Johan Cruyff had son Jordi in the team and son-in law Angoy on the bench.

● United still haven't beaten a Spanish club in Spain in a European competition.

● Scoreline equals Reds worst ever Champions' Cup defeat (but not their worst ever European defeat) inflicted by AC Milan on the post Munich side.

Score Sheet

STOICHKOV 9 min – 1-0
ROMARIO 45 min – 2-0
STOICHKOV 52 min – 3-0
FERRER 88 min – 4-0

Referee:
Mr J. Quiniou (France)

UEFA Champions' League – Group A

	P	W	D	L	F	A	Pts
IFK Gothenburg	4	3	0	1	6	5	6
Barcelona	4	2	1	1	9	5	5
Manchester United	4	1	2	1	6	8	4
Galatasary	4	0	1	3	1	4	1

Outpassed, Outgunned, Outclassed

United sprang a surprise prior to the game by opting to leave out Peter Schmeichel in order to play an extra 'foreign' outfield player. But this was nothing to the surprise that awaited the Reds once the game got under way as the Spanish champions outpassed, outgunned, outplayed and, by the end, outclassed United. If it had been a boxing match it would have been stopped after the third goal went in and, in truth, it could have been even worse. Not that Ferguson's side were dreadful, they weren't – it was just that Barcelona had one of *those* nights.

Things got off to a bright start for United with Koeman booked as early as the second minute for a foul on Hughes and, with the Dutchman now having to step warily, visions were held of United gaining the upperhand. Hughes, himself, was very fortunate to escape a booking when he blatantly flattened Stoichkov minutes before he put the Spaniards into an early ninth minute lead. It was the manager's son, Jordi Cruyff, who did the damage with a skillful ball inside Parker for Romario. It looked as though it might run out but the Brazilian caught it and pulled the ball back to Cruyff whose shot was cleared off the line by Ince but only straight back to Cruyff who now squared the ball to Stoichkov. A blistering shot across the face of the goal was going wide until it hit Pallister and deflected on to the post before nestling in the net.

To United's great credit, they weathered the storm and actually got on top for the final ten minutes of the first period although they failed to turn their possession into anything resembling even a half chance. Then, in the second minute of injury time, came the killer blow. There appeared no danger as Stoichkov walked with the ball into the United half on the right. There still appeared no danger as he lofted the ball high towards the United area from some sixty yards out in the general direction of Romario. Pallister, however, simply didn't get to it but there still seemed little threat of danger as Romario chested the ball down with the United central defender in close proximity. However, a shift of the hips made a yard of space for the Brazilian World Cup star and his aim under an outstretched Gary Walsh was unerring in its accuracy. United were poleaxed.

Inevitably another goal came early in the second half and what a goal it was! Stoichkov's pace down the left did the damage and, as he played the ball into the box for Romario, the Bulgarian kept running across the edge of the area. A deft back heel from the Brazilian, who seemed to know instinctively where his team mate would be, unhinged the Reds' defence and Stoichkov's famed left foot did the rest. United appeared to have saved themselves from further embarrassment when full back Ferrer popped up on the wing with just two minutes left. His attempted cross was only hacked back to him by a hapless Pallister and, given a second chance, Ferrer opted this time to drive the ball home to set the seal on a wonderful home performance.

European Record

	P	W	D	L	F	A	W	D	L	F	A
		Home					*Away*				
Champions' Cup	49	21	3	0	75	21	8	8	9	39	38
All Euro Comps	109	39	14	0	138	38	17	17	22	77	82

	Home	Away	Total
European Attendances	73,689	145,000	218,689

Aston Villa (1) 1
Manchester United (1) 2

Sunday, 6th November 1994, Villa Park   Att: 32,136

Aston Villa

1	Nigel	SPINK
2	Earl	BARRETT
3	Steve	STAUNTON (*58)
15	Peter	KING
5	Paul	McGRATH – *Booked*
6	Kevin	RICHARDSON
7	Ray	HOUGHTON (+78)
16	Ugo	EHIOGU
9	Dean	SAUNDERS
10	Dalian	ATKINSON
11	Andy	TOWNSEND

Manchester United

13	Gary	WALSH
16	Roy	KEANE
3	Denis	IRWIN
4	Steve	BRUCE – *Booked*
6	Gary	PALLISTER
14	Andrei	KANCHELSKIS
8	Paul	INCE
19	Nicky	BUTT (*6)
11	Ryan	GIGGS
7	Eric	CANTONA
24	Paul	SCHOLES (+78)

Subs

13	Mark	BOSNICH (G)
18	Dwight	YORKE *
14	Garry	PARKER +

25	Kevin	PILKINGTON (G)
31	Keith	GILLESPIE + – *Booked*
9	Brian	McCLAIR *

Match Facts

- First FAPL start for Paul Scholes.
- Andrei Kanchelskis' match winner was ample revenge for being sent off the last time the two teams met which was in the League Cup Final at Wembley.
- The result left Villa with just one point from their last eight league games.

Score Sheet

D. ATKINSON 29 min – 1-0
P. INCE 44 min – 1-1
A. KANCHELSKIS 51 min –1-2

Referee:
Mr P. Don (Hanworth Park)

FA Carling Premiership

		P	W	D	L	F	A	Pts
1	Newcastle United	13	10	2	1	31	13	32
2	Blackburn Rovers	14	9	3	1	28	12	30
3	**Manchester United**	**13**	**9**	**1**	**3**	**23**	**10**	**28**
4	Nottingham Forest	13	8	3	2	25	14	27
5	Liverpool	13	8	2	3	29	13	26

Reds Shake Off Blues in Black

United took to the pitch in the all-black kit they had worn when suffering in Barcelona a few days prior to this league game and, to be honest, the display at Villa Park wasn't a great deal better. The difference was that Villa were no Barcelona and, having been dismissed themselves from Europe during the previous midweek by Trabzonspor, they allowed United to shake off their blues.

Ferguson had been given problems when both Schmeichel and Hughes reported unfit and the Old Trafford boss had no option but to carry on with Gary Walsh in net whilst giving young Paul Scholes the nod over Brian McClair. Cantona was back after serving the last of his four game European ban with Keane moving to full back in place of Parker in order to accommodate the Frenchman.

United almost made a nightmare start when Kanchelskis tried passing back to Walsh only for the 'keeper to slice his clearance straight to Staunton who, fortunately shot wide of the empty net from fifteen yards! United's poor start became even more disjointed when they lost Nicky Butt after only six minutes following a collision with Ehiogu that resulted in the youngster suffering concussion. The classy confrontation these two teams usually put on was sadly missing with both sides frequently giving the ball needlessly away and bystanders could easily see why Villa had won just five of their last 27 league games. The opening goal, when it came on the half hour, was the result of yet another sloppy piece of work, this time from Keane who gave the ball away when under no pressure. Dalian Atkinson, having been given the ball didn't look the gift horse in the mouth and let fly. The ball struck Bruce, looped up in the air and over the stranded Walsh for a goal that summed the game up.

United equalised on the stroke of half time when Ehiogu headed out of defence straight to Ince. The United player chested the ball down and hit a shot from 20 yards that Spink should have got to. But he didn't and, after hitting the woodwork on numerous occasions during the course of the campaign, Ince would have been more than pleased to register his first goal since the FA Charity Shield match. Having struck just prior to the interval, United also hit Villa within five minutes of the restart. Scholes released Irwin down the left flank for the Irishman to cross into the area. Cantona stepped over the ball allowing it to run to Kanchelskis. The Russian, about sixteen yards out on the right was confronted by King but, nevertheless, opted to shoot. The Villa defender obligingly left his legs apart and the ball found the gap to beat an unsighted Spink.

Villa threw everything at United in search of the equaliser but Walsh was in fine form between the posts with nothing better than his excellent effort to turn aside Staunton's late attempt that again took a wicked change of direction off Bruce. It had been a poor game but it was another three points gathered.

League Record

| | Home | | | | | | Away | | | | |
	P	W	D	L	F	A	W	D	L	F	A
94/95 FAPL	13	6	0	0	12	0	3	1	3	11	10
All time FAPL	97	34	11	3	90	27	26	13	10	80	52
FAPL/FL	3653	1070	421	335	3640	1811	558	425	794	2486	3108

	Home	Away	Total
FAPL Attendances	261,787	204,366	466,153

Manchester United (2) 5
Manchester City (0) 0

Thursday, 10th November 1994, Old Trafford   Att: 43,738

Manchester United

1	Peter	SCHMEICHEL
16	Roy	KEANE
3	Denis	IRWIN
4	Steve	BRUCE
6	Gary	PALLISTER
14	Andrei	KANCHELSKIS
8	Paul	INCE
9	Brian	McCLAIR
11	Ryan	GIGGS (*45)
7	Eric	CANTONA
10	Mark	HUGHES – *Booked*

Subs

13	Gary	WALSH (G)
24	Paul	SCHOLES *
26	Gary	NEVILLE

Manchester City

32	Simon	TRACEY
22	Richard	EDGEHILL – *Booked*
12	Ian	BRIGHTWELL – *Booked*
6	Michel	VONK
3	Terry	PHELAN – *Booked*
16	Nicky	SUMMERBEE – *Booked*
10	Gary	FLITCROFT – *Booked*
21	Steve	LOMAS
11	Peter	BEAGRIE
8	Paul	WALSH
9	Niall	QUINN

33	John	BURRIDGE (G)
18	David	BRIGHTWELL
24	Adie	MIKE

Match Facts

- Kanchelskis becomes first United player to score a hat-trick in the FAPL.
- The match is played 100 years to the week after the first ever 'derby' clash.
- The 5-0 scoreline is United's biggest ever win against City and equals United's biggest ever FAPL win to date.
- City not won at Old Trafford since Denis Law's goal beat the Reds in 1974.

Score Sheet

E. CANTONA 24 min – 1-0
A. KANCHELSKIS 43 min – 2-0
A. KANCHELSKIS 47 min – 3-0
M. HUGHES 70 min – 4-0
A. KANCHELSKIS 89 min – 5-0

Referee:
Mr K. Cooper (Pontypridd)

FA Carling Premiership

		P	W	D	L	F	A	Pts
1	Newcastle United	14	10	3	1	31	13	33
2	**Manchester United**	14	10	1	3	28	10	31
3	Blackburn Rovers	14	9	3	2	28	12	30
4	Liverpool	14	9	2	3	32	14	29
5	Nottingham Forest	14	8	4	2	25	14	28

History Repeats Itself as City are Crushed

The 121st League meeting between the two clubs took place exactly 100 years to the week after the first ever encounter when, strangely, United also put five past City with Smith becoming the first United player to score four times in a Football League match. On this November night, Kanchelskis was to finish one short of Smith's haul but still had the satisfaction of becoming the first United player to score a hat trick in the Premiership whilst City didn't even have the consolation of the two goals they had managed in reply a hundred years earlier.

The whistle had no sooner gone than Hughes was in the book and a second caution came ninety seconds later when Summerbee's name was taken for clattering Giggs. But once the football got under way, City began the game reasonably well with Beagrie causing makeshift right-back Keane some problems as the Blues had the better of the early exchanges without ever threatening to score.

But the City fan's taunts of "Barcelona" rebounded on them when Kanchelskis and Cantona combined to open the scoring. Kanchelskis, on the half way line, released a fifty yard ball, from the right towards Cantona, who was marked by Brightwell. A quick shuffle from the Frenchman gave him five yards of space and he thundered the ball past City's on-loan 'keeper, Simon Tracey from fifteen yards to record his sixth goal in two years against them since he moved to Old Trafford. United now stepped up the pace and, just before the break, United doubled their lead. A long ball from Pallister found Cantona who helped it on to Kanchelskis. The Russian cut in and let fly from his favourite angle with the ball taking a slight deflection on its way into Tracey's net.

The second period was hardly under way when the Reds went further in to the lead and again it was Cantona and Kanchelskis who were responsible for the damage. Set on his way by a flick from the Frenchman, the Russian outpaced Phelan over forty yards before coming face to face with Tracey. The 'keeper blocked the first effort but was powerless to do anything about the follow up. United were now in full flow with City totally outclassed. The Reds always looked likely to increase their lead and on seventy minutes they proceeded to do so when Keane's strong run down the right enabled him to play the ball into Hughes. His first effort from near the penalty spot was blocked by a despairing tackle that floored the United player.

But he was on his feet in a flash to toe poke the ball past Tracey for United's fourth. City looked like conceding plenty more but somehow survived until the dying minutes when Cantona redirected Schmeichel's long throw to Kanchelskis who again took two attempts to beat Tracey to make it 5-0. City captain Niall Quinn said after the game "This has to be the worst night of my football career". It certainly wasn't that, though, for the United fans who sang long into the night!

League Record

	Home					Away				
	P	W	D	L	F	A	W	D	L	F	A
94/95 FAPL	14	7	0	0	17	0	3	1	3	11	10
All Time FAPL	98	35	11	3	95	27	26	13	10	80	52
FAPL/FL	3654	1071	421	335	3645	1811	558	425	794	2486	3108

	Home	Away	Total
FAPL Attendances	305,525	204,366	509,891

Manchester United (2) 3
Crystal Palace (0) 0

Match 23

Saturday, 19th November 1994, Old Trafford   Att: 43,788

Manchester United

1	Peter	SCHMEICHEL (**7)
27	Gary	NEVILLE
3	Denis	IRWIN
12	David	MAY
6	Gary	PALLISTER
14	Andrei	KANCHELSKIS (*52)
8	Paul	INCE
9	Brian	McCLAIR
18	Simon	DAVIES (+71)
7	Eric	CANTONA
10	Mark	HUGHES

Crystal Palace

1	Nigel	MARTYN
2	John	HUMPHREY
3	Dean	GORDON
4	Gareth	SOUTHGATE – Booked
14	Richard	SHAW
6	Chris	COLEMAN
22	Darren	PATTERSON – Booked (*69)
23	Ricky	NEWMAN
9	Chris	ARMSTRONG
18	Andy	PREECE
11	John	SALAKO

Subs

24	Paul	SCHOLES +
25	Kevin	PILKINGTON (G)**
31	Keith	GILLESPIE *

15	Robert	BOWRY *
16	Darren	PITCHER
19	Rhys	WILMOT (G)

Match Facts

- FAPL debut for Simon Davies.
- First team debut for Kevin Pilkington.
- First goal of the season for Denis Irwin.
- Palace came to Old Trafford on the back of five straight wins.
- United hit top spot for the first time in 94/95.
- Palace not scored at Old Trafford since they won there in December 1989.

Score Sheet

D. IRWIN 7 min – 1-0

E. CANTONA 37 min – 2-0

A. KANCHELSKIS 50 min – 3-0

Referee:
Mr B. Hill (Market Harborough)

FA Carling Premiership

		P	W	D	L	F	A	Pts
1	**Manchester United**	15	11	1	3	31	10	34
2	Blackburn Rovers	15	10	3	2	31	13	33
3	Newcastle United	15	10	3	2	33	16	33
4	Liverpool	14	9	2	3	32	14	29

86

No Lottery for United

On the day that the National Lottery made its bow, United made sure their game against Crystal Palace was nowhere near a lottery as they put on one of their best displays of the campaign to demolish the London side who, themselves, came North on the back of five straight victories. Alex Ferguson certainly had plenty of selection problems with Keane, Parker, Giggs, and Butt all out of contention through injury and Bruce suspended due to the number of bookings he had picked up. The United boss was forced to put young Kevin Pilkington on the bench, standing in as sub 'keeper in the absence of Gary Walsh who had been laid low with a stomach strain. Pilkington, having begun the morning in obscurity, was to have a day he would remember for the rest of his life.

Things, initially, looked bleak for the Reds when Schmeichel collided with Pallister in collecting a high ball after only six minutes. The Dane carried on briefly but was in obvious trouble with his back and a minute later young Pilkington was on for his debut in front of a full Old Trafford house. United took the blow in their stride, however, and within seconds of the substitution were in front. Irwin was tripped by Humphrey when foraging down the left and, from the resulting free kick, the Irishman himself blasted the Reds ahead from just outside the box. The kick took a wicked deflection off the wall to leave Martyn stranded on one side of his goal as the ball thudded home in the opposite corner. Davies, also on his FAPL debut, had settled well and was causing Palace problems with one mazy run ending with a good cross for Cantona to head narrowly wide. At the other end, Pilkington made a marvellous one handed save pushing the ball round the post to deny Preece whilst Neville, a seasoned campaigner by the standards of Davies and Pilkington, with one previous outing in the league, was also playing a prominent part and it was his link up with Kanchelskis that put the Champions two up. A quick interchange of passes down the right between Neville and the Russian left Kanchelskis to cross from the right. The ball to the far post was weighted perfectly for Cantona to head home from point blank range after losing his marker and the points looked secure.

There were let offs especially when Armstrong came as close as anyone to becoming the first visiting player to score an FAPL goal at Old Trafford in 1994/95 when he thumped the post with a header. Just before the break both Patterson and Southgate were booked for violent tackles as United threatened to run rampant.

The mood continued in the second period with United making it three within five minutes of the kick off as Hughes quickly took a throw-in near the half way line on the right to release Kanchelskis. His pace was too much for Palace and, as he cut in from the right, his shot beat Martyn at the near post for pace. Ferguson took the opportunity to give both Gillespie and Scholes more experience of the big time as the Reds began to treat the crowd to a top class show. It certainly wasn't a lottery!

League Record

| | P | Home | | | | | Away | | | | |
		W	D	L	F	A	W	D	L	F	A
FAPL 94/95	15	8	0	0	20	0	3	1	3	11	10
All Time FAPL	99	36	11	3	98	27	26	13	10	80	52
FAPL/FL	3655	1072	421	335	3648	1811	558	425	794	2486	3108

	Home	Away	Total
FAPL Attendances	349,313	204,366	553,679

IFK Gothenburg (1) 3
Manchester United (0) 1

Wednesday, 23rd November 1994, Ullevi Stadium   Att: 36,350

IFK Gothenburg

1	RAVELLI
2	KAMARK
3	BJORKLUND
4	JOHANSSON
5	NILSSON
6	MARTINSSON (*48)
7	REHN
8	LINDQVIST – *Booked*
9	BLOMQVIST
10	ERLINGMARK
11	PETTERSSON (+78)

Subs

12	ANDERSSON *
13	LAST (G)
14	ANEGRUND
15	BENGTSSON +
16	WAHlSTEDT

Manchester United

1	Gary	WALSH
2	David	MAY (*68)
3	Denis	IRWIN
4	Steve	BRUCE
5	Andrei	KANCHELSKIS
6	Gary	PALLISTER
7	Eric	CANTONA – *Booked*
8	Paul	INCE – *Sent Off*
9	Brian	McCLAIR
10	Mark	HUGHES – *Booked*
11	Simon	DAVIES (+75)

12	Gary	NEVILLE *
13	Kevin	PILKINGTON (G)
14	Nicky	BUTT +
15	Paul	SCHOLES
16	David	BECKHAM

Match Facts

- European debut for Simon Davies.
- First Euro start for Brian McClair since 1992.
- Gothenburg only lost twice at home in over forty European ties.
- Erlingmark was scoring for the fourth successive UEFA Champions League match.
- United's longest run in European competition without a win now stretched to four games.

Score Sheet

BLOMQVIST 10 min – 1-0
M. HUGHES 64 min – 1-1
ERLINGMARK 65 min – 2-1
KAMARK 71min Pen – 3-1

Referee:
Mr A. Trentalange (Italy)

UEFA Champions' League – Group A

	P	W	D	L	F	A	Pts
IFK Gothenburg	5	4	0	1	9	6	8
Barcelona	5	2	1	2	10	7	5
Manchester United	**5**	**1**	**2**	**2**	**7**	**11**	**4**
Galatasary	5	1	1	3	3	5	3

Another Sorry Mess

As if United's previous European match when they were hammered by Barcelona was not sufficient to knock them out of the competition, the Reds proceeded to put on another inept display in Gothenburg to leave themselves in a sorry mess and facing almost certain elimination. True, they were without established players such as Schmeichel, Keane, Sharpe, Giggs and Parker through injury but there was an apathy about their first half performance that belied the fact that they needed at least a draw in Sweden to keep alive a reasonable hope of progressing in the competition.

This was Mr Trentalange's first game in the UEFA Champions League and he wasted no time in making a name for himself by booking Mark Hughes for an innocuous encroachment at a free kick as early as the third minute. But even before this, the Swedes, who had already won their domestic title a month earlier, had given their supporters a fright when a bad pass back from the kick off saw Ravelli struggle to beat Hughes to the ball. Gothenburg, however, settled to their task quicker than United who looked strangely lethargic considering the task in hand. The Reds paid the penalty for their casual approach when they went behind after ten minutes, being caught very square by a through ball from Rehn. The former Everton player was in the centre circle when he released Blomqvist whose run was perfectly timed to leave Irwin, on the far side, playing him on as the rest of United's back four stood flat footed. Walsh spread himself but was powerless to stop the Swedes gaining an early advantage. United were clearly out of sorts but a brilliant header from Cantona gave Kanchelskis a good opportunity only for the winger to fire against Ravelli. Play, however, was mainly at the other end and a bad pass back from Pallister almost let in Martinsson.

Ferguson obviously had plenty to say in the break for United looked a keener outfit after the interval and got on level terms after 63 minutes when May's long ball from the right was brilliantly dropped into the path of Hughes from the head of Cantona and the Welshman drilled home a goal that seemed to have secured United's immediate future in the competition. But their concentration lapsed and within seconds the Swedes were back in front. Blomqvist, as he had done in the first match at Old Trafford, beat May for the umpteenth time and his cross was hit crisply home by Erlingmark. May was immediately substituted but his replacement, Gary Neville, experienced immediate disaster when he slipped to allow in Blomqvist. The flying winger was promptly felled by Pallister with Walsh unable to prevent Kamark converting the resultant spot kick. It was all too much for Ince who had too much to say to Mr Trentalange and found himself sent off as United's evening degenerated still further with the most infuriating news still to come. As the players trooped off the pitch, the unexpected result from Turkey of Galatasary beating Barcelona would almost certainly have been good enough to put United through had they held on to a 1-1 scoreline!

European Record

	Home						Away				
	P	W	D	L	F	A	W	D	L	F	A
Champions' Cup	50	21	3	0	75	21	8	8	10	40	41
All Euro Comps	110	39	14	0	138	38	17	17	23	78	85

	Home	Away	Total
European Attendances 94/95	73,689	181,350	255,039

Arsenal (0) 0
Manchester United (0) 0

Match 25

Saturday, 26th November 1994, Highbury — Att: 38,301

Arsenal

1	David	SEAMAN
2	Lee	DIXON
12	Steve	BOULD
6	Tony	ADAMS
3	Nigel	WINTERBURN
21	Steve	MORROW
17	John	JENSEN (+68)
11	Eddie	McGOLDRICK – *Booked*
19	Jimmy	CARTER (*45)
8	Ian	WRIGHT
9	Alan	SMITH

Subs

27	Paul	DICKOV * – *Booked*
14	Martin	KEOWN +
13	Vince	BARTRAM (G)

Manchester United

13	Gary	WALSH
12	David	MAY
27	Gary	NEVILLE
6	Gary	PALLISTER
3	Denis	IRWIN
14	Andrei	KANCHELSKIS (*56)
8	Paul	INCE – *Booked*
9	Brian	McCLAIR
10	Mark	HUGHES – *Booked/ Sent Off*
7	Eric	CANTONA
31	Keith	GILLESPIE – *Booked* (+73)

Subs

18	Simon	DAVIES +
19	Nicky	BUTT * – *Booked*
25	Kevin	PILKINGTON (G)

Match Facts

- United's 100th FAPL game.
- Arsenal still to beat United in the FAPL.
- Second season in succession that United had a player dismissed at Highbury following Eric Cantona's sending off in 93/94.

Score Sheet

Referee:
Mr K. Morton (Bury St Edmunds)

FA Carling Premiership

		P	*W*	*D*	*L*	*F*	*A*	*Pts*
1	Blackburn Rovers	16	11	3	2	35	13	36
2	**Manchester United**	**16**	**11**	**2**	**3**	**31**	**10**	**35**
3	Newcastle United	16	10	4	2	34	17	34
4	Liverpool	16	9	3	4	33	17	30
5	Nottingham Forest	16	8	4	4	25	16	28

No Shot in the Arm

United, reeling from their midweek defeat in Gothenburg, met an Arsenal side trying to recover from the sensational disclosure made just before the game that their England international Paul Merson had a £150 a day cocaine habit but neither side could find the shot in the arm to forget their problems. The game was as drab as the late November day and, in the case of United, things got worse rather than better, when Hughes was sent off to become the second United player to be dismissed in the space of four days.

For two of England's top trophy winners over the past few seasons, there was a strange look about the respective line ups with unfamiliar names everywhere. United fielded Walsh, May, Neville, Gillespie, Davies, Butt and Pilkington whilst Arsenal had Morrow, Carter and Dickov. Gillespie, left out in Gothenburg because of his Irish nationality, was too keen to make an impression and was booked after just 23 seconds for a late tackle on Dixon that was to set the tone for the afternoon. As Arsenal pushed forward at every opportunity, United were in the wars with Irwin, Hughes and Neville all requiring attention. McGoldrick was booked for a foul on Gillespie and then Hughes seemed to push Jensen to the ground by running into him from behind to earn yet another caution. Thirty minutes had passed before United got a shot in but Seaman was equal to the blistering effort from Kanchelskis and pushed it over the bar. Then McClair should have done better with an effort from inside the box after good work by Cantona and Kanchelskis down the right as United finished a poor half with a Hughes shot being pushed round by Seaman.

Arsenal, the better team in the first period, began the second half by forcing Walsh into two excellent saves as he pushed a Dickov bender round the post before blocking a Wright strike that had *goal* written all over it. He couldn't hang on to the ball, however, and it was Pallister to the rescue as he chested down the follow up effort in a goalmouth scramble. It seemed that Ferguson had decided the best he could hope for out of the game was a draw when he withdrew winger Kanchelskis and reinforced his midfield with Butt. Almost immediately Pallister nearly opened up the Gunners with a long run that suddenly saw him at the edge of the Arsenal penalty area. Just as he looked to be running out of ideas, the central defender slipped a superb pass through to Cantona but Seaman was quickly at the feet of the Frenchman to deny him. Ten minutes from time Hughes was off. After being fouled by Morrow, the Welshman needlessly lunged back at the perpetrator of the incident to receive his second caution and dismissal.

The Reds could have been down to nine men with Ince's extraordinary mid air, studs showing, follow through on Jensen – surely a sending off in its own right never mind a second booking. The referee apparently saw nothing wrong as Jensen limped off to be replaced by Keown.

League Record

	Home					Away				
	P	W	D	L	F	A	W	D	L	F	A
94/95 FAPL	16	8	0	0	20	0	3	2	3	11	10
All Time FAPL	100	36	11	3	98	27	26	14	10	80	52
FAPL/FL	3656	1072	421	335	3648	1811	558	426	794	2486	3108

	Home	Away	Total
FAPL Attendances	349,313	242,667	591,980

Manchester United (1) 1
Norwich City (0) 0

Saturday, 3rd December 1994, Old Trafford   Att: 43,789

Manchester United

13	Gary	WALSH
27	Gary	NEVILLE – *Booked*
3	Denis	IRWIN
12	David	MAY
6	Gary	PALLISTER
14	Andrei	KANCHELSKIS (+68)
8	Paul	INCE
9	Brian	McCLAIR
18	Simon	DAVIES (*56)
7	Eric	CANTONA
10	Mark	HUGHES

Norwich City

1	Bryan	GUNN
2	Mark	BOWEN
3	Rob	NEWMAN (*62)
4	Ian	CROOK
5	Jon	NEWSOME
16	Carl	BRADSHAW
15	Daryl	SUTCH
18	Robert	ULLATHORNE
9	Mark	ROBINS
10	John	POLSTON
11	Jeremy	GOSS

Subs

25	Kevin	PILKINGTON (G)
19	Nicky	BUTT +
31	Keith	GILLESPIE *

8	Mick	MILLIGAN
25	Jamie	CURETON *
24	Andy	MARSHALL (G)

Match Facts

- Norwich still without a win over United in the FAPL after five attempts.
- United stretch their record to 12 FAPL games without conceding a goal at home.
- The clean sheet also meant that the Reds had conceded just one goal (at Aston Villa) anywhere in the FAPL in 579 minutes of play.

Score Sheet

E. CANTONA 36 min – 1-0

Referee:
Mr T.J. Holbrook (Walsall)

FA Carling Premiership

		P	W	D	L	F	A	Pts
1	Blackburn Rovers	17	12	3	2	38	13	39
2	**Manchester United**	**17**	**12**	**2**	**3**	**32**	**10**	**38**
3	Newcastle United	17	10	4	3	36	21	34
4	Liverpool	17	9	4	4	34	18	31
5	Nottingham Forest	17	8	5	4	27	18	29

Cantona's Command Performance

On the day that the Royal Command Performance went out on TV, Eric Cantona appropriately put on a show of his own that was as regal in its presentation as the variety acts placed before the Royal Family in a London theatre. Manager Alex Ferguson had serious problems on the injury and suspension front and of the fourteen man squad on duty, no fewer than half had played little or no part in bringing the double to Old Trafford whilst an eighth, Brian McClair, had been little more than a bit player in the fabulous 1993/94 campaign.

United pressed from the start and, after only two minutes, Cantona linked up with Davies to forge an opening for Hughes only for the Welshman to fire wide. A brilliant piece of juggling from Cantona, which had the crowd drooling, then freed Ince but the acting skipper was also wide of the mark with his effort. It wasn't all United, however, and Gary Walsh, making his first home league appearance of the campaign, played his part in keeping the United record of not conceding a goal at home in the FA Premiership since April intact with several smart interceptions.

Around the twenty-five minute mark, United began to take a firmer hold on the game as their attacks began to flow more freely. In the space of five minutes, Ince and Irwin both had shots blocked whilst McClair drove over after good work by Davies. Goss also cleared the bar at the other end but it was a brief excursion into United territory and the Reds took a justified lead in the 36th minute with Cantona playing a part in the build up before converting with aplomb. Neville played the ball into Cantona from the right midfield and in a flash the Frenchman had whipped it back out to McClair further upfield on the right wing. When the Scot crossed the ball back in from the edge of the area in a slick one-two, the Frenchman sweetly swept the ball home for his fifth goal in his last seven league outings.

Gillespie was sent on after ten minutes of the second period for Davies who had impressed with a good display and the new boy was immediately in the action with a stinging effort that was only just off target but then, in a rare Norwich attack, Robins surprised United only to be ruled fractionally offside.

The warning was taken by Ferguson who withdrew Kanchelskis as the Russian had not looked fully recovered from a bout of 'flu but the Canaries were definitely coming into the game as an attacking force. United were thrown back on their heels as Norwich won a series of corners and it was now the turn of Pallister to shine. He was the rock on which the Norwich ship foundered but, amid all the backpedalling, Cantona managed to almost make it two in the dying minutes and only a last ditch challenge from Newsome and Gunn's block prevented the Frenchman ending the game on an even higher note after a display which had Ferguson purring afterwards "Unbelievable, incredible – easily the best he has played all season".

League Record

	Home						Away				
	P	W	D	L	F	A	W	D	L	F	A
94/95 FAPL	17	9	0	0	21	0	3	2	3	11	10
All time FAPL	101	37	11	9	99	27	26	14	10	80	52
FAPL/FL	3657	1073	421	335	3649	1811	558	426	794	2486	3108

	Home	Away	Total
FAPL Attendances	393,102	242,667	635,769

Manchester United
Galatasary

Wednesday 7th December 1994, Old Trafford

Att: 39,220

	Manchester United			**Galatasary**	
1	Gary	WALSH	1	STAUCE	
2	Gary	NEVILLE	2	ERGUN	
3	Denis	IRWIN	3	BULENTS	
4	Steve	BRUCE	4	SEDAT	
5	Roy	KEANE	5	MERT	
6	Gary	PALLISTER	6	TUGAY (+63)	
7	Eric	CANTONA – *Booked*	7	ARIF	
8	Nicky	BUTT	8	HAMZA (*45)	
9	Brian	McCLAIR	9	HAKAN	
10	David	BECKHAM	10	SUAT	
11	Simon	DAVIES – *Booked*	11	KUBILAY – *Booked*	

Subs

12	David	MAY	12	NEZIHI (G)	
13	Kevin	PILKINGTON (G)	13	UGUR *	
14	Paul	SCHOLES	14	YUSUF +	
15	John	O'KANE	15	SAFFET	
16	David	JOHNSON	16	BEKIR	

Match Facts

- European debut for Beckham and first European goals for both Davies and Beckham.
- United unbeaten at Old Trafford in European matches stretching back almost 38 years.
- First success for United over Galatasary in four attempts.

Score Sheet

S. DAVIES 2 min – 1-0

D. BECKHAM 37 min – 2-0

R. KEANE 48 min – 3-0

BULENTS og 87 min – 4-0

Referee:
Mr R. Wojcik (Poland)

UEFA Champions' League – Final Group A Table

	P	W	D	L	F	A	Pts
IFK Gothenburg	6	4	1	1	10	7	9
Barcelona	6	2	2	2	11	8	6
Manchester United	6	2	2	2	11	11	6
Galatasary	6	1	1	4	3	9	3

The Dream Is Over

The banners read "Welcome to Heaven" in reference to the flags that had greeted United in Turkey saying "Welcome to Hell" but United boss Alex Ferguson wouldn't have thought there was much very heavenly about his team selection problems. The side was decimated by injury and suspension with Schmeichel, Hughes, Ince, Giggs, Sharpe and Kanchelskis all missing. This gave a European debut to David Beckham and places on the subs bench for the first time in Europe to John O'Kane and David Johnson. With Butt and Neville also in the starting line up it gave United four teenagers on the park from the kick-off, all who turned in an exhibition well beyond their years.

Indeed, as early as the second minute three of them combined to put the Reds into the lead. Butt intercepted on the halfway line and fed Keane who slipped the ball wide to Neville on the right. His long cross saw Bulents put under pressure in the air by McClair and when both players missed the ball, it fell to Davies who put the ball wide of Stauce from the narrowest of angles to score at the far post. The Reds increased the tempo even further and a second goal came with Cantona's tackle seeing the ball rebound to McClair whose shot was blocked but only as far as Beckham on the right. The youngster seized his chance and beat Stauce to the keeper's right to score on his European debut. But the half ended on a sour note when Bulents elbowed Beckham down by the corner flag and Neville was spat at as some fifteen players or so piled into a melee.

United started the second period almost as quickly as they had the first with another goal just three minutes after the restart. Again Cantona was instrumental with a cross from the left that was headed on by Beckham to fall to Keane in the inside right slot. The Irishman cleverly beat three lunging tackles and then curled the ball along ground in crown green bowling style to score a superbly executed goal off Stauce's right hand post.

United's dominance was now total and the final nail in Galatasary's coffin was hammered home by their own Bulents. A strong driving run by Cantona down the left saw him try to pick out Keane with his cross but Bulents got there first to volley past a surprised Stauce. The game ended United's longest run in European competition without a win but it wasn't enough to save them from elimination. As the final whistle went, so did another one some two thousand miles distant.

That one signalled that Barcelona had drawn 1-1 with IFK Gothenburg to give the Spanish champions the point they needed to finish ahead of the Reds on goal difference with the last word going to the Swede's goalkeeper Ravelli who said "United were unlucky – Bakero won't score another goal like he did tonight if he plays for the next twenty years". United's European dream was over for another year.

European Record

	Home						Away				
	P	W	D	L	F	A	W	D	L	F	A
Champions' Cup	51	22	3	0	79	21	8	8	10	40	41
All Euro Comps	111	40	14	0	142	38	17	17	23	78	85

	Home	Away	Total
European Attendances	112,909	181,350	294,259

Queens Park Rangers (1) 2
Manchester United (2) 3

Saturday, 10th December 1994, Loftus Road   Att: 18,948

Queens Park Rangers

13	Sieb	DYKSTRA
3	Clive	WILSON
16	Danny	MADDIX
2	David	BARDSLEY
6	Alan	MCDONALD – *Booked*
7	Andrew	IMPEY
25	Steve	HODGE
14	Simon	BARKER
9	Les	FERDINAND – *Booked*
20	Kevin	GALLEN
11	Trevor	SINCLAIR

Manchester United

13	Gary	WALSH
27	Gary	NEVILLE – *Booked (+77)*
3	Denis	IRWIN – *Booked*
4	Steve	BRUCE
6	Gary	PALLISTER
16	Roy	KEANE – *Booked*
8	Paul	INCE – *Booked*
9	Brian	McCLAIR
14	Andrei	KANCHELSKIS
24	Paul	SCHOLES
18	Simon	DAVIES (*67)

Subs

23	Peter	CALDWELL (G)
8	Ian	HOLLOWAY
10	Bradley	ALLEN

19	Nicky	BUTT *
31	Keith	GILLESPIE +
25	Kevin	PILKINGTON

Match Facts

- The officials for this game had an average age of just 30 – the youngest ever for an FAPL game.
- The win maintained United's 100% record in the FAPL at Loftus Road and left the Reds unbeaten in six games in the FAPL against QPR.

Score Sheet

L. FERDINAND 23 min – 1-0

P. SCHOLES 34 min – 1-1

R. KEANE min – 1-2

P. SCHOLES 47 min – 1-3

L. FERDINAND 64 min – 2-3

Referee:
Mr G.Poll (Reading)

FA Carling Premiership

		P	W	D	L	F	A	Pts
1	Blackburn Rovers	18	13	3	2	41	15	42
2	**Manchester United**	**18**	**13**	**2**	**3**	**35**	**12**	**41**
3	Newcastle United	18	11	4	3	39	22	37
4	Nottingham Forest	18	9	5	4	31	19	32
5	Liverpool	17	9	4	4	34	18	31

Scholes at the Double

In a quite extraordinary game of all-out attacking football from both sides, a double strike from young Paul Scholes gave United the points but he would have still been looking over his shoulder as Les Ferdinand, long thought to be a target for United, also scored a brace to give United a red-hot reminder of just what he could do. With Eric Cantona on international duty and Ferguson still shorn of many of his stars (Hughes not one to do things by half was suspended and on international duty), the United boss was again relying on his youth policy paying dividends with no fewer than five of his starlets playing some part in the match.

But it was Rangers who were first into their stride and the Reds looked to have gone behind after eleven minutes when Gallen smacked the crossbar but they were saved by the woodwork again when Hodge's follow-up effort from the rebound also cracked the bar! There was no denying Rangers were on top and they took the lead on 24 minutes. There appeared little danger when Ferdinand got the ball some thirty yards out and slightly to the left of goal. The England striker brought the ball inside onto his right foot and then thundered the ball into Walsh's top right hand corner leaving the 'keeper helpless. United's reply was swift but unlucky when Scholes hit the bar within a minute with a spectacular overhead kick and then Ince went close with a strong drive from the edge of the area. United were coming more into the game now and just past the half-hour mark they got the equaliser when Scholes powerfully headed home an Irwin cross from some 14 yards. United were now on top and just before half-time they took the lead. McClair won the ball on the half-way line and slipped it square to Scholes. The Salford youngster split the Rangers' defence with a brilliant ball through to Keane who took it all the way into the area before clipping it past Dykstra for his first league goal of the season.

Having hit the London side with a goal just before the interval, United looked to have put the game beyond recall when they scored again straight after the interval and, again, it was Scholes. Davies took a corner kick on the right that completely confused the Rangers' defence and as it bobbled up at the edge of the six yard box, Scholes twisted his neck muscles to get some pace on the header which Hodge could only help into the roof of the net. For a player standing just 5ft 8ins two headed goals on only his second FAPL start was quite an amazing contribution. But just when the points appeared in safe keeping, Les Ferdinand again stepped up to put United under pressure when he headed home an Impey cross.

Ferguson's reaction was immediate and he sent on the hard tackling Butt to replace the more attack minded Davies in an effort to tighten things up. United's defence was now put under intense scrutiny and both Ince and Irwin picked up bookings as the Reds defended their slim lead in desperate fashion. They survived two penalty claims in a grandstand finish but the Reds held on to nick the points.

League Record

	Home					Away				
	P	W	D	L	F	A	W	D	L	F	A
94/95 FAPL	18	9	0	0	21	0	4	2	3	14	12
All time FAPL	102	37	11	3	99	27	27	14	10	83	54
FAPL/FL	3658	1073	421	335	3649	1811	559	426	794	2489	3110

	Home	Away	Total
FAPL Attendances	393,102	261,615	654,717

Manchester United (0) 1
Nottingham Forest (1) 2

Saturday, 17th December 1994, Old Trafford   Att: 43,744

Manchester United

13	Gary	WALSH
16	Roy	KEANE – *Booked*
3	Denis	IRWIN
4	Steve	BRUCE
6	Gary	PALLISTER
14	Andrei	KANCHELSKIS (+88)
8	Paul	INCE
9	Brian	McCLAIR
11	Ryan	GIGGS – *Booked* (*76)
7	Eric	CANTONA
10	Mark	HUGHES

Subs

19	Nicky	BUTT *
27	Gary	NEVILLE +
25	Kevin	PILKINGTON (G)

Nottingham Forest

1	Mark	CROSSLEY
2	Des	LYTTLE – *Booked*
3	Stuart	PEARCE – *Booked*
18	Alf	HAALAND
5	Steve	CHETTLE – *Booked*
7	David	PHILLIPS
22	Bryan	ROY– *Booked* (*84)
8	Scott	GEMMILL
14	Ian	WOAN – *Booked*
10	Stan	COLLYMORE
11	Steve	STONE – *Booked*

9	Lars	BOHINEN *
20	Paul	McGREGOR
13	Tommy	WRIGHT (G)

Match Facts

- United fail to equal record of 12 consecutive home games without conceding a goal.
- First goal conceded by United at Old Trafford in 1134 minutes of league action.
- Forest maintain their good recent record at Old Trafford with a fourth victory in their last six visits.
- United's goal is their 100th at home in the FAPL.

Score Sheet

S. COLLYMORE 35 min – 0-1

S. PEARCE 62 min – 0-2

E. CANTONA 68 min – 1-2

Referee:
Mr KW. Burge (Tonypandy)

FA Carling Premiership

		P	W	D	L	F	A	Pts
1	Blackburn Rovers	19	13	4	2	41	15	43
2	**Manchester United**	**19**	**13**	**2**	**4**	**36**	**14**	**41**
3	Newcastle United	19	11	5	3	39	22	38
4	Nottingham Forest	19	10	5	4	33	20	35
5	Liverpool	18	9	5	4	34	18	32

Lost in the Forest

United went into this game with the recall of three internationals as they went in search of equalling the all time record for English football of keeping twelve consecutive blank sheets at home set by Notts County in 1971/72 and later equalled by Cambridge United in 1982/83. The return of Cantona, Hughes and Giggs, however, was not sufficient to stop Forest not only breaking the United stranglehold on opposition forwards but also taking all three points as United got lost in the dense Forest defence.

Collymore was quick to impress but was just thwarted as he closed in on Walsh by a superb tackle from Ince. But United were also keen to show their attacking paces and Hughes rattled the bar at the other end within sixty seconds with one of his specials from a Cantona cross. Collymore had the ball in the net only for his celebrations to be cut short as the referee ruled he had wrestled Ince to the ground in the process of winning the ball. In the 35th minute the goal that broke United's long 100% defensive record came with a classic that was worthy of breaking a record and, once again, it was Stan the Man who was proving to be a right handful. Roy played the ball in from the Forest right to Collymore who was fully 25 yards out from goal. He took the ball down and, despite the close attention of defenders, then smashed it high past Walsh's right hand into the roof of the net for a truly memorable goal.

When the second period got under way, there was a let off for the Reds when Irwin slipped and allowed Woan to find Collymore whose rocket clipped the post. But it was only a brief respite for United as Forest went two up in the 62nd minute. By now Forest were raiding only spasmodically, concentrating on getting eight or nine men behind the ball as United attacks foundered in the Forest penalty area due to sheer numbers. But when they did move forward, the Midlanders always looked likely to catch United out and they did just that when United only cleared a left wing corner as far as Stuart Pearce. The former England captain latched onto the ball and struck a fierce shot from 25 yards out. His effort took a wicked deflection off Bruce to wrong foot Walsh and the Reds looked down and out. Roy then flattened Ince with an outrageous high tackle that earned him only a yellow card when surely if his name had been Cantona or Hughes he would have walked and then Stone and Giggs were booked after an altercation near the corner flag. United pulled a goal back with just over twenty minutes left when a right wing in-swinging corner was flicked on by Cantona's head, probably intended for the far post but instead found its way into the net.

The Reds stepped up their attacks and laid siege to the Forest goal and Ince had a shot kicked off the line by Stone with Crossley beaten. United had lost in the League at Old Trafford for the first time in sixteen games.

League Record

	Home						Away				
	P	W	D	L	F	A	W	D	L	F	A
94/95 FAPL	19	9	0	1	22	2	4	2	3	14	12
All time FAPL	103	37	11	4	100	29	27	14	10	83	54
FAPL/FL	3659	1073	421	336	3650	1813	559	426	794	2489	3110

	Home	Away	Total
FAPL Attendances	436,846	261,615	698,461

Chelsea (0) 2
Manchester United (1) 3

Monday, 26th December 1994, Stamford Bridge   Att: 31,161

Chelsea

1	Dmitri	KHARINE
3	Andy	MYERS
5	Erland	JOHNSEN
6	Frank	SINCLAIR
7	John	SPENCER – *Booked*
10	Gavin	PEACOCK
12	Steve	CLARKE
17	Nigel	SPACKMAN
24	Craig	BURLEY – *Booked* (*54)
20	Glenn	HODDLE (+73)
9	Paul	FURLONG

Manchester United

13	Gary	WALSH
16	Roy	KEANE – *Booked*
4	Steve	BRUCE
6	Gary	PALLISTER
3	Denis	IRWIN
8	Paul	INCE (*45)
19	Nicky	BUTT – *Booked* (+76)
9	Brian	McCLAIR
11	Ryan	GIGGS
7	Eric	CANTONA – *Booked*
10	Mark	HUGHES

Subs

18	Eddie	NEWTON
21	Mark	STEIN *
13	Kevin	HITCHCOCK (G)

27	Gary	NEVILLE * – *Booked*
14	Andrei	KANCHELSKIS +
25	Kevin	PILKINGTON (G)

Match Facts

- First success at Stamford Bridge in the FAPL for United.
- United's three goalscorers the same three players who scored in the 1994 FA Cup Final against Chelsea.
- All three penalties conceded by Chelsea in this game and the FA Cup Final were all due to fouls by the same player Frank Sinclair.

Score Sheet

M. HUGHES 21 min
E. CANTONA 46 min Pen
J. SPENCER 58 min Pen
E. NEWTON 77 min
B. McCLAIR 78 min

Referee:
Mr M.Reed (Birmingham)

FA Carling Premiership

		P	W	D	L	F	A	Pts
1	Blackburn Rovers	20	14	4	2	44	16	46
2	**Manchester United**	20	14	2	4	39	16	44
3	Newcastle United	20	11	6	3	39	22	39
4	Liverpool	20	10	6	4	36	19	36
5	Nottingham Forest	20	10	6	4	33	20	36

Brian's Last Word

Brian McClair, who scored United's last goal in their 4-0 1994 FA Cup Final triumph at Wembley over Chelsea, once again had the last word at the expense of the Londoners. This time, however, it was worth much more than just the icing on the cake as it gave Alex Ferguson's side all three points in a Boxing Day game that was a real Christmas cracker. A 12.00 noon kick off irritated United fans who had to set off at the break of light in order to get to a Stamford Bridge ground now so narrow that Ferguson elected to play just one winger rather than his customary two but the big surprise was that he preferred an out of form Giggs to the electric pace of Kanchelskis. He was to be quickly rewarded for his judgement.

After 21 minutes McClair freed Giggs down the left and the youngster's speed saw him hit the byeline before crossing low and firm into the centre where Hughes was arriving just ahead of Myers to slide the ball home from close range. But there was a blow for the Reds just before half-time when Ince pulled up with a hamstring that prevented him re-appearing in the second period.

That, however, did not prevent the Reds from making a splendid start after the interval and within seconds of the game getting back under way they were awarded a penalty. Keane made a powerful run into the area from the inside-right position only to be cynically brought down by Sinclair, the perpetrator of both FA Cup Final penalties. On that occasion, Cantona had hit both spot kicks to Kharine's left and this time the Russian 'keeper dived in that direction only to find that the Frenchman had outwitted him again and delivered the ball into the opposite corner. *C'est la vie.*

United seemed to ease up once they had a two goal cushion but in the 57th minute Chelsea had a penalty of their own when substitute Stein was brought down by Pallister although television replays made it very questionable as to whether it was actually inside the area. Spencer hit the ball hard and high to Walsh's right for only Chelsea's second goal in five games. The goal gave the London outfit fresh hope and they took the game to United. A long unhindered run to the left corner flag by Furlong was the prelude to a far post cross which Walsh came for but missed. Newton, who had only been on the pitch four minutes, arrived behind Walsh and made the most of the 'keeper's mistake with a high looping header that went back across the face of the goal before nestling in the side of the net.

Chelsea's joy was obvious but also destined to be short-lived. Within seconds of the kick-off, United were back in front as Irwin fed the ball to Keane in the centre circle. The Irishman, who was having a splendid game, surged forward yet again to the edge of the box before passing to Cantona. The Frenchman's return pass was probably meant as a one-two with Keane but it took a nice deflection off a Chelsea leg to land in the path of the on-coming McClair who seized the opportunity with glee. The goal gave United their ninth win in eleven league outings.

League Record

	Home						Away				
	P	W	D	L	F	A	W	D	L	F	A
94/95 FAPL	20	9	0	1	22	2	5	2	3	17	14
All time FAPL	104	37	11	4	100	29	28	14	10	86	56
FAPL/FL	3660	1073	421	336	3650	1813	560	426	794	2492	3112

	Home	Away	Total
FAPL Attendances	436,846	292,776	729,622

Manchester United (0) 1
Leicester City (0) 1

Wednesday, 28th December 1994, Old Trafford   Att: 43,789

Manchester United

13	Gary	WALSH
27	Gary	NEVILLE
4	Steve	BRUCE
6	Gary	PALLISTER
3	Denis	IRWIN
16	Roy	KEANE
14	Andrei	KANCHELSKIS
9	Brian	McCLAIR
11	Ryan	GIGGS
7	Eric	CANTONA
10	Mark	HUGHES – *Booked* (*69)

Subs

12	David	MAY
25	Kevin	PILKINGTON (G)
24	Paul	SCHOLES *

Leicester City

33	Kevin	POOLE
2	Simon	GRAYSON
3	Mike	WHITLOW
4	Jimmy	WILLIS
6	Steve	AGNEW
21	Lee	PHILPOTT – *Booked* (+75)
19	Colin	HILL
9	Iwen	ROBERTS
10	Mark	DRAPER
20	David	OLDFIELD (*69)
16	Steve	THOMPSON

Subs

8	Mark	BLAKE +
25	David	LOWE *
1	Gavin	WARD (G)

Match Facts

- Leicester ended a disastrous run of eight straight defeats on visits to Old Trafford with this result.
- Leicester have still not won at Old Trafford since the season United were relegated in 1973.
- Prior to this result, Leicester had won just one point out of 27 on their travels.

Score Sheet

A. KANCHELSKIS 61 min – 1-0
M. WHITLOW 65 min – 1-1

Referee:
Mr D. Gallagher (Banbury)

FA Carling Premiership

		P	W	D	L	F	A	Pts
1	Blackburn Rovers	20	14	4	2	44	17	46
2	**Manchester United**	21	14	3	4	40	17	45
3	Liverpool	21	11	6	4	38	19	39
4	Newcastle United	20	11	6	3	39	22	39
5	Nottingham Forest	21	11	6	4	34	20	39

The Master and the Pupil

Alex Ferguson's helping hand throughout his footballing career counted for nought when his pupil Mark McGhee visited Old Trafford just days after taking over the managerial reins at struggling Leicester City. The Leicester boss had played as a bustling striker for five years under Ferguson at Aberdeen and the United boss recommended him for his first stab at management with Reading but McGhee was in no mood to repay his mentor with any favours as his side battled every inch of the way for an unlikely point that prevented the Reds from regaining the lead at the top of the table with Blackburn rained off at home to Leeds.

Despite United doing virtually all the attacking, they didn't look like breaching the Leicester rearguard and Hughes showed his frustration as early as the seventh minute when stamping on Thompson's toes long after the ball had gone to earn a caution. This was not, however, a dismal display by United and both Kanchelskis and Giggs had their markers at full stretch whilst Cantona, although not at his brilliant best, still had enough party pieces to light up a dismal, rain sodden Old Trafford night, with nothing better than his eloquent shimmy that left Thompson pondering a close encounter with the rain soaked turf. But they couldn't turn their domination into goals. A brilliant ball from Pallister set on Giggs on one of his weaving, bobbing runs that had been missing from his game all season as he rounded the 'keeper with aplomb and then froze. It was almost as if the Welsh youngster couldn't believe he had found his touch at last and he put the ball into the side netting with an open goal beckoning.

In an attempt to break down the Leicester stubbornness, United's wingers changed flanks after the interval and it seemed likely to be the answer but, whenever the Reds did break through, they found former Hartlepool and Northampton goalkeeper Kevin Poole in as resolute mood as the rest of his defence. But even he couldn't keep out a Kanchelskis rocket on the hour after Hughes had caught Colin Hill in possession some thirty yards out. The goal, and especially the manner in which it was conceded, should have deflated the Midlanders but they fought back and within five minutes had forced their second corner of the game. Yes, it really was that one sided but the corner was to gift them the equaliser with a comedy of errors in the underworked United defence. From the corner, Walsh and Neville collided, Willis poked the ball goalwards only for it to hit Bruce and allow Whitlow to jab home from four yards. Hughes was then lucky not to get sent off and Ferguson sensibly removed him from the fray but his replacement, young Scholes, found that his first touch wasn't good enough and a great chance for a winner went begging when he recovered the ball but could only hit Poole's legs. The corner count of 16-2 told it all but Leicester still went home with a share of the spoils!

League Record

		Home						Away				
	P	W	D	L	F	A	W	D	L	F	A
94/95 FAPL	21	9	1	1	23	3	5	2	3	17	14
All Time FAPL	105	37	12	4	101	30	28	14	10	86	56
FAPL/FL	3661	1073	422	336	3651	1814	560	426	794	2492	3112

	Home	Away	Total
FAPL Attendances	480,635	292,776	773,411

Southampton   (1) 2
Manchester United   (0) 2

Saturday, 31st December 1994, The Dell   Att: 15,204

Southampton			**Manchester United**		
1	Bruce	GROBBELAAR	13	Gary	WALSH
2	Jeff	KENNA	12	David	MAY
3	Francis	BENALI – Booked	4	Steve	BRUCE
4	Jim	MAGILTON	6	Gary	PALLISTER
6	Ken	MONKOU	27	Gary	NEVILLE – Booked
7	Matthew	LE TISSIER	9	Brian	McCLAIR – Booked
9	Iain	DOWIE	16	Roy	KEANE
18	David	HUGHES	19	Nicky	BUTT – Booked
21	Tom	WIDDRINGTON	11	Ryan	GIGGS
24	Ronnie	EKLUND (*66)	7	Eric	CANTONA – Booked
15	Jason	DODD – Booked	10	Mark	HUGHES – Booked

Subs

8	Craig	MASKELL	24	Paul	SCHOLES
12	Neil	HEANEY *	31	Keith	GILLESPIE
13	Dave	BEASANT (G)	25	Kevin	PILKINGTON (G)

Match Facts

- First points dropped by United to Southampton in the FAPL.
- United unbeaten by Southampton in eleven league games dating back to May 1989.
- First senior goal for Nicky Butt.
- First game for Alex Ferguson as a CBE.
- Only one win in last four games for the Reds.

Score Sheet

J. MAGILTON 44 min – 1-0

N. BUTT 51 min – 1-1

D. HUGHES 74 min – 2-1

G. PALLISTER 79 min – 2-2

Referee:

Mr M. Bodenham (Cornwall)

FA Carling Premiership

		P	W	D	L	F	A	Pts
1	Blackburn Rovers	21	15	4	2	45	16	49
2	**Manchester United**	**22**	**14**	**4**	**4**	**42**	**19**	**46**
3	Liverpool	22	12	6	4	40	19	42
4	Newcastle United	21	11	6	4	40	24	39
5	Nottingham Forest	22	11	6	5	35	23	39

Unrecognisable

With six internationals, Schmeichel, Parker, Ince, Kanchelskis, Sharpe, and Irwin missing from the line up and the side sporting yet another new kit (blue and white stripes) United were hardly identifiable as the team that did the double in 1993/94. But it wasn't just their appearance that made the Champions unrecognisable but rather a lack lustre performance that did little to celebrate the New Years Honour of a CBE bestowed on manager Alex Ferguson. But it could have been worse had it not been for a late equaliser from Gary Pallister.

With some one hundred names of past and present players etched into the new kit it was somewhat surprising, perhaps, to discover the name of Paul Ince missing and it was also probably the omission from the team sheet of his name that contributed most to a poor performance from United after an encouraging start that saw them attack from the kick off with a back header from Monkou leaving Grobbelaar exposed only for Nicky Butt to slip at the critical moment as he closed in on the error. Then Widdrington handled the ball in the area but the referee considered it to be unintentional and play switched to the other end where it was to stay for a considerable period. After United's promising start Eklund grazed the bar with a third minute header when it seemed easier to score from four yards out and the same player again cleared the bar a minute later with an empty net beckoning as Walsh lay on the floor after colliding with Southampton's David Hughes.

The Saints kept up the pressure with a Dowie header bringing a full length save out of Walsh and, in a similar incident to the Widdrington hand ball earlier, the referee denied Southampton's claims for a spot kick when the ball hit Neville's hand as he tried to cut out a Le Tissier cross. May's return to the team was not a success and he was being given a torrid time of it especially by opposing full back Jeff Kenna. It was no surprise that Kenna should be the provider of the cross that finally deflated the Reds just before half-time when Magilton swept the ball past Walsh for only his second goal of the 1994/95 campaign.

United came out for the second period in a more determined mood and were rewarded after 51 minutes with a classic equaliser quite out of context from their performance. May got Cantona in the clear down the right and the Frenchman's inch perfect cross was volleyed home by Butt for his first senior goal. In a grandstand finish, play was held up for Cantona to be revived after falling unconscious in the area after an incident which nobody appeared to witness and then Southampton regained the lead with a goal executed as clinically as United's equaliser. David Hughes met Heaney's low cross from the left near the penalty spot and shot strongly past Walsh's right hand. But United were not done for and with eleven minutes remaining Pallister's head buried a Cantona cross from the right to give United a share of the spoils that, on the day, they probably did not deserve.

League Record

	Home						Away				
	P	W	D	L	F	A	W	D	L	F	A
94/95 FAPL	22	9	1	1	23	3	5	3	3	19	16
All Time FAPL	106	37	12	4	101	30	28	15	10	88	58
FAPL/FL	3662	1073	422	336	3651	1814	560	427	794	2494	3112

	Home	Away	Total
FAPL Attendances	480,635	307,980	788,615

Manchester United   (1) 2
Coventry City   (0) 0

Wednesday, 3rd January 1995, Old Trafford   Att: 43,103

Manchester United

13	Gary	WALSH
27	Gary	NEVILLE – *Booked*
3	Denis	IRWIN
4	Steve	BRUCE – *Booked*
6	Gary	PALLISTER
19	Nicky	BUTT
16	Roy	KEANE (*64)
31	Keith	GILLESPIE
11	Ryan	GIGGS
7	Eric	CANTONA
24	Paul	SCHOLES

Subs

9	Brian	McCLAIR *
25	Kevin	PILKINGTON (G)
12	David	MAY

Coventry City

1	Steve	OGRIZOVIC
17	Ally	PICKERING
6	Kevin	PRESSLEY – *Booked/Sent Off*
3	Steve	MORGAN
12	John	WILLIAMS
7	Sean	FLYNN (+86)
15	Paul	COOK – *Booked*
14	Leigh	JENKINSON
8	Roy	WEGERLE (*53)
19	Dion	DUBLIN
25	Mike	MARSH

13	Jonathon	GOULD (G)
4	Julian	DARBY *
24	Cobi	JONES +

Match Facts

• First senior goal at Old Trafford for Paul Scholes.

• First full 90 minutes of FAPL action for Keith Gillespie.

• Coventry have not scored a league goal against United since 15th December 1994.

• Coventry have not beaten United in a league game since April 1989.

Score Sheet

P. SCHOLES 29 min – 1-0

E.CANTONA 49 min Pen 2-0

Referee:

Mr G. Willard (Worthing)

FA Carling Premiership

		P	W	D	L	F	A	Pts
1	Blackburn Rovers	22	16	4	2	49	18	52
2	**Manchester United**	**23**	**15**	**4**	**4**	**49**	**19**	**49**
3	Liverpool	23	13	6	4	44	19	45
4	Nottingham Forest	23	12	6	5	36	23	42
5	Newcastle United	22	11	7	4	40	24	40

Killer Instinct Missing

The task of halving Blackburn Rovers' six point lead at the top of the table was, in the end, comfortably achieved by United but not before they had confirmed that the killer instinct that was the hallmark of their *double* year was somehow missing this time round. True, United still had massive injury problems with five internationals all still out and a sixth, Mark Hughes, voluntarily omitted by Alex Ferguson after failing to set the world alight in recent matches. But Coventry were also missing some five or six regulars. As it was, United seemed content to pull out their party pieces in the second period and that, allied to some mysterious refereeing decisions, let the light blues off the hook.

Despite United's early territorial advantage, however, it was Coventry should have taken the lead. Dion Dublin, on his return to Old Trafford following his early season move, almost made a fairy tale start when he met Wegerle's cross but Bruce just got a block in as the former Red took aim from ten yards. Having survived these early escapes, along with strong claims for a penalty when a header from Dublin hit Pallister on the arm, United began to impose themselves with Keane playing a particularly dominant role in midfield whilst Cantona, later to be voted Man of the Match, began to orchestrate things up front. Just on the half hour, the Frenchman released Gillespie down the right and the Irishman's pace took him clear to cut in and fire a hard low cross. Butt back heeled it in much the same manner Sharpe had done to score against Barcelona but, on this occasion, Ogrizovic palmed the close range effort away only for Scholes to whip the ball home from all of three yards.

The second period began with early United pressure being rewarded with a penalty that also saw the dismissal for a second bookable offence of Pressley. There appeared to be little threat to Coventry as Pressley took the ball clear of his own area but the tenacious Scholes chased back to harry the Coventry defender and pinched the ball off him. Once he had possession, a quick turn saw Scholes heading for goal only to be brought down just inside the box by Pressley whose dismissal seemed hard justice although it was a foul. Cantona rammed home his spot kick and Coventry manager Phil Neal, obviously fearing a rout with his side minus a defender, took off Wegerle and sent on defender Darby. The replacement was very fortunate to stay on the pitch when he clearly pulled Cantona back by the shirt when the Frenchman was clean through on goal and the Reds were denied yet another blatant penalty when Williams upended Cantona as he was about to score.

Both decisions had a distinct look of a referee making up for the earlier decision to dismiss Pressley. United now tore through Coventry on a regular basis but seemed content to show off with flicks and back heels rather than go for the jugular as Keane was removed from the fray to be saved for more arduous tasks ahead and the Reds missed out on a great opportunity to improve their goal difference.

League Record

| | Home | | | | | | Away | | | | |
	P	W	D	L	F	A	W	D	L	F	A
94/95 FAPL	23	10	1	1	25	3	5	3	3	19	16
All Time FAPL	107	38	12	4	103	30	28	15	10	88	58
FAPL/FL	3663	1074	422	336	3653	1814	560	427	794	2494	3112

	Home	Away	Total
FAPL Attendances	523,738	307,980	831,718

Sheffield United   (0) 0
Manchester United   (0) 2

Monday, 9th January 1995, Bramall Lane   Att: 22,322

Sheffield United

1	Alan	KELLY
2	Kevin	GAGE
3	Roger	NILSON
4	Charlie	HARTFIELD – *Sent Off*
5	Brian	GAYLE
6	Dane	WHITEHOUSE (+86)
7	Paul	ROGERS – *Booked*
8	Carl	VEART
9	Nathan	BLAKE
10	Glyn	HODGES
11	Andy	SCOTT (*75)

Manchester United

1	Peter	SCHMEICHEL
30	John	O'KANE (*64)
3	Denis	IRWIN – *Booked*
4	Steve	BRUCE
6	Gary	PALLISTER
9	Brian	McCLAIR (+78)
19	Nicky	BUTT
16	Roy	KEANE – *Booked*
11	Ryan	GIGGS
7	Eric	CANTONA
10	Mark	HUGHES

Subs

12	Phil	STARBUCK *
13	Billy	MERCER (G)
14	Justin	FLO +

25	Kevin	PILKINGTON
5	Lee	SHARPE *
24	Paul	SCHOLES +

Match Facts

- FA Cup debut for John O'Kane.
- Second successive season that United had beaten Sheffield United at Bramall Lane in the FA Cup.
- Second successive season that a player has been sent off at Bramall Lane in a United v Sheff United FA Cup tie following dismissal of Mark Hughes in the 1993/94 FA Cup tie.
- Cantona's goal was United's 300th FA Cup goal away from home.

Score Sheet

M. HUGHES 80 min – 0-1
E. CANTONA 81 min – 0-2

Referee:
Mr R.Hart (Darlington)

Ten Men Count for Nothing

The almost annual clash of the the two Uniteds in the FA Cup saw a man dismissed for the second successive year when Charlie Hartfield was shown the red card for cuffing Eric Cantona about the ear in the thirteenth minute as the two sides met in the Cup for the fourth time since 1990. A win for the Old Trafford side would be looked upon as a good omen for they had gone on to win the FA Cup on both occasions they had beaten the *Blades* in 1990 and 1994. In the event, Hartfield's dismissal served initially to inspire Sheffield to even greater efforts but, in atrocious conditions on a wind swept night, the extra exertions eventually took a heavy toll as the Reds scored twice in the last ten minutes.

United had an early let-off when Schmeichel, playing his first game for several weeks, couldn't hold a close range effort from Blake and O'Kane's clearance off the line struck Hodges to swirl back in the wind towards the net only for the 'keeper to recover in the nick of time. The *Blades* then had strong claims for a penalty turned down when Blake tumbled following a tackle from Bruce. But, if that was bad luck, then Hartfield only had himself to blame when he was dismissed in the 13th minute for clipping Cantona's ear with a punch after a melee.

When the game got restarted, Giggs was looking rejuvenated and it was from his left wing cross that Hughes smacked Kelly's right hand post with a stooping header which had the 'keeper well beaten. At the other end, Schmeichel had to be alert to pounce on a back heel effort from Rogers but a scintillating run from Giggs brought a corner which almost produced a football rarity as the Welshman went within a whisker of scoring with his head from Irwin's kick!

Although Sheffield's ten men had held their own until the interval, the second period saw Ferguson's side begin to dominate with Giggs, looking much more like the Giggs of twelve months earlier, beginning to cause serious trouble for the Yorkshire outfit. The Reds looked sure to take the lead when Cantona curled a ball out of reach of Kelly only to see Butt's flick go agonisingly close. But Sheffield showed they weren't done for when Schmeichel was forced to make a breathtaking save from Rogers whilst Hodges hammered a long range effort just wide. But it was mainly United and it seemed they must take the lead when Cantona shot from point blank range only for Kelly to make a magnificent reflex stop.

But he was powerless to stop the Reds taking the lead with ten minutes to go. Butt won the ball in midfield and found Keane who quickly moved the ball out left to the dangerman Giggs. The youngster lobbed the ball into the area where Hughes had lost his marker to head down and in. Within a minute United had made it two with a classic goal from Cantona who had picked the ball up just outside his own penalty area. He pushed it infield to Hughes and set off on a sprint as his colleague whisked it left to Giggs. An inch perfect pass found Cantona with acres of room on the right from where he spotted Kelly some three yards off his line and placed a delicate chip just out of the keeper's reach. C'est magnifique.

United's all time FA Cup Record

	Home					Away				
P	W	D	L	F	A	W	D	L	F	A
347	99	31	28	333	148	79	53	57	300	268

	Home	Away	Total
FA Cup Attendances	-	22,322	22,322

Newcastle United   (0) 1
Manchester United   (1) 1

Sunday, 15th January 1995, St James' Park   Att: 34,471

Newcastle United

1	Pavel	SRNICEK
12	Marc	HOTTIGER
15	Darren	PEACOCK
6	Steve	HOWEY
3	John	BERESFORD – *Booked*
2	Barry	VENISON
5	Ruel	FOX
10	Lee	CLARK
26	Robbie	ELLIOTT – *Booked*
7	Robert	LEE
27	Paul	KITSON

Subs

14	Alex	MATTHIE
19	Steve	WATSON
30	Mike	HOOPER (G)

Manchester United

1	Peter	SCHMEICHEL
3	Denis	IRWIN
4	Steve	BRUCE
5	Lee	SHARPE – *Booked*
6	Gary	PALLISTER
16	Roy	KEANE – *Booked*
9	Brian	McCLAIR
19	Nicky	BUTT (+46)
11	Ryan	GIGGS
7	Eric	CANTONA
10	Mark	HUGHES (*16)

12	David	MAY +
13	Gary	WALSH (G)
24	Paul	SCHOLES *

Match Facts

- Third 1-1 draw in four FAPL meetings between the two sides.
- Newcastle not yet beaten United in FAPL.
- United's 850th drawn game in all time FAPL/Football League games.
- Newcastle have not beaten United in a league game since December 1987.

Score Sheet

M. HUGHES 13 min – 0-1
P. KITSON 67 min – 1-1

Referee:
Mr S. Lodge (Barnsley)

FA Carling Premiership

		P	W	D	L	F	A	Pts
1	Blackburn Rovers	23	17	4	2	52	18	55
2	**Manchester United**	24	15	5	4	45	20	50
3	Liverpool	24	13	6	5	44	20	45
4	Nottingham Forest	24	12	6	6	36	26	42
5	Newcastle United	23	11	8	4	41	25	41

Rearguard Action

Following the euphoria of Andy Cole's arrival in midweek from Newcastle, United were soon brought down to earth when they immediately met up with Cole's former club. Although the man under most pressure from Cole's transfer, Mark Hughes, began the game in typical fighting fashion to give the Reds an early lead, he was badly injured in the incident leading to the goal and, by the interval, manager Alex Ferguson had run out of options. He needed to replace Bruce, who during the first forty-five minutes had felt flu' like symptoms come on, but was unable to do so as not only had Scholes gone on for Hughes but David May had also been thrust into action as Butt was withdrawn suffering badly from concussion. With the Newcastle side already bristling from the fans' criticism of their manager Kevin Keegan for selling Andy Cole, it was hardly surprising that the reshaped United side were faced with a rearguard action.

By the time kick off approached, it seemed that the Newcastle fans' anger at the sale of Cole had subsided and, faced with the certainty of not being able to do anything about the sale, they had decided to get right behind their team and manager. They were temporarily silenced after only thirteen minutes but at a crippling cost to the Reds. A typical Keane surge down the right flank brought a cross that was dummied by Cantona leaving Hughes to volley at full stretch. Newcastle 'keeper Srnicek had been quick to see the danger and rushed out to try to block Hughes' effort only to collide heavily with the United man who went down in a heap with his knee gashed and badly twisted under him. With Hughes out of the game.

Having claimed the initiative before the interval, Newcastle dominated the early exchanges in the second period. Keane's thrusting attacks were blunted as he tried to shore up the defence which Ferguson ordered to become a five man formation with May, Bruce and Pallister all sitting in the middle of defence and Irwin and Sharpe in the full back positions. But the Reds were being swamped and it was no surprise when Keegan's outfit equalised. Lee fed Elliott down the left and he helped the ball on with a deft lob which saw Pallister and Kitson in an aerial duel to the left of the area with no apparent immediate danger for United. Neither player, however, made good contact but the ball fell nicely into the path of the Newcastle striker as he recovered his feet a shade more quickly than Pallister. A well struck left foot shot from a fairly acute angle beat Schmeichel through his legs to send the home fans wild.

Moments later Kitson almost doubled up only to see Schmeichel fingertip his twisting header over the bar and it seemed only a matter of time before Newcastle grabbed the winner. But the Reds hung on and, incredibly, in the last ten minutes almost won it themselves. The Geordies began to leave gaps at the back as they pushed forward in ever increasing numbers and Keane and Cantona, twice, both missed clear opportunities to commit grand larceny.

League Record

| | Home | | | | | | Away | | | | |
	P	W	D	L	F	A	W	D	L	F	A
94/95 FAPL	24	10	1	1	25	3	5	4	3	20	17
All time FAPL	108	38	12	4	103	30	28	16	10	89	59
FAPL/FL	3664	1074	422	336	3653	1814	560	428	794	2495	3113

	Home	Away	Total
FAPL Attendances	523,738	342,451	866,189

Manchester United (0) 1
Blackburn Rovers (0) 0

Sunday, 22nd January 1995, Old Trafford   Att: 43,742

Manchester United

1	Peter	SCHMEICHEL
16	Roy	KEANE
3	Denis	IRWIN
4	Steve	BRUCE – Booked
5	Lee	SHARPE (*77)
6	Gary	PALLISTER
7	Eric	CANTONA – Booked
8	Paul	INCE
9	Brian	McCLAIR
11	Ryan	GIGGS
17	Andy	COLE

Blackburn Rovers

1	Tim	FLOWERS
20	Henning	BERG
24	Paul	WARHURST
5	Colin	HENDRY
6	Graeme	LE SAUX – Booked
11	Jason	WILCOX (+89)
4	Tim	SHERWOOD
22	Mark	ATKINS (*89)
3	Alan	WRIGHT – Booked
9	Alan	SHEARER
16	Chris	SUTTON – Booked

Subs

12	David	MAY
13	Gary	WALSH (G)
14	Andrei	KANCHELSKIS *

13	Bobby	MIMMS (G)
25	Ian	PEARCE *
10	Mike	NEWALL +

Match Facts

- Debut match for United's £7m Andy Cole.
- The win broke a Blackburn run of eleven wins and a draw since United beat them 4-2 at Ewood Park earlier in the season.
- The result continued Dalglish's poor record at Old Trafford as a manager – just one win.
- Blackburn extended their record of not having won at Old Trafford since Oct 1962.

Score Sheet

E. CANTONA 80 min – 1-0

Referee:
Mr P. Durkin (Portland)

FA Carling Premiership

		P	W	D	L	F	A	Pts
1	Blackburn Rovers	24	17	4	3	52	19	55
2	**Manchester United**	25	16	5	4	46	20	53
3	Liverpool	24	13	6	5	44	20	45
4	Newcastle United	24	11	9	4	41	25	42
5	Nottingham Forest	25	12	6	7	37	28	42

Dalglish Ploy Backfires

Blackburn Rovers came into this crunch game five points clear of United and on the back of 34 points out of 36 since the Reds had beaten them 4-2 at Ewood Park in October but, nevertheless, manager Kenny Dalglish was clearly feeling the strain more than his United counterpart Alex Ferguson in the run up to the fixture. At a Press Conference two days prior to the game Dalglish made an appeal to the match officials to take no notice of "the partisan stadium and the crowd that can influence decisions. The referee's decisions must be based on what happens, not on what the crowd thinks. It has happened to us before".

The game also saw the debut of United's record buy Andy Cole and the new boy had a glorious opportunity within the first sixty seconds to make a sensational start to his Old Trafford career. A long ball from McClair down the centre of the park was poorly judged by Warhurst and Cole seized on the loose ball. Unfortunately his first touch didn't control the ball sufficiently to stop it bouncing about waist high and his lashed attempt went wide. But that moment set the tempo for the game with the Reds swamping Blackburn in a one sided first half that was remarkable for the fact that United didn't score despite so much fabulous approach work, particularly by Giggs who was back to his old self. Flowers was having an inspirational game, but the Blackburn 'keeper couldn't hold a 25 yard Ince blockbuster and had to flap desperately at the ball to stop it bouncing over the line.

Rovers came more into the game after the break but Shearer, a lone front runner starved of the ball in the first period, clearly had not been able to set his sights and when presented with two opportunities failed to hit the target. Down at the other end, Flowers denied Cantona on the hour with a brave dive at the Frenchman's feet after Hendry had been left bemused and, with ten minutes left, yet another chance seemed to have gone begging when Giggs tamely gave the ball away to Berg when in a promising position. Berg could, and should, have booted the ball anywhere but he proceeded to dwell on it as he progressed out of the area on Blackburn's right. Giggs chased back and slid into a tackle which saw him regain the ball and, back on his feet in a flash, cross it deep towards the far post. Cantona came rushing in at speed and, despite looking likely to lose the race, just got to the ball in time to send a header rocketing into Flowers' top left hand angle.

Rovers now stormed to the attack and their efforts seemed to have been rewarded in the last minute when a long ball from the right was headed back across goal for Sherwood to head home from close range. The referee, however, was of the opinion that Shearer had pushed Keane in their initial challenge for the ball and the goal was disallowed. Certainly there had been contact but it was insignificant and an incredible let off for the Reds. But, perhaps Dalglish was simply a victim of his own desire to exert pressure on the referee!

League Record

	Home					Away					
	P	W	D	L	F	A	W	D	L	F	A
94/95 FAPL	25	11	1	1	26	3	5	4	3	20	17
All time FAPL	109	39	12	4	104	30	28	16	10	89	59
FAPL/FL	3665	1075	422	336	3654	1814	560	428	794	2495	3113

	Home	Away	Total
FAPL Attendances	567,480	342,451	909,931

Crystal Palace (0) 1
Manchester United (0) 1

Wednesday, 25th January 1995, Selhurst Park   Att: 18,223

Crystal Palace

1	Nigel	MARTYN
22	Darren	PATTERSON
6	Chris	COLEMAN – *Booked*
14	Richard	SHAW
3	Dean	GORDON
4	Gareth	SOUTHGATE
16	Darren	PITCHER
23	Ricky	NEWMAN
11	John	SALAKO
9	Chris	ARMSTRONG
8	Iain	DOWIE (*82)

Subs

19	Rhys	WILMOT (G)
15	Bobby	BOWRY
18	Andy	PREECE *

Manchester United

1	Peter	SCHMEICHEL
16	Roy	KEANE – *Booked*
12	David	MAY
6	Gary	PALLISTER
3	Denis	IRWIN
9	Brian	McCLAIR
8	Paul	INCE
5	Lee	SHARPE (82)
11	Ryan	GIGGS
7	Eric	CANTONA – *Sent Off*
17	Andy	COLE

13	Gary	WALSH (G)
24	Paul	SCHOLES
14	Andrei	KANCHELSKIS *

Match Facts

- First FAPL goal against United for Crystal Palace against United.
- First time United had failed to beat Palace in the FAPL.
- Cole's 11th consecutive game without scoring including nine with Newcastle.
- May's first league goal for United.
- Cantona's fifth sending off in United colours in sixteen months.

Score Sheet

D. MAY 58 min 0-1
G. SOUTHGATE 79 min – 1-1

Referee:
Mr A. Wilkie (Co Durham)

FA Carling Premiership

		P	W	D	L	F	A	Pts
1	Blackburn Rovers	24	17	4	3	52	19	55
2	**Manchester United**	26	16	6	4	47	21	54
3	Liverpool	25	13	7	5	44	20	46
4	Newcastle United	25	13	9	4	43	26	45
5	Nottingham Forest	26	13	6	7	39	28	45

L'enfant Terrible Loses Les Marbles

Manchester United travelled south to Selhurst Park for their match with Crystal Palace in eager anticipation of going back to the top of the FA Premiership above Blackburn Rovers but returned home a club in crisis after one of the most extraordinary scenes ever witnessed on an English football field. For the man at the centre of the events, Eric Cantona, this was sensational even by his own standards and was the first item on every news bulletin for the next forty-eight hours.

Strangely, the actual game up to the incident which saw Cantona sent off, was almost devoid of action of any serious consequence and the match was still goalless at the 52 minute mark when the Frenchman received his marching orders for the fifth time in sixteen months after a kick aimed at Richard Shaw as they chased a long ball. But that was not the end of the matter by any means. Indeed, the controversy was only just about to unfurl as a spectator rushed down several flights of steps and began to hurl abuse at Cantona who appeared to simply flip his lid to launch a karate style kick to the spectator's chest over the top of the advertising boards. Picking himself up quickly, Cantona then aimed a punch with some force at his verbal assailant before United kit man, Norman Davies, managed to pull him away. As Schmeichel and Ince moved in to also pull Cantona away they were hit by cups of tea thrown from the crowd but there was little doubt that Cantona would be in extremely serious trouble with the authorities. And so it proved to be with a ban for the rest of the season and a £20,000 fine to boot.

As for the game itself, the first half produced nothing of note except yet another booking for Keane but the action did warm up after the Cantona incident. It took the ten men just six minutes to get themselves in front. A Giggs free kick from the United right fell loose on the far side where May did well to win the ball and pass to Sharpe. The England man played a good one two with Pallister and set off down the left wing before crossing to the far post where May headed home after being initially involved at the start of the move on the other wing. Cole then missed a glorious opportunity to make the game safe when put clean through with just the 'keeper to beat only to miss the target by yards rather than inches. United were to soon rue that missed opportunity for Crystal Palace equalised with eleven minutes left to deprive the Reds of top spot. The Palace 'keeper, Martyn, brought the ball to almost the half way line before hoisting a long ball forward for Armstrong to head on. May, the hero a few minutes beforehand, now became the villain as he completely failed to prevent a comparatively simple situation becoming a melee as Salako and Southgate for Palace and Schmeichel and May for United all attempted to get something of some significance on the loose ball. Southgate won and United headed home with a point.

League Record

| | Home | | | | | | Away | | | | |
	P	W	D	L	F	A	W	D	L	F	A
94/95 FAPL	26	11	1	1	26	3	5	5	3	21	18
All time FAPL	110	39	12	4	104	30	28	17	10	90	60
FAPL/FL	3666	1075	422	336	3654	1814	560	429	794	2496	3114

	Home	Away	Total
FAPL Attendances	567,480	360,675	928,155

115

Manchester United (2) 5
Wrexham (1) 2

Saturday, 28th January 1995, Old Trafford   Att: 43,222

Manchester United

1	Peter	SCHMEICHEL
3	Denis	IRWIN
23	Phil	NEVILLE
12	David	MAY
6	Gary	PALLISTER
16	Roy	KEANE (*69)
8	Paul	INCE
11	Ryan	GIGGS
9	Brian	McCLAIR (+73)
24	Paul	SCHOLES
5	Lee	SHARPE

Wrexham

1	Andrew	MARRIOTT
2	Barry	JONES
3	Phil	HARDY
4	Bryan	HUGHES (+80)
5	Barry	HUNTER
6	Tony	HUMES
7	Gary	BENNETT
8	Gareth	OWEN
9	Karl	CONNOLLY (*71)
10	Steve	WATKIN
11	Kieron	DURKAN

Subs

28	David	BECKHAM +
14	Andrei	KANCHELSKIS *
13	Gary	WALSH (G)

12	Jonathon	CROSS *
13	Mark	CARTWRIGHT (G)
14	Wayne	PHILLIPS +

Match Facts

- First team debut for Phil Neville.
- FA Cup debuts for Scholes and Beckham.
- 100th home victory in the competition.
- Wrexham's second goal was the 150th conceded at home in the competition by United.
- Wrexham's opening goal was the first they have ever scored against United.
- The win maintained United's 100% record against the Welsh club in five meetings in various cup competitions with a goal difference of 17-2.

Score Sheet

K. DURKAN 9 min – 0-1

D. IRWIN 17 min – 1-1

R. GIGGS 26 min 2-1

B. McCLAIR 67 min 3-1

D. IRWIN 73 min Pen 4-1

T. HUMES og 80 min 5-1

J. CROSS 89 min – 5-2

Referee:
Mr M.J. Bodenham (Looe)

A Cup of Cheer

United went in to this Fourth Round FA Cup tie in something of a crisis following the Cantona affair at Crystal Palace just days earlier. With the Frenchman suspended, Hughes out injured and new boy Andy Cole cup-tied, the Reds had no recognised strike force and turned to the untried partnership of veteran Brian McClair, restored to his front running role after a long sojourn in midfield, and young Paul Scholes. To add to their worries they tried yet another player in the problem right back position with Denis Irwin moving across from left back and Gary Neville's younger brother Phil coming in at left back. With such problems, the last thing they needed was Wrexham to take the lead.

But the Welsh Dragons had come out breathing fire and take the lead they did after only nine minutes. Giggs lost out in a tussle on the halfway line and the ball was played forward to Durkan who was closed down by McClair. The Wrexham player slipped the ball inside to Owen and went for a one-two. McClair lost his man leaving Durkan to steer the return in between Schmeichel's legs to send the Welsh fans delirious. "Are you Chester in disguise" chanted the visiting supporters as they sensed a shock. But the Reds hit back to take full control with Irwin leading the way. He forced a corner on the right after being put through by Keane and, when Giggs' flag kick was only partially cleared after challenges from Ince and Pallister, he was on hand to send a thunderous shot from the edge of the area high into Marriott's net with the 'keeper beaten by sheer pace. United were soon two up when Scholes and Neville linked up on the left. A neat one-two sent the debutant skipping to the bye line before pulling the ball across the face of the goal to be met by Giggs who clipped home his first strike since September.

The Second Division side held out for more than twenty minutes in the second period and should have levelled after 65 minutes when Neville slipped as he tried to cut out a Bennett cross. The slip allowed the ball to travel to the scorer of the first goal but this time Durkan's shot was straight into Schmeichel's arms. United then punished their guests' miss when McClair sealed the tie with a quite exquisite curling shot from out on the left side of the area. Scholes and Ince had forced a corner which was cleared only as far as Pallister at the edge of the area. He deftly played McClair clear and, as he cut in from the left, the Scot curled the ball round Marriott and just inside the far post. Within minutes, a surging run from Ince was ended by Humes scything down the United captain to earn the Reds a penalty which Irwin tucked away to the 'keeper's right. United made it a nap hand with ten minutes left when a Giggs cross from the right had Humes at full stretch to clear.

The defender got the merest touch of his head to the ball which lifted the cross sufficiently to clear Marriott and finish up in the net. But with United now in relaxed mood, Wrexham were able to snatch a consolation effort when substitute Cross fired in a 25 yarder that took a nasty deflection off a defender to leave Schmeichel stranded. But, following their problems of the previous seventy two hours, at least United had found a cup of cheer.

United's all time FA Cup Record

	Home					Away				
P	W	D	L	F	A	W	D	L	F	A
348	100	31	28	338	150	79	53	57	300	268

	Home	Away	Total
FA Cup Attendances 94/95	43,222	22,322	65,544

Manchester United (1) 1
Aston Villa (0) 0

Saturday, 4th February 1995, Old Trafford   Att: 43,795

Manchester United			**Aston Villa**		
1	Peter	SCHMEICHEL	13	Mark	BOSNICH
27	Gary	NEVILLE (+64)	22	Gary	CHARLES
3	Denis	IRWIN	3	Steve	STAUNTON – *Booked*
4	Steve	BRUCE	4	Shaun	TEALE
5	Lee	SHARPE	5	Paul	McGRATH – *Booked*
6	Gary	PALLISTER	20	Bryan	SMALL
24	Paul	SCHOLES	18	Dwight	YORKE (+61)
8	Paul	INCE – *Booked*	8	John	FASHANU (*43)
9	Brian	McCLAIR	9	Dean	SAUNDERS
17	Andy	COLE	17	Ian	TAYLOR
11	Ryan	GIGGS (*44)	11	Andy	TOWNSEND

Subs

12	David	MAY +	7	Ray	HOUGHTON +
13	Gary	WALSH (G)	25	Tommy	JOHNSON *
14	Andrei	KANCHELSKIS *	1	Nigel	SPINK (G)

<table>
<tr><td>

Match Facts

• Andy Cole's first goal for United and his first goal in twelve games including his last nine at Newcastle.

• Villa have won just one league game at Old Trafford in 40 years. That was in 1983 when Peter Withe scored twice.

</td><td>

Score Sheet

A. COLE – 18 min 1-0

Referee:
Mr D. Elleray (Harrow)

</td></tr>
</table>

FA Carling Premiership

		P	W	D	L	F	A	Pts
1	Blackburn Rovers	26	18	5	3	57	21	59
2	**Manchester United**	27	17	6	4	48	21	57
3	Newcastle United	27	13	9	5	45	29	48
4	Liverpool	26	13	8	5	45	21	47
5	Nottingham Forest	27	13	7	7	40	29	46

Goal for Cole

Prior to the kick off, United paraded the injured Mark Hughes on the pitch and announced to a receptive full house that the Welsh striker had signed a new two year contract. With the stadium flags flying at half mast on the weekend nearest to the anniversary of the Munich Air Disaster, the Reds welcomed back captain Steve Bruce from suspension and Andy Cole, who had been cup tied against Wrexham, but lost Roy Keane who was the latest player to be suspended.

Virtually straight from the kick off, Cole and Small clashed down the United right leaving the United record signing nursing, if the pun can be excused, a black eye. But he quickly recovered to latch on to a good ball from Giggs and cut in along the right bye-line. His low hard cross was pushed out by Bosnich but only as far as Sharpe some seven yards out and right in the centre of goal. Somehow, though, Sharpe contrived to hit Bosnich's right hand post when it seemed impossible to miss. United were motoring in top gear at this point and Irwin was the next to test Bosnich with a strong shot from way out on the left wing that took a wicked deflection. But the Villa goalkeeper, once on United's books of course, brought off a fabulous diving save to his left to keep his goal intact. But the Reds in this mood are not often denied and Cole forced Charles into conceding a corner down the left. When the kick came over from Giggs, Pallister got the knock down and Cole, with his back to goal, twisted like lightning to smack the ball into the roof of the net from all of three yards. It was vintage stuff as the £7m man scored for the first time since 26th November when he netted his final goal for Newcastle against Ipswich Town. A terrible tackle by Fashanu on Giggs saw the match held up for five minutes and both players went out of the game with the Villa man stretchered off immediately and the Welshman being substituted a minute before the interval.

The second period began with Cole causing danger when his cross from the left went right across the face of goal but Fashanu's deputy, Tommy Johnson, was beginning to get into the game and was causing definite problems for United's rearguard. Pallister did well to block a good effort from the Villa striker and a cross from the same source deserved better than to drift harmlessly to safety. Johnson then sent a shot fizzing across Schmeichel's goal before United hit back in a rare attack. Scholes did well down the left before hitting a good shot from the edge of the box. The ball was deflected into the path of Cole who reacted quickly to turn it against the bar from where it bounced down and was hooked to safety by the Villa defence. Saunders had the ball in the United net only for the effort to be disallowed as the referee adjudged the ball to have gone out of play before Charles crossed it. The Midlanders piled on the pressure and United were fortunate that Johnson fluffed a great opportunity. United were certainly grateful to hear the final whistle.

League Record

		Home					Away				
	P	W	D	L	F	A	W	D	L	F	A
94/95 FAPL	27	12	1	1	27	3	5	5	3	21	18
All Time FAPL	111	40	2	4	105	30	28	17	10	90	60
FAPL/FL	3667	1076	422	336	3655	1814	560	429	794	2496	3114

	Home	Away	Total
FAPL Attendances	611,275	360,675	971,950

Manchester City   (0) 0
Manchester United   (0) 3

Saturday, 11th February 1995, Maine Road   Att: 26,368

Manchester City

125	Andy	DIBBLE
16	Nick	SUMMERBEE
18	David	BRIGHTWELL *Booked*
4	Maurizio	GAUDINO
5	Keith	CURLE
15	Alan	KERNAGHAN
12	Ian	BRIGHTWELL
8	Paul	WALSH
28	Uwe	ROSLER *Booked*
10	Gary	FLITCROFT
11	Peter	BEAGRIE *Booked* *63

Subs

9	Niall	QUINN * *Booked*
2	Andy	HILL
33	John	BURRIDGE (G)

Manchester United

1	Peter	SCHMEICHEL
3	Denis	IRWIN
4	Steve	BRUCE
5	Lee	SHARPE
6	Gary	PALLISTER
8	Paul	INCE *Booked*
9	Brian	McCLAIR
11	Ryan	GIGGS
14	Andrei	KANCHELSKIS +82
17	Andy	COLE
23	Phil	NEVILLE *53

12	David	MAY +
13	Gary	WALSH (G)
24	Paul	SCHOLES *

Score Sheet

P. INCE 58 min – 0-1

A.KANCHELSKIS 74 min – 0-2

A. COLE 77 min – 0-3

Referee
Mr. P. Don (Middlesex)

FA Carling Premiership

		P	W	D	L	F	A	Pts
1	**Manchester United**	28	18	6	4	51	21	60
2	Blackburn Rovers	27	18	5	4	58	24	59
3	Newcastle United	28	14	9	5	47	30	51
4	Liverpool	27	13	9	5	46	22	48
5	Nottingham Forest	28	13	7	8	41	31	46

The 'Guvnor takes Charge

There was a nasty scare for the fans when torrential rain put the game in doubt with the final decision to allow the game to proceed only being taken some 90 minutes before kick off. Despite much conjecture that Mark Hughes would be back after his injury at Newcastle, the Welshman didn't appear and Ferguson gave a League debut to Phil Neville to give the team a strange look with McClair and Sharpe in a five man midfield leaving Cole to forage alone up front.

With such a defensive formation, it was little surprise that City took the game to the Reds with Beagrie's mazy dribbling causing problems but not nearly as many as young Neville was suffering on the right flank under Summerbee's attacks. But for all City's pressure it was United who could, and should, have been in the lead by the half way mark as their occasional lightning counter thrusts lay the City defence bare. The first of those raids came after ten minutes with Giggs breaking at pace down the left.Reinforcements were arriving and his far post cross was met by Kanchelskis but unfortunately the Russian does not head the ball as well as he shoots and Dibble was able to palm the ball away at full stretch. The same two players linked up again after 36 minutes with Curle getting in a lunging tackle on the Russian in the nick of the time, only for Dibble to pick the ball up and find himself penalised as the referee judged it to be a back pass. The crowd were incensed and it was perhaps as well that the free kick came to nothing.

A tactical substitution by Ferguson early in the second period changed the course of the game. Scholes came on to give Cole support and Neville, who had had a torrid time, was withdrawn allowing Sharpe to drop into the left back position where he immediately became more effective than in his earlier midfield role. Having secured their own ramparts, United now set about attacking City's and produced one of those purple patches that not many teams are capable of living with. Pallister played a superb ball out of defence to Cole on the left who took on and beat Kernaghan before pulling the ball back to the edge of the area from where Ince let fly. The ball took a deflection to wrong foot Dibble and the Reds were in front. They could have been two up moments later when the normally unselfish Kanchelskis elected to shoot from an acute angle and found the side netting when a rolled ball to Scholes would only have needed a tap in. But he made amends after 74 minutes when Ince gave Kanchelskis the ball on the right leaving the Russian to shimmy past David Brightwell before beating Dibble at his near post. The goal, and the ease with which Dibble conceded it, totally deflated the Blues and it became a procession towards the City goal. The third was not long in arriving and what a gem it was. Cole almost casually strolled onto the ball in his own half before involving McClair. The Scot's precision pass to the left gave Giggs the opportunity to run at the City defence and, as he cut in along the bye line, the Welshman nonchalantly cut the ball back to leave Cole the simplest of tap ins.

League Record

	Home						Away					
	P	W	D	L	F	A	W	D	L	F	A	
94/95 FAPL	28	12	1	1	27	3	6	5	3	24	18	
All time FAPL	112	40	12	4	105	30	29	17	10	93	60	
FAPL/FL	3668	1076	422	336	3655	1814	561	429	794	2499	3114	

	Home	Away	Total
FAPL Attendances	611,275	387,043	998,318

Manchester United   (2) 3
Leeds United   (0) 1

Sunday, 19 February 1995, Old Trafford   Att: 43,214

Manchester United

1	Peter	SCHMEICHEL
3	Denis	IRWIN
4	Steve	BRUCE
6	Gary	PALLISTER
5	Lee	SHARPE
14	Andrei	KANCHELSKIS
8	Paul	INCE
16	Roy	KEANE
11	Ryan	GIGGS
9	Brian	McCLAIR
10	Mark	HUGHES

Subs

13	Gary	WALSH (G)
19	Nicky	BUTT
24	Paul	SCHOLES

Leeds United

1	John	LUKIC
2	Gary	KELLY
3	Tony	DORIGO *Booked*
6	David	WETHERALL
8	Rod	WALLACE +45
10	Gary	McALLISTER *Booked*
11	Gary	SPEED
12	John	PEMBERTON
14	David	WHITE
19	Noel	WHELAN *Booked*
26	Phil	MASINGA *45

13	Mark	BEENEY (G)
21	Tony	YEBOAH *
15	Nigel	WORTHINGTON +

Match Facts

- Leeds United came into this game unbeaten in 1995.
- Leeds not beaten United in six attempts in Cup competitions since the three match 1970 FA Cup semi final.
- Leeds have never beaten United at Old Trafford in a Cup Tie.
- Leeds not beaten United at Old Trafford in any competition since 1981.
- Yeboah's first goal for Leeds.

Score Sheet

S. BRUCE 1 min – 1-0
B. McCLAIR 4 min – 2-0
T. YEBOAH 53 min – 2-1
M. HUGHES 72 min – 3-1

Referee:
Mr. M Reed (Birmingham)

Heading On

United headed on in their attempt to retain the FA Cup in more ways than one, for all three of the goals that deflated Leeds came from headers. In fact, not only did the Yorkshire side fall to pieces, they fell to set pieces as United hit them with two goals in the first four minutes of a tie that had appeared likely to be a tricky confrontation for the Reds. United simply floored Leeds with a pounding inside those four opening minutes.

The Reds forced a corner on the left within a minute of the start and the flag kick from Giggs was met with unerring accuracy and tremendous power by Bruce who, amazingly, was virtually unmarked. The next corner three minutes later was taken again by Giggs but this time from the right flank. Pallister got the flick on at the near post for McClair to head home leaving the Yorkshire supporters shell shocked. Howard Wilkinson's side were minus Carlton Palmer and Brian Deane, two six foot plus performers who would have come in handy in the aerial duels that put the game virtually beyond recall but without them it was too tall an order.

United were taking an inept Leeds team apart and it was a surprise that not more goals came prior to the interval. But they didn't and Leeds boss Howard Wilkinson was grateful to get his men into the dressing room for a reorganisation. The degree to which the Yorkshire side were being over-run could be measured by the fact that their manager introduced both his substitutes for unforced changes during the break to leave himself without any options for the remaining 45 minutes.

The changes almost paid immediate dividends when Yeboah incredibly missed from a few yards after only sixty seconds and a few minutes later Sharpe somehow managed to get a toe poke away from the same player to concede a corner when a goal looked the more likely outcome. But after 53 minutes Leeds were back in it with a vengeance. A long ball from Whelan on the left found White raiding down the right. His cross eluded everybody but Yeboah who did his best to emulate his earlier miss but from two yards couldn't as the ball bobbled off his legs to roll over the line.

Match on, and the Reds were quick to resurrect their game. Giggs was back to his teasing best, Keane more than formidable in midfield, McClair tireless and all should have increased United's lead. But the pressure eventually told when McClair released Kanchelskis on the right. He cut into the box where he was faced with a wall of three defenders before chipping to the far post. Hughes had been going to the near post presumably expecting one of the Russian's cannonball shots cum crosses and had to quickly back pedal. But the sheer strength of the man enabled him to still get sufficient power into his header, despite still being in reverse gear, to beat Lukic by putting the ball back in the direction from where it had arrived.

The goal drained Leeds of any further thoughts of resistance and the Reds won in a canter. Their reward was swift with the draw for the next round being made immediately after the final whistle and presenting the Cup holders with a home tie against QPR, managed by former Red, Ray Wilkins.

United's all time FA Cup Record

		Home					Away				
P	W	D	L	F	A	W	D	L	F	A
349	101	31	28	341	151	79	53	57	300	268

	Home	Away	Total
FA Cup Attendances	85,966	22,322	108,288

Norwich City (0) 0
Manchester United (2) 2

Wednesday, 22nd February 1995, Carrow Road   Att: 21,824

Norwich City			**Manchester United**		
24	Andy	MARSHALL	1	Peter	SCHMEICHEL
16	Carl	BRADSHAW	16	Roy	KEANE
5	Jon	NEWSOME	4	Steve	BRUCE
10	John	POLSTON – *Booked*	6	Gary	PALLISTER
2	Mark	BOWEN	5	Lee	SHARPE
6	Neil	ADAMS	14	Andrei	KANCHELSKIS
19	Andy	JOHNSON	8	Paul	INCE
8	Mick	MILLIGAN	9	Brian	McCLAIR
20	Darren	EADIE	11	Ryan	GIGGS
33	Mike	SHERON	17	Andy	COLE
7	Ashley	WARD	10	Mark	HUGHES

Subs

15	Daryl	SUTCH	3	Denis	IRWIN
3	Rob	NEWMAN	13	Gary	WALSH (G)
34	Simon	TRACEY (G)	19	Nicky	BUTT

Match Facts

• United's first goal was their 2,500th away from home in league matches.

• United's second strike was their 200th FAPL goal.

• The attendance pushed the total league attendances for United in 94/95 past the one million mark.

• Kanchelskis played 90 minutes in a league game for the first time in 1995.

Score Sheet

P. INCE 2min – 0-2

A. KANCHELSKIS 17 min – 0-2

Referee:
Mr. T. Holbrook (Walsall)

FA Carling Premiership

		P	W	D	L	F	A	Pts
1	Blackburn Rovers	29	20	5	4	63	26	65
2	**Manchester United**	**29**	**19**	**6**	**4**	**53**	**21**	**63**
3	Newcastle United	28	14	9	5	47	30	51
4	Liverpool	27	13	9	5	46	22	48
5	Nottingham Forest	29	13	7	9	41	32	46

Canaries Crushed

Despite Eric Cantona's continued absence, United boss Alex Ferguson still had sufficient talent available to allow him the luxury of leaving Denis Irwin on the bench as Roy Keane and Lee Sharpe took over the full back positions. Up front, Andy Cole and Mark Hughes appeared together for the first time to leave a Norwich team humiliated 5-0 by Everton in their previous game pondering the probability of another uphill struggle.

And after only three minutes it was exactly that as the Reds followed their barnstorming start three days earlier against Leeds with another rapid goal, again from a Giggs corner. Alert to the dangers that United's corners had been posing for other sides, Newsome climbed high to head the left wing flag kick out of the area but, unfortunately for Norwich, only as far as Ince. The England player's aim from 25 yards was as unerring as an Exocet missile and easily beat Norwich's young 'keeper, Marshall, at his right hand post. There was worse to come for the youngster when he was powerless to prevent another United strike less than 15 minutes later.

The move began with United defending a corner kick but six seconds later the ball was nestling nicely in the back of the Canaries cage for a quite magnificent goal. Pallister headed out the Norwich flag kick to Hughes just outside the United area where the Welshman initially struggled to control the ball which had dropped awkwardly for him. He was, however, able to find McClair who, in turn, fed Giggs to sprint deep into Norwich territory. A precision pass switched play to the right from where Kanchelskis cut in at pace to fire a rasping drive across Marshall and into the far corner for his fourteenth goal of the season and a truly memorable one.

Norwich didn't collapse after the second goal and they brought the best out of Schmeichel when he had to dive full length to his right to beat away a powerful 20 yard Mark Bowen effort. So vicious was the shot that the rebound off Schmeichel's hands carried the ball into touch!

The second period was a formality with the only danger to United being the ceaseless downpour driven by high winds which saw most of the other scheduled games called off. But Norwich, to their credit, never made it easy for the Reds and, whilst they rarely troubled the United rearguard after the break, they defended well. Cole looked all set to score for the third successive game when he chested down a Giggs cross but Bowen dived in smartly to save the day and Hughes should undoubtedly have been awarded a penalty when felled by Polston. He then beat Marshall only for his aim to be slightly adrift allowing the woodwork to intercept with ten minutes left. But the most telling moment of the second period came half way through when a spectator berated Keane as he retrieved the ball for a throw-in. Keane turned quickly on his verbal assailant and everybody's mind went back in time to Crystal Palace and Eric Cantona. But there was no karate kick or ranting back, the Irishman merely took a long look and then blew a mocking kiss to the idiot involved.

League Record

| | | Home | | | | | Away | | | | |
	P	W	D	L	F	A	W	D	L	F	A
94/95 FAPL	29	12	1	1	27	3	7	5	3	26	18
All time FAPL	113	40	12	4	105	30	30	17	10	95	60
All time FAPL/FL	3669	1076	422	336	3655	1814	562	429	794	2501	3114

	Home	Away	Total
FAPL Attendances	611,275	408,867	1,020,142

Everton   (0) 1
Manchester United   (0) 0

Saturday, 25th February 1995, Goodison Park   Att: 40,011

Everton

1	Neville	SOUTHALL
4	Earl	BARRETT
5	Dave	WATSON
26	David	UNSWORTH
3	Andy	HINCHCLIFFE
14	John	EBBRELL *Booked* *71
10	Barry	HORNE
18	Joe	PARKINSON
17	Anders	LIMPAR
9	Duncan	FERGUSON
19	Stuart	BARLOW

Subs

7	Vinnie	SAMWAYS *
11	Daniel	AMOKACHI
31	Steve	REEVES (G)

Manchester United

1	Peter	SCHMEICHEL
3	Denis	IRWIN
4	Steve	BRUCE
6	Gary	PALLISTER
5	Lee	SHARPE
8	Paul	INCE – *Booked*
9	Brian	McCLAIR *66
16	Roy	KEANE
11	Ryan	GIGGS
17	Andy	COLE
10	Mark	HUGHES

14	Andrei	KANCHELSKIS *
19	Nicky	BUTT
13	Gary	WALSH (G)

Match Facts

- First Goodison goal conceded by United since September 1989.
- First success at home for Everton over United in the FAPL.
- Result maintained Everton's 100% record at Goodison on 1995.
- United had only lost one of their previous nineteen FAPL games.

Score Sheet

D. FERGUSON 58 min – 1-0

Referee:
Mr. J. Worrall (Warrington)

FA Carling Premiership

		P	W	D	L	F	A	Pts
1	Blackburn Rovers	30	20	6	4	63	26	66
2	**Manchester United**	**30**	**19**	**6**	**5**	**53**	**21**	**63**
3	Newcastle United	29	15	9	5	50	31	54
4	Liverpool	28	14	9	5	48	23	51
5	Nottingham Forest	29	13	7	9	41	32	46

Ferguson at the Double

With Everton languishing in the bottom four places before the game, United went into the match as hot favourites but anybody with a nose for outsiders would have noted that Everton had a 100% home record in 1995 that had yielded 15 goals. The game was, in the event, to evolve around two men, both named Ferguson. The United boss, Alex, who many people felt lost the League title in 1991/92 through making unforced team changes, made the unbelievable decision to demote leading goalscorer Andrei Kanchelskis to the subs bench and by the time the Russian was brought into the action it was too late with Everton in front and their confidence as high as their sky-line main stand. The other Ferguson to make an impact on the game was Everton's Duncan whose goal settled the issue.

The high balcony of Goodison's main stand gives, quite literally, a bird's eye view of the play deep below but unfortunately there were no pretty patterns to admire as Everton hustled and bustled United at every opportunity. The Blues "Toffee Lady" had gone round the ground prior to kick off giving sweets away but, as far as United were concerned, that was the last of the goodies for the afternoon even though the start was delayed twenty minutes to allow all the Reds supporters in. There was little inkling of what was to come as United made the first clear cut chance in the 15th minute when a cross from the left by Keane eluded everybody to fall at the far post for Hughes only for the Welshman to also completely miss the ball with the net beckoning. Cole was then left hanging his head when, after looking worth £7m with some brilliant control to make an opening, he looked a free transfer man as he fluffed the chance he had created for himself from ten yards.

United again created chances at the start of the second period but Cole tried to sidefoot the ball home from the edge of the area to give Southall little problem with what was a clear sight of goal. The Reds paid dearly for this miss as the ball was cleared upfield where Horne thundered a great shot against the angle of the woodwork although, had it gone in, it would have been interesting to see if a goal would have been allowed as the linesman was flagging for offside. Still shaken by this let off, United conceded a series of corners and the winning goal came from a Hinchcliffe flag kick on the Everton right. For once, Ferguson got away from Pallister and rocketed a header into the unguarded net as Schmeichel came out.

Kanchelskis was belatedly introduced but Everton's tiring legs were rejuvenated by the goal and they were now quite happy to leave Ferguson upfield on his own and defend in depth. Cole managed a shot but it was as powder puff as his earlier miss and he then completed a miserable afternoon by heading over an Irwin cross in the dying minutes when he should at least have hit the target. Two questions were on the lips of every United fan as they left the ground – had Newcastle seen the best of Cole and why, oh why, had Kanchelskis been left out? The answer to the first was that time would tell whilst only the manager knew the answer to the second.

League Record

	Home						Away				
	P	W	D	L	F	A	W	D	L	F	A
94/95 FAPL	30	12	1	1	27	3	7	5	4	26	19
All time FAPL	114	40	12	4	105	30	30	17	11	95	61
All time FAPL/FL	3670	1076	422	336	3655	1814	562	429	795	2501	3115

	Home	Away	Total
FAPL Attendances	611,275	448,878	1,060,153

Manchester United (3) 9
Ipswich Town (0) 0

Saturday, 4th March 1995, Old Trafford   Att: 43,804

Manchester United			Ipswich Town		
1	Peter	SCHMEICHEL	1	Craig	FORREST *Booked*
16	Roy	KEANE *45	19	Frank	YALLOP
3	Denis	IRWIN	3	Neil	THOMPSON
4	Steve	BRUCE +80	5	John	WARK
6	Gary	PALLISTER	6	David	LINIGHAN *Booked*
8	Paul	INCE	18	Steve	PALMER
9	Brian	McCLAIR	7	Geraint	WILLIAMS
14	Andrei	KANCHELSKIS	14	Steve	SEDGELEY
17	Andy	COLE	21	Stuart	SLATER
10	Mark	HUGHES	33	Alex	MATHIE
11	Ryan	GIGGS	11	Lee	CHAPMAN *64
Subs			Subs		
5	Lee	SHARPE *	10	Ian	MARSHALL *
19	Nicky	BUTT +	23	Philip	MORGAN (G)
13	Gary	WALSH (G)	4	Paul	MASON

Match Facts

- The 9-0 scoreline smashed the FA Premiership record previously held by Newcastle Utd and Aston Villa at 7-1
- Andy Cole became the first United player to ever score four goals in a FAPL game and first ever to score five in a FAPL or Football League game. His first goal is his 100th of his career
- United's biggest league victory for 103 years

Score Sheet

R. KEANE 15 min – 1-0

A. COLE 19 min – 2-0

A. COLE 37 min – 3-0

A. COLE 53 min – 4-0

M. HUGHES 55 min – 5-0

M. HUGHES 59 min – 6-0

A. COLE 65 min – 7-0

P. INCE 72 min – 8-0

A. COLE 87 min – 9-0

FA Carling Premiership

		P	W	D	L	F	A	Pts
1	Blackburn Rovers	31	21	6	4	64	26	69
2	**Manchester United**	31	20	6	5	62	22	66
3	Newcastle United	31	16	9	6	52	33	57
4	Liverpool	29	15	9	5	50	23	54
5	Nottingham Forest	31	13	9	9	44	35	48

Referee:
Mr. G. Poll
(Tilehurst)

Cole's Galore on Cloud Nine

This was next to top playing next to bottom and the Ipswich manager George Burley said prior to the game "We will not put nine men behind the ball like last season" in reference to the goalless draw that was the worst game Old Trafford had endured in the FAPL. Unfortunately he did not mention anything about United depositing the ball in the net nine times. As for the Reds, they went into the game with the Hughes, Cole partnership having failed to produce a goal in their previous two games together – they ended the match with seven!

Ipswich fielded six players aged 30 or over and Wark, at 37 the daddy of them all, broke up the first United raid. But that was the end of their success for the afternoon as the Reds ran riot with the first goal coming after 15 minutes. Irwin crossed to Hughes at the edge of the area and the Welshman held it up before rolling it into the path of Keane. From the right hand edge of the area, Keane's aim to the far post was unerring with the ball finding the net off the woodwork. The second came when Giggs won a rebound on the half way line off Yallop and sprinted down the left before cutting in and slipping the ball to Cole who picked his spot from eight yards. Next a Kanchelskis cross brought a magnificent overhead scissors kick from Hughes that smacked the bar leaving Cole to tap home but, if the East Anglians thought that half time would bring relief, they were very badly mistaken.

The slaughter continued unabated in the second period with the only dispute being who scored the fourth. An Irwin cross was headed by Yallop and appeared to hit Cole on the way into the net but there was no dispute over the fifth, a typical smashed Hughes volley onto the roof of the net from Giggs and he headed home his second and United's sixth from close range following a Giggs effort that had bounced high in the air after being blocked. McClair tried to get in on the act but his shot hit Forrest's body to fall for Cole to notch number seven. The eighth came when Forrest actually managed to get a hand on something but unfortunately for him he was well outside his area when he did so. Fearing a red card, there was positive relief on his face when only a yellow was produced but his look altered dramatically as he cantered back to goal only to see the ball sail over his shoulder and bounce into the empty net as Ince took a quick free kick. In a close game, the goal would undoubtedly have been hotly disputed but such was their morale that it was meekly accepted. Hughes smashed the bar again but the Reds were not finished yet. Ipswich failed to clear a corner and Cole rammed the ball home for United's ninth.

When the final whistle eventually put Town out of their misery, Manager Alex Ferguson simply said "That was as near perfection as it is possible to get". Not many contested that.

League Record

		Home					Away				
	P	W	D	L	F	A	W	D	L	F	A
94/95 FAPL	31	13	1	1	36	3	7	5	4	26	19
All time FAPL	115	41	12	4	114	30	30	17	11	95	61
All time FAPL/FL	3671	1077	422	336	3664	1814	562	429	795	2501	3115

	Home	Away	Total
FAPL Attendances	55,079	448,878	1,103,957

Wimbledon (0) 0
Manchester United (0) 1

Tuesday, 7th March 1995, Selhurst Park   Attendance 18,224

Wimbledon

1	Hans	SEGER
2	Warren	BARTON – Booked
20	Marcus	GAYLE *86
12	Gary	ELKINS – Booked
4	Vinnie	JONES
16	Alan	KIMBLE – Booked and Sent Off
15	Alan	REEVES
10	Dean	HOLDSWORTH Booked
21	Chris	PERRY
37	Kenny	CUNNINGHAM
36	John	GOODMAN

Subs

26	Neil	ARDLEY *
30	Mick	HARFORD
23	Neil	SULLIVAN (G)

Manchester United

1	Peter	SCHMEICHEL
27	Gary	NEVILLE
4	Steve	BRUCE
6	Gary	PALLISTER
3	Denis	IRWIN
11	Ryan	GIGGS
9	Brian	McCLAIR
8	Paul	INCE
5	Lee	SHARPE
10	Mark	HUGHES
17	Andy	COLE

13	Gary	WALSH (G)
18	Simon	DAVIES
26	Chris	CASPER

Match Facts

● The Dons failed in their bid to become the first team to beat United in three consecutive FAPL seasons.

● Changing times – in the previous season's encounter, Wimbledon boss Joe Kinnear had received the Manager of the Month Award for March. This time he received a red card.

Score Sheet

S. BRUCE 84 min – 0-1

Referee:
Mr R. Hart (Darlington)

FA Carling Premiership

		P	W	D	L	F	A	Pts
1	**Manchester United**	32	21	6	5	63	22	69
2	Blackburn Rovers	31	21	6	4	64	26	69
3	Newcastle United	31	16	9	6	53	33	57
4	Liverpool	29	15	9	5	50	23	54
5	Nottingham Forest	31	13	9	9	44	35	48

Red Mist at the Palace

Less than six weeks had passed since United had visited Crystal Palace and ended up with Paul Ince and Eric Cantona receiving summonses to appear in Court on charges of assault. Back at Selhurst Park to take on Wimbledon, the red mist of frayed tempers again exploded but this time it was Don's boss Joe Kinnear who lit the blue touchpaper and then failed to stand back after United had scored the only goal of the game six minutes from time. Wimbledon had already had five yellow cards including Kimble's two that resulted in him being dismissed after 79 minutes when Kinnear exploded on the touchline where he was ably assisted by Club Chairman Sam Hammam. Although it was the goal that prompted the incident, Kinnear strangely said afterwards that "The goal was fair enough but I'm bitter about the bookings and sending off" adding that referee Mr. Hart was "his usual Hitler fashion". United boss Alex Ferguson simply said "It was a bit quieter than the last time we were here".

On a sticky pitch, United carved out just two solitary chances in the first period, the first when Gary Neville almost opened his first team account with a rasping left footer from some thirty yards out only to see Segers make a fine diving save to his right and the other when a Hughes snap shot was straight at the Wimbledon 'keeper. The Reds, without the injured Keane and the sulking Kanchelskis who had opted to play for his country in a meaningless friendly after being dropped against Everton, found themselves struggling particularly as Ince was only a shadow of his usual self having been told just hours before the game that he was to face prosecution for his part in the Cantona fracas. Certainly they could have gone in at the interval trailing as Gayle beat Neville down the Wimbledon left and cut in only to be denied by the right hand of Schmeichel. The ball bounced high in the air and Gayle's follow up effort was then cleared off the line by Pallister.

In the second half, Wimbledon rarely troubled the United defence but the Reds, too, struggled to create anything. Cole had half a chance from an acute angle and even the dismissal of Kimble failed to open things up. It was, perhaps, fitting for such a nondescript game that the goal should be fashioned out of nothing. McClair did well to keep the ball in play on the half way line on the United right and immediately hoisted a long ball, more in hope it seemed than anything else, towards the Don's penalty area. Segers came out to the penalty spot but fumbled his catch. So desperate were the Reds by this stage that they had thrown Steve Bruce up front and the big central defender was on hand to stab the dropped ball through the legs of Segers before running round the stricken 'keeper to tap the ball home left footed. Now there's a rarity – a Steve Bruce goal from his left foot, no wonder Joe Kinnear saw red!

League Record

	Home						Away				
	P	W	D	L	F	A	W	D	L	F	A
94/95 FAPL	32	13	1	1	36	3	8	5	4	27	19
All time FAPL	116	41	12	4	114	30	31	17	11	96	61
All time FAPL/FL	3672	1077	422	336	3664	1814	563	429	795	2502	3115

	Home	Away	Total
FAPL Attendances	655,079	467,102	1,122,181

131

Manchester United (1) 2
Queens Park Rangers (0) 0

Sunday, 12th March 1995, Old Trafford   Att: 42,830

Manchester United		
1	Peter	SCHMEICHEL
27	Gary	NEVILLE
4	Steve	BRUCE
6	Gary	PALLISTER
3	Denis	IRWIN
14	Andrei	KANCHELSKIS
8	Paul	INCE
9	Brian	McCLAIR
5	Lee	SHARPE
10	Mark	HUGHES (Booked)
11	Ryan	GIGGS *45

Subs

13	Gary	WALSH (G)
16	Roy	KEANE *
23	Phil	NEVILLE

Queens Park Rangers		
1	Tony	ROBERTS
2	David	BARDSLEY
3	Clive	WILSON
6	Alan	McDONALD *Booked*
16	Danny	MADDIX *Booked*
8	Ian	HOLLOWAY *Booked*
15	Rufus	BREVETT *62
14	Simon	BARKER
7	Andrew	IMPEY
9	Les	FERDINAND *Booked*
20	Keith	GALLEN

12	Gary	PENRICE *
13	Sieb	DYKSTRA (G)
5	Karl	READY

Match Facts

- United had never met QPR in the FA Cup until 1977 but have now played them six times in the competition without being defeated.
- QPR have not beaten United in eight meetings since thrashing the Reds 4-1 at Old Trafford on New Year's Day 1992.
- United's 350th FA Cup tie.
- Lee Sharpe's first ever FA Cup goal for United.
- The first goals conceded in the 1994/95 FA Cup competition by QPR were their last.

Score Sheet

L. SHARPE 23 min – 1-0
D. IRWIN 53 min – 2-0

Referee:
Mr D. Gallagher (Banbury)

Twin Towers in Sight Again

United maintained their assault on the FA Cup with something in hand for, despite being without Parker, Cantona and Keane in their starting line up from the 1994 Final team and minus the cup tied Cole, the Reds were never seriously threatened by a QPR side that worked hard but created only two clear cut chances in the entire ninety minutes.

The commitment shown by QPR manifested itself in bookings for Maddix and Ferdinand before twenty minutes had been played and there were further yellow cards for McDonald and Holloway. Kanchelskis, back in action after his absence on international duty, was proving to be a handful for the Londoners and one of his runs almost produced the first goal when Giggs easily beat Maddix to the cross from the right only to steer the ball narrowly wide of Roberts' left hand post. QPR replied with Gallen sending a long ball for Ferdinand to chase and the England striker's speed down United's left flank found Bruce wanting for pace. As Ferdinand cut in from the angle of the area he fired across Schmeichel and past the far post.

Neville, Kanchelskis and Hughes then combined down the right to give Sharpe a clear opportunity but he wanted to get the ball on his left foot and a great chance went begging. Sharpe, however, quickly atoned after a long punt upfield by Schmeichel was killed stone dead by Hughes who then fed Giggs. The youngster quickly slipped the ball further left still for Sharpe but Bardsley should have intercepted. He didn't and Sharpe cut in with the ball this time on his favoured left to slot home his first ever FA Cup goal for the Reds and his first strike since his fabulous back heel against Barcelona in October.

After only eight minutes of the second period, United wrapped the game up with one of Irwin's free kick specials. Once again, Hughes was involved in the build up when Bruce made the Welsh international the target for a free kick. As Hughes attempted to hold the ball, Maddix wrestled him to the ground and, having already been booked, was extremely fortunate in the prevailing climate of discipline to escape dismissal. But the let off for Maddix did not extend to QPR with Irwin bending the free kick from the edge of the box on United's left past Roberts' despairing left hand for a fabulous strike.

United seemed to ease up and QPR had their best spell of the game with Brevett threatening to score his first ever goal for Rangers only to see the ball bobble just wide of the post and then slack defending gave Ferdinand a good sight of goal. His hard hit drive, however, was excellently blocked by Schmeichel for Irwin to complete the clearance. United heeded the warning and tightened up again to ensure a smooth passage into the semi-final leaving themselves still on course for the double, double.

United's all time FA Cup Record

| | Home | | | | | Away | | | | |
	P	W	D	L	F	A	W	D	L	F	A
	350	102	31	28	343	151	79	53	57	300	268

	Home	Away		Total
FA Cup Attendances	128,796	22,322		151,118

Manchester United (0) 0
Tottenham Hotspur (0) 0

Match 47

Wednesday, 15th March 1995, Old Trafford · Att: 43,802

Manchester United			**Tottenham Hotspur**		
1	Peter	SCHMEICHEL	13	Ian	WALKER
3	Denis	IRWIN	5	Colin	CALDERWOOD *Booked*
4	Steve	BRUCE	2	Dean	AUSTIN
6	Gary	PALLISTER	3	Justin	EDINBURGH *Booked*
5	Lee	SHARPE *Booked*	6	Gary	MABBUTT
14	Andrei	KANCHELSKIS	9	Darren	ANDERTON
8	Paul	INCE	11	Ronnie	ROSENTHAL
9	Brian	McCLAIR *78	15	David	HOWELLS
11	Ryan	GIGGS *Booked*	7	Nicky	BARMBY
17	Andy	COLE	18	Jurgen	KLINSMANN
10	Mark	HUGHES	10	Teddy	SHERINGHAM

Subs					
13	Gary	WALSH (G)	20	Darren	CASKEY
27	Gary	NEVILLE	1	Eric	THORSTVEDT (G)
19	Nicky	BUTT *	14	Stuart	NETHERCOTT

Match Facts

• First time United had failed to score at Old Trafford in 1994/95.

• Spurs not beaten United in last ten meetings.

• Only Ryan Giggs' third booking of the season in FAPL but two of them were home and away against Spurs!

Score Sheet

Referee:
Mr K. Morton (Bury St. Edmonds)

FA Carling Premiership

		P	W	D	L	F	A	Pts
1	Blackburn Rovers	33	22	7	4	68	28	73
2	**Manchester United**	**33**	**21**	**7**	**5**	**63**	**22**	**70**
3	Newcastle United	32	17	9	6	54	33	60
4	Liverpool	30	15	9	6	52	26	54
5	Nottingham Forest	33	15	9	9	50	38	54

Reds Thwarted by Spurs

With both these sides in the semi-finals of the FA Cup and having missed one another in the draw, most people looked forward to this game as the "hors d'oeuvre" for the Cup Final itself and the game, though goalless, lived up to everybody's expectations. Indeed, it was quite incredible that neither side managed a goal in a ninety minutes that had everybody on the edge of their seats throughout. But if United dominated the first period, Spurs certainly had the better of the exchanges thereafter and the result could easily have gone either way.

United almost took the lead after only thirty seconds when a fierce Bruce challenge on the half way line against Klinsmann saw the ball break to Hughes. He quickly fed the ball out to Kanchelskis on the right and the pacey Russian set off like a sprinter from the blocks. As he hit the byeline, Kanchelskis cleverly chipped the ball to the far post where Hughes, having started the move, now got on the end of the cross and his powerful header beat Walker all ends up only for the ball to rebound to safety off a post. But Spurs hit back when a long kick from Walker was flicked on by Sheringham for Klinsmann. The German was free and bearing in on goal with Schmeichel committed to coming out to the edge of his area and the classy World Cup star looked like he must score. But the Reds had a big let off when his lob not only cleared the United 'keeper but also the unguarded net.

It was the Reds turn to bounce back next with a brilliant move that began with an interception by Ince at halfway. He slipped the ball to Irwin on the right who proceeded to play a couple of one-twos with Kanchelskis which left the Russian again causing the Londoner's defence all sorts of problems. His cross from the byeline this time came in hard and low and seemed that Cole only had to touch the ball home from five yards. He touched it all right but could only look up in anguish as he scooped the ball against the bar when it appeared impossible to miss. Giggs fastened on to the rebound and it seemed he had got Cole off the hook only for his goalbound effort to take a deflection for a corner. The danger, however, for Spurs was still not over as Ince powered in a great header from the resulting flag kick that had goal written all over it only for Walker, under intense pressure from Cole, to produce a superb save.

The second period saw a much more confident Spurs and they limited United's chances whilst both Anderton and Klinsmann could have given the London side the lead. But, with time running out, United almost stole it only to find Spurs saved by an unlikely hero. Butt won the ball at the edge of the Spurs area and found Kanchelskis who was immediately closed down by three defenders. He squeezed the ball out to Giggs and his cross was going in when Rosenthal, a scorer of a hat-trick against Southampton when Spurs had trailed 0-2 two weeks earlier, somehow kicked it off the line as he raced back into his own net to maintain the stalemate.

League Record

	P	W	D	L	F	A	W	D	L	F	A
			Home						*Away*		
94/95 FAPL	33	13	2	1	36	3	8	5	4	27	19
All time FAPL	117	41	13	4	114	30	31	17	11	96	61
All time FAPL/FL	3673	1077	423	336	3664	1814	563	429	795	2502	3115

	Home	*Away*	*Total*
FAPL Attendances	698,881	467,102	1,165,983

Liverpool   (1) 2
Manchester United   (0) 0

Match 48

Liverpool			**Manchester United**		
1	David	JAMES	1	Peter	SCHMEICHEL
12	John	SCALES	16	Roy	KEANE *Booked* +84
5	Mark	WRIGHT	4	Steve	BRUCE *Booked*
6	Phil	BABB	6	Gary	PALLISTER
25	Neil	RUDDOCK	3	Denis	IRWIN
20	Stig	BJORNEBYE	14	Andrei	KANCHELSKIS
15	Jamie	REDKNAPP *Booked*	8	Paul	INCE
17	Steve	McMANAMAN	9	Brian	McCLAIR
10	John	BARNES *62	5	Lee	SHARPE *45
9	Ian	RUSH +87	11	Ryan	GIGGS
23	Robbie	FOWLER	10	Mark	HUGHES

Subs

30	Anthony	WARNER (G)	17	Andy	COLE *
11	Mark	WALTERS +	19	Nicky	BUTT +
16	Michael	THOMAS * *Booked*	13	Gary	WALSH (G)

Match Facts

- First FAPL win for Liverpool over United.
- Andy Cole became the most expensive substitute in British football.
- First time United had failed to score in consecutive FAPL games since October 1992.
- Apart from the 9-0 drubbing handed out to Ipswich, United had now scored just one goal in their last four FAPL games teenager.

Score Sheet

J. REDKNAPP – 25 min – 1-0

S. BRUCE (og) 84 min – 2-0

Referee:
Mr G. Ashby (Worcester)

FA Carling Premiership

		P	W	D	L	F	A	Pts
1	Blackburn Rovers	34	23	7	4	70	29	76
2	**Manchester United**	**34**	**21**	**7**	**6**	**63**	**24**	**70**
3	Newcastle United	33	18	9	6	55	33	63
4	Liverpool	31	16	9	6	54	26	57
5	Nottingham Forest	34	16	9	9	53	38	57

Bad Boy Bruce

Events on the pitch dramatically revised the original intended headline which had been served up off the pitch when Alex Ferguson dropped more than a bombshell when he relegated £7m signing Andy Cole to the bench making the Reds' latest capture the British game's most expensive substitute. The decision seemed all the more remarkable given the fact that Liverpool are one of Cole's favourite opponents – he scored four times against them in 1993/94 for Newcastle! But Steve Bruce had an even worse day when he was booked, causing him to miss the FA Cup semi-final, and then compounding his woe by turning the ball past Schmeichel for Liverpool's second goal to put the game beyond recall. Rounding off Bruce's unhappy day, the final result also seemed to spell the end of United's Championship chances just as a 2-0 defeat at Anfield in 1992 had allowed Leeds United to pip the Old Trafford side to the title. Strange how history repeats itself.

Liverpool, for their part, had lost their previous two home games and had not lost three home games on the trot since 1963. They were not about to allow such arch enemies as United the honour of repeating the feat. Their manager Roy Evans brought back the man who had been missing so long that he had become referred to on Merseyside as Lord Lucan, Mark Wright, in an attempt to right the ship as Liverpool played five across the back in a home match. Hughes, on his own up front, and faced with Wright, Babb and Ruddock was hopelessly outnumbered whilst in midfield it once again seemed that Ince's determination and tenacity had been blighted by his impending court case for his part in the Crystal Palace fracas. The end result was that United rarely troubled James in the Liverpool net and by the time Cole was introduced during the break, the Anfield boys had their tails up.

For all that, there had been nothing to particularly worry Schmeichel prior to the first goal but, when it came, the strike was a first class effort from Redknapp. Ince missed his tackle on Rush allowing the ball to run to Redknapp who then proceeded to achieve what very few others have by speeding past Irwin down Liverpool's left. As he cut into the angle of the penalty area, Redknapp let fly with a powerful drive across Schmeichel and into the far corner of the net for an excellent finish.

The nearest United came to equalising was in the 55th minute when Hughes headed down for Giggs but the youngster's shot shaved the bar. Hughes also had a snap shot saved but, in truth, there seemed little prospect of the Reds breaching the Anfield defence. What lingering hopes they had were finally killed off six minutes from time. A right wing cross from Thomas was met by McManaman whose shot seemed to be covered by Schmeichel going to his right when Bruce stuck out a leg and deflected the ball past the Dane's left. That just about summed the day up.

League Record

	P	W	D	L	F	A	W	D	L	F	A
		Home					*Away*				
94/95 FAPL	34	13	2	1	36	3	8	5	5	27	21
All time FAPL	118	41	13	4	114	30	31	17	12	96	63
All time FAPL/FL	3674	1077	423	336	3664	1814	563	429	796	2502	3117

	Home	Away	Total
FAPL Attendances	698,881	506,008	1,204,889

Manchester United   (2) 3
Arsenal   (0) 0

Wednesday, 22nd March 1995, Old Trafford   Att: 43,623

Manchester United

1	Peter	SCHMEICHEL
16	Roy	KEANE
4	Steve	BRUCE *Booked*
6	Gary	PALLISTER
3	Denis	IRWIN
14	Andrei	KANCHELSKIS
8	Paul	INCE
5	Lee	SHARPE
11	Ryan	GIGGS
10	Mark	HUGHES
17	Andy	COLE

Subs

25	Kevin	PILKINGTON (G)
9	Brian	McCLAIR
19	Nicky	BUTT

Arsenal

13	Vince	BARTRAM
2	Lee	DIXON
6	Tony	ADAMS
12	Steve	BOULD *Booked*
3	Nigel	WINTERBURN
23	Ray	PARLOUR *57
14	Martin	KEOWN *Booked*
21	Steve	MORROW
10	Paul	MERSON
31	Chris	KIWOMYA
8	Ian	WRIGHT *Booked*

26	Lee	HARPER (G)
11	Eddie	McGOLDRICK
32	Glenn	HELDER *

Match Facts

- Paul Merson remains the only Arsenal player to have scored against United in the FAPL in six attempts. Their only other strike was a Gary Pallister own goal in 1993/94.
- The Gunners have not scored at Old Trafford in a league game since October 1991.
- Reds still to lose to the Gunners in the FAPL.

Score Sheet

M. HUGHES 26 min – 1-0

L. SHARPE 31 min – 2-0

A. KANCHELSKIS 80 min – 3-0

Referee:

Mr K. Cooper (Pontypridd)

FA Carling Premiership

		P	W	D	L	F	A	Pts
1	Blackburn Rovers	34	23	7	4	70	29	76
2	**Manchester United**	**35**	**22**	**7**	**6**	**66**	**24**	**73**
3	Newcastle United	34	18	9	7	56	36	63
4	Nottingham Forest	35	17	9	9	56	38	60
5	Liverpool	32	16	10	6	54	26	58

Lifeline

After the massive swing in Championship fortunes away from Old Trafford towards Ewood Park in the previous week, United knew they had probably to take maximum points from their remaining eight Championship games if they were to have any realistic hope of retaining their Crown. Nothing less than outright victory against Arsenal, therefore, would do but the odds were against them. Not only had they managed just one goal in their previous four league games (apart from the nine goal barrage against Ipswich) but they had never scored in open play against the Gunners at Old Trafford in the FAPL, the Reds only goal against Arsenal having come courtesy of a phenomenal Eric Cantona free kick in 93/94.

The omens, then, were not good for United and nothing that happened in the first 25 minutes suggested that they were about to change against a side that had just reached the semi-final stage of the European Cup-Winners' Cup. Indeed, it was Arsenal who almost opened the scoring as Wright tried a spectacular fifty yard, yes, fifty yard effort that bounced only narrowly wide after the Gunner spotted Schmeichel out of position. But the turning point came after 26 minutes when Bartram failed to hold a routine cross from Giggs and, after Sharpe had tried unsuccessfully to force the loose ball home, Hughes bludgeoned it through a mass of defenders.

The anxiety visibly drained away from the Reds and five minutes later the points were in the bag as Hughes laid the ball into Sharpe's path for the England man to drive home. Just before the interval, Steve Bruce, already awaiting a visit to the FA for topping forty disciplinary points, received yet another caution when he tangled with Wright and the two apparently continued the skirmish in the sanctuary of the dressing room corridor after leaving the field for the break.

Arsenal, facing their fourth successive league defeat, seemed unable to raise their game whilst United were content to sit on their lead. Andy Cole added to his catalogue of missed sitters since arriving at Old Trafford when he first of all missed the target completely from six yards and then, with his sights straightened, tamely diverted a Kanchelskis cross directly into Bartram's waiting arms from the same distance. The visiting 'keeper, however, had no chance ten minutes from time when Kanchelskis became United's leading goalscorer with his fifteenth of the campaign as he threaded the ball home after Bartram had parried a low drive from Giggs.

Ferguson had castigated his players in the match programme and said afterwards that "I had to ask the players if they still had the hunger for success. I was beginning to wonder how we were going to score a goal". The players responded by giving themselves a lifeline, albeit a frayed one, to the title.

League Record

		Home					Away				
	P	W	D	L	F	A	W	D	L	F	A
94/95 FAPL	35	14	2	1	39	3	8	5	5	27	21
All time FAPL	119	42	13	4	117	30	31	17	12	96	63
All time FAPL/FL	3675	1078	423	336	3667	1814	563	429	796	2502	3117

	Home	Away	Total
FAPL Attendances	742.504	506,008	1,248,512

Manchester United (0) 0
Leeds United (0) 0

Sunday, 2nd April 1995, Old Trafford   Att: 43,712

Manchester United			**Leeds United**		
1	Peter	SCHMEICHEL	1	John	LUKIC
27	Gary	NEVILLE	2	Gary	KELLY
16	Roy	KEANE	3	Tony	DORIGO
6	Gary	PALLISTER	4	Carlton	PALMER
3	Denis	IRWIN	6	David	WETHERALL
28	David	BECKHAM	8	Rod	WALLACE +88
8	Paul	INCE	10	Gary	McALLISTER
9	Brian	McCLAIR	23	Andrew	COUZENS
11	Ryan	GIGGS	12	John	PEMBERTON
10	Mark	HUGHES	9	Brian	DEANE *83
17	Andy	COLE	21	Tony	YEBOAH
Subs					
13	Gary	WALSH (G)	13	Mark	BEENEY (G)
19	Nicky	BUTT	15	Nigel	WORTHINGTON +
24	Paul	SCHOLES	19	Noel	WHELAN *

Match Facts

- First League start for David Beckham.
- Leeds still to score a goal at Old Trafford in the FAPL.
- United not lost to Leeds at Old Trafford in a league game since 1980/81.

Score Sheet

Referee:
Mr R. Gifford (Mid Glamorgan)

FA Carling Premiership

		P	W	D	L	F	A	Pts
1	Blackburn Rovers	35	24	7	4	72	30	79
2	**Manchester United**	**36**	**22**	**8**	**6**	**66**	**24**	**74**
3	Newcastle United	36	18	10	7	57	37	64
4	Nottingham Forest	36	18	9	9	63	39	63
5	Liverpool	32	16	10	6	54	26	58

Goalless but Decisive

It was a game that United simply had to win but, already shorn of Cantona, Bruce and Sharpe through suspension, the Reds were dealt a further major blow when it was announced that speed merchant Andrei Kanchelskis would also sit out the game due to a stomach strain received on international duty. It transpired that the Russians had given Kanchelskis no fewer than eight separate injections to get him on to the pitch in the midweek qualifier against Scotland and Alex Ferguson was far from happy about it saying "I find it remarkable, we simply wouldn't even consider it. I'm very disappointed and we shall be taking the matter up with the Russians". Two hours and no goals later, Ferguson was even unhappier.

United drafted in David Beckham for his League debut in place of the Russian and, in a first half that is best forgotten, it was the youngster who looked United's best bet to prise open the ten man defence that even included amongst its numbers Brian Deane, normally an out and out front runner. Indeed, one of Beckham's crosses from the right eluded everybody only to float past the far post as well. But, in a turgid forty five minutes, it was Leeds who came closest to scoring with virtually their only attack in the first period. A McAllister run freed Yeboah on the right and his cross was well hit by Wallace. Schmeichel parried and it looked as if the ball would drop to Deane to tap in from close range only for Schmeichel to lunge and flap at the ball with his right hand to deny the Yorkshire side on the stroke of half-time.

The second period was better but the first chance again fell to Leeds and what a bizarre goal it would have been if Schmeichel's fly kick clearance that struck Carlton Palmer had gone in. In fact, after bouncing back over the 'keeper's head, the spin on the ball actually prevented it going in the net as it spun back to a grateful Schmeichel. Then Cole missed a great chance when he took too long from an inviting position and had his effort blocked whilst a Hughes snap shot rocket was unfortunately straight at Lukic. McClair shaved a post after good work down the right by Neville and Cole and then Giggs had a shot blocked as United desperately searched for the winner.

Leeds seemed to have little attacking ambition but, against all out defence, the Reds without Cantona definitely miss the spark of genius that can, in one moment of time, prise the door open. The longer the game went, the more obvious it became that the game would finish goalless and United's last chance came and went as a drive from Ince was deflected for a corner.

All of which left Alex Ferguson saying "The result is very disappointing. It's not crucial, it's decisive".

League Record

		Home					Away				
	P	W	D	L	F	A	W	D	L	F	A
94/95 FAPL	36	14	3	1	39	8	5	8	5	27	21
All time FAPL	120	42	14	4	117	30	31	17	12	96	63
All time FAPL/FL	3676	1078	424	336	3667	1814	563	429	796	2502	3117

	Home	Away	Total
FAPL Attendances	786,216	506,008	1,292,224

Manchester United (0) 2
Crystal Palace (1) 2

Sunday, 9th April 1995, Villa Park   Att: 38,256

Manchester United			Crystal Palace		
1	Peter	SCHMEICHEL	1	Nigel	MARTYN
27	Gary	NEVILLE	22	Darren	PATTERSON
3	Denis	IRWIN *Booked*	5	Eric	YOUNG
16	Roy	KEANE	14	Richard	SHAW
6	Gary	PALLISTER *Booked*	6	Chris	COLEMAN *45
28	David	BECKHAM *49	20	Ray	HOUGHTON
8	Paul	INCE	16	Darren	PITCHER *Booked*
9	Brian	McCLAIR	4	Gareth	SOUTHGATE
5	Lee	SHARPE	11	John	SALAKO
11	Ryan	GIGGS	9	Chris	ARMSTRONG
10	Mark	HUGHES	8	Iain	DOWIE

Subs					
19	Nicky	BUTT *	19	Rhys	WILMOT (G)
24	Paul	SCHOLES	21	Ian	COX
13	Gary	WALSH (G)	3	Dean	GORDON *

Match Facts

- First time United and Palace had ever been drawn against one another in the FA Cup – the only other time they had met was in the 1990 Final.
- United's 20th FA Cup semi-final appearance put them into clear second place in front of Liverpool in the number of appearances they have made at this stage of the competition. Everton lead with 23.
- Denis Irwin's goal made him United's leading goalscorer in the 94/95 FA Cup with four goals.
- Gary Pallister's first booking of the season.

Score Sheet

I. DOWIE 33 min – 0-1

D. IRWIN 70 min – 1-1

C. ARMSTRONG 92 min – 1-2

G. PALLISTER 96 min – 2-2

Referee:

Mr D. Elleray (Harrow)

Dowie Gives United Second Chance

United went into this game short of scoring power. Not only was the suspended Cantona out as a result of his misdemeanour against Palace in January but also Kanchelskis due to his recurring stomach injury. That was thirty goals missing and to cap it all, Andy Cole was cup-tied. The Reds also had problems at the back with Bruce suspended and obvious replacements, Paul Parker and David May both injured. By comparison, Palace were at full strength.

United started the better of the two teams and Sharpe very nearly got Beckham in before the first sixty seconds had passed. But Martyn dived bravely at Beckham's feet to save, albeit at the cost of what later proved to be a broken finger. Giggs tried an audacious lob from 45 yards when he caught Martyn off his line but the 'keeper recovered his ground and then Keane was just wide with a header. Palace hit back and Schmeichel had to concede several corners as the Londoners began to turn the tide. Just past the half hour mark, United went behind when they failed to clear a long throw on the Palace left from Salako. The ball eventually found its way to Armstrong on the opposite flank and his cross to the far post was headed back across goal by Salako for Dowie to enjoy a simple nod in.

It was Dowie's fourth goal in five FA Cup ties since he joined the "Eagles" from Southampton in January. Not a bad return for the £450,000 Palace paid out for him, but the hero turned villain in the 64th minute with a miss that proved to be the turning point of the game. Deadline day signing, Ray Houghton, curled over a superb cross which left the unmarked Dowie with what looked to be a simple chance but his header inexplicably missed the target from about five yards. Three minutes later United were level and what should have been 2-0 as Palace conceded a free kick in "Denis Irwin country". His thunderbolt clipped Houghton causing it to loop and bend even more than his normal mercurial specials and Martyn had no chance.

Extra time and within seconds, as at the start of the game, the Reds almost went in front. Sharpe got in a dangerous cross from the left and McClair lunged to get a toe on the ball but it went inches wide. From the goal kick, Palace went ahead when Southgate headed on. United's concentration seemed to have been broken by the interval so quickly followed by the near miss and there was precious little cover as the ball fell nicely for Armstrong. He ran in between Pallister and Keane and beat the advancing Schmeichel with a lob from the edge of the area. The Reds had it all to do but they bounced back to grab an equaliser when Pallister got just enough on a long throw from Neville to deflect the ball gently past Martyn. A fair result to a good game but it would surely have been all over had Dowie not missed the simple chance that would have made it 2-0.

United's all time FA Cup Record

	Home						Away				
	P	W	D	L	F	A	W	D	L	F	A
All time	351	102	31	28	343	151	79	54	57	302	270

	Home	Away	Total
94/95 FA Cup Attendances	128,796	60,578	189,374

Manchester United   (2) 2
Crystal Palace   (0) 0

Semi-Final Replay   Match 52

Wednesday, 12 April 1995, Villa Park   Att: 17,897

Manchester United

1	Peter	SCHMEICHEL
27	Gary	NEVILLE
4	Steve	BRUCE
6	Gary	PALLISTER *Booked*
3	Denis	IRWIN
16	Roy	KEANE (Sent Off)
19	Nicky	BUTT
8	Paul	INCE
5	Lee	SHARPE
11	Ryan	GIGGS *58
10	Mark	HUGHES *Booked*

Subs

13	Gary	WALSH (G)
24	Paul	SCHOLES
9	Brian	McCLAIR *

Crystal Palace

19	Rhys	WILMOT
22	Darren	PATTERSON *Sent Off*
5	Eric	YOUNG *Booked*
14	Richard	SHAW
3	Dean	GORDON
20	Ray	HOUGHTON
4	Gareth	SOUTHGATE
16	Darren	PITCHER *Booked* +81
11	John	SALAKO *Booked*
8	Iain	DOWIE *81
9	Chris	ARMSTRONG

21	Ian	COX +
23	Ricky	NEWMAN *
25	James	GLASS (G)

Match Facts

- Smallest attendance for an FA Cup semi final since the Second World War.
- Crystal Palace still to beat United in the FA Cup in four attempts.
- United have not lost in six semi finals at Villa Park.
- After going all season without a booking until the first game against Palace 72 hours earlier, Pallister immediately earned his second caution.

Score Sheet

S. BRUCE 30 min – 1-0
G. PALLISTER 41 min – 2-0

Referee:
Mr D. Elleray (Harrow)

Many Happy Returns

United captain Steve Bruce returned from his suspension and immediately brought a better shape to the United line up with his presence being enough to lift the Reds to a victory which saw them return to Wembley just twelve months after lifting the FA Cup against Chelsea. Indeed, it was his goal that paved the way for the success. With Butt also making the starting line up for the replay, the unlucky men were McClair, relegated to the bench, and Beckham whilst Palace had Rhys Wilmot, a veteran of just 3 minutes league action in the season prior to the semi, standing in for 'keeper Nigel Martyn who had broken a finger in the first game. Prior to kick off, both managers were out on the pitch to appeal for sanity in the wake of the death of Palace supporter Paul Nixon in a pub car park brawl before the first meeting and a minute's silence was observed after a wreath had been laid on the centre spot as a poignant reminder of the seriousness of the occasion.

Unlike the first game, United never looked like losing the replay and it was undoubtedly the return of Bruce that made the difference. Sometimes, certain players are never fully appreciated until they are not playing and so it is with Bruce. Many critics commented on his lack of pace in 1994/95 but the Reds were a much better balanced outfit in his presence. He opened the door for another visit to Wembley by capitalising on Denis Irwin's fine left wing overlap which Ray Houghton only stopped at the expense of a corner. Having conceded two set piece goals to the Reds in the first game Palace should have been more alert but when Sharpe slung over the flag kick, Dowie, who had been delegated the task of shadowing Bruce at set pieces, was on the halfway line looking for his contact lens. Patterson realised the danger too late and couldn't hold Bruce's late run that finished with a rocket header into the roof of the net, high to Wilmot's right. Another Irwin left flank sortie caused trouble for Palace ten minutes later and was halted by Shaw fouling the United full back. Sharpe's delivery was again perfect with Bruce's partner, Pallister, on hand to score with the reverse of his captain's earlier effort. This header was low and to the 'keeper's left.

The only bit of football played in the second period came when Giggs totally bemused Gordon and Houghton with an outlandish sliding turn but after the good, came the bad and the ugly. Keane was high with a tackle on Southgate who attempted to return the compliment a moment later. As he went down, Southgate slid under Keane who then quite clearly stamped on the Palace captain. Houghton ran in, blood boiling, and was the catalyst around the ensuing melee which brought disgrace to both sides and dismissals for Keane and Patterson who raised his fist at the Irishman. The minute's silence had quickly been forgotten.

United's all time FA Cup Record

		Home					Away						
P	W	D	L	F	A	W	D	L	F	A			
352	102	31	28	343	151	80	54	57	304	270			

	Home	Away	Total
FA Cup attendances	128,796	78,565	207,361

Leicester City   (0) 0
Manchester United   (2) 4

Saturday, 15 April 1995, Filbert Street   Att: 21,281

Leicester City

33	Kevin	POOLE
2	Simon	GRAYSON *55
3	Mike	WHITLOW
4	Jimmy	WILLIS
19	Colin	HILL
10	Mark	DRAPER
18	Gary	PARKER
22	Jamie	LAWRENCE
9	Iwan	ROBERTS
6	Mark	ROBINS
25	David	LOWE +75

Subs

15	Brian	CAREY +
8	Mark	BLAKE *
1	Gavin	WARD (G)

Manchester United

1	Peter	SCHMEICHEL
27	Gary	NEVILLE
4	Steve	BRUCE
6	Gary	PALLISTER
3	Denis	IRWIN
9	Brian	McCLAIR
8	Paul	INCE
19	Nicky	BUTT
5	Lee	SHARPE *45
10	Mark	HUGHES +55
17	Andy	COLE

28	David	BECKHAM *
24	Paul	SCHOLES +
13	Gary	WALSH (G)

Match Facts

- United's biggest away winning margin in the FAPL.
- Cole's double confirmation of his liking for Leicester – he scored for Newcastle against them on the opening day of the season and scored a hat-trick against them on the final day of the 1992/93 campaign.
- United's fourth goal their 100th away goal in the FAPL, their first goal was their 100th of the season in all competitions.

Score Sheet

L. SHARPE 33 min – 0-1
A. COLE 42 min – 0-2
A. COLE 52 min – 0-3
P. INCE 90 min – 40-4

Referee:
Mr M. Bodenham (Cornwall)

FA Carling Premiership

		P	W	D	L	F	A	Pts
1	Blackburn Rovers	37	25	8	4	74	31	83
2	**Manchester United**	37	23	8	6	70	24	77
3	Nottingham Forest	38	19	10	9	65	40	67
4	Newcastle United	37	19	10	8	60	39	67
5	Liverpool	36	18	10	8	59	30	64

Cole Double

United made two changes to their successful FA Cup semi final side with injuries to Keane and Giggs bringing in McClair and the cup-tied Andy Cole. For Cole it was to prove a happy return with two goals but neither were going to change the minds of the doubters as both were mere tap-ins from barely a yard.

Unlike the earlier drawn game against Leicester at Old Trafford, this was a mis-match from the start with United quickly into their stride only to see Cole waste an excellent chance by shooting over after good work by McClair and Hughes. But their early pressure could have counted for nothing had Neville not been alert enough to hack the ball clear from under the feet of former Red, Mark Robins, in City's first attack after 12 minutes. Draper had caused the problem with a powerful drive that Schmeichel could only parry leaving Neville to complete the clearance. Sharpe, operating in his favourite left wing position, was causing all sorts of problems for the Leicester defence and he went close to opening the scoring on no fewer than three occasions. Cole, too, twice had decent chances that were wasted and Leicester showed with a second attack that if United didn't turn their superiority into goals then they could pay a heavy penalty. It took a great save from Schmeichel to deny Willis before the Reds took the hint and, not for the first time in recent games, it was a long throw from Neville that did the damage. Headed on by Pallister at the near post, it fell to Sharpe on the United left and the winger drove calmly home with a low, angled shot that gave Poole no chance.

Cole missed yet another good opportunity when put clear down the centre but, seconds before the interval, the £7m man did get on the scoresheet when he slid a cross shot from Sharpe home from less than a yard. It was Sharpe's last touch of the game for he was pulled off at the interval with an injury and it was his replacement, David Beckham, who supplied the corner kick for the third United goal. Bruce got in a good header from the flag kick to leave the ball bobbing about on the line. Action replays later showed that Cole had already just forced the ball over the line before Leicester scrambled it away only for Bruce to make sure. With the £7m player coming in for a lot of criticism there was little doubt as to who would claim the goal!

United put on Scholes for Hughes and the Reds now had no fewer than four of their 1992 Youth team on the pitch. And it was one of the youngsters, David Beckham, who slung over a long ball from the right for Ince to stretch and direct home at the far post to complete an easy victory. So easy, in fact, that Leicester boss, Mark McGhee afterwards simply said "We were outclassed".

League Record

	P	W	D	L	F	A	W	D	L	F	A
			Home					**Away**			
94/95 FAPL	37	14	3	1	39	3	9	5	5	31	21
All time FAPL	121	42	14	4	117	30	32	17	12	100	63
All time FAPL/FL	3677	1078	424	336	3667	1814	564	429	796	2506	3117

	Home	Away	Total
FAPL Attendances	786,216	527,289	1,313,505

Manchester United (0) 0
Chelsea (0) 0

Monday, 17th April 1995, Old Trafford   Att: 43,725

Manchester United

1	Peter	SCHMEICHEL
27	Gary	NEVILLE
4	Steve	BRUCE
6	Gary	PALLISTER
3	Denis	IRWIN
28	David	BECKHAM *45
8	Paul	INCE
19	Nicky	BUTT
9	Brian	McCLAIR
10	Mark	HUGHES
17	Andy	COLE

Subs

13	Gary	WALSH
24	Paul	SCHOLES +
18	Simon	DAVIES *74+

Chelsea

13	Kevin	HITCHCOCK
2	Steve	CLARKE
6	Frank	SINCLAIR (Booked)
5	Erland	JOHNSEN
27	Gareth	HALL
21	David	ROCASTLE *61
17	Nigel	SPACKMAN
25	David	LEE (Booked)
10	Gavin	PEACOCK
8	Paul	FURLONG *Booked* +67
9	Mark	STEIN *Booked*

24	Craig	BURLEY *
7	John	SPENCER +
33	Nick	COLGAN (G)

Match Facts

- United's miserable record against Chelsea continues. Only one win in a league fixture at Old Trafford in the last six meetings and only three wins in the last twelve league clashes home or away with the Londoners.
- Third goalless Old Trafford draw for United in their last four home games since beating Ipswich 9-0.

Score Sheet

Referee:
Mr S. Lodge (Barnsley)

FA Carling Premiership

		P	W	D	L	F	A	Pts
1	Blackburn Rovers	38	25	8	5	76	34	83
2	**Manchester United**	**38**	**23**	**9**	**6**	**70**	**24**	**78**
3	Nottingham Forest	39	20	10	9	67	40	70
4	Liverpool	37	19	10	8	61	30	67
5	Newcastle United	38	19	10	9	61	41	67

United Miss their Way

The Reds went into this match knowing that nothing short of an outright victory would keep their slim hopes of retaining the Championship alive. In the event, they wasted enough chances to have won several games as the London side yet again proved to be United's hoodoo team.

A left wing raid by Denis Irwin quickly brought United the first corner of the game that was only cleared at the expense of another flag kick on the right which Hitchcock completely missed. Cole chested the loose ball down for Bruce who had a clear sight of goal but he failed to control the ball leaving Hughes to step in with a toe poke that was wide and a great early chance had gone begging. Unfortunately, that set the tone for the rest of the afternoon as the Reds create glorious opportunities in the downpour that ruined the Bank Holiday. Ince and Hughes opened up the Chelsea defence for Cole but his lob cleared the bar before the signing made some amends with a deft back heel flick that set up Hughes for a shot from 25 yards that caused Hitchcock severe problems before Sinclair helped get the rebound away to safety.

Pallister then sent Neville away down the right and the youngster's deep cross was inch perfect for Butt to come running on to at full speed. His header was powerful but straight at the 'keeper and what looked a certain goal wasn't. McClair was the next to find himself unmarked as Chelsea lived dangerously but the Scot didn't even hit the target with a poor header from a good position. The Reds almost paid the price for their profligacy when Peacock broke clear down the Chelsea left. Peacock, of course, was the player who, in 1993/94, scored the two goals that gave Chelsea a league double over United but, just as he appeared to be about to score again, Schmeichel made a brave diving save at his feet with Furlong promptly being booked for his follow through after Peacock had jumped clear of the keeper.

The second period continued with a procession towards the Chelsea goal and a super cross form Davies on the left was acrobatically played back into the area by Hughes on the opposite flank. Cole got his head to the ball but so did Sinclair to clear off the line at the expense of a corner from which the Reds had strong claims for a penalty turned down when a defender appeared to handle in the congested area. A long ball in from Bruce was poorly dealt with by Sinclair which enabled Cole to lob over Hitchcock but Johnssen cleared off the line. Then, just as in the first half, in their one attack, Chelsea looked odds on to score when Bruce make a horrendous mistake to allow in Stein only for the diminutive striker to clear the bar. United's day was just about summed up when a Neville long throw was clearly handled by Johnssen with the referee unsighted and that was goodbye to the title with the miserable weather matching the feelings of the fans.

League Record

		Home					Away				
	P	W	D	L	F	A	W	D	L	F	A
94/95 FAPL	38	14	4	1	39	3	9	5	5	31	21
All time FAPL	122	42	15	4	117	30	32	17	12	100	63
All time FAPL/FL	3678	1078	424	336	3667	1814	564	429	796	2506	3117

	Home	Away	Total
FAPL Attendances	829,944	527,289	1,357,233

Coventry City (1) 2
Manchester United (1) 3

Monday, 1st May 1995, Highfield Road   Att: 21,885

Coventry City			**Manchester United**		
13	Jonathon	GOULD	1	Peter	SCHMEICHEL
2	Brian	BORROWS *Booked*	27	Gary	NEVILLE *Booked*
5	David	RENNIE	12	David	MAY
6	Steve	PRESSLEY	6	Gary	PALLISTER
25	Marcus	HALL (Booked)	3	Denis	IRWIN
31	Gordon	STRACHAN	19	Nicky	BUTT
28	Kevin	RICHARDSON	9	Brian	McCLAIR
15	Paul	COOK	24	Paul	SCHOLES * 77
8	Roy	WEGERLE	5	Lee	SHARPE *Booked*
19	Dion	DUBLIN	17	Andy	COLE *Booked*
9	Peter	NDLOVU	10	Mark	HUGHES

Subs

30	John	FILAN	28	David	BECKHAM *
17	Ally	PICKERING	21	Pat	McGIBBON
26	Mike	MARSH	13	Gary	WALSH (G)

Match Facts

- United continue their 100% FAPL record at Highfield Road.
- Coventry not beaten United in the FAPL in six attempts.
- Peter Ndlovu's goal is first Coventry goal against the Reds in the FAPL.
- First Booking in United colours for Andy Cole.
- Gary Neville booked in both games against Coventry.

Score Sheet

P. SCHOLES 32 mins 0-1

P. NDLOVU 39 mins 1-1

A. COLE 55 mins 1-2

S. PRESSLEY 72 mins 2-2

A. COLE 79 mins 2-3

Referee
Mr P.Don (Middlesex)

FA Carling Premiership

		P	W	D	L	F	A	Pts
1	Blackburn Rovers	40	26	8	6	78	37	86
2	**Manchester United**	**39**	**24**	**9**	**6**	**73**	**26**	**81**
3	Nottingham Forest	40	21	10	9	69	41	73
4	Liverpool	38	20	10	8	63	31	70
5	Newcastle United	39	19	11	9	61	41	68

Cole Keeps Title Fire Burning

With both teams desperate to win for vastly different reasons, this was the best game between the sides for many years. United went into the game knowing that nothing short of victory would be sufficient to keep alive their title hopes but took the field denuded of most of their household names. There was no Bruce, Ince, Giggs, Cantona, Kanchelskis or Keane but that didn't stop the Reds being committed to all out attack.

In a game that was as enthralling as it was entertaining, it was sad to record that the first action of note was the booking of Gary Neville for a foul on the flying Peter Ndlovu. Young Neville held his face in his hands as he realised the enormity of perhaps missing the FA Cup Final after accumulating over 40 disciplinary points. But the football flowed as fast as Cole who provided the first goal, skipping inside two defenders down the United right before letting go a rasping left shot from an angle. Gould parried but when the ball fell to Scholes, the United youngster rifled it home from just inside the area.

The lead, however, was shortlived and within seven minutes Coventry were level. There appeared little danger as former United star Gordon Strachan put in a cross that was headed away by Pallister. The clearance went only as far as another former United player, Dion Dublin, but even his effort from outside the box showed little sign of eluding Schmeichel until Ndlovu stuck out a heel and deflected it past the wrong-footed Dane.

After the break, the tempo increased still further and United regained the lead ten minutes into the second period. A high long ball from Butt dropped from the night sky in the direction of Cole and Pressley. It was the type of ball that defenders should always win but Cole judged its flight the better of the two before wheeling away past the Coventry defender to drill the ball powerfully below, and beyond, Gould. But the title appeared once more to have slipped away from the Reds when Pressley atoned for his earlier mistake by heading a second equaliser with just eighteen minutes left. Paul Cook's cross from the right found Pressley completely unmarked and he beat Schmeichel with a simple flick of his head from eight yards.

But there was still time for a further twist to the story when Kevin Richardson, under no pressure at all, for some reason best known to himself attempted to head back some thirty five yards to his 'keeper. The ball was never going to arrive at its destination and Cole latched onto it before lobbing it over Gould and then rounding the 'keeper to score with ease. So United kept their title fire burning with the aid of Cole.

League Record

| | | Home | | | | | Away | | | | |
	P	W	D	L	F	A	W	D	L	F	A
94/95 FAPL	39	14	4	1	39	3	10	5	5	34	23
All time FAPL	123	42	15	4	117	30	33	17	12	103	65
All time FAPL/FL	3679	1078	424	336	3667	1814	565	429	796	2509	3119

	Home	Away	Total
FAPL Attendances	829,944	549,174	1,379,118

Manchester United (1) 1
Sheffield Wednesday (0) 0

Match 56

Sunday, 7th May 1995, Old Trafford   Att: 43,868

Manchester United

1	Peter	SCHMEICHEL
27	Gary	NEVILLE
12	David	MAY *24
6	Gary	PALLISTER
3	Denis	IRWIN
9	Brian	McCLAIR
8	Paul	INCE
24	Paul	SCHOLES +52
5	Lee	SHARPE
17	Andy	COLE
10	Mark	HUGHES – Booked

Subs

23	Phil	NEVILLE *
19	Nicky	BUTT +
13	Gary	WALSH

Sheffield Wednesday

1	Chris	WOODS
2	Peter	ATHERTON
12	Andy	PEARCE – Booked
17	Des	WALKER – Booked
3	Ian	NOLAN
25	Mike	WILLIAMS
11	John	SHERIDAN
16	Graham	HYDE *62
14	Bart	WILLIAMS
30	Guy	WHITTINGHAM +82
10	Mark	BRIGHT

7	Adam	PORIC +
8	Chris	WADDLE *
13	Kevin	PRESSMAN (G)

Match Facts

- Gary and Phil Neville become the first pair of brothers to play in the same United side in a League game since Brian and Jimmy Greenhoff played against West Bromwich Albion at the Hawthorns on 5th May 1979.
- United's 100% FAPL home record against Wednesday is maintained.
- Not lost to Wednesday at Old Trafford in a league game since 13th April 1986.

Score Sheet

D.MAY 5 mins – 1-0

Referee
Mr G. Poll (Tilehurst)

FA Carling Premiership

		P	W	D	L	F	A	Pts
1	Blackburn Rovers	40	26	8	6	78	37	86
2	**Manchester United**	40	25	9	6	74	26	84
3	Nottingham Forest	41	22	10	9	70	41	76
4	Liverpool	40	20	11	9	63	33	71
5	Newcastle United	40	19	12	9	64	44	69

May Day

With United rapidly running out of games in the race to catch Blackburn at the top and Sheffield Wednesday themselves badly in need of three points to head off a very serious threat of relegation, the two clubs were sending out SOS calls. United, once more shorn of most of their stars, had their May Day distress signals appropriately answered by none other than David May whose goal after five minutes ensured the Reds just days earlier at Coventry. gap on his former Blackburn colleagues to just two points.

Indeed, the former Manchester City season ticket holder came close to being made Man of the Match despite the fact that he was only in the fray for 24 minutes, such was the lack of cohesion from either side. To be blunt, it was an awful game in direct contrast to the thriller served up by the Reds just days earlier at Coventry.

But things didn't immediately go too well for May, standing in again for the injured Bruce, for he should have scored after only four minutes. The chance came when an Irwin thunderbolt brought a smart save from Chris Woods to provide the Reds with a right wing corner. Sharpe's flag kick was flicked on by the head of Pallister towards his defensive partner May. But the resulting finish from May was not good and gave Woods the chance to get the ball on to a post and away for another corner. May, however, was to quickly make amends from this kick, taken from the opposite flank by Paul Scholes. The initial cross was cleared by Pearce but only back to Scholes who had now retreated into the inside left slot. Moving quickly forward the youngster outwitted Bright to reach the byeline from where he cut the ball back to May for the defender to shoot crisply home from ten yards.

May was not destined to play much further part in the proceedings and was helped off less than twenty minutes later with a back problem which saw the introduction of Phil Neville to play alongside his brother Gary. This was the first time a pair of brothers had played for United in the same team in a league match since the Greenhoffs in the late seventies leaving their father, Neville Neville, Commercial Manager at Bury FC a proud man in the stands. Gary moved into central defence to take over from May whilst Phil went to full back. Both did well although, in truth, Wednesday's attack was so lacking in fire power, it was easy to see why this was their fourth consecutive game without a goal.

The game did acquire a little life late on with Cole's downward header scrambled frantically away by Woods and then the 'keeper showed shades of his former England form to deny both Butt and Cole to ensure that at the end of a lack lustre game United were grateful for May's intervention.

League Record

| | Home | | | | | | Away | | | | |
	P	W	D	L	F	A	W	D	L	F	A
94/95 FAPL	40	15	4	1	40	3	10	5	5	34	23
All time FAPL	124	43	15	4	118	30	33	17	12	103	65
All time FAPL/FL	3680	1079	424	336	3668	1814	565	429	796	2509	3119

	Home	Away	Total
FAPL Attendances	873,812	549,174	1,422,986

Manchester United (1) 2
Southampton (1) 1

Wednesday, 10th May , Old Trafford   Att: 43,479

Manchester United			**Southampton**		
1	Peter	SCHMEICHEL	13	Dave	BEASANT
27	Gary	NEVILLE	14	Simon	CHARLTON
4	Steve	BRUCE (Booked)	6	Ken	MONKOU
6	Gary	PALLISTER	16	Neil	SHIPPERLEY
3	Denis	IRWIN	3	Francis	BENALI *57
8	Paul	INCE	5	Richard	HALL
9	Brian	McCLAIR	4	Jim	MAGILLTON
19	Nicky	BUTT	15	Jason	DODD *Booked*
5	Lee	SHARPE	10	Neil	MADDISON
17	Andy	COLE	9	Gordon	WATSON
10	Mark	HUGHES *76	7	Matthew	LE TISSIER *Booked*+76

Subs

24	Paul	SCHOLES *	12	Neil	HEANEY *
13	Gary	WALSH (G)	1	Bruce	GROBBELAAR (G)
28	David	BECKHAM	21	Tom	Widdrington + *Booked*

<table>
<tr><td>

Match Facts

- Southampton's goal is the first conceded by Peter Schmeichel at Old Trafford in the FAPL all season! The previous three were conceded by Gary Walsh.
- United kept an incredible 18 clean sheets at home in the FAPL in 94/95.
- Southampton still to beat Reds in the FAPL.

</td><td>

Score Sheet

S. CHARLTON 5 mins 0-1

A. COLE 21 mins 1-1

D. IRWIN 80 mins (pen) 2-1

Referee

Mr P.Danson (Leicester)

</td></tr>
</table>

FA Carling Premiership

		P	W	D	L	F	A	Pts
1	Blackburn Rovers	41	27	8	6	79	37	89
2	**Manchester United**	**41**	**26**	**9**	**6**	**76**	**27**	**87**
3	Nottingham Forest	41	22	10	9	70	41	76
4	Leeds United	41	20	12	9	58	37	72
5	Liverpool	41	20	11	10	63	36	71

154

Irwin Spot On

Blackburn's win over Newcastle 48 hours earlier left United lining up against Southampton in the knowledge that nothing less than outright victory would be good enough to take the Championship to a final day decider. But the "Saints" arrived north with only one defeat in their previous nine games to give the Reds just the sort of game they could do without as they continued their belated efforts to retain their crown.

Things started badly when a left wing cross from Irwin found Hughes completely unmarked at the far post with the goal at his mercy but the Welshman stubbed his toe as he pulled the trigger and his poor effort went harmlessly wide. United paid dearly for the miss when Southampton broke down the right after five minutes. Le Tissier headed on to Shipperley who, in turn, set Watson free. As Schmeichel came out to narrow the angle, Watson's chipped shot didn't quite clear the big Dane's fingers but the 'keeper couldn't get enough hand on the ball to prevent it looping up before falling kindly for Charlton to stoop and head into the empty net. It was the first league goal conceded by Schmeichel at Old Trafford all season in the final game. That miserly total, however, could have quickly doubled when Pallister gave the ball away to Le Tissier who presented Watson with a glorious chance to double the lead but fortunately the striker's shot was just wide. Pallister almost made amends with a great header that hit Beasant's post from a Sharpe left wing corner and then, thanks to McClair's never give up spirit, United equalised. A long cross from Neville on the right was poor and much too long but, when everybody else assumed the ball would go out, McClair chased and saved it. His cross was dummied by Cole and hit two defenders before bouncing back for the £7m man to rifle home left footed from seven yards.

United swarmed all over the "Saints" in the second period but Beasant was in spectacular form with nothing better than the point blank reflex save from an Ince header after the 'keeper had just denied Hughes. Butt was next to try his luck only to find Beasant once again the stumbling block with a tremendous parry whilst Cole couldn't quite convert the rebound. Then came the little bit of luck that the Reds needed. Irwin played in Cole who was challenged by Monkou. As Cole went down, nobody in the United team or the crowd made any sort of appeal for a penalty but the referee was pointing to the spot. It was, in fact, a quite brilliant piece of refereeing as TV replays showed clearly that Monkou had tugged Cole's shirt and Southampton boss Alan Ball himself said he agreed totally with the decision. Irwin hammered the spot kick to Beasant's right with such force that he actually fell over in completing the kick. But it was a good job that Irwin hit it so hard because Beasant guessed correctly and was within a fingertip of saving it. The title race was going to the wire!

League Record

		Home					Away				
	P	W	D	L	F	A	W	D	L	F	A
94/95 FAPL	41	16	4	1	42	4	10	5	5	34	23
All time FAPL	125	44	15	4	120	31	33	17	12	103	65
All time FAPL/FL	3681	1080	424	336	3670	1815	565	429	796	2509	3119

| | Home | Away | Total |
| FAPL Attendances | 917,291 | 549,174 | 1,466,465 |

West Ham United (1) 1
Manchester United (0) 1

Sunday, 14th May 1995, Upton Park   Att: 24,783

West Ham United

1	Ludek	MIKLOSKO
2	Tim	BREAKER *Booked*
8	Marc	RIEPER *Booked*
4	Steve	POTTS
12	Keith	ROWLAND
17	Michael	HUGHES +88 *Booked*
26	Don	HUTCHISON *85
7	Ian	BISHOP
10	John	MONCUR
11	Matt	HOLMES
9	Trevor	MORLEY

Subs

13	Les	SEALEY (G)
6	Martin	ALLEN *
18	Simon	WEBSTER +

Manchester United

1	Peter	SCHMEICHEL
27	Gary	NEVILLE
4	Steve	BRUCE (Booked)
6	Gary	PALLISTER
3	Denis	IRWIN
16	Roy	KEANE +79
8	Paul	INCE
9	Brian	McCLAIR
19	Nicky	BUTT *45
5	Lee	SHARPE
17	Andy	COLE

24	Paul	SCHOLES +
10	Mark	HUGHES * (Booked)
13	Gary	WALSH (G)

Match Facts

• United's final tally of 88 points is the highest ever recorded by a team not winning the Championship.

• West Ham's goal stopped United setting a new record for the FAPL of fewest goals conceded in an FAPL season. Their final figure of 28 only equalled Arsenal's total in 93/94.

• Under the old two points for a win system, United would have been Champions again.

Score Sheet

M. HUGHES 31 mins 1-0

B. McCLAIR 54 mins 1-1

Referee

Mr A.Wilkie

(Chester-Le-Street)

FA Carling Premiership

		P	W	D	L	F	A	Pts
1	Blackburn Rovers	42	27	8	7	80	39	89
2	**Manchester United**	42	26	10	6	77	28	88
3	Nottingham Forest	42	22	11	9	72	43	77
4	Liverpool	42	21	11	10	65	37	74
5	Leeds United	42	20	13	9	59	38	73

156

White Knuckle Ride

United travelled to Upton Park for their final league match of the season knowing that old rivals Liverpool had to do them a massive favour by preventing Blackburn winning whilst the Reds themselves had to beat West Ham. It was to prove a day of contrast for the Redknapp family with Dad Harry attempting to plot the downfall of Alex Ferguson's side whilst son Jamie was to score the winner for Liverpool at Anfield that had Blackburn fans in despair for just a couple of seconds. Then it was time for the Rovers to celebrate as the radios around the ground gave the news that United's siege of the West Ham goal had not prevailed.

All season the Reds had made hard work of things and the final league match was no different. Holmes had already thundered a shot against Schmeichel's bar when he beat Neville and crossed to an on rushing Michael Hughes whose mid-air volley from twelve yards could have gone anywhere but landed firmly in the back of the net. By now, news had filtered through that Blackburn were in front at Anfield and United once more had a mountain to climb if they were to hold onto their title.

But the Reds had proved to be tenacious mountaineers on more than one occasion in 94/95 and this May afternoon was to be no exception. Ferguson had caused surprise by relegating Mark Hughes to the bench and his introduction at the break brought such a revival in the fortunes of his side that it bellowed criticism at the original decision. Not so, according to Ferguson who said afterwards "It was the right decision on the day". Be that as it may, United were a different team after the interval and virtually laid siege to the West Ham goal. But Miklosko was in irrepressible form in the Hammers' goal despite needing the woodwork to come to his aid in stopping a Cole daisy cutter in the first period.

He had no chance, however, when a Neville free kick on the right was firmly headed home by the totally unmarked McClair and then came a roar from the Reds fans that signified Liverpool had equalised some 200 miles away. The roller coaster ride seemed to be on one final upward curve for United and the Reds swamped West Ham. Miklosko made two fabulous diving saves to turn away headers from Sharpe and Hughes whilst McClair blasted over on the turn from six yards. Then, with only four minutes of the campaign left, the pendulum looked to have swung towards United when Cole burst through in a one on one situation but Miklosko to deny him. Three minutes later Cole was again denied by the brilliance of the West Ham 'keeper and, as United peppered the Londoner's goal, a desperate defence simply hurled bodies in the way of shots. One flick in the dying seconds and the title would have remained at Old Trafford but the white knuckle ride came to its last stop with Blackburn very relieved to get off.

League Record

		Home					Away				
	P	W	D	L	F	A	W	D	L	F	A
94/95 FAPL	42	16	4	1	42	4	10	6	5	35	24
All time FAPL	126	44	15	4	120	31	33	18	12	104	66
FAPL/FL	3682	1080	424	336	3670	1815	565	430	796	2510	3120

	Home	Away	Total
FAPL Attendances	917,291	573,957	1,491,248

Everton
Manchester United

(1) 1
(0) 0

20th May 1995, Wembley   Att: 79,592

Everton

1	Neville	SOUTHALL
2	Matthew	JACKSON
3	Andy	HINCHCLIFFE
5	Dave	WATSON
6	Gary	ABLETT
18	Joe	PARKINSON
10	Barry	HORNE *Booked*
8	Graham	STUART
15	Paul	RIDEOUT *51
17	Anders	LIMPAR +69
26	David	UNSWORTH

Subs

9	Duncan	FERGUSON *
11	Daniel	AMOKACHI +
13	Jason	KEARTON (G)

Manchester United

1	Peter	SCHMEICHEL
27	Gary	NEVILLE *Booked*
4	Steve	BRUCE *45
6	Gary	PALLISTER
3	Denis	IRWIN
19	Nicky	BUTT
8	Paul	INCE
9	Brian	McCLAIR
16	Roy	KEANE
5	Lee	SHARPE +72
10	Mark	HUGHES

24	Paul	SCHOLES +
11	Ryan	GIGGS *
13	Gary	WALSH (G)

Match Facts

- United set a new record of 13 FA Cup Final appearances, one more than Arsenal and Everton.
- The Reds, however, fail to secure their ninth FA Cup Final success which would have put them clear of Spurs at the top of the leader board.
- United fail to become only the third team after Newcastle and Spurs to retain the trophy this century
- Everton's fifth FA Cup Final in twelve years
- The last game referee Gerald Ashby officiated in prior to the FA Cup Final was a Sunday morning game in Division Three of the Worcester League between Archdales and Monkswood!

Score Sheet

P.RIDEOUT 30 mins

Referee
Mr G.Ashby – (Worcester)

Double Disappointment

Having seen their chance of the "double, double" disappear a week earlier when their final ten minute barrage of the West Ham goal failed to produce the successful strike that would have clinched the Championship, United were to suffer a double disappointment with defeat at Wembley that left the Reds without a trophy for the first time in six seasons.

The pre-match talk was all about the threat that £4M signing Duncan Ferguson would be to Alex Ferguson's side in his come back game but, in the event, all he got he was a place on the subs bench. Instead, the Everton hero was Paul Rideout who, almost unnoticed alongside the rave notices pinned on Ferguson, had climbed gracefully up the goalscoring ladder to become his club's leading marksman. On Cup Final day he was again to climb gracefully to score his sixteenth, and most important, goal of the campaign following a move that had all the hallmarks of United circa 1993/94.

In a physical start both Ince and Hughes were flattened by the team Joe Royle himself had dubbed the "Dogs of War" but Sharpe had already scored a good chance straight from the kick off when he headed over from Butt's cross. The Reds appeared to be gaining the upperhand when Bruce tweaked a hamstring after 21 minutes and this was to prove decisive nine minutes later when the Merseysiders took the lead.

Despite there being still an hour left for play, United were on all out attack when Ince tried to thread the ball through the Everton defence. Watson intercepted and released Limpar well inside his own half. His pace was reminiscent of Kanchelskis at his flying best as he ran half the length of the pitch. United were caught with only two defenders, Pallister and the still hobbling Bruce, between the Everton counter attack and Schmeichel. Coming up at even greater pace than Limpar on a right wing overlap was Jackson and, as Pallister closed down the Swede, the ball was released into the path of Jackson. He looked well placed for a shot but squared instead to Stuart who appeared to have let United off the hook when he shot against the under-side of the bar from ten yards. As the ball arced back up into the air after bouncing down on the line, Rideout jumped to pick his spot and headed home from the edge of the six yard box with Bruce immobile on the line.

The introduction of Giggs for Bruce at half time gave United hope and the Welshman produced a cross for McClair to head against the bar after 68 mins before then setting up Scholes who was denied by a good double save by Southall. The veteran 'keeper then made an even better save from a Pallister header as United's season came to its final catastrophic conclusion.

United's all time FA Cup Record

	Home					Away				
P	W	D	L	F	A	W	D	L	F	A
353	102	31	28	343	151	80	54	58	304	271

	Home	Away	Total
FA Cup Attendances	128,796	158,157	286,953

The Road to the 1995 FA Cup Final

Manchester United

Round		Club	Venue	Score	Players
3rd	v	Sheffield United	(a)	2-0	Hughes, Cantona
4th	v	Wrexham	(h)	5-2	Irwin 2, Giggs, McClair, og.
5th	v	Leeds United	(h)	3-1	Bruce, McClair, Hughes
6th	v	QPR	(h)	2-0	Irwin, Sharpe
S/Final	v	Crystal Palace	(n)	2-2	Irwin, Pallister
Replay	v	Crystal Palace	(n)	2-0	Bruce, Pallister
		Goals		16-5	

Everton

Round		Club	Venue	Score	Players
3rd	v	Derby County	(h)	1-0	Hinchcliffe
4th	v	Bristol City	(a)	1-0	Jackson
5th	v	Norwich City	(h)	5-0	Limpar, Parkinson, Ferguson, Rideout, Stuart
6th	v	Newcastle United	(h)	1-0	Watson
S/Final	v	Tottenham H.	(n)	4-1	Jackson, Stuart, Amokachi 2
		Goals		12-1	

FINAL TABLE 1994-95

FA Carling Premiership

	P	HOME					AWAY					Pts
		W	D	L	F	A	W	D	L	F	A	
Blackburn Rovers	42	17	2	2	54	21	10	6	5	26	18	89
MANCHESTER UNITED	42	16	4	1	42	4	10	6	5	35	24	88
Nottingham Forest	42	12	6	3	36	18	10	5	6	36	25	77
Liverpool	42	13	5	3	38	13	8	6	7	27	24	74
Leeds United	42	13	5	3	35	15	7	8	6	24	23	73
Newcastle United	42	14	6	1	46	20	6	6	9	21	27	72
Tottenham Hotspur	42	10	5	6	32	25	6	9	6	34	33	62
Queens Park Rangers	42	11	3	7	36	26	6	6	9	25	33	60
Wimbledon	42	9	5	7	26	26	6	6	9	22	39	56
Southampton	42	8	9	4	33	27	4	9	8	28	36	54
Chelsea	42	7	7	7	25	22	6	8	7	25	33	54
Arsenal	42	6	9	6	27	21	7	3	11	25	28	51
Sheffield Wednesday	42	7	7	7	26	26	6	5	10	23	31	51
West Ham United	42	9	6	6	28	19	4	5	12	16	29	50
Everton	42	8	9	4	31	23	3	8	10	13	28	50
Coventry City	42	7	7	7	23	25	5	7	9	21	37	50
Manchester City	42	8	7	6	37	28	4	6	11	16	36	49
Aston Villa	42	6	9	6	27	24	5	6	10	24	32	48
Crystal Palace	42	6	6	9	16	23	5	6	10	18	26	45
Norwich City	42	8	8	5	27	21	2	5	14	10	33	43
Leicester City	42	5	6	10	28	37	1	5	15	17	43	29
Ipswich Town	42	5	3	13	24	34	2	3	16	12	59	27

Composite Table with Prize Money

	P	W	D	L	F	A	Pts	Prize Money	Psn
Blackburn Rovers	42	27	8	7	80	39	89	£897,820	1
MANCHESTER UNITED	42	26	10	6	77	28	88	£857,010	2
Nottingham Forest	42	22	11	9	72	43	77	£816,200	3
Liverpool	42	21	11	10	65	37	74	£775,390	4
Leeds United	42	20	13	9	59	38	73	£734,580	5
Newcastle United	42	20	12	10	67	47	72	£693,770	6
Tottenham Hotspur	42	16	14	12	66	58	62	£652,960	7
Queens Park Rangers	42	17	9	16	61	59	60	£612,150	8
Wimbledon	42	15	11	16	48	65	56	£571,340	9
Southampton	42	12	18	12	61	63	54	£530,530	10
Chelsea	42	13	15	14	50	55	54	£489,720	11
Arsenal	42	13	12	17	52	49	51	£448,720	12
Sheffield Wednesday	42	13	12	17	49	57	51	£408,100	13
West Ham United	42	13	11	18	44	48	50	£367,290	14

Everton	42	11	17	14	44	51	50	£326,480	15
Coventry City	42	12	14	16	44	62	50	£285,670	16
Manchester City	42	12	13	17	53	64	49	£244,860	17
Aston Villa	42	11	15	16	51	56	48	£204,050	18
Crystal Palace	42	11	12	19	34	49	45	£163,240	19
Norwich City	42	10	13	19	37	54	43	£122,430	20
Leicester City	42	6	11	25	45	80	29	£81,620	21
Ipswich Town	42	7	6	29	36	93	27	£40,810	22

All-time Tables 1992-95

Positions Based on Total Points

Psn		P	W	D	L	F	A	Pts	Yrs
1	MANCHESTER UTD ...	126	77	33	16	224	97	264	3
2	Blackburn Rovers ...	126	72	28	26	211	121	244	3
3	Leeds United	126	50	44	32	181	139	194	3
4	Liverpool	126	54	31	41	186	147	193	3
5	QPR	126	50	33	43	186	175	183	3
6	Aston Villa	126	47	38	41	154	146	179	3
7	Arsenal	126	46	40	40	145	115	178	3
8	Wimbledon	126	47	34	45	160	173	175	3
9	Sheffield Wednesday	126	44	42	40	180	162	174	3
10	Norwich City	126	43	39	44	163	180	168	3
11	Tottenham Hotspur ...	126	43	37	46	180	183	166	3
12	Chelsea	126	40	41	45	150	162	161	3
13	Coventry City	126	39	41	46	139	164	158	3
14	Manchester City	126	36	43	47	147	164	151	3
15	Newcastle United	84	43	20	21	149	88	149	2
16	Everton	126	38	33	55	139	169	147	3
17	Southampton	126	37	36	53	164	190	147	3
18	Ipswich Town	126	28	38	60	121	206	122	3
19	Nottingham Forest ...	84	32	21	31	113	105	117	2
20	West Ham United	84	26	24	34	91	106	102	2
21	Crystal Palace	84	22	28	34	82	110	94	2
22	Sheffield United	84	22	28	34	96	113	94	2
23	Oldham Athletic	84	22	23	39	105	142	89	2
24	Middlesbrough	42	11	11	20	54	75	44	1
25	Swindon Town	42	5	15	22	47	100	30	1
26	Leicester City	42	6	11	25	45	80	29	1

Positions Based on Points-Games Average

Psn		P	W	D	L	F	A	Pts	Ave
1	MANCHESTER UTD ...	126	77	33	16	224	97	264	69.84
2	Blackburn Rovers	126	72	28	26	211	121	244	64.55
3	Newcastle United	84	43	20	21	149	88	149	59.13
4	Leeds United	126	50	44	32	181	139	194	51.32
5	Liverpool	126	54	31	41	186	147	193	51.06
6	QPR	126	50	33	43	186	175	183	48.41
7	Aston Villa	126	47	38	41	154	146	179	47.35
8	Arsenal	126	46	40	40	145	115	178	47.09
9	Nottingham Forest	84	32	21	31	113	105	117	46.43
10	Wimbledon	126	47	34	45	160	173	175	46.30
11	Sheffield Wednesday ...	126	44	42	40	180	162	174	46.03
12	Norwich City	126	43	39	44	163	180	168	44.44
13	Tottenham Hotspur	126	43	37	46	180	183	166	43.92
14	Chelsea	126	40	41	45	150	162	161	42.59
15	Coventry City	126	39	41	46	139	164	158	41.80
16	West Ham United...	84	26	24	34	91	106	102	40.48
17	Manchester City	126	36	43	47	147	164	151	39.95
18	Everton	126	38	33	55	139	169	147	38.89
19	Southampton	126	37	36	53	164	190	147	38.89
20	Crystal Palace	84	22	28	34	82	110	94	37.30
21	Sheffield United	84	22	28	34	96	113	94	37.30
22	Oldham Athletic	84	22	23	39	105	142	89	35.32
23	Middlesbrough	42	11	11	20	54	75	44	34.92
24	Ipswich Town	126	28	38	60	121	206	122	32.28
25	Swindon Town	42	5	15	22	47	100	30	23.81
26	Leicester City	42	6	11	25	45	80	29	23.02

	Arsenal	Aston Villa	Blackburn R	Chelsea	Coventry City	Crystal Palace	Everton	Ipswich Town	Leeds United	Leicester City	Liverpool
Arsenal	•	0-0	0-0	3-1	2-1	1-2	1-1	4-1	1-3	1-1	0-1
Aston Villa	0-4	•	0-1	3-0	0-0	1-1	0-0	2-0	0-0	4-4	2-0
Blackburn Rovers	3-1	3-1	•	2-1	4-0	2-1	3-0	4-1	1-1	3-0	3-2
Chelsea	2-1	1-0	1-2	•	2-2	0-0	0-1	2-0	0-3	4-0	1-1
Coventry City	0-3	0-0	1-1	2-2	•	1-4	0-0	3-0	2-1	4-2	1-6
Crystal Palace	1-1	2-2	0-1	0-1	0-2	•	1-0	3-0	1-2	2-0	2-0
Everton	0-2	0-1	1-2	3-3	0-2	3-1	•	4-1	3-0	1-1	1-3
Ipswich Town	1-0	1-0	1-3	2-2	2-0	0-2	0-0	•	2-0	4-1	0-2
Leeds United	2-1	1-1	1-1	2-3	3-0	3-1	1-0	4-0	•	2-1	1-2
Leicester City	3-0	2-1	0-0		2-2	3-1	2-2	2-0	1-3	•	0-2
Liverpool	1-2	3-2	2-1	3-1	2-3	0-0	0-0	0-1	0-1	2-0	•
Manchester City	3-0	2-2	1-3	1-2	0-0	1-1	4-0	2-0	0-0	0-1	1-2
Manchester United	1-0	1-0	1-0	0-0	2-0	3-0	2-0	9-0	1-2	3-1	2-0
Newcastle United	0-0	3-1	1-1	4-2	4-0	3-2	2-0	1-1	2-1	3-1	1-2
Norwich City	2-2	1-1	2-1	3-0	2-2	0-0	0-0	3-0	2-1	1-0	1-1
Nottingham Forest	2-2	1-2	0-2	0-1	2-0	1-0	2-1	4-1	3-0	2-0	1-1
QPR	3-1	2-0	0-1	1-0	2-2	0-1	2-3	1-2	3-2	2-2	2-1
Sheffield Wednesday	3-1	1-2	1-1	1-1	5-1	1-0	0-0	4-1	1-1	1-0	2-1
Southampton	1-0	2-1	0-0	1-1	0-0	3-1	2-1	3-1	1-3	1-0	2-1
Tottenham Hotspur	1-0	3-4	3-1	0-0	1-3	0-0	2-1	3-0	1-1	1-0	2-2
West Ham United	0-2	1-0	2-0	1-2	0-1	1-0	2-2	1-1	0-0	1-0	0-0
Wimbledon	1-3	4-3	0-3	1-1	2-0	2-0	2-1	1-1	0-0	2-1	0-0

RESULTS 1994-95

Home \ Away	Manchester City	Manchester United	Newcastle Utd	Norwich City	Nottingham Forest	QPR	Sheffield Wed	Southampton	Tottenham Hot	West Ham Utd	Wimbledon
Arsenal	3-0	0-0	2-3	5-1	1-0	1-3	0-0	1-1	1-1	0-1	0-0
Aston Villa	1-1	1-2	0-2	1-1	0-2	2-1	1-1	1-1	1-0	0-2	7-1
Blackburn Rovers	2-3	2-4	1-0	0-0	3-0	4-0	3-1	3-2	2-0	4-2	2-1
Chelsea	3-0	2-3	1-1	2-0	0-0	1-0	1-0	0-2	1-1	1-2	1-1
Coventry City	1-0	2-3	0-0	1-0	0-0	0-0	2-0	1-3	0-4	2-0	1-1
Crystal Palace	2-1	1-1	0-1	0-1	1-2	0-0	0-0	0-0	1-1	1-0	0-0
Everton	1-1	1-0	2-0	2-1	1-2	2-2	1-4	0-0	0-0	1-0	0-0
Ipswich Town	1-2	3-2	0-0	1-2	0-1	0-1	1-2	2-1	1-3	1-1	2-2
Leeds United	2-0	2-1	1-3	1-0	0-0	4-0	0-1	0-1	1-1	2-2	3-1
Leicester City	0-1	0-4	2-0	1-0	2-4	1-1	0-1	4-3	3-1	1-2	3-4
Liverpool	2-0	2-0	0-0	4-0	1-0	1-1	4-1	3-1	1-1	0-0	3-0
Manchester City	•	0-3	0-0	1-0	3-3	2-3	3-2	3-3	5-2	3-0	2-0
Manchester United	5-0	•	1-1	3-0	1-2	2-1	1-0	2-1	3-3	1-0	2-1
Newcastle United	0-0	1-1	•	2-1	2-1	2-1	2-1	5-1	0-2	2-0	1-2
Norwich City	1-1	0-2	2-1	•	0-1	4-2	0-0	2-2	2-2	1-0	3-1
Nottingham Forest	1-0	1-1	3-0	1-0	•	3-2	4-1	3-0	3-4	2-1	0-1
QPR	1-2	2-3	0-0	2-0	1-1	•	3-2	2-1	4-3	2-1	0-1
Sheffield Wednesday	1-1	1-0	3-1	0-0	1-7	0-2	•	1-1	3-1	1-0	2-3
Southampton	2-2	2-2	0-0	1-1	1-1	2-1	0-0	•	1-2	1-1	1-2
Tottenham Hotspur	2-1	0-1	2-2	1-1	1-4	1-1	3-1	1-2	•	3-1	3-0
West Ham United	3-0	1-1	1-3	2-2	3-1	0-0	0-2	2-0	1-2	•	1-0
Wimbledon	2-0	0-1	3-2	1-0	2-2	1-3	0-1	0-2	1-2	1-0	•

Season's Records 94-95

Attendances by Number – FA Premier League

Home			Away		
7/05/95	Sheffield Wednesday	43,868	25/05/95	Everton	40,011
4/03/95	Ipswich Town	43,804	11/09/94	Leeds United	39,396
1/10/94	Everton	43,803	19/03/95	Liverpool	38,906
15/03/95	Tottenham Hotspur	43,802	26/11/94	Arsenal	38,301
15/10/95	West Ham United	43,795	26/10/94	Newcastle United	34,471
29/10/94	Newcastle United	43,795	8/10/94	Sheffield Wednesday	33,441
04/02/95	Aston Villa	43,795	6/11/94	Aston Villa	32,136
03/12/94	Norwich City	43,789	26/12/94	Chelsea	31,161
28/12/94	Leicester City	43,789	23/10/94	Blackburn Rovers	30,260
19/11/94	Crystal Palace	43,778	11/02/95	Manchester City	26,368
17/12/94	Notts Forest	43,744	14/05/95	West Ham United	24,783
22/01/95	Blackburn Rovers	43,742	27/08/94	Tottenham Hotspur	24,502
17/09/94	Liverpool	43,740	24/09/94	Ipswich Town	22,559
10/11/94	Manchester City	43,738	22/08/94	Notts Forest	22,072
17/04/95	Chelsea	43,728	1/05/95	Coventry City	21,885
2/04/95	Leeds United	43,712	22/02/95	Norwich City	21,824
22/03/95	Arsenal	43,623	15/04/95	Leicester City	21,281
10/03/95	Southampton	43,479	10/12/94	Queens Park Rangers	18,498
31/08/94	Wimbledon	43,440	21/01/95	Crystal Palace	18,224
20/08/94	Queens Park Rangers	43,214	7/03/95	Wimbledon	18,224
3/01/95	Coventry City	43,103	31/12/94	Southampton	15,204
	Total	917,291		*Total*	573,957

Attendances by Number – European Cup

Home			Away		
19/10/94	Barcelona	40,064	2/11/94	Barcelona	114,273
14/09/94	IFK Gothenburg	33,625	23/11/94	IFK Gothenburg	36,350
7/12/94	Galatasary	30,000	28/9/94	Galatasary	30,000
	Total	112,909		*Total*	180,623

Attendances by Number – Coca Cola Cup

Home			Away		
5/10/94	Port Vale	31,615	26/10/94	Newcastle United	34,178
	Total	31,615	12/09/94	Port Vale	18,605
				Total	57,783

Attendances by Number – FA Cup

Home			Away		
12/03/94	Charlton Athletic	44,340	9/01/95	Sheffield United	22,322
28/01/95	Wrexham	43,222	9/04/95	Crystal Palace (n)	38,256
19/02/95	Leeds United	42,744	12/04/95	Crystal Palace (n)	17,987
12/05/95	Queens Park Rangers	42,830	20/05/95	Everton (n)	79,592
				Total	158,157

Sending Offs

Eric	CANTONA	6/8/94	v	Glasgow Rangers	(a)
Paul	PARKER	20/8/94	v	Queens Park Rangers	(h)
Paul	INCE	23/11/94	v	IFK Gothenburg	(a)
Mark	HUGHES	26/11/94	v	Arsenal	(a)
Eric	CANTONA	25/1/95	v	Crystal Palace	(a)
Roy	KEANE	12/4/95	v	Crystal Palace	(n)

Bookings

Steve	BRUCE	14/8/94	v	Blackburn Rovers	(n)
		17/9/94	v	Liverpool	(h)
		1/10/94	v	Everton	(h)
		8/10/94	v	Sheff Wed	(a)
		23/10/94	v	Blackburn Rovs	(a)
		29/10/94	v	Newcastle United	(h)
		6/11/94	v	Aston Villa	(a)
		3/01/95	v	Coventry City	(h)
		22/1/95	v	Blackburn Rovers	(h)
		19/3/95	v	Liverpool	(a)
		22/3/95	v	Arsenal	(h)
		10/5/95	v	Southampton	(h)
		14/5/95	v	West Ham Utd	(a)
Nicky	BUTT	15/10/94	v	West Ham Utd	(h)
		27/10/94	v	Newcastle United	(a)
		26/11/94	v	Arsenal	(a)
		26/12/94	v	Chelsea	(a)
		31/12/94	v	Southampton	(a)
Eric	CANTONA	17/9/94	v	Liverpool	(h)
		23/11/94	v	IFK Gothenburg	(a)
		7/12/94	v	Galatasary	(h)
		26/12/94	v	Chelsea	(a)
		31/12/94	v	Southampton	(a)

				v		
		22/1/95	v	Blackburn Rovers	(h)
Andy	COLE	1/05/95	v	Coventry City	(a)
Simon	DAVIES	5/8/94	v	Newcastle United	(n)
		7/12/94	v	Galatasary	(h)
Ryan	GIGGS	14/8/94	v	Blackburn Rovers	(n)
		27/8/94	v	Tottenham H	(a)
		17/12/94	v	Notts Forest	(h)
		15/3/95	v	Tottenham H	(h)
Keith	GILLESPIE	6/11/94	v	Aston Villa	(a)
		26/11/94	v	Arsenal	(a)
Mark	HUGHES	28/9/94	v	Galatasary	(a)
		8/10/94	v	Sheff Wed	(a)
		8/11/94	v	Man City	(h)
		23/11/94	v	IFK Gothenburg	(a)
		26/11/94	v	Arsenal	(a)
		28/12/94	v	Leicester City	(h)
		31/12/94	v	Southampton	(a)
		12/3/95	v	QPR	(h)
		12/4/95	v	Crystal Palace	(n)
		6/05/95	v	Sheffield Wednesday	(h)
		14/5/95	v	West Ham Utd	(a)
Paul	INCE	2/11/94	v	Barcelona	(a)
		26/11/94	v	Arsenal	(a)
		10/12/94	v	QPR	(a)
		4/02/95	v	Aston Villa	(h)
		11/2/95	v	Man City	(a)
		25/2/95	v	Everton	(a)
Denis	IRWIN	24/9/94	v	Ipswich Town	(a)
		10/12/94	v	QPR	(a)
		9/01/95	v	Sheffield United	(a)
		9/04/95	v	Crystal Palace	(n)
Roy	KEANE	22/8/94	v	Notts Forest	(a)
		24/9/94	v	Ipswich Town	(a)
		28/9/94	v	Galatasary	(a)
		10/12/94	v	QPR	(a)
		17/12/94	v	Notts Forest	(h)
		26/12/94	v	Chelsea	(a)
		9/01/95	v	Sheffield United	(a)
		14/1/95	v	Newcastle Utd	(a)
		25/1/95	v	Crystal Palace	(a)
		19/3/95	v	Liverpool	(a)
Brian	McCLAIR	31/12/94	v	Southampton	(a
David	MAY	11/9/94	v	Leeds United	(a)
		17/9/94	v	Liverpool	(h)

		28/9/94	v	Galatasary	(a)
		19/10/94	v	Barcelona	(h)
Gary	NEVILLE	21/9/94	v	Port Vale	(a)
		3/12/94	v	Norwich City	(h)
		10/12/94	v	QPR	(a)
		26/12/94	v	Chelsea	(a)
		31/12/94	v	Southampton	(a)
		3/01/95	v	Coventry City	(h)
		1/05/95	v	Coventry City	(a)
		20/5/95	v	Everton	(n)
Paul	PARKER	2/11/94	v	Barcelona	(a)
Gary	PALLISTER	9/04/95	v	Crystal Palace	(n)
		12/4/95	v	Crystal Palace	(n)
Paul	SCHOLES	27/10/94	v	Newcastle Utd	(a)
Lee	SHARPE	14/8/94	v	Blackburn Rovers	(n)
		28/9/94	v	Galatasary	(a)
		1/10/94	v	Everton	(h)
		8/10/94	v	Sheff Wed	(a)
		15/10/95	v	West Ham Utd	(h)
		14/1/95	v	Newcastle Utd	(a)
		7/03/95	v	Wimbledon	(a)
		15/3/95	v	Tottenham H.	(h)
		1/05/95	v	Coventry City	(a)

Suspensions

Eric	CANTONA	3 matches	August-94
Steve	BRUCE	3 matches	November-94
Mark	HUGHES	2 matches	December-94
Paul	INCE	1 match	December-94
Roy	KEANE	2 matches	January-95
Steve	BRUCE	2 matches	January-95
Gary	NEVILLE	2 matches	January-95
Eric	CANTONA	until 30th Sept 1995	January-95
Roy	KEANE	2 matches	February-95
Lee	SHARPE	1 match	April-95
Steve	BRUCE	2 matches	April-95
Paul	INCE	1 match	May-95

European Bans

Eric	CANTONA	4 matches
Mark	HUGHES	1 match
Paul	INCE	1 match

Summary of Appearances

No.	Player		Lge	EC	CCC	FAC
1	Peter	SCHMEICHEL	32	3	-/-	7
2	Paul	PARKER	1/1	2/1	-/-	-/-
3	Denis	IRWIN	40	5	2	7
4	Steve	BRUCE	35	5/1	1	5
5	Lee	SHARPE	26/2	3	-/2	6/1
6	Gary	PALLISTER	42	6	2	7
7	Eric	CANTONA	21	2	-/-	1
8	Paul	INCE	36	5	-/-	6
9	Brian	McCLAIR	34/5	2	3	6/1
10	Mark	HUGHES	33/1	5	-/-	6
11	Ryan	GIGGS	30	3	-/-	6/1
12	David	MAY	15/4	4	2	1
13	Gary	WALSH	10	3	3	-/-
14	Andrei	KANCHELSKIS	25/5	5	-/-	2/1
15	Graeme	TOMLINSON	-/-	-/-	-/2	-/-
16	Roy	KEANE	23/1	4	1	6/1
17	Andy	COLE	17	-/-	-/-	-/-
18	Simon	DAVIES	3/2	2	3	-/-
19	Nicky	BUTT	11/10	5/1	3	3/1
23	Phil	NEVILLE	1/1	-/-	-/-	1
24	Paul	SCHOLES	6/11	-/2	3	1/2
25	Kevin	PILKINGTON	-/1	-/-	-/-	-/-
26	Chris	CASPER	-/-	-/-	1	-/-
27	Gary	NEVILLE	16/2	1/1	2-1	4
28	David	BECKHAM	2/2	1/-	3	1/1
30	John	O'KANE	-/-	-/-	1-1	1
31	Keith	GILLESPIE	3/6	-/-	3	-/-

Goalscorers

No.	Player		Lge	EC	CCC	FAC
14	Andrei	KANCHELSKIS	14	1	-	-
7	Eric	CANTONA	12	-	-	1
17	Andy	COLE	12	-	-	-
10	Mark	HUGHES	8	2	-	2
8	Paul	INCE	5	-	-	-
9	Brian	McCLAIR	5	-	1	2
24	Paul	SCHOLES	5	-	2	-
5	Lee	SHARPE	3	2	-	1
4	Steve	BRUCE	2	-	-	2
3	Denis	IRWIN	2	-	-	4

No.	Player		Lge	EC	CCC	FAC
16	Roy	KEANE	2	1	-	-
12	David	MAY	2	-	1	-
6	Gary	PALLISTER	2	-	-	2
11	Ryan	GIGGS	1	2	-	2
19	Nicky	BUTT	1	-	-	-
31	Keith	GILLESPIE	1	-	-	-
18	Simon	DAVIES	-	1	-	-
28	David	BECKHAM	-	1	-	-
	Own	Goals	-	1	-	-

List of Scores by Number (League Games Only)

0-0	1-0	1-1	2-0
Arsenal (a)	Spurs (a)	Forest (a)	QPR (h)
Spurs (h)	West Ham (h)	Leicester C (h)	Liverpool (h)
Leeds (h)	Norwich C (h)	Newcastle U (a)	Everton (h)
Chelsea (h)	Blackburn R (h)	C.Palace (a)	Newcastle U (h)
	Aston V (h)	West Ham (a)	Coventry C (h)
	Wimbledon (a)		Norwich C (a)
	Sheff Wed (h)		

2-1	2-2	3-0	3-2
Aston V (a)	Southampton (a)	Wimbledon (h)	QPR (a)
Southampton (h)	C.Palace (a)		Chelsea (a)
	Man City (a)		Coventry (a)
	Arsenal (h)		

0-1	0-2	1-2	2-3
Sheff.Wed (a)	Liverpool (a)	Leeds U (a)	Ipswich T (a)
Everton(a)		Notts Forest (h)	

4-0	4-2	5-0	9-0
Leicester (a)	Blackburn R (a)	Man City (h)	Ipswich T (h)

League Sequences

Consecutive Wins	6
Consecutive Home Wins	9
Consecutive Away Wins	2
Games Without Defeat	9
Games Without a Win	2

United's Record Against Other Clubs in the FAPL

Club	P	W	D	L	F	A	W	D	L	F	A
Arsenal	6	2	1	0	4	0	1	2	0	3	2
Aston Villa	6	2	1	0	5	2	2	0	1	4	3
Blackburn Rovers	6	2	1	0	5	2	1	1	1	4	4
Chelsea	6	1	1	1	3	1	1	1	1	4	4
Coventry City	6	2	1	0	7	0	3	0	0	5	2
Crystal Palace	4	2	0	0	4	0	1	1	0	3	1
Everton	6	2	0	1	3	3	2	0	1	3	1
Ipswich Town	6	1	2	0	10	1	1	0	2	5	6
Leeds United	6	1	2	0	2	0	1	1	1	3	2
Leicester City	2	0	1	0	1	1	1	0	0	4	0
Liverpool	6	2	1	0	5	2	1	1	1	5	6
Manchester City	6	3	0	0	9	1	2	1	0	7	3
Middlesbrough	2	1	0	0	3	0	0	1	0	1	1
Newcastle United	4	1	1	0	3	1	0	2	0	2	2
Norwich City	6	2	1	0	4	2	3	0	0	7	1
Nottingham Forest	4	1	0	1	3	2	1	1	0	3	1
Oldham Athletic	4	2	0	0	6	2	1	0	1	5	3
QPR	6	2	1	0	4	1	3	0	0	9	5
Sheffield United	4	2	0	0	5	1	1	0	1	4	2
Sheffield Wednesday	6	3	0	0	8	1	1	1	1	6	6
Southampton	6	3	0	0	6	2	2	1	0	6	3
Swindon Town	2	1	0	0	4	2	0	1	0	2	2
Tottenham Hotspur	6	2	1	0	6	2	2	1	0	3	1
West Ham United	4	2	0	0	4	0	0	2	0	3	3
Wimbledon	6	2	0	1	6	2	2	0	1	3	2
Total	126	44	15	4	120	31	33	18	12	104	66

Transfers to Manchester United

Player		Date Bought	From	Fee
David	MAY	June 1994	Blackburn Rovers	£1,250,000
Graeme	TOMLINSON	June 1994	Bradford City	£100,000
Andy	COLE	January 1995	Newcastle United	£7,000,000

Transfers from Manchester United

Player	Date Sold	To	Fee
Bryan Robson	May 1994	Middlesbrough	Free
Clayton Blackmore	May 1994	Middlesbrough	Free
Les Sealey	May 1994	Blackpool	Free
Mike Phelan	June 1994	West Bromwich Albion	Free
Craig Lawton	June 1994	Port Vale	Free
Ian Hart	June 1994	Crewe Alexandra	Free
Robert Savage	June 1994	Crewe Alexandra	Free
Neil Whitworth	Sept 1994	Kilmarnock	joint deal
Colin McKee	Sept 1994	Kilmarnock	worth £530,000
Dion Dublin	Sep 1994	Coventry City	£2,000,000
Keith Gillespie	January 1995	Newcastle Utd	Estimated £1,000,000

Appearances – FA Carling Premiership

Player Number	1	2	3	4	5	6	7	8	9	10	11	12	13	14	27	16	18	19	20	24	25	31
Queens Park Rangers	*	70	*	*	*	*	*	*	*	*	*	s	*	*	*	s	.	.	.	.	s	.
Nottingham Forest	*	s	*	*	*	*	*	*	*	s	s	s	*	*	*	55	.	.	.	.	s	.
Tottenham Hotspur	*	*	*	*	*	*	.	*	*	*	*	*	*	*	.	.	.	.	.	.	s	.
Wimbledon	*	.	.	*	*	*	*	*	s	*	*	*	*	*	.	.	.	s	.	.	s	.
Leeds United	*	.	.	.	63	.	.	.	59	s	.	.	.	.	.	.	63	63	.	.	s	.
Liverpool	*	.	.	.	.	.	.	*	s	s	*	*	.	.	.	.	s	s	.	62	s	.
Ipswich Town	*	.	.	.	.	.	.	*	75	s	.	.	*	.	.	.	s	s	.	76	s	.
Everton	*	s	*	.	.	.	.	.	*	.	*	.	60	s	.	.	45	45	.	.	s	.
Sheffield Wednesday	*	.	.	.	.	.	.	*	s	*	*	s	s	*	.	.	.	.	.	.	s	s
West Ham	*	.	*	*	*	*	.	*	82	*	.	s	s	*	.	.	s	s	.	.	s	s
Blackburn Rovers	*	No23	*	*	*	*	*	*	*	*	.	*	s	*	*	.	.	.	.	.	s	65
Newcastle United	*	P	*	*	*	*	*	*	*	*	*	*	s	*	*	.	.	s	.	s	s	78
Aston Villa	*	N	.	.	.	.	.	.	6	*	*	*	*	*	*	.	.	s	.	s	s	.
Manchester City	*	E	.	.	.	.	.	*	*	*	*	*	*	*	*	.	.	71	.	45	7	52
Crystal Palace	s	V	.	.	.	.	.	*	*	*	*	*	*	s	s	.	73	56	.	71	.	s
Arsenal	*	I	.	.	.	.	.	*	*	*	*	*	*	s	s	.	s	68	.	.	s	56
Norwich City	*	L	.	.	.	.	.	*	*	*	*	*	*	s	s	.	s	68	.	.	s	s
Queens Park Rangers	*	L	.	.	.	.	.	*	*	*	*	*	*	s	s	.	s	67	.	.	s	77
Nottingham Forest	*	E	.	.	.	.	.	*	*	*	*	*	s	*	88	.	76	No17	.	.	s	.
Chelsea	.	.	.	.	.	.	.	s	*	*	*	.	76	45	*	.	.	*	C	.	s	.
Leicester City	*	.	.	.	.	.	.	*	*	*	s	*	s	.	.	.	.	*	O	69	s	.
Southampton	*	.	.	.	.	.	64	*	*	*	*	s	*	.	.	.	.	*	L	.	s	79
Coventry City	*	.	.	.	.	.	.	*	*	s	s	*	46	.	.	.	s	*	E	16	s	*
Newcastle United	*	.	.	.	.	.	.	*	.	.	.	.	S	S	77	.	.	s	.	.	s	.
Blackburn Rovers	*	*	.	.	s	.	.	.	.	.	.	.	s	s	.	.	.	.	.	.	s	.

174

Player Number	1	2	3	4	5	6	7	8	9	10	11	12	13	14	16	27	18	19	20	24	25	28
Crystal Palace	*	-	*	*	s	*	*	*	*	*	*	*	*		*				*	s		B
Aston Villa	*	*	*	*	*	*	*	*	*	*	*		82	44	s	s			*			E
Manchester City	*	s	s	*	*	*	-	*	*	*	*		64	s	s	s			*			C
Norwich City	*		s	*	*	*	-	*	*	*	*		82	s	s					53		K
Everton	*	*	*	*	*	*	*	*	s	*	*		66				s	s	*			H
Ipswich Town	*	*	*	s	45	*	*	*	*	*	*			s	s			80	*			A
Wimbledon	*		*	*	*	*	-	*	s	*	*		s			s	s					M
Tottenham Hotspur	*	*	*	*	*	*	*	*	*	s	*		s		s	s					s	-
Liverpool	*		*	*	*	*	-	*	*	*	*				s		s	78	45			-
Arsenal	*		*	*	*	*	*	*	*	*	*		s		s	s		84	45		s	-
Leeds United	*		*	-	-	*	*	*	*	*	*				s			s	*			-
Leicester City	*		*	*	s	*	*	*	*	*	*		s		s		s	s	*	55	s	-
Chelsea	*	*	*	*	*	*	*	*	*	*	*		s		45	*	s	*	*	74		45
Coventry City	*	*	*	*	*	*	*	-	*	*	*		s	*		*		*	s	s		77
Sheffield United	*	24	*	*	*	*	-	-	s	s	*	s	s	*		*		52	*			s
Southampton	*	*	*	*	*	*	*	*	*	s	*	s	s	*	s	*		s	*	76		s
West Ham United	*	*	*	*	*	*	-	*	45	*	*		s		s	*		s	*	79		s

Chris Casper (26) was included as substitute against Wimbledon (a) but not used
Pat McGibbon (21) was included as substitute against Coventry City (a) but not used

Coca-Cola League Cup

Player Number	3	4	5	6	9	12	13	15	16	18	19	24	25	26	27	28	30	31
Port Vale	*	-	84	-	*	*	*	*	*	s	s	*	*	s	s	*	75	*
Port Vale	-	-	-	*	*	*	*	65	-	*	*	*	*	s	76	*	*	s
Newcastle	s	*	52	*	*	*	-	72	-	*	*	*	*	-	*	*	*	*

FA Cup

Player Number	1	2	3	4	5	6	7	8	9	10	11	12	13	14	27	16	18	19	23	24	25	28	30
Sheff Utd	*	-	-	*	64	*	*	-	s	*	*	-	-	-	*	*	*	*	-	78	s	-	s
Wrexham	*	-	-	*	*	*	*	*	s	-	*	*	s	*	-	s	s	*	*	*	s	73	-
Leeds Utd	*	-	*	*	*	*	-	*	*	*	s	-	s	69	*	-	-	s	s	s	-	-	-
QPR	*	-	*	*	*	*	-	*	*	*	45	s	-	*	*	45	*	*	*	-	-	-	-
Crystal Pal	*	-	*	-	*	*	-	*	58	*	*	s	s	-	-	*	49	*	-	s	s	s	-
Crystal Pal	*	-	*	s	s	*	*	*	*	*	45	-	s	-	*	*	*	*	*	72	s	s	-
Everton	*	-	*	s	s	*	*	*	*	-	-	*	s	-	*	*	*	*	*	72	-	-	-

European Cup

Player Number	1	2	3	4	5	6	7	8	9	10	11	12	13	14	27	16	18	19	23	24	25	28	30
IFK Goth'g	*	-	*	*	*	*	-	*	-	*	*	*	*	*	s	-	s	*	*	s	s	s	-
Galatasary	*	65	-	*	*	*	-	*	*	*	s	*	s	*	s	*	-	-	*	s	s	-	-
Barcelona	*	-	*	69	*	*	-	*	*	*	s	s	s	*	s	*	*	*	*	79	67	-	-
IFK Goth'g	-	-	*	*	-	*	*	-	*	s	-	*	*	*	68	-	*	75	*	s	s	s	s
Galatasary	*	-	-	*	*	*	*	-	-	-	-	s	*	-	*	*	*	*	*	s	s	s	s

Other Sub in European Matches not used - D.Johnson (1)

Squad Nos

1 Schmeichel, 2 Parker, 3 Irwin, 4 Bruce, 5 Sharpe, 6 Pallister, 7 Cantona, 8 Ince, 9 McClair, 10 Hughes, 11 Giggs, 12 May, 13 Walsh, 14 Kanchelskis, 15 Tomlinson, 16 Keane, 17 Cole, 18 Davies, 19 Butt, 20 Dublin, 23 P.Neville 24 Scholes, 25 Pilkington, 26 Casper, 27 G.Neville, 28 Beckham, 30 O'Kane 31 Gillespie

S – Sub not used – s denotes the player substituted

A figure shows the number of minutes played when that player was introduced to the game.

General Records

Football Alliance

Biggest Home Win:	10-1 v Lincoln City	21/11/1891
Biggest Away Win:	6-1 v Lincoln City	02/04/1892
Biggest Home Defeat:	1-3 v Birmingham St George	14/03/1891
Biggest Away Defeats:	0-7 v Grimsby Town	08/02/1890
	2-8 v Notts Forest	22/11/1890
Highest Home Attendance:	16,000 v Nottingham Forest (1-1)	01/01/1892
Most Appearances:	62 WS Stewart	
Leading Goalscorer:	25 AH Farman	
Most Goals in a Season:	20 R Donaldson	1891/1892
Most Consecutive Wins:	5 31/10/1891 to 12/12/1891	
Most Consecutive Defeats:	5 07/03/1891 to 12/09/1891	
Longest Run Without a Win:	6 21/02/1891 to 12/09/1891	
Longest Unbeaten Run:	15 19/09/1891 to 20/02/1892	

United's longest unbeaten run in the Alliance came immediately after their longest sequence of defeats and their longest run without a win!

Football League

Biggest Home Win:	10-1 v Wolverhampton Wanderers	15/10/1892
Biggest Away Win:	7-0 v Grimsby Town	26/12/1899
Biggest Home Defeat:	1-7 v Newcastle United	10/09/1927
	0-6 v Aston Villa	14/03/1914
	v Huddersfield Town	10/09/1930*

* In their next home match on 13th September 1930, United were beaten 7-4 by Newcastle United which made a total of thirteen goals conceded at home in a period of four days! They had also conceded six goals at Chelsea in their previous away game.

Biggest Away Defeat:	0-7 v Blackburn Rovers	10/04/1926
	v Aston Villa	27/12/1930
	v Wolverhampton Wanderers	26/12/1931*

* This was United's second consecutive Christmas 7-0 defeat.

Highest Home Attendance:	70,504 v Aston Villa (lost 1-3)	27/12/1920
	83,260 v Arsenal (1-1)*	17/01/1948

* This game was played at Maine Road and set a record Football League attendance which still stands today

177

Most Appearances:	604 plus 2 as substitute R Charlton	
Leading Goalscorer:	199 R Charlton	
Most Goals in a Season:	32 D Viollet	1959/1960
Most Goals in a Game:	There have been numerous instances of players scoring 4 in a game but nobody has achieved five or more.	
Most Consecutive Wins:	14 15/10/1904 to 03/01/1905	
Most Consecutive Defeats:	14 26/04/1930 to 25/10/1930	

The 12 consecutive defeats United suffered in this spell from the beginning of the 1930/31 season is still a Football League record for the number of defeats from the opening of a season.

Longest Unbeaten Run:	26	04/02/1956 to 13/10/1956
Longest Run Without a Win:	16	19/04/1930 to 25/10/1930
		03/11/1928 to 09/02/1929

FA Premiership

Biggest Home Win:	9-0 v Ipswich Town	4/03/95
Biggest Home Defeat:	0-3 v Everton	19/08/93
Biggest Away Win:	5-2 v Oldham Athletic	29/12/93
	4-0 v Leicester City	15/04/95
Biggest Away Defeat:	0-2 v Blackburn Rovers	02/04/94
	0-2 v Liverpool	19/03/95
Highest Home Attendance:	44,751 v Liverpool (1-0)	30/03/94
Lowest Home Attendance:	29,736 v Crystal Palace	02/09/92
Most Appearances:	125 G. Pallister	
Leading Goalscorer:	39 E. Cantona, M. Hughes	
Most Goals in a Season:	18 E. Cantona 1993/94	
Most Consecutive Wins:	9 05/04/1993 to 18/08/1993	
Most Goals in a Game:	5 A. Cole v Ipswich Town (h) 4/03/95	
Games Without Defeat:	22 19/09/1993 to 26/02/1994	

Note: In 38 league games between 14/03/1993 and 26/03/1994 United lost just once.

FA Cup

Biggest Home Win:	8-0 v Yeovil Town – 5th Round	12/02/1949
Biggest Away Win:	8-2 v Northampton Town – 5th Round	07/02/1970
Biggest Home Defeat:	2-7 v Sheffield Wednesday 4th Round replay	01/02/1961

Biggest Away Defeat:	1-7 *v* Burnley – 1st Rnd replay	13/02/1901
	0-6 *v* Sheffield Wednesday (2nd Round)	20/02/1904
Highest Home Attendance:	81,565 *v* Yeovil Town – 5th Round	
	(at Maine Road)	12/02/1949
	66,350 *v* Sheffield Wed – 5th Round	
	(at Old Trafford)	20/02/1960
Most Appearances:	79 R Charlton	
Leading Goalscorer:	34 D Law	
Most Goals in a Game:	6 G Best *v* Northampton Town	07/02/1970
Longest Unbeaten Run:	13 10/01/1948 to 26/03/1949	
	11/01/94 to 20/05/95	
Longest Run Without a Win:	5 12/02/1898 to 28/10/1899	
	31/01/1920 to 13/01/1923	
	11/01/94 to 20/05/95	
	24/01/1931 to 17/01/1934	

Between January 1929 and January 1935 United won just one FA Cup tie – a replay against Liverpool. From 18th February 1928 to 16th January 1937 United failed to win a single FA Cup tie at Old Trafford.

Football League Cup

Biggest Home Win:	7-2 *v* Newcastle United	27/10/1976
Biggest Away Win:	6-2 *v* Arsenal	28/11/1990
Biggest Home Defeat:	0-3 *v* Everton	01/12/1976
	v Tottenham Hotspur	25/10/1989
Biggest Away Defeat:	1-5 *v* Blackpool	14/09/1966

United's team for this game was virtually full strength with nine internationals

Highest Home Attendance:	63,418 *v* Manchester City (2-2)	17/12/1969
	Semi-Final	
Most Appearances:	52 B Robson	
Leading Goalscorer:	19 B McClair	
Most Goals in a Game:	3 G Hill, M Hughes (twice), B McClair and	
	L Sharpe	
Longest Unbeaten Run:	10 25/09/1991 to 28/10/1992	
Longest Run Without a Win:	5 26/09/1979 to 28/10/1981	

UEFA Champions' League (nee Cup)

| Biggest Home Win: | 10-0 *v* Anderlecht (at Maine Road) | 26/09/1956 |
| Biggest Win at Old Trafford: | 7-1 *v* Waterford | 02/10/1968 |

Biggest Away Win:	6-0 v Shamrock Rovers	25/09/1957
Biggest Home Defeat:	None	
Biggest Away Defeat:	0-4 v A.C. Milan	14/05/58
	0-4 v Barcelona	2/11/94
Highest Home Attendance:	65,000 v Real Madrid (2-2)	25/04/1957
	Semi-Final	

The crowd was equalled for the visit of Atletico Bilbao on 6/2/1957 but that game was played at Maine Road.

Most Appearances:	35	W Foulkes	
Most Goals:	14	D Law	
Most Goals in a Game:	4	D Viollet v Anderlecht	26/09/56
		D Law v Waterford	02/10/68

Law scored 7 in total during this tie having netted a hat-trick in the First Leg.

Most Consecutive Wins:	6	22/09/1965 to 09/03/1966
Longest Unbeaten Run:	6	22/09/1965 to 09/03/1966
		20/04/1966 to 28/02/1968
		24/04/1968 to 13/11/1969
Longest Run Without a Win:	4	28/09/1994 to 23/11/94

European Cup-Winners' Cup

Biggest Home Win:	6-1 v Willem II	15/10/1963

United set their record score in this competition in their first home game – as they had done in the European Cup.

Biggest Away Win:	3-1 v Legia Warsaw	10/04/1991
Biggest Home Defeat:	None	
Biggest Away Defeat:	0-5 v SC Lisbon	18/03/1964

This result overturned a 4-1 lead that United held from the First Leg.

Biggest Home Attendance:	60,000 v SC Lisbon (won 4-1)	26/02/1964
Most Appearances:	16	M Hughes	
Leading Goalscorer:	6	D Law	
Most Goals in a Game:	3	D Law v Willem II	15/10/1963
		D Law v SC Lisbon	26/02/1964
Most Consecutive Wins:	4	19/09/1990 to 07/11/1990	
Longest Unbeaten Run:	11	19/09/1990 to 02/10/1991	
Longest Run Without a Win:	4	Galatasary (a). Barce;pma (h). barce;pma (a), IFK Gothenburg (a), in Group A 1994/95	

Biggest Home Win: 6-1 v Djurgardens   27/10/1964

This completed United's unusual hat-trick of recording their biggest home win in each of the three major European tournaments in their first home game in each respective competition.

Biggest Away Win:	6-1 v Borussia Dortmund	11/11/1964
Biggest Home Defeat:	None	
Biggest Away Defeat:	0-3 v Juventus	03/11/1976
Highest Home Attendance:	59,000 v Juventus (won 1-0)	20/10/1976
Most Appearances:	11 R Charlton	
Leading Goalscorer:	8 R Charlton	
Most Goals in a Game:	3 D Law v Djurgardens	27/10/1964
	R Charlton v Borussia Dortmund	11/11/1964
Most Consecutive Wins:	3 27/10/1964 to 02/12/1964	
Most Consecutive Defeats:	2 06/06/1965 to 16/06/1965	

Both defeats were by Hungarian side, Ferencvaros who thus became the first and, to date, only team to defeat United in consecutive European matches. The second defeat came in a play-off after the first two matches had failed to produce a winner.

Longest Unbeaten Run: 9   23/09/1964 to 31/05/1965

These were United's first nine games in the competition.

Longest Run Without a Win: 5   30/11/1976 to 29/09/1982

Pot Pourri Facts

The 39 steps

When Manchester United took on Blackburn Rovers at Old Trafford in January 1995 the match witnessed the most expensive line up in the history of League football in Britain. One of the teams was certain to win the title and the cost of the two line ups, *not* counting injured players such as Batty (£2.75m), Gallagher (£1.5m), Hughes (£1.5m), Parker (£2m), and Ripley (£1.3m), was in excess of a colossal £39,000,000! The 39 steps to the title were made up as follows:

Manchester United		Blackburn Rovers	
Schmeichel	£850,000	Flowers	£2.3m
Irwin	£650,000	Berg	£400,000
Bruce	£800,000	Hendry	£800,000
Pallister	£2.3m	Warhurst	£2.75m
Sharpe	£185,000	Le Saux	£650,000
McClair	£850,000	Sherwood	£500,000
Keane	£3.75m	Atkins	£45,000
Ince	£1.8m	Wilcox	no fee
Giggs	no fee	Shearer	£3.5m
Cantona	£1.2m	Sutton	£5m
Cole	£7m	Wright	£400,000
Kanchelskis	£650,000	Mimms	£250,000
May	£1.2m	Newall	£1.1m
Walsh	no fee	Pearce	£300,000
Total	£21,210,000	Total	£17,995,000

Semi United

Manchester United's FA Cup semi final clash with Crystal Palace moved them into second place in the all time list of last four appearances. But they failed to make up ground on the leaders, Everton, who also made it through to the Final in 1994/95.

United's appearance was their 20th in the semi final whilst Everton increased their number to 23.

The leading positions are:

Everton	23
Man United	20
Liverpool	19
WBA	19
Arsenal	18
Aston Villa	17
Blackburn Rovers	16
Sheffield Wednesday	16
Tottenham	15

There have been 57 different semi finalists with three clubs, Norwich City, Oldham Athletic, and Stoke City having reached the last four on three occasions without ever progressing to the Final itself. United, who have never lost a semi final at Villa Park, have played at nine different venues at the last four stage. Altogether, there have been 42 different venues for the FA Cup semi finals with Old Trafford ranking high on the list despite United's success in reaching so many semi finals automatically ruling the ground out of contention on many occasions:

Villa Park	44
Hillsborough	32
Bramall Lane	19
Maine Road	18
Kennington Oval	17
Old Trafford	12
White Hart Lane	12
Highbury	11
Goodison Park	10
Stamford Bridge	10
Elland Road	9
Molyneux	9
St Andrews	9

United's opponents in the Final, Everton broke a remarkable hoodoo to reach the Final when beating Spurs 4-1 at Elland Road. They had never won there in either the FA Cup or League Cup and had not won at the ground in the League since 1951/52!

The highest number of goals scored in a semi final is eight with United being involved in one of three such matches, a 5-3 win over Fulham in a replay in 1958 when Alex Dawson became only the second United player in history to score a hat-trick in a semi-final. The first player to perform this feat for the Reds was Stan Pearson in the 3-1 victory over Derby County in 1948.

Busby Players

134 players had the privilege of playing a competitive match for United whilst Sir Matt Busby was manager. In alphabetical order, they are:

Reg Allen	Tony Dunne	Ken Morgans
John Anderson	Pat Dunne	Johnny Morris
Willie Anderson	Duncan Edwards	Bobby Noble
John Aston Jnr	Paul Edwards	Jimmy Nicholson
John Aston Snr	Sonny Feehan	Les Olive
Bill Bainbridge	Bill Fielding	Tommy O'Neil
John Ball	John Fitzpatrick	Mark Pearson
Geoff Bent	Billy Foulkes	Stan Pearson
John Berry	David Gaskell	David Pegg
George Best	Don Gibson	Ken Pegg
Brian Birch	Johnny Giles	Mike Pinner
Cliff Birkett	Freddie Goodwin	Albert Quixall
Jackie Blanchflower	Alan Gowling	Billy Redman
Tommy Bogan	Ian Greaves	Jimmy Rimmer
Ernie Bond	Harry Gregg	John Roach
Warren Bradley	John Hanlon	Jack Rowley
Harold Bratt	Bobby Harrop	Jimmy Ryan
Shay Brennan	Tony Hawksworth	David Sadler
Ronnie Briggs	Frank Haydock	Carlo Sartori
Bob Brown	David Herd	Albert Scanlon
Ted Buckle	Tommy Heron	John Scott
Ronnie Burke	Reg Hunter	Maurice Setters
Francis Burns	Steve James	Jack Smith
Roger Byrne	Mark Jones	Alex Stepney
Noel Cantwell	Peter Jones	Nobby Stiles
Johnny Carey	Paddy Kennedy	Ernie Taylor
Joe Carolan	Brian Kidd	Tommy Taylor
Laurie Cassidy	Albert Kinsey	Wilf Tranter
Bobby Charlton	Frank Kopel	Ian Ure
Allenby Chilton	Joe Lancaster	Dennis Viollet
Phil Chisnall	Denis Law	Dennis Walker
Gordon Clayton	Nobby Lawton	Joe Walton
Frank Clempson	Eddie Lewis	Jack Warner
Henry Cockburn	Tommy Lowrie	Colin Webster
Cliff Collinson	Sam Lynn	Bert Whalley
Eddie Colman	Noel McFarlane	Billy Whelan
John Connelly	Billy McGlen	Jeff Whitefoot
Ronnie Cope	Wilf McGuinness	Walter Whitehurst
Pat Crerand	Eddie McIlvenny	Ray Wood
Jack Crompton	Sammy McMillan	Harry Worrall
Stan Crowther	Tommy McNulty	Billy Wrigglesworth
Joe Dale	Harry McShane	Willie Morgan
Alex Dawson	Charlie Mitten	
Jimmy Delaney	Ian Moir	
John Downie	Graham Moore	

Match Rigging

With the 1994/95 season containing, amongst its many other unsavoury incidents, allegations of match rigging perhaps it is an appropriate time to reflect that fixing results has gone on for many years. United, themselves, were caught up in it as long ago as 1915.

When United played Liverpool on 2nd April 1915, bookmakers noticed that a flood of bets had gone on United to win the game 2-0. The amounts staked on the individual bets were not sufficient, in themselves, to raise suspicion but collectively the money bet was substantial and, with the odds on that particular scoreline standing at 7-1, there was a killing to be made.

When the result came up 2-0, the bookmakers smelt a rat and refused to pay out calling for an investigation. It took over seven months for the investigation to announce its findings but, when it did, the results were damning.

The Anfield club had been accused twice previously in the preceding four years of match rigging and the 1915 plot had been hatched in a Manchester pub with the ringleader alleged to be Jackie Sheldon, a Liverpool player who had played for United between 1910 and 1912. Although it was thought that most of the players in the game were involved, just four from each club were found guilty. Besides Sheldon, the other Liverpool players were Tommy Fairfoul (not sure if that's a joke or not), Tommy Miller and Bob Purcell. The United players included a virtually unknown Reserve player called Laurence Cook but Arthur Whalley had played over a century of games for the club whilst the other two were big names indeed.

Sandy Turnbull scored exactly one hundred goals for the club in 245 games including the goal that brought United their first FA Cup success in 1909. He was also the side's leading goalscorer when United won their first league title in 1908 and he landed a second Championship medal in 1911. Ominously, he was one of several Manchester City players suspended in 1906 over illegal payments.

Enoch 'Knocker' West had joined United prior to the start of the 1910/11 season and went on to score 80 goals in 181 appearances, being leading goalscorer in 1911/12 and 1912/13. He had been the First Division's leading goalscorer in 1907/08 when with Nottingham Forest and had scored almost a hundred goals for them when United bought him and went on to win representative honours for the Football League.

All eight players were banned for life by the FA despite the fact that seven of them had not even played in the game. The life ban, sadly, was exactly that for Sandy Turnbull who was killed in action in France on 3rd May 1917 whilst serving with the Manchester Regiment. The six other players who had not participated in the game had their bans lifted at the cessation of war hostilities in 1919 as recognition of the fact that they had fought for their country. But the life ban stayed on Enoch West, the one player to have appeared in the rigged game. Despite a long battle to clear his name, West was never successful and by the time the ban was lifted at the end of the Second World War thirty years later, it was purely academic. His suspension remains the longest in Football League history.

Johnny Berry – Obituary

Johnny Berry died in a Hampshire hospital on 19th September 1994 aged 68 after a short illness. He had first come to the notice of the legendary Matt Busby when, as a Birmingham City player, he virtually destroyed United single handed with a wing display that culminated in him scoring what many observers of the time reckoned was one of the best goals seen at Old Trafford since the war. When Jimmy Delaney was transferred to Aberdeen in November 1950, Busby was in need of a right winger and nine months later brought the diminutive Berry to Manchester in exchange for £15,000. Berry made his debut for the Reds at Burnden Park in a 1-0 defeat (United at that time invariably lost at Bolton) early in the 1951/52 campaign and, despite that disappointing start to his Old Trafford career, went on to win a First Division Championship medal in his first season.

The next time United won the title, in 1955/56, only Berry and captain Roger Byrne survived from the 1952 side. He went on to capture a third Championship medal as the 'Busby Babes' dominated that period of British football. Although only 5' 5" Berry packed a lethal shot and scored 44 goals in his 273 appearances for United. His fast, tricky wing play earned Berry four caps on the right wing against Argentina, Chile, Uruguay and Sweden during the era of Matthews and Finney, two other outstanding right–wingers who surely denied Berry more international caps. In addition to his three Championship medals, Berry also appeared in the 1957 FA Cup Final before his career was finished by injuries received in the Munich Air Crash.

Manchester United
Player by Player

Stephen Roger BRUCE

Date of Birth: 31st December 1960, Corbridge

Signed for United in 1987 for £800,000 and made his debut against Portsmouth in a game he is unlikely to ever forget as he broke his nose and conceded a penalty in United's 2-1 victory. In the early nineties he was probably the unluckiest player never to win an England cap as Graham Taylor appeared to award them to almost everybody else and his chances now seem to have gone. He does, however, have international honours at both Youth and "B" levels and has been one of the most consistent performers for the Reds over a long period. Many people reckon it was Bruce's two goals during injury time against Sheffield Wednesday in April 1993 that landed United the elusive championship after twenty-six years of toil. Indeed, Bruce has had the knack of scoring a big tally of goals for a central defender and in 1990/91 netted 19, a total many strikers would be proud of. Hailing from the North-East where he learned his football in the famous Wallsend Boys Club youth sides, Bruce began his Football League career with Gillingham and when he made his debut against Blackpool in August 1979 he could hardly have dreamed of the honours he would go on to win in United colours. He was, more or less, an ever-present thereafter clocking up over 200 appearances before signing for Norwich City in 1984 for a fee in the region of £125,000. Whilst at Carrow Road he appeared at Wembley in the Canaries side which beat Sunderland in the 1985 Milk Cup before gaining honours galore with United.

Previous Clubs and Appearance Record

Clubs	Signed	Fee	Appearances			Goals		
			Lge	FLC	FAC	Lge	FLC	FAC
Gillingham	10/78	–	203+2	15	14	29	6	1
Norwich City	8/84	£125,000	141	20	9	14	5	1
Man Utd	12/87	£800,000	162	19	21	26	4	1
FA Premier League Record								
	92/93		42	3	3	5		
	93/94		41	8/1	7	3	2	
	94/95		35	1	5	2		

There is little doubt that Bruce will finish his football career with United and it is likely that he will be found a job on the coaching staff when his days are numbered. In the unlikely event of him wanting to move on then United have a proven track record of not standing in players way when they have given the sort of service that Bruce has given. In view of this and his age, it is most unlikely that United would insist on a fee.

Estimated value: Free Transfer

Nicky BUTT

Date of Birth: 21st January 1975, Manchester

First came to prominence with the Manchester Schoolboys side and his early promise at Youth level was fulfilled when playing in the 'Class of '92' that won the FA Youth Cup. Further Youth honours came his way when he played alongside club mates Chris Casper, Gary Neville and Paul Scholes in the England Under 18 side that participated in the ninth European Under 18 Tournament in 1992/93. After helping England beat France (2-0), Holland (4-1) and Spain (5-1), Butt was unable to play in the Final at Nottingham Forest's City Ground due to injury and had to watch from the stands as his team mates beat Turkey 1-0. Made his first team debut on 21st November 1992 in the home game against Oldham Athletic when he came on as substitute but had to wait almost a further twelve months before making another appearance, again as substitute, in October 1993 against Spurs. His third appearance, also as substitute, was a dream come true for the youngster as it was in the FA Cup semi final at Wembley against Oldham Athletic. 1994/95 saw his graduation with a first full start coming in United's 4-2 win over IFK Gothenburg on 14th September 1994 and his first start in the FAPL coincided with another 4-2 victory, this time at Blackburn Rovers. Strangely, Butt is virtually the same weight as when he first arrived at Old Trafford at the age of fifteen. Although slight of build he is a tigerish tackler but needs to improve on his distribution whilst Youth Coach Eric Harrison professes to his only disappointment regarding Butt as being his difficulty in finding the net at senior level. "He was a regular scorer at Youth and Reserve level and should have had more goals by now in the first team".

Appearance Record

	Appearances			Goals			
	Lge	FLC	FAC	Lge	FLC	FAC	FAC
92/93	-/1						
93/94	-/1		-/1				
94/95	11/10	3	3/1	1			

Estimated value: £2,000,000

Eric CANTONA

Date of Birth: 24th May 1966, Paris

Many critics at the time considered his signing in November 1992 from Leeds United in exchange for £1.2m as confirmation that Alex Ferguson had finally flipped his lid in the frustration of not being able to land the coveted title. The signing of the wayward genius seemed totally out of character for Ferguson who had previously always erred on the side of caution. It was, however, to prove to be the final piece of the jigsaw as United with the talented, but erratic Frenchman, in their side mounted a charge up the table that was to prove unstoppable. The value of Cantona's presence in the side can be gauged by the fact that of his first sixty appearances in United colours, they only lost twice – a remarkable statistic. But Cantona had equal cause to be thankful to United. At last it seemed, after a nomadic football career, that the Frenchman had found peace of mind, at last playing on a stage he thought worthy of his skills. But after early indications that he had put his disciplinary problems behind him, Cantona was sent off at Galatasary, Swindon and Arsenal in 1993/94 and then at Rangers in a pre-season game at the beginning of the 94/95 campaign. Then followed his moment of madness at Crystal Palace which leaves his future at United still clouded. Although he says he is staying, there is little doubt that opposing players and fans alike will attempt to bait the Frenchman into fresh trouble. It remains to be seen whether he regains the enthusiasm for the game that his move to Old Trafford rekindled. He had arrived at Leeds in February 1992 on loan from Nimes via a week's training at Sheffield Wednesday, but the move was soon made permanent in a deal worth £900,000 and with him in their line up, Leeds overtook United to pinch the Championship from under the noses of the Old Trafford faithful. Cantona began his career with Auxerre in 1986 before moving to Marseille during 1988 in a £2.2m deal that was not successful with Cantona making just 40 appearances and spending time on loan at both Montpellier and Bordeaux before moving on to Nimes for £1m in June 1991. Eight months later he was at Leeds and nine months further down the road he was at Old Trafford where it seemed until his sendings off he had found stability for the first time. Even his international career led a chequered existence with him walking out of the French set up at one stage but one thing is for sure, United fans will always have a place in their heart for the man who became the only Frenchman to win English Championship medals with two different clubs

Previous Clubs and Appearance Record

Clubs	Signed	Fee	Appearances			Goals		
			Lge	FLC	FAC	Lge	FLC	FAC
Auxerre			81	23				
Martiques		loan	–	–				
Marseille	1988	£2.2m	55	13				

190

Bordeaux		loan	11	6				
Montpellier		loan	33	10				
Nimes	1991	£1m	n/k	n/k				
Leeds Utd	2/92	£900,000	16		3			

FA Premier League Record

Leeds Utd			13	1		6		
Man Utd	11/92	£1.2m	22			9		
	93/94		34	5	5	18	1	4
	94/95		21		1	12	-	1

Because of his unpredictable nature it is difficult to assess how much a club would be prepared to risk on someone who could walk out after a few weeks. Without this side of his nature Cantona would be in the £10m class but anybody buying him from Old Trafford would almost certainly only want to pay a down payment and then so much per game.

Cantona's Crime Sheet

The uproar which followed Eric Cantona's attack on the Crystal Palace spectator in January was not, of course, the first time that controversy had stalked the Frenchman. His full catalogue of disputes reads as follows:

1987	Fined heavily by Auxerre for punching his own goalkeeper Bruno Martini, giving him a black eye in the process.
1988	Banned for a year by the French Football Federation after calling the former international team coach Henri Michel a "shitbag".
1989	Suspended indefinitely by Marseille after kicking the ball into the crowd, throwing his shirt at the referee and storming off the pitch. Loaned out to Bordeaux and Montpellier.
1990	Smashed his boots into Montpellier team mate Jean Claude Lemoult and was banned for ten days by the club, prompting him to return to Marseille.
1991	Sold to Nimes where he was banned for three games after throwing the ball at the referee. When he appeared at the disciplinary hearing he muttered "Idiots". When asked to repeat himself he walked up to each member of the three man board in turn and shouted "Idiot". The ban was increased to two months and Cantona immediately announced his retirement from the game.
1991	Brought to England by Trevor Francis for a trial at Sheffield Wednesday. Bad weather limited his 'trial' to a six aside game on plastic and when Francis said he wanted to see him play in a eleven side match under proper conditions Cantona said he was insulted and left for Leeds.
1993	Sent off at the end of United's game against Galatasary in Turkey for accusing referee Kurt Rothlisberger of cheating. Involved in the tunnel in an altercation with the Turkish police. Received a four match European ban.

March 1994	Sent off at Swindon and Arsenal in successive games resulting in a five match ban.
June 1994	Cantona is ejected from the Pasadena Rose Bowl for throwing a punch at an official before the World Cup semi-final between Brazil and Sweden on which he was supposed to be acting as summariser for French TV.
August 1994	Sent off against Glasgow Rangers in a curtain raiser to the season at Ibrox Park. Receives a three match ban for his fourth dismissal in nine months.
January 1995	Is dismissed at Crystal Palace and then becomes embroiled in his infamous punch up. Banned for the rest of the season and fined £20,000. The Football Association later add a further £10,000 fine and extend the ban to 30th September. A Court Hearing then sentences Cantona to two weeks in prison for the attack. Amid uproar, Cantona is freed on bail and later has the sentence reduced to 120 hours community service.

Estimated value: £7,500,000

Andrew COLE

Date of Birth: 19th October 1971, Nottingham

Alex Ferguson and Kevin Keegan surprised everybody when the *Magpies'* boss agreed to sell his leading goalscorer to United in exchange for Keith Gillespie and a cool £6m. Cole first came to prominence in the Nottingham Schools side and in December 1985 became an Associated Schoolboy with Arsenal for whom he made his Football League debut against Sheffield United in December 1990 when he came on as a substitute. In May 1992 he represented England at Under 21 level against Czechoslovakia but just two months later was allowed to join Bristol City for £500,000 still having made only the one substitute appearance for the London club. Prior to his move to Bristol, Cole scored three times in thirteen games whilst on loan to Fulham. But it was at Bristol that his career really began to take off with 20 goals in 41 games prompting interest from Kevin Keegan who wanted some more fire power to see his side's promotion bid sealed. Cole joined the Geordies in March 1993 for £1.75m and promptly picked up a First Division Championship medal. His following campaign proved to be nothing short of sensational as he became the first player to score 40 league goals in a season for Newcastle and he finished the country's leading goalscorer to also land the PFA's Young Player of the Year award. Strange to relate, then, that at the time of his transfer to United Cole had not scored in his last nine outings for Newcastle. On joining the Reds, Cole became the first United player to ever score five times in a league game, a feat he performed against Ipswich Town, and soon secured his first England cap against Uruguay in March.

Previous Clubs and Appearance Record

Clubs	Signed	Fee	Appearances			Goals		
			Lge	FLC	FAC	Lge	FLC	FAC
Arsenal	10/89	---	-/1	-	-	-	-	-
Fulham	5/91	Loan	13	-	-	3	-	-
Bristol City	7/92	£0.5m	41	-	-	20	-	-
Newcastle Utd	3/93	£1.75m	64/1	5	4	59	6	1
Man Utd	1/95	£7m	17	-	-	12	-	-
FA Premier League Record								
	93/94		40			34		
Newcastle United	94/95		18	5	1	9	-	

Estimated value: £7,000,000

Ryan Joseph GIGGS

Date of Birth: 29th November 1973, Cardiff

Although born in Cardiff, Ryan Giggs first came under the eye of United fans when he captained England Schoolboys against Scotland at Old Trafford under the name of Ryan Wilson having been brought up in Manchester when his father, good enough at his chosen sport to play for Great Britain, moved to the area to take up Rugby League after a successful Rugby Union career. The young Wilson was actually first spotted by Manchester City and played for one of their junior sides but it was to United that the gifted youngster turned on leaving school. At about this time his mother changed her name to Giggs and that name is now the one on everybody's lips. Giggs was quickly recognised as something very special and was elevated through the ranks at a surprisingly quick rate. He made his first team debut on 2nd March 1991 at the age of 17 when he came on as substitute against Everton in a 2-0 home defeat. By the following season he was a regular, making 38 league appearances and winning a League Cup medal against Notts Forest, a month before he won a FA Youth Cup winners medal against Crystal Palace. Giggs became the youngest ever Welsh full international when he played against Germany on 16th October 1991 aged 17 years 321 days to complete an unusual quartet of home country *youngest* records for United. Duncan Edwards had become the youngest player to play for England, Northern Ireland's Norman Whiteside was the youngest ever player to appear in the Final stages of the World Cup during his days at Old Trafford and the youngest player ever to turn out for Scotland, Denis Law, also later played for the Reds. Giggs also set another record when he became the first player to win the PFA's Young Player of the Year Award in successive seasons, a feat he achieved in 1992 and 1993. He also won the Barclay's Bank Young Eagle of the Year award in 1992.

Previous Clubs and Appearance Record

Clubs	Signed	Fee	Appearances			Goals		
			Lge	FLC	FAC	Lge	FLC	FAC
Man Utd	12/90		33+7	8	1	5	3	
FA Premier League Record								
	92/93		41	2	2	9		2
	93/94		32+6	6+2	7	13	3	1
	94/95		30	-	6/1	1	-	2

No British club could surely afford to prise Giggs away from Old Trafford but Continental clubs would also be looking at the youngster's form towards the end of the season when he didn't really look the finished article. His youth would boost the fee, however, although not to the reported £10m that Italian clubs were said to be prepared to pay.

Estimated value: £7,500,000

194

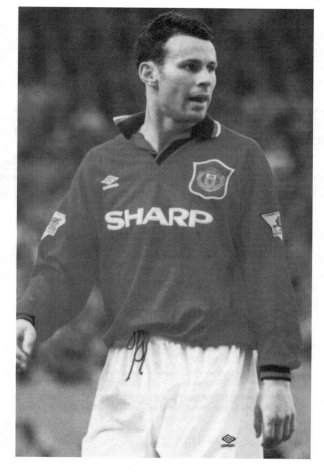

Roy KEANE

Date of Birth: 10 August 1971, Cork

Roy Keane set a record for a transfer deal between English clubs when signing for United in the summer of 1993 for a £3.75m fee from Nottingham Forest. It gave Forest a massive profit on their lay out of £25,000 which it had cost them to bring the former amateur boxer over from Republic of Ireland outfit Cobh Ramblers. Manager Alex Ferguson saw his costliest player as the replacement for his ageing midfield general Bryan Robson, but the younger Keane looked far from that in his early games for United. He was quite definitely not match fit and looked positively overweight during the pre match friendlies and people were quick to question the wisdom of the outlay. As the season progressed, however, Keane's importance to the cause became apparent with his ability not only to win the ball but to then do something constructive with it. Equally vital Keane seems to have developed the knack of arriving late from deep positions to score goals, much like Robson. Having brought Keane over from the comparative obscurity of Cobh Ramblers in 1990, Brian Clough quickly pushed him into his first team line up and in his first full season Keane had a FA Cup runners-up medal after Spurs beat Forest 2-1 after extra-time. The following season he had another runners-up medal when Forest were beaten at Wembley in the League Cup Final by United but Forest did win the Zenith Data Systems Cup that year which led to the honours laden United team nick naming Keane 'ZDS'. He was, of course, to have the last laugh on most of his colleagues when he was one of only three United players to participate in the 1994 World Cup Finals in the USA. Keane, once at Forest, had not taken long to attract the attention of the Republic of Ireland's team boss, Jack Charlton, and he won his first cap against Chile on 22nd May 1991.

Previous Clubs and Appearance Record

Clubs	Signed	Fee	Appearances			Goals		
			Lge	FLC	FAC	Lge	FLC	FAC
Notts Forest	5/90	£25,000	74	12	14	16	5	2
FA Premier League Record								
Notts Forest	92/93		42	5	4	6	1	1
Man Utd	93/94		34+3	6+1	6	5	-	1
	94/95		23+1	1	6/1	2	-	-

Thought by many to be overpriced when bought for £3.75m but has since proved his worth and would now fetch a price well in advance of that figure.

Estimated value: £4,500,000

Denis Joseph IRWIN

Date of Birth: 31st October 1965, Cork

An established international and an important part of United's set up, he made his start by way of the junior ranks at Leeds United, making his debut against Fulham at Elland Road on 21st January 1984 just three months after signing professional forms. After playing some 80 games for the Yorkshire club he received a free transfer in the summer of 1986 from Leeds to Oldham Athletic and is quick to acknowledge the part played in his career by Oldham's Joe Royle and his assistant Willie Donachie. He became a vital part of the best team Oldham ever had and appeared in their 1990 League Cup Final defeat at the hands of Nottingham Forest. In the same season Oldham had two titanic duels against United in the semi-final of the FA Cup and Irwin impressed the United management throughout that campaign. By the end of the summer Ferguson had landed Irwin and he was to play in United's League Cup Finals in 1991 and 1992 to become the only player to appear in the first three League Cup Finals of the 1990's. He was later to make it four League Cup Finals in five years when playing against Aston Villa. By the time he left Boundary Park he was game short of 200 appearances. He had been signed as a right back, a position he plays in regularly when on international duty, and it was in that position that he made his debut for the Reds in August 1990 when United enjoyed a 2-0 home win over Coventry City. Ferguson, however, was struggling with his left back position with Mal Donaghy, Clayton Blackmore, a young Lee Sharpe, and Lee Martin all trying and failing to hold their place in that position. Paul Parker arrived from QPR, ostensibly as a central defender but he was soon converted to right back with Irwin asked to switch to the problematic left back slot, a position he has held ever since for United despite playing right back for his country! He made his international debut just after his move to Old Trafford on 12th September 1990 in Dublin against Morocco and has been first choice ever since and one of only three players to represent United in the 1994 World Cup Finals. The full caps won by Irwin complete the full set as he had already played for his country at School, Youth and Under 21 levels.

Previous Clubs and Appearance Record

Clubs	Signed	Fee	*Appearances*			*Goals*		
			Lge	FLC	FAC	Lge	FLC	FAC
Leeds United	10/83	-	72	5	3	1		
Oldham Athletic	5/86	-	167	19	13	4	3	
Man Utd	6/90	£625,000	72	15	6	4		
FA Premier League Record								
	92/93		40	3	3	5		
	93/94		42	8+1	7	2		2
	94/95		40	2	7	2		4

Estimated value: £3,500,000

197

Brian John McCLAIR

Date of Birth: 8th December 1963, Bellshill

One of the few Scots currently on United's books, McClair joined the Old Trafford set up in 1987 for £850,000 after Celtic had originally been pushing for a fee of £2m. Whilst with Celtic he had netted 99 goals in 145 league appearances after joining the Glasgow club from Motherwell for £100,000 in 1983. Strangely, after dropping out of University to concentrate on making a career in football, McClair had failed to make the grade with his first club, Aston Villa, who were later to beat United in the 1994 Coca Cola Cup Final. After being leading goalscorer in all four seasons he was with Celtic, McClair immediately hit the goal trail at Old Trafford becoming, in his first season at the club, the first Red since George Best to hit twenty League goals in a campaign. However, after the arrival back home of United's prodigal son, Mark Hughes, McClair found goalscoring a lot more difficult and was gradually withdrawn to a more midfield role but still completed a century of goals in the United cause in the last game of the 1991/92 season against Spurs after making his debut at the Dell in a 2-2 draw. McClair played in all three of United's League Cup appearances in the nineties but his first winners medal with the club was in the 1990 FA Cup Final against Crystal Palace quickly followed by his place in the successful European Cup-winners Cup Final side. He won the first of thirty caps against Luxembourg in 1987 shortly before his move to United and was an ever present in the United side that regained the Championship in 1993. With the emergence of Giggs, the signing of Cantona, and the return from illness of Lee Sharpe, however, his role in 1993/94 was mainly as substitute and, given his list of success, it is a great tribute to his loyalty that he stayed throughout a season where he could have commanded a regular first team spot in almost any other FA Premiership side. Alex Ferguson said of him *"If sides were made up of thirteen players out on the pitch, he would be playing every game"*. McClair was voted Scottish Player of the Year in 1987.

Previous Clubs and Appearance Record

Clubs	Signed	Fee	Appearances			Goals		
			Lge	FLC	FAC	Lge	FLC	FAC
Aston Villa	1980	--	-	-	-	-	-	-
Motherwell	1981	--	39	15				
Celtic	1983	£100,000	145	99				
Man Utd	1987	£850,000	190/3	28	24	70	14	11
FA Premier League Record								
	92/93		41/1	3	3	9		
	93/94		12+14	6+1	1+4	1	4	1
	94/95		34+5	3	6+1	5	1	2

Estimated value: £850,000

Gary NEVILLE

Date of Birth: 18th February 1975, Bury

The youngster first came to prominence as captain of the successful 'Class of 92' that captured the FA Youth Cup but was destined to be a professional sportsman from a much earlier age. His father, Neville Neville, is Commercial manager at Bury FC where his mother is Club Secretary whilst his sister, Alison, is an England international at Netball. Adding to the family's sporting links is younger brother Phil who played alongside Gary against Sheffield Wednesday to become the first pair of brothers to play in the same United side since the Greenhoffs some twenty years earlier. His Wembley appearance in the FA Cup Final was his first game on the hallowed turf and was followed a week later by his father and mother visiting the world famous stadium with Bury in the Third Division play-offs. Brother Phil had already beaten the three of them to it by playing there for England Schoolboys. Neville made his FAPL debut for the Reds in the final home game of 93/94 against Coventry City but had already made three brief appearances as substitute in European competition. Injury to Paul Parker in 94/95 gave Neville the opportunity to stake his place for a first team position and he grabbed it to such an extent that by the end of the campaign Terry Venables had included him in his international squad. The youngster has also made a name for himself as a long throw specialist.

Appearance Record

FA Premier League Record

		Appearances			Goals		
Signed	Fee	Lge	FLC	FAC	Lge	FLC	FAC
93/94		1	-	-	-	-	-
94/95		16/2	2/1	4	-	-	-

Estimated value: £2,000,000

Gary Andrew PALLISTER

Date of Birth: 30th June 1965, Ramsgate

When United signed Gary Pallister in August 1989 the fee of £2.3m was not only a club record but a British record. His early games at Old Trafford suggested to many people that he had been overpriced but once he was settled in and, perhaps even more importantly, the team began winning, Pallister went on to prove that he has been a sound investment. His early days were spent in non-league football with Billingham Town and Middlesbrough were the first full-time club to show interest in him. He joined Middlesbrough in November 1984 making his debut in August 1985 at Wimbledon in a 3-0 defeat. The Ayresome Park club, however, were in bad state at that time and were relegated that season to Division Three with Pallister going on loan to Darlington for whom he would have signed had the Feethams outfit been able to afford the £4,000 fee! He returned to Middlesbrough and was a virtual regular as they bounced straight back up with a club record points total of 94 to finish runners-up in 1986/87. By 1988 he had made his international debut against Holland and had also played against Saudi Arabia when United signed him. He made his United debut in a dreadful 2-0 home defeat by Norwich but by the end of his first season in United colours he was the proud owner of a FA Cup winners medal. He was also a member of the United sides that appeared in three League Cup Finals in four years and lifted the European Cup-winners Cup in Rotterdam. After his move to Old Trafford he lost his England place but when his form took an upturn along with United's, he came back into international reckoning with a substitute appearance against Cameroon in 1991 and since 1993 has been a regular member of the England set up to take his number of caps to well into double figures. Pallister was voted the PFA's Player of the Year in 1992.

Previous Clubs and Appearance Record

Clubs	Signed	Fee	Appearances			Goals		
			Lge	FLC	FAC	Lge	FLC	FAC
Middlesbrough	11/84	--	156	10	10	5	1	
Darlington	10/85	loan	7					
Man Utd	8/89	£2.3m	111	20	14	4		
FA Premier League Record								
	92/93		42	3	3	1		
	93/94		41	9	7	1		
	94/95		42	2	7	2		2

Many said United paid over the odds for Pallister but they have had the best out of him for some time now. Still looking as strong as ever and still has a good number of years service left in him.

Estimated value: £3,800,000

Paul Andrew PARKER

Date of Birth: 4th April 1964, West Ham

Capped at Under 21, 'B' and Full international levels by England, Paul Parker arrived at Old Trafford in August 1991 from QPR for a fee of £2m but it took him over eighteen months to register his first goal for the club which came in a 4-1 defeat of Spurs in January 1993. Born in West Ham, Parker made the short trip across London on leaving school to link up with Fulham for whom he made his debut at the age of 17 years and 21 days against Reading in a 2-1 home defeat. That was his only game that season and he managed only five more the following campaign but by 1984 he was a regular and in 1987 he moved the short distance to QPR for £300,000. He was noted as one of the fastest defenders in the game and he made his full international debut for England against Albania in 1989. He became a regular in the England set up and United moved for him in August 1991 but, strangely, after arriving at Old Trafford his international career went on the back burner after just one more appearance against Germany in September 1991. His United debut was against Notts County in a 2-0 Old Trafford victory and he picked up a League Cup winners medal in his first season when playing in the side that beat Notts Forest 1-0. He was also a regular in the side that lifted the Championship for the first time in 1992/93 and his performances during the early part of 1993/94 saw him win back his England shirt.

Previous Clubs and Appearance Record

Clubs	Signed	Fee	Appearances			Goals		
			Lge	FLC	FAC	Lge	FLC	FAC
Fulham	4/82	--	153	16	11	2	1	
QPR	6/87	£300,000	125	14	16	1		
Man Utd	8/91	£2m	26	6	3			
FA Premier League Record								
	92/93		31	2	3	1		
	93/94		39+1	6	7			
	94/95		1+1					

United would almost certainly have to take a loss on what they paid for Parker due to his age and the fact that he missed virtually all the 1994/95 campaign through injury. He has also lost his England place whilst at Old Trafford and is the wrong side of thirty.

Estimated value: £1,000,000

201

Peter Boleslaw SCHMEICHEL

Date of Birth: 18th November 1968, Gladsaxe, Denmark

With respect to Les Sealey who was United's Number 1 when Alex Ferguson plunged for Peter Schmeichel in August 1991, the arrival of the Great Dane solved what has traditionally been a problem position at Old Trafford. Whilst truly great 'keepers such as Frank Swift and Bert Trautmann had prospered at rivals Manchester City, United had always struggled, by and large, in the custodian stakes. Paddy Roche, Pat Dunne, Dave Gaskell, and Ronnie Briggs are just some names that crop up in discussion about United 'keepers but there can be no arguing about Schmeichel's position as the best United 'keeper ever. When Alex Ferguson signed him in August 1991 for £850,000 Schmeichel was already an established Danish international but his best was still to come. After helping United to win the League Cup against Forest in his first season, Schmeichel was to become one of the stars of the 1992 European Nation's Championships when Denmark were let in by the backdoor just days prior to the start of the Championships. The fighting in Yugoslavia brought about the decision to expel them with the Danes taking their place. He kept a clean sheet against England in the Group matches and against Germany in the Final itself to become the first ever United player to win a European Nations' medal. He kept clean sheets in his first four games for the Reds and seventeen in the League in his first season, a figure he bettered by one in United's FA Premier Championship success the following campaign. As well as stopping goals, however, he has also set up on more than one occasion, goals with his magnificent throws to beyond the half way line. Indeed, the extrovert character was seen marauding in the opposing penalty area in the last seconds of the Old Trafford game against Blackburn as United desperately sought an equaliser!

Previous Clubs and Appearance Record

Clubs	Signed	Fee	Appearances			Goals		
			Lge	FLC	FAC	Lge	FLC	FAC
Man Utd	8/91	£850,000	40	6	3			
FA Premier League Record								
	92/93		42	3	3			
	93/94		40	8	7			
	94/95		37		7			

Possibly United's best buy in terms of value for money. Now acknowledged as the best in Europe if not the world and only the fact that there are so many good number 1's about would keep his value below £4m.

Estimated value: £3,750,000

Paul SCHOLES

Date of Birth: 16th November 1974, Salford

Paul Scholes was not, as many think, one of the famed 'Class of '92' but actually came to prominence a year later once the likes of Giggs and McKee had become too old for the Youth team. He played in the 1993 FA Youth Cup Final side that was surprisingly beaten 4-1 on aggregate by Leeds United in front of gates totalling over 60,000 and the same year played in the Final of the European Under 18 Championship when England beat Turkey 1-0. Scholes made a sensational first team debut in September 1994 when he scored both goals in a 2-1 Coca Cola victory. The last player to score twice on a debut for United was no less than Bobby Charlton! His first FAPL appearance saw him score within eleven minutes of coming on as substitute in a 3-2 defeat at Ipswich Town and his goalscoring prowess was to net him seven goals in ten full starts and fifteen substitute appearances. But despite his above average strike rate, Youth Coach Eric Harrison reckons his best position is central midfield because "he has such craft, intelligence, vision and awareness".

Appearance Record

FA Premier League Record

	Appearances			Goals		
	Lge	FLC	FAC	Lge	FLC	FAC
94/95	6/11	3	1/2	5	2	

Estimated value: £2,000,000

Lee Stuart SHARPE

Date of Birth: 27th May 1971, Halesowen

Although still not 23 at the end of the 93/94 season, Lee Sharpe's career has been blighted by a series of serious injuries and illnesses. It is testament to his ability that, despite the lengthy set backs he has taken, Sharpe has by still such a young age accumulated so many honours in the game. A native of Halesowen, Sharpe's first chance in football was as a YTS apprentice at Torquay United but United quickly spotted his potential and after only nine full games plus five more as substitute they plunged £185,000 in May 1988 for the unknown 17 year old. Sharpe signed professional forms for Torquay on his seventeenth birthday but within days was signing for United. He had played his first Football League game for Torquay coming on as substitute in the local *derby* against Exeter City at the ripe old age of 16 in October 1987. Strangely, the first time he actually started a game was also against Exeter in the return fixture at Plainmoor the following February. If anybody harboured any thoughts about the new young signing being one to watch for the future they were quickly put in their place by a young man determined to make his way to the top in the shortest time possible. The 1988/89 season was just five games old when Sharpe was put in against West Ham United at Old Trafford where the Reds enjoyed a 2-0 victory and he was to play over twenty games that season. He also won the first of his eight Under 21 caps that season when he played against Greece in Patras on 7th February 1989 and he went on to become the most capped United player at Under 21 level other than former 'keeper Gary Bailey. But whereas Bailey won most of his caps as an 'over age' player, Sharpe had won all his prior to his 20th birthday. He missed the first big chunk of his fledgling career when he was out for the second half of the 1989/90 campaign but by September 1990 he was back and was to play a significant part in getting United to the League Cup Final, scoring against Liverpool, netting a hat-trick against Arsenal at Highbury and two of the three goals by which United beat Leeds in the semi-final. His form had not gone unnoticed at international level and he became the youngest player to represent England since the late Duncan Edwards when he played against the Republic of Ireland on 27/3/91, still two months short of his 20th birthday. Despite missing a further eight months between April 91 and November 91, and a total of six months during the first two FAPL competitions, Sharpe has still managed to total over 150 appearances for United. Sharpe was voted the PFA's *Young Player of the Year* in 1991.

Previous Clubs and Appearance Record

Clubs	Signed	Fee	Appearances			Goals		
			Lge	FLC	FAC	Lge	FLC	FAC
Torquay United	5/88	--	14	--	--	3	--	--

Manchester Utd	5/88	£185,000	77	15	10	3	7
FA Premier League Record							
92/93			27	--	3	1	
93/94			26+4	2+2	1+2	9	2	3
94/95			26+2	0+2	6+1	3		1

Very difficult to estimate his worth on the transfer market due to his history of injury and illness. Any buyer would probably insist on a down payment only with a fee per game thereafter.

Estimated value: £3,000,000

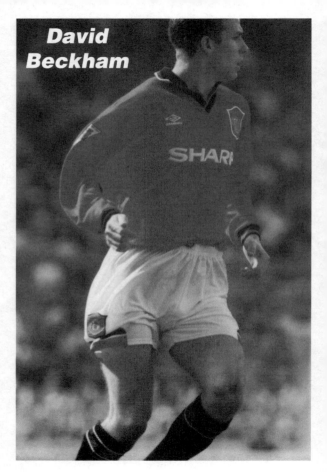

David
Beckham

FA Carling Premiership
Stadium Guide

Arsenal

Arsenal Stadium, Highbury, London N5

Nickname: Gunners
All-seater Capacity: 39,497

Colours: Red/White sleeves, White, Red
Pitch: 110 yds x 71 yds

Directions:

From North: M1, J2 follow sign for the City. After Holloway Road station (c 6 miles) take third left into Drayton Park. Then right into Aubert Park after ¼ mile and 2nd left into Avenell Road.

From South: Signs for Bank of England then Angel from London Bridge. Right at traffic lights towards Highbury roundabout. Follow Holloway Road then third right into Drayton Park, thereafter as above. *From West:* A40(M) to A501 ring road. Left at Angel to Highbury roundabout, then as above.

Rail: Drayton Park/Finsbury Park.   Tube (Piccadilly line): Arsenal.

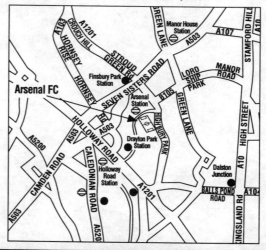

Club: 0171 226 0304 Recorded: 0171 359 0131

Aston Villa

Villa Park, Trinity Rd, Birmingham, B6 6HE

Nickname: The Villains
All-seater Capacity: 40,530

Colours: Claret/Blue, White, Blue/Claret
Pitch: 115 yds x 75 yds

Directions:

M6 J6, follow signs for Birmingham NE. third exit at roundabout then right into Ashton Hall Rd after ½ mile.
Rail: Witton.

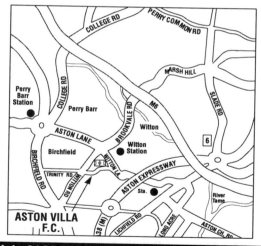

Club: 0121 327 2299 Ticket Info: 0891 121848

Blackburn Rovers

Ewood Park, Blackburn, BB2 4JF

Nickname: Blue and Whites
All-seater Capacity: 30,591

Colours: Blue/White, White, Blue
Pitch: 115yds x 76yds

Directions:

From North, South & West: M6 J31 follow signs for Blackburn then Bolton Road.
Turn left after 1½ miles into Kidder Street.
From East: A677 or A679 following signs for Bolton Road, then as above.
Rail: Blackburn Central.

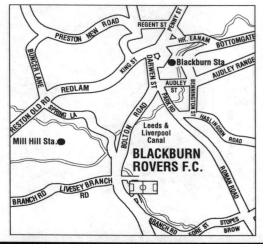

Club: 01254 698888 Ticket Info: 0891 121179

Bolton Wanderers

Burden Park, Bolton

Nickname: The Trotters   **Colours:** White/Navy, Navy, Navy
All-seater Capacity: 25,000

Directions:

From North: M61, J5. Follow signs towards Farnworth B653 onto Manchester
Road. After half mile turn left into Croft Lane.
From South, East & West: M62, J14 onto M61. Leave M61 at roundabout end
(about two miles). Take first exit on roundabout – B6536. After two miles turn right
into Croft Lane.

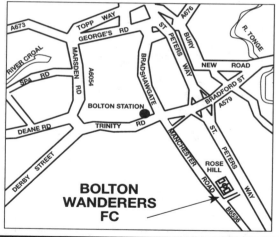

Club: 01204 389200 Ticket Info: 01204 521101

Chelsea

Stamford Bridge, London SW6

Nickname: The Blues
All-seater Capacity: 41,050

Colours: Royal Blue, Royal Blue, White
Pitch: 110 yds x 72 yds

Directions:

From North & East: A1 or M1 to central London and Hyde Park corner. Follow signs for Guildford (A3) and then Knightsbridge (A4). After a mile turn left into Fulham Road. *From South:* A219 Putney Bridge then follow signs for West End joining A308 and then into Fulham Road. *From West:* M4 then A4 to central London. Follow A3220 to Westminster, after ¼ mile right at crossroads into Fulham Road.

Rail/Tube: Fulham Broadway (District line).

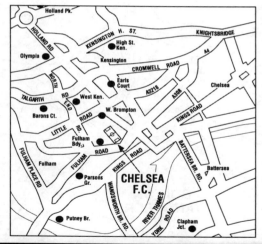

Club: 0171 385 5545 Ticket Info: 0891 121011

Coventry City

Highfield Road Stadium, King Richard Street, Coventry, CV2 4FW

Nickname: Sky Blues
All-seater Capacity: 24,021

Colours: All Sky Blue
Pitch: 110 yds x 75 yds

Directions:

From North & West: M6 J3, after 3½ miles turn left into Eagle Street and straight on to Swan Lane. *From South & East:* M1 to M45 then A45 to Ryton-on-Dunsmore where third exit at roundabout is A423. After one mile turn right into B4110. Left at T-junction then right into Swan Lane.
Rail: Coventry.

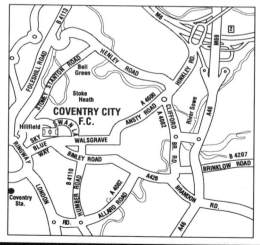

Club: 01203 223535

Everton

Goodison Park, Liverpool, L4 4EL

Nickname: The Toffees
All-seater Capacity: 40,160

Colours: Royal Blue, White, Blue
Pitch: 112 yds x 78 yds

Directions:

From North: M6 J8 take A58 to A580 and follow into Walton Hall Avenue.
From South & East: M6 J21A to M62, turn right into Queen's Drive then, after 4 miles, left into Walton Hall Avenue.
From West: M53 through Wallasey Tunnel, follow signs for Preston on A580. Walton Hall Avenue is signposted.
Rail: Liverpool Lime Street

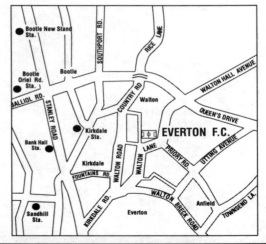

Club: 0151 521 2020 Ticket Info: 0891 121599

Leeds United

Elland Road, Leeds, LS11 0ES

Nickname: United
All-seater Capacity: 39,704

Colours: All White
Pitch: 117 yds x 76 yds

Directions:

From North & East: A58, A61, A63 or A64 into city centre and then onto M621. Leave motorway after 1½ miles onto A643 and Elland Road.
From West: take M62 to M621 then as above.
From South: M1 then M621 then as above.
Rail: Leeds City.

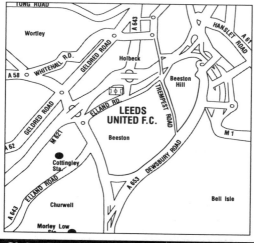

Club: 0113 271 6037 Info: 0891 121180

Liverpool

Anfield Road, Liverpool 4 0TH

Nickname: Reds or Pool
All-seater Capacity: 44,243

Colours: All Red/White Trim
Pitch: 110 yds x 75 yds

Directions:

From North: M6 J8, follow A58 to Walton Hall Avenue and pass Stanley Park turning left into Anfield Road. *From South/East:* To end of M62 and right into Queens Drive (A5058). After three miles turn left into Utting Avenue and right after one mile into Anfield Road. *From West:* M53 through Wallasey Tunnel, follow signs for Preston then turn into Walton Hall Avenue and right into Anfield Road before Stanley Park. *Rail:* Liverpool Lime Street.

Club: 0151 263 2361 Match: 0151 260 9999

Manchester City

Maine Road, Moss Side, Manchester, M14 7WN

Nickname: Blues or City
All-seater Capacity: 45,053

Colours: Sky Blue, White, Sky Blue
Pitch: 117 yds x 77 yds

Directions:

From North & West: M61 to M63 J9. Follow signs into Manchester (A5103). Right after three miles into Claremont Road. Right after 400 yards into Maine Road.
From South: M6 J19 to A556 joining M56. Leave at J3 following A5103 as above.
From East: M62 J17 following signs for Manchester Airport (A56 and A57(M)). Then follow Birmingham signs to A5103. Left into Claremont Road after one mile then right into Maine Road. *Rail:* Manchester Piccadilly.

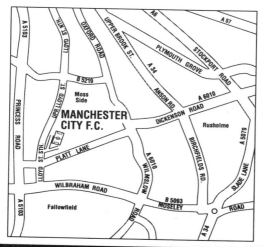

Club: 0161 226 1124 Ticket Info: 0891 121591

Middlesbrough

Cellnet Riverside Stadium, Middlesbrough Harbour

Nickname: The Boro

All-seater Capacity: 31,000

Colours: Red with White/Black, White, Red/Black

Pitch:

Directions:

From South: Al onto A19. Follow signs to Teesside/Middlesbrough and then to Cellnet Riverside Stadium.

From West: A66 towards Middlesbrough and then follow signs off to Cellnet Riverside Stadium.

From North: Take A19 towards Teesside/Middlesbrough. Cross Tees Bridge and join A66 eastbound. Follow signs to Cellnet Riverside Stadium at harbour.

Rail: Middlesbrough (600 yards).

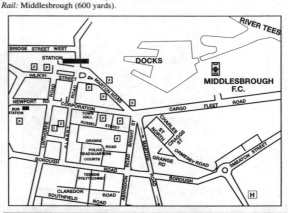

Club: 01642 819659 Tickets: 01642 815996

Newcastle United

St James' Park, Newcastle-upon-Tyne, NE1 4ST

Nickname: Magpies
All-seater Capacity: 36,401

Colours: Black/White, Black, Black
Pitch: 115 yds x 75 yds.

Directions:

From South: Follow A1, A68 then A6127 to cross the Tyne. At roundabout, first exit into Moseley Street. Left into Neville Street, right at end for Clayton Street and then Newgate Street. Left for Leaze Park Road. *From West:* A69 towards city centre. Left into Clayton Street for Newgate Street, left again for Leaze Park Road. *From North:* A1 then follow signs for Hexham until Percy Street. Right into Leaze Park Road.

Rail: Newcastle Central (½ mile).

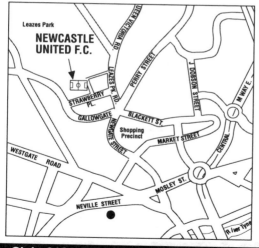

219

Nottingham Forest

City Ground, Nottingham, NG2 5FJ

Nickname: The Reds or Forest
All-seater Capacity: 30,500

Colours: Red, White, Red
Pitch: 115 yds x 78 yds

Directions:

From North: Leave the M1 J26 for the A610 and the A606. Left into Radcliffe Road for the ground. *From South:* Leave the M1 J24 to Trent Bridge, turning right into Radcliffe Road. *From East:* A52 to West Bridgeford and right for the ground. *From West:* A52 to A606 and then as for the North.
Rail: Nottingham.

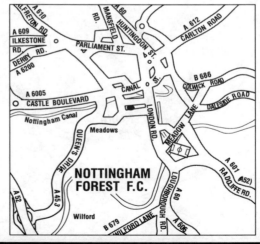

Club: 0115 952 6000 Tickets: 0115 952 6002

Queens Park Rangers

South Africa Road, W12 7PA

Nickname: Rangers or Rs
All-seater Capacity: 19,300

Colours: Blue/White, White, White
Pitch: 112 yds x 72 yds

Directions:

From North: M1 to north circular A406 towards Neasden. Left onto A404 for Hammersmith, past White City Stadium then right into South Africa Road. *From South:* A3 across Putney Bridge and signs for Hammersmith. A219 to Shepherd's Bush and join A4020 towards Acton. Turn right after ¼ mile into Loftus Road. *From East:* From A40(M) towards M41 roundabout. Take third exit at roundabout to A4020 then as above. *From West:* M4 to Chiswick then A315 and A402 to Shepherd's Bush joining A4020 then as for South.

Rail: Shepherd's Bush   *Tube:* White City (Central Line).

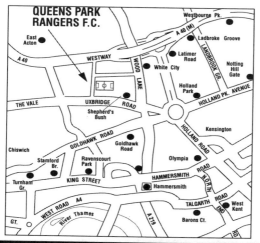

Club: 0181-743 0262 Info: 0181 749 7798

Sheffield Wednesday

Hillsborough, Sheffield, S6 1SW

Nickname: The Owls
All-seater Capacity: 40,000

Colours: Blue/White, Blue, Blue
Pitch: 115 yds x 75 yds

Directions:

From North: M1 J34 then A6109 to Sheffield. At roundabout after 1½ miles take third exit then turn left after three miles into Harries Road.

From South & East: M1 J31 or 33 to A57. At roundabout take Prince of Wales Road exit. A further six miles then turn left into Herries Road South.

From West: A57 to A6101 then turn left after four miles at T junction into Penistone Road.

Rail: Sheffield Midland.

Club: 0114 243 3122 Tickets: 0114 233 7233

Southampton

The Dell, Milton Road, Southampton, SO9 4XX

Nickname: The Saints
All-seater Capacity: 15,288

Colours: Red/White, Black, Black
Pitch: 110 yds x 72 yds

Directions:

From North: A33 into The Avenue then right into Northlands Road. Right at the end into Archer's Road. *From East:* M27 then A334 and signs for Southampton along A3024. Follow signs for the West into Commercial Road, right into Hill Lane then first right into Milton Road.
From West: Take A35 then A3024 towards city centre. Left into Hill Lane and first right into Milton Road.
Rail: Southampton Central.

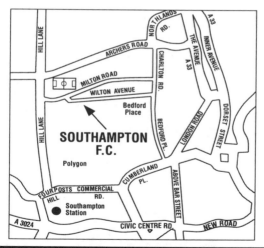

Club: 01703 220505 Tickets: 01703 228575

223

Tottenham Hotspur

748 High Road, Tottenham, London, N17 0AP

Nickname: Spurs
All-seater Capacity: 30,246

Colours: White, Navy Blue, White
Pitch: 110 yds x 73 yds

Directions:

A406 North Circular to Edmonton. At traffic lights follow signs for Tottenham along A1010 then Fore Street for ground.
Rail: White Hart Lane (adjacent).
Tube: Seven Sisters (Victoria Line) or Manor House (Piccadilly Line).

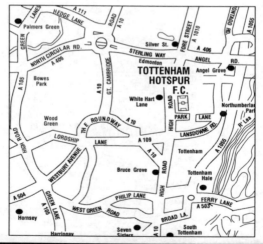

Club: 0181 365 5000 Tickets: 0181 365 5050

West Ham United

Boleyn Ground, Green Street, Upton Park, London E13

Nickname: The Hammers

All-seater Capacity: 24,500

Colours: Claret, White, White

Pitch: 112 yds x 72 yds

Directions:

From North & West: North Circular to East Ham then Barking Rd for 1½ miles until traffic lights. Turn right into Green Street.

From South: Blackwall Tunnel then A13 to Canning Town. Then A124 to East Ham, Green Street on left after two miles.

From East: A13 then A117 and A124. Green Street on right after ¼ miles.

Rail/Tube: Upton Park (¼ mile).

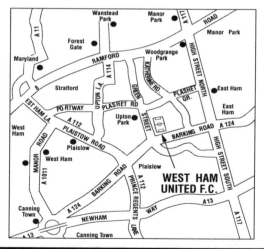

Club: 0181 548 2748 Tickets: 0181 548 2700

Wimbledon

Selhurst Park, South Norwood, London E5

Nickname: The Dons
All-seater Capacity: 26,995

Colours: All Blue with Yellow trim
Pitch: 110 yds x 74 yds

Directions:

From North: M1/A1 to North Circular A406 and Chiswick. Follow South Circular A205 to Wandsworth then A3 and A214 towards Streatham and A23. Then left onto B273 for one mile and turn left at end into High Street and Whitehorse Lane.
From South: On A23 follow signs for Crystal Palace along B266 going through Thornton Heath into Whitehorse Lane. *From East:* A232 Croydon Road to Shirley joining A215, Norwood Road. Turn left after 2¹/₂ miles into Whitehorse Lane.
From West: M4 to Chiswick then as above.
Rail: Selhurst, Norwood Junction or Thornton Heath.

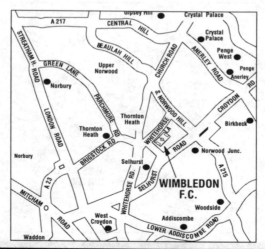

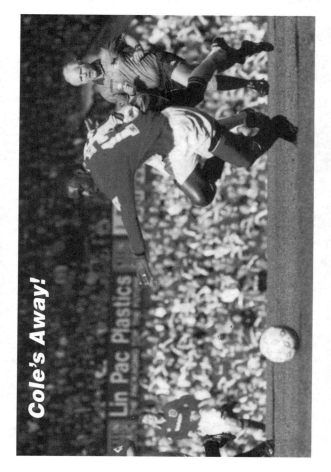

Cole's Away!

All-time Records and Statistics

United Against Other Clubs – *Football Alliance*

Club	Home						Away				
	P	W	D	L	F	A	W	D	L	F	A
Ardwick	2	1	0	0	3	1	0	1	0	2	2
Birmingham St George	6	2	0	1	6	4	1	0	2	5	12
Bootle	6	3	0	0	9	1	0	1	2	2	10
Burton Swifts	2	1	0	0	3	1	0	0	1	2	3
Crewe Alexandra	6	2	0	1	12	8	2	1	0	5	2
Darwen	4	2	0	0	6	3	0	0	2	2	6
Grimsby Town	6	1	1	1	6	5	0	1	2	3	12
Lincoln City	2	1	0	0	10	1	1	0	0	6	1
Long Eaton	2	1	0	0	3	0	1	0	0	3	1
Nottingham Forest	6	0	2	1	2	3	1	0	2	5	12
Sheffield Wednesday	6	0	2	1	3	4	2	0	1	7	6
Small Heath	6	2	1	0	15	5	0	1	2	4	6
Stoke City	2	1	0	0	0	1	0	0	1	1	2
Sunderland Albion	4	1	0	1	5	6	0	0	2	1	4
Walsall Town Swifts	6	2	1	0	10	4	1	0	2	5	7
Total	66	20	7	6	93	47	9	5	19	53	86

United Against Other Clubs – *Football League*

Manchester United met 78 other clubs during their time in the Football League. The following list gives their record against each of those 78 clubs. Where clubs have changed their names, the latest name only is used but the list includes all games against that club under either name (ie Small Heath became Birmingham City, therefore the record shown below in respect of Birmingham City also includes games against Small Heath).

Club	Home						Away				
	P	W	D	L	F	A	W	D	L	F	A
Accrington Stanley	2	0	1	0	3	3	0	1	0	2	2
Arsenal	146	41	20	12	143	70	18	11	44	84	151
Aston Villa	118	37	12	10	127	59	14	15	30	88	128
Barnsley	30	12	2	1	35	7	5	7	3	20	14
Birmingham City	80	23	8	9	60	34	10	15	15	53	62
Blackburn Rovers	62	15	8	8	61	38	10	7	14	55	66
Blackpool	80	26	8	6	83	34	17	9	14	66	60
Bolton Wanderers	92	23	9	14	78	53	11	11	24	52	88

Club	Home						Away				
	P	W	D	L	F	A	W	D	L	F	A
Bradford Park Avenue	18	5	0	4	17	12	3	1	5	13	24
Bradford City	42	13	6	2	35	9	5	7	9	26	28
Brentford	10	2	1	2	9	7	2	1	2	10	12
Brighton & Hove Alb	8	3	1	0	7	2	2	1	1	5	2
Bristol City	34	9	3	5	30	18	5	7	5	17	21
Bristol Rovers	2	1	0	0	2	0	0	1	0	1	1
Burnley	102	30	8	13	116	66	17	8	26	64	91
Burton United	24	9	3	0	39	6	5	3	4	22	23
Burton Wanderers	6	1	1	1	5	3	1	0	2	3	7
Bury	38	9	2	8	24	23	10	5	4	34	23
Cardiff City	26	5	6	2	28	19	8	1	4	22	18
Charlton Athletic	41	13	4	3	45	20	8	5	8	27	33
Chelsea	101	21	16	13	81	47	25	12	14	97	75
Chesterfield	20	10	0	0	26	7	3	1	6	15	15
Coventry City	56	15	7	6	49	21	8	8	12	34	37
Crewe Alexandra	4	2	0	0	11	1	2	0	0	4	0
Crystal Palace	24	8	2	2	22	7	5	3	4	21	22
Darwen	12	4	1	1	20	5	2	2	2	7	8
Derby County	76	19	10	9	70	39	9	13	16	58	84
Doncaster Rovers	8	3	1	0	16	0	1	2	1	3	6
Everton	126	32	17	14	107	64	12	16	35	71	140
Fulham	42	17	3	1	44	15	6	7	8	34	32
Gainsborough Trinity	20	8	2	0	26	7	5	3	2	10	7
Glossop North End	14	6	1	0	20	5	5	1	1	14	5
Grimsby Town	37	13	2	4	42	26	4	4	10	26	37
Huddersfield Town	42	11	9	1	46	21	7	6	8	32	39
Hull City	16	7	1	0	22	4	2	2	4	8	13
Ipswich Town	40	13	2	5	31	13	6	4	10	26	40
Leeds City	2	0	0	1	0	3	1	0	0	3	1
Leeds United	68	13	13	8	51	32	11	12	11	41	40
Leicester City	96	32	11	5	115	51	12	11	25	72	90
Leyton Orient	12	3	3	0	13	5	3	1	2	5	3
Lincoln City	28	10	3	1	34	12	3	1	10	12	28
Liverpool	118	27	21	11	100	55	13	16	30	62	103
Loughborough Town	10	5	0	0	23	2	2	2	1	6	5
Luton Town	38	18	0	1	58	10	9	7	3	30	16
Manchester City	116	23	21	14	87	74	18	22	18	75	86
Middlesbrough	74	23	6	8	77	47	12	9	16	56	73
Millwall	12	5	1	0	22	3	3	2	1	6	4
Nelson	2	0	0	1	0	1	1	0	0	2	0
New Brighton Town	6	2	0	1	4	3	2	0	1	7	3

Club	Home						Away				
	P	W	D	L	F	A	W	D	L	F	A
Newcastle United	110	33	13	9	125	67	17	12	26	78	111
Northampton Town	2	1	0	0	6	2	0	1	0	1	1
Norwich City	42	13	5	3	34	10	9	6	6	37	28
Nottingham Forest	86	24	11	8	90	54	13	10	20	55	68
Notts County	48	11	9	4	41	27	9	5	10	33	33
Oldham Athletic	32	9	3	4	32	17	5	6	5	31	23
Oxford United	8	4	0	0	13	3	2	0	2	5	4
Plymouth Argyle	12	4	1	1	12	7	2	1	3	8	13
Port Vale	36	16	1	1	52	10	5	4	9	24	27
Portsmouth	44	13	3	6	38	21	5	9	8	23	30
Preston North End	66	15	11	7	51	35	11	9	13	56	55
Queen's Park Rangers	30	12	2	1	33	11	4	6	5	18	22
Rotherham United	6	3	0	0	9	2	1	1	1	5	5
Sheffield United	82	26	4	11	83	47	11	9	21	49	74
Sheffield Wednesday	96	30	12	6	91	46	11	9	28	62	89
Southshields	6	2	1	0	5	1	2	0	1	5	2
Southampton	64	18	7	7	56	35	9	12	11	38	37
Stockport County	18	7	2	0	21	7	2	0	7	8	11
Stoke City	70	17	13	5	63	29	9	11	15	40	60
Sunderland	96	25	12	11	96	60	12	11	25	61	104
Tottenham Hotspurs	110	34	11	10	104	58	13	20	22	67	99
Walsall	12	5	1	0	24	1	2	3	1	7	7
Watford	12	4	2	0	13	4	2	2	2	4	7
West Bromwich Alb	100	26	13	11	102	65	13	11	26	72	98
West Ham United	80	24	6	10	91	48	7	10	23	49	70
Wimbledon	12	3	2	1	5	3	2	2	2	9	8
Wolverhampton Wndrs	80	26	5	9	80	44	10	9	21	55	81
York City	2	1	0	0	2	1	1	0	0	1	0
Total	3556	410		3550		532		784		3057	
		1036		332		1784		462		2406	

United's Full League Record

Year	Home						Away						
	P	W	D	L	F	A	W	D	L	F	A	Pts	Pos
Football Alliance													
1889/90	22	7	0	4	27	11	2	2	7	13	34	20	8th
1890/91	22	5	3	3	25	22	2	0	9	12	31	17	9th
1891/92	22	7	4	0	41	14	5	3	3	28	19	31	2nd
Football League – First Division													
1892/93	30	6	3	6	39	35	0	3	12	11	50	18	16th
1893/94	30	5	2	8	29	33	1	0	14	7	39	14	16th
Second Division													
1894/95	30	9	6	0	52	18	6	2	7	26	26	38	3rd
1895/96	30	12	2	1	48	15	3	1	11	18	42	33	6th
1896/97	30	11	4	0	37	10	6	1	8	19	24	39	2nd
1897/98	30	11	2	2	42	10	5	4	6	22	25	38	4th
1898/99	34	12	4	1	51	14	7	1	9	16	29	43	4th
1899/1900	34	15	1	1	44	11	5	3	9	19	16	44	4th
1900/01	34	11	3	3	31	9	3	1	13	11	29	32	10th
1901/02	34	10	2	5	27	12	1	4	12	11	41	28	15th
1902/03	34	9	4	4	32	15	6	4	7	21	23	38	5th
1903/04	34	14	2	1	42	14	6	6	5	23	19	48	3rd
1904/05	34	16	0	1	60	10	8	5	4	21	20	53	3rd
1905/06	38	15	3	1	55	13	13	3	3	35	15	62	2nd
First Division													
1906/07	38	10	6	3	33	15	7	2	10	20	41	42	8th
1907/08	38	15	1	3	43	19	8	5	6	38	29	52	1st
1908/09	38	10	3	6	37	33	5	4	10	21	35	37	13th
1909/10	38	14	2	3	41	20	5	5	9	28	41	45	5th
1910/11	38	14	4	1	47	18	8	4	7	25	22	52	1st
1911/12	38	9	5	5	29	19	4	6	9	16	41	37	13th
1912/13	38	13	3	3	41	14	6	5	8	28	29	46	4th
1913/14	38	8	4	7	27	23	7	2	10	25	39	36	14th
1914/15	38	8	6	5	27	19	1	6	12	19	43	30	18th
1919/20	42	6	8	7	20	17	7	6	8	34	33	40	12th
1920/21	42	9	4	8	34	26	6	6	9	30	42	40	13th
1921/22	42	7	7	7	25	26	1	5	15	16	47	28	22nd
Second Division													
1922/23	42	10	6	5	25	17	7	8	6	26	19	48	4th
1923/24	42	10	7	4	37	15	3	7	11	15	29	40	14th
1924/25	42	17	3	1	40	6	6	8	7	17	17	57	2nd

Year		Home					Away						
	P	W	D	L	F	A	W	D	L	F	A	Pts	Pos
First Division													
1925/26	42	12	4	5	40	26	7	2	12	26	47	44	9th
1926/27	42	9	8	4	29	19	4	6	11	23	45	40	15th
1927/28	42	12	6	3	51	27	4	1	16	21	53	39	18th
1928/29	42	8	8	5	32	23	6	5	10	34	53	41	12th
1929/30	42	11	4	6	39	34	4	4	13	28	54	38	17th
1930/31	42	6	6	9	30	37	1	2	18	23	78	22	22nd
Second Division													
1931/32	42	12	3	6	44	31	5	5	11	27	41	42	12th
1932/33	42	11	5	5	40	24	4	8	9	31	44	43	6th
1933/34	42	9	3	9	29	33	5	3	13	30	52	34	20th
1934/35	42	16	2	3	50	21	7	2	12	26	34	50	5th
1935/36	42	16	3	2	55	16	6	9	6	30	27	56	1st
First Division													
1936/37	42	8	9	4	29	26	2	3	16	26	52	32	21st
Second Division													
1937/38	42	15	3	3	50	18	7	6	8	32	32	53	2nd
First Division													
1938/39	42	7	9	5	30	20	4	7	10	27	45	38	14th
1946/47	42	17	3	1	61	19	5	9	7	34	35	56	2nd
1947/48	42	11	7	3	50	27	8	7	6	31	21	52	2nd
1948/49	42	11	7	3	40	20	10	4	7	37	24	53	2nd
1949/50	42	11	5	5	42	20	7	9	5	27	24	50	4th
1950/51	42	14	4	3	42	16	10	4	7	32	24	56	2nd
1951/52	42	15	3	3	55	21	8	8	5	40	31	57	1st
1952/53	42	11	5	5	35	30	7	5	9	34	42	46	8th
1953/54	42	11	6	4	41	27	7	6	8	32	31	48	4th
1954/55	42	12	4	5	44	30	8	3	10	40	44	47	5th
1955/56	42	18	3	0	51	20	7	7	7	32	31	60	1st
1956/57	42	14	4	3	55	25	14	4	3	48	29	64	1st
1957/58	42	10	4	7	45	31	6	7	8	40	44	43	9th
1958/59	42	14	4	3	58	27	10	3	8	45	39	55	2nd
1959/60	42	13	3	5	53	30	6	4	11	49	50	45	7th
1960/61	42	14	5	2	58	20	4	4	13	30	56	45	7th
1961/62	42	10	3	8	44	31	5	6	10	28	44	39	15th
1962/63	42	6	6	9	36	38	6	4	11	31	43	34	19th
1963/64	42	15	3	3	54	19	8	4	9	36	43	53	2nd
1964/65	42	16	4	1	52	13	10	5	6	37	26	61	1st
1965/66	42	12	8	1	50	20	6	7	8	34	39	51	4th

232

Year			Home						Away					
	P	W	D	L	F	A	W	D	L	F	A	Pts	Pos
1966/67	42	17	4	0	51	13	7	8	6	33	32	60	1st
1967/68	42	15	2	4	49	21	9	6	6	40	34	56	2nd
1968/69	42	13	5	3	38	18	2	7	12	19	35	42	11th
1969/70	42	8	9	4	37	27	6	8	7	29	34	45	8th
1970/71	42	9	6	6	29	24	7	5	9	36	42	43	8th
1971/72	42	13	2	6	39	26	6	8	7	30	35	48	8th
1972/73	42	9	7	5	24	19	3	6	12	20	41	37	18th
1973/74	42	7	7	7	23	20	3	5	13	15	28	32	21st
Second Division													
1974/75	42	17	3	1	45	12	9	6	6	21	18	61	1st
First Division													
1975/76	42	16	4	1	40	13	7	6	8	28	29	56	3rd
1976/77	42	12	6	3	41	22	6	5	10	30	40	47	6th
1977/78	42	9	6	6	32	23	7	4	10	35	40	42	10th
1978/79	42	9	7	5	29	25	6	8	7	31	38	45	9th
1979/80	42	17	3	1	43	8	7	7	7	22	27	58	2nd
1980/81	42	9	11	1	30	14	6	7	8	21	22	48	8th
1981/82	42	12	6	3	27	9	10	6	5	32	20	78	3rd
1982/83	42	14	7	0	39	10	5	6	10	17	28	70	3rd
1983/84	42	14	3	4	43	18	6	11	4	28	23	74	4th
1984/85	42	13	6	2	47	13	9	4	8	30	34	76	4th
1985/86	42	12	5	4	35	12	10	5	6	35	24	76	4th
1986/87	42	13	3	5	38	18	1	11	9	14	27	56	11th
1987/88	40	14	5	1	41	17	9	7	4	30	21	81	2nd
1988/89	38	10	5	4	27	13	3	7	9	18	22	51	11th
1989/90	38	8	6	5	26	14	5	3	11	20	33	48	13th
1990/91	38	11	4	4	34	17	5	8	6	24	28	59	6th
1991/92	42	12	7	2	34	13	9	8	4	29	20	78	2nd
FA Premier League													
1992/93	42	14	5	2	39	14	10	7	4	28	17	84	1st
1993/94	42	14	6	1	39	13	13	5	3	41	25	92	1st
1994/95	42	16	4	1	42	4	10	6	5	35	24	88	2nd

Players' Career Records

NB League appearances/goals entries include games played in the Football Alliance but not in the FA Premier League which has its own column. Where an asterisk * appears in the European column this denotes the number of 'Test Match' appearances made in the early days of the Football League's promotion and relegation method, not European games. The chart does not include wartime games when innumerable players turned out for whichever club they were stationed closest to at the time.

Player	FAPL App	FAPL Goals	League App	League Goals	FACup App	FACup Goals	LgeCup App	LgeCup Goals	Europe App	Europe Goals	Totals App	Totals Goals
A Ainsworth (1933)	–	–	2	–	–	–	–	–	–	–	2	–
J Aitken (1895)	–	–	2	1	–	–	–	–	–	–	2	1
G Albison (1920)	–	–	–	–	1	–	–	–	–	–	1	–
AR Albiston (1974/88)	–	–	364/15	6	36	–	38/2	1	26/1	–	464/18	7
JT Allan (1904/06)	–	–	35	21	1	1	–	–	–	–	36	22
RA Allen (1950/52)	–	–	75	–	5	–	–	–	–	–	80	–
A Allman (1914)	–	–	12	–	–	–	–	–	–	–	12	–
A Ambler (1899/1900)	–	–	10	–	–	–	–	–	–	–	10	–
G Anderson (1911/14)	–	–	80	37	6	2	–	–	–	–	86	39
J Anderson (1947/48)	–	–	33	1	6	1	–	–	–	–	39	2
T Anderson (1972/73)	–	–	13/6	2	–	–	–	–	–	–	13/6	2
VA Anderson (1987/91)	–	–	50/4	2	7	2	6/1	–	1	–	64/5	4
WJ Anderson (1963/66)	–	–	7/2	–	2	–	–	–	1	–	10/2	–
TA Arkesden (1902/05)	–	–	70	28	9	5	–	–	–	–	79	33
B Asquith (1939)	–	–	1	–	–	–	–	–	–	–	1	–
JE Astley (1925/26)	–	–	2	–	–	–	–	–	–	–	2	–
J Aston snr (1946/53)	–	–	253	29	29	1	–	–	–	–	282	30
J Aston jnr (1964/71)	–	–	139/16	25	5/2	1	12/3	–	8	1	164/21	27
GR Bailey (1978/87)	–	–	294	–	31	–	28	–	20	–	373	–
D Bain (1922/23)	–	–	22	9	1	–	–	–	–	–	23	9
J Bain (1899)	–	–	2	–	–	–	–	–	–	–	2	–
J Bain (1924/27)	–	–	4	1	–	–	–	–	–	–	4	1
W Bainbridge (1945)	–	–	–	–	1	1	–	–	–	–	1	1
HC Baird (1936/37)	–	–	49	15	4	3	–	–	–	–	53	18
T Baldwin (1974)	–	–	2	–	–	–	–	–	–	–	2	–

Player	FAPL App	FAPL Goals	League App	League Goals	FACup App	FACup Goals	LgeCup App	LgeCup Goals	Europe App	Europe Goals	Totals App	Totals Goals
J Ball (1947/49)	-	-	22	-	1	-	-	-	-	-	23	-
JT Ball (1929/34)	-	-	47	17	3	1	-	-	-	-	50	18
WH Ball (1902)	-	-	4	-	-	-	-	-	-	-	4	-
T Bamford (1934/37)	-	-	98	53	11	4	-	-	-	-	109	57
J Banks (1901/02)	-	-	40	7	4	1	-	-	-	-	44	8
J Bannister (1906/09)	-	-	57	-	4	1	-	-	-	-	61	1
J Barber (1922/23)	-	-	3	1	1	1	-	-	-	-	4	2
C Barlow (1919/21)	-	-	29	-	1	-	-	-	-	-	30	-
PS Barnes (1985/87)	-	-	19/1	2	-	-	5	2	-	-	24/1	4
F Barrett (1896/97)	-	-	118	-	14	-	-	-	4*	-	136	-
F Barson (1922/27)	-	-	140	4	12	-	-	-	-	-	152	4
A Beardsworth (1902)	-	-	9	1	3	1	-	-	-	-	12	2
RH Beale (1912/14)	-	-	105	-	7	-	-	-	-	-	112	-
PA Beardley (1982)	-	-	-	-	-	-	1	-	-	-	1	-
RP Beardsmore (1988/92)	-	-	30/26	4	4/4	-	3/1	-	1/2	-	38/33	4
T Beckett (1886)	-	-	-	-	-	-	-	-	-	-	-	-
D Beckham (1992)	2/2	-	-	-	1/1	-	3/1	1	1	-	7/3	1
JH Beddow (1904/06)	-	-	33	12	1	3	-	-	-	-	34	15
W Behan (1933)	-	-	1	-	-	-	-	-	-	-	1	-
A Bell (1902/12)	-	-	278	10	28	-	-	-	-	-	306	10
SR Bennion (1921/32)	-	-	286	2	15	-	-	-	-	-	301	3
G Bent (1954/56)	-	-	12	-	-	-	-	-	-	-	12	-
JJ Berry (1951/57)	-	-	247	37	15	4	-	-	11	3	273	44
W Berry (1906/08)	-	-	13	1	1	-	-	-	-	-	14	1
G Best (1963/73)	-	-	361	137	46	21	25	9	34	11	466	178

Player	FAPL App	FAPL Goals	League App	League Goals	FACup App	FACup Goals	LgeCup App	LgeCup Goals	Europe App	Europe Goals	Totals App	Totals Goals
PA Bielby (1973)	–	–	2/2	–	–	–	–	–	–	–	2/2	–
B Birch (1949/51)	–	–	11	4	4	1	–	–	–	–	15	5
H Birchenough (1902)	–	–	25	–	5	–	–	–	–	–	30	–
C Birkett (1950)	–	–	9	2	4	–	–	–	–	–	13	2
G Birtles (1980/82)	–	–	57/1	11	4	–	2	–	–	–	63/1	12
G Bissett (1919/21)	–	–	40	10	2	–	–	–	–	–	42	10
R Black (1931/33)	–	–	8	3	–	–	–	–	–	–	8	3
CG Blackmore (1983/	12/2	–	138/34	19	15/6	–	23/2	3	12	2	200/44	25
P Blackmore (1899)	–	–	1	–	1	–	–	–	–	–	2	–
T Blackstock (1903/06)	–	–	34	–	4	–	–	–	–	–	38	–
J Blanchflower (1951/57)	–	–	105	26	6	1	–	–	5	–	116	27
WH Blew (1905)	–	–	1	–	–	–	–	–	–	–	1	–
SP Blott (1909/12)	–	–	19	2	–	–	–	–	–	–	19	2
T Bogan (1949/50)	–	–	29	7	4	–	–	–	–	–	33	7
JE Bond (1951/52)	–	–	20	4	1	–	–	–	–	–	21	4
RP Bonthron (1903/06)	–	–	119	3	15	–	–	–	–	–	134	3
W Booth (1900)	–	–	2	–	–	–	–	–	–	–	2	–
M Bosnich (1989/91)	–	–	3	–	–	–	–	–	–	–	3	–
H Boyd (1896/98)	–	–	52	32	7	1	–	–	3*	2	62	35
WG Boyd (1934)	–	–	6	4	–	–	–	–	–	–	6	4
TW Boyle (1928/29)	–	–	16	6	1	–	–	–	–	–	17	6
L Bradbury (1938)	–	–	2	1	–	–	–	–	–	–	2	1
W Bradley (1958/61)	–	–	63	20	3	–	–	–	–	–	66	21
H Bratt (1960)	–	–	–	–	–	–	1	–	–	–	1	–
AB Brazil (1984/85)	–	–	18/13	8	–/1	–	4/3	3	2	1	27/17	12

Player	FAPL		League		FACup		LgeCup		Europe		Totals	
	App	Goals	App	Goals	App	Goals	App	Goals	App	Goals	App	Goals
DM Brazil (1988/92)	–	–	-/2	–	–	–	–	–	–	–	-/2	–
J Breedon (1935/39)	–	–	38	–	–	–	–	–	–	–	38	–
T Breen (1936/38)	–	–	65	–	6	–	–	–	–	–	71	–
SA Brennan (1957/69)	–	–	291/1	3	36	3	4	–	24	–	355/1	6
FB Brett (1921)	–	–	10	–	–	–	–	–	–	–	10	–
WR Briggs (1960/61)	–	–	9	–	2	–	–	–	–	–	11	–
WH Brooks (1898)	–	–	3	–	–	–	–	–	–	–	3	–
AH Broome (1922)	–	–	1	–	–	–	–	–	–	–	1	–
H Broomfield (1907)	–	–	9	–	–	–	–	–	–	–	9	–
J Brown (1932/33)	–	–	40	17	1	–	–	–	–	–	41	17
J Brown (1935/38)	–	–	102	1	8	–	–	–	–	–	110	1
RB Brown (1947/48)	–	–	4	–	–	–	–	–	–	–	4	–
W Brown (1892)	–	–	7	–	–	–	–	–	–	–	7	–
W Brown (1896)	–	–	7	2	–	–	–	–	–	–	7	2
SR Bruce (1987/	118	10	162	25	36	2	23	4	19/1	4	370/2	50
W Bryant (1896/99)	–	–	109	27	14	6	–	–	–	–	127	33
W Bryant (1934/39)	–	–	151	44	9	–	4*	–	–	–	160	44
G Buchan (1973)	–	–	-/3	–	–	–	-/1	–	–	–	-/4	–
MM Buchan (1971/82)	–	–	376	4	39	–	30	–	10	–	455	4
EW Buckle (1946/49)	–	–	20	6	4	1	–	–	–	–	24	7
FC Buckley (1906)	–	–	3	–	–	–	–	–	–	–	3	–
KJ Bullock (1930)	–	–	10	3	–	–	–	–	–	–	10	3
W Bunce (1902)	–	–	2	–	–	–	–	–	–	–	2	–
H Burgess (1906/09)	–	–	49	–	3	–	–	–	–	–	52	–
RS Burke (1946/48)	–	–	28	16	6	6	–	–	–	–	34	22

Player	FAPL App	FAPL Goals	League App	League Goals	FACup App	FACup Goals	LgeCup App	LgeCup Goals	Europe App	Europe Goals	Totals App	Totals Goals
T Burke (1886)	–	–	5	–	–	–	–	–	–	–	6	–
FS Burns (1967/71)	–	–	111/10	6	11/1	–	10/1	–	10/1	1	142/13	7
N Butt (1992/)	11/12	1	–	–	3/2	–	3	–	5/1	–	22/15	1
D Byrne (1933)	–	–	4	3	–	–	–	–	–	–	4	3
RW Byrne (1951/57)	–	–	245	17	18	2	–	–	14	–	277	19
J Cairns (1894/98)	–	–	2	1	–	–	–	–	–	–	2	1
WC Campbell (1893)	–	–	5	–	–	–	–	–	–	–	5	–
E Cantona (1992/)	76/1	39	–	–	7	5	5	1	6	2	94/1	47
N Cantwell (1960/66)	–	–	123	6	14	2	5	–	7	–	144	8
JP Cape (1933/36)	–	–	59	18	1	–	–	–	–	–	60	18
A Capper (1911)	–	–	1	–	–	–	–	–	–	–	1	–
JJ Carey (1937/52)	–	–	306	17	38	1	–	–	–	–	344	18
J Carman (1897)	–	–	3	1	–	–	–	–	–	–	3	1
JF Carolan (1958/60)	–	–	66	–	4	–	1	–	–	–	71	–
A Carson (1892)	–	–	13	3	–	–	–	–	–	–	13	3
HR Cartman (1922)	–	–	3	–	–	–	–	–	–	–	3	–
WG Cartwright (1895/1903)	–	–	228	8	27	–	–	–	2*	–	257	8
AA Cashmore (1913)	–	–	3	–	–	–	–	–	–	–	3	–
C Casper (1994/)	–	–	–	–	–	–	–	–	–	–	–	–
J Cassidy (1892/99)	–	–	152	90	15	9	–	–	7*	1	174	100
L Cassidy (1947/51)	–	–	4	1	–	–	–	–	–	–	4	1
WS Chalmers (1932/33)	–	–	34	1	1	–	–	–	–	–	35	1
W Chapman (1926/27)	–	–	26	–	–	–	–	–	–	–	26	–
R Charlton (1956/72)	–	–	604/2	199	79	19	24	7	45	22	752/2	247
RA Chester (1935)	–	–	13	1	–	–	–	–	–	–	13	1

238

Player	FAPL		League		FACup		LgeCup		Europe		Totals	
	App	Goals	App	Goals	App	Goals	App	Goals	App	Goals	App	Goals
A Chesters (1929/31)	–	–	9	–	–	–	–	–	–	–	9	–
AC Chilton (1939/54)	–	–	353	3	37	–	–	–	–	–	390	3
JP Chisnall (1961/63)	–	–	35	8	8	–	–	–	4	1	47	10
T Chorlton (1913)	–	–	4	–	–	–	–	–	–	–	4	–
D Christie (1908)	–	–	2	–	–	–	–	–	–	–	2	–
J Christie (1902)	–	–	1	–	–	–	–	–	–	–	1	–
J Clark (1899)	–	–	9	–	–	–	–	–	–	–	9	–
J Clark (1976/77)	–	–	0/1	–	–	–	–	–	–	–	0/1	–
J Clarkin (1893/95)	–	–	67	23	5	–	–	–	–	–	74	23
G Clayton (1956)	–	–	2	–	–	–	–	–	2*	–	2	–
H Cleaver (1902)	–	–	1	–	–	–	–	–	–	–	–	–
JE Clements (1891/93)	–	–	72	–	4	–	–	–	2*	–	78	2
F Clempson (1949/52)	–	–	15	2	–	–	–	–	–	–	15	2
H Cockburn (1946/54)	–	–	243	4	32	–	–	–	–	–	275	4
A Cole (1995/	17	12	–	–	–	–	–	–	–	–	17	12
C Collinson (1946)	–	–	7	–	–	–	–	–	–	–	7	–
J Collinson (1895/1900)	–	–	62	16	9	1	–	–	–	–	71	17
E Colman (1955/57)	–	–	85	1	9	–	–	–	13	–	107	1
J Colville (1892)	–	–	9	1	1	–	–	–	–	–	10	1
J Connachan (1898)	–	–	4	–	–	–	–	–	–	–	4	–
JP Connaughton (1971)	–	–	3	–	–	–	–	–	–	–	3	–
TE Connell (1978)	–	–	2	–	–	–	–	–	–	–	2	–
JM Connelly (1964/66)	–	–	79/1	22	13	2	2	1	19	11	112/1	35
E Connor (1909/10)	–	–	15	2	–	–	–	–	–	–	15	2
SP Cookson (1914)	–	–	12	–	1	–	–	–	–	–	13	–

Player	FAPL App	FAPL Goals	League App	League Goals	FACup App	FACup Goals	LgeCup App	LgeCup Goals	Europe App	Europe Goals	Totals App	Totals Goals
R Cope (1956/60)	–	–	93	2	10	–	1	–	2	–	106	2
SJ Coppell (1974/82)	–	–	320/2	54	36	4	25	9	11/1	3	392/3	70
J Coupar (1892/1901)	–	–	32	9	–	–	–	–	2*	1	34	10
PD Coyne (1975)	–	–	1/1	1	–	–	–	–	–	–	1/1	1
T Craig (1889/90)	–	–	25	5	2	1	–	–	–	–	27	6
C Craven (1938)	–	–	11	2	2	–	–	–	–	–	13	2
PT Crerand (1962/70)	–	–	304	10	43	4	4	–	41	1	392	15
J Crompton (1945/56)	–	–	191	–	20	–	–	–	–	–	211	–
GA Crooks (1983)	–	–	6/1	2	–	–	–	–	–	–	6/1	2
S Crowther (1957/58)	–	–	13	–	5	–	–	–	2	–	20	–
J Cunningham (1898)	–	–	15	2	2	–	–	–	–	–	17	2
LP Cunningham (1982)	–	–	3/2	1	–	–	–	–	–	–	3/2	1
JJ Curry (1908/10)	–	–	13	–	1	1	–	–	–	–	14	1
A Dale (1890)	–	–	–	–	–	–	–	–	–	–	–	–
J Dale (1947)	–	–	2	–	–	–	–	–	–	–	2	–
W Dale (1928/31)	–	–	64	–	4	–	–	–	–	–	68	–
E Dalton (1907)	–	–	1	–	–	–	–	–	–	–	1	–
GA Daly (1973/76)	–	–	107/4	23	9/1	5	17	4	4	–	137/5	32
P Davenport (1985/89)	–	–	72/19	22	2/2	–	8/2	4	–	–	83/23	26
WR Davidson (1893/94)	–	–	40	2	3	–	–	–	1*	–	44	2
A Davies (1981/83)	–	–	6/1	–	2	–	–	–	–/1	–	8/2	–
JE Davies (1886/89)	–	–	21	2	2	–	–	–	–	–	23	2
J Davies (1892)	–	–	10	–	1	–	–	–	2*	–	13	–
L Davies (1886)	–	–	–	–	1	–	–	–	–	–	1	–
RT Davies (1974)	–	–	–/8	–	–/2	–	–	–	–	–	–/10	–

Player	FAPL		League		FACup		LgeCup		Europe		Totals	
	App	Goals	App	Goals	App	Goals	App	Goals	App	Goals	App	Goals
S Davies (1994	3/2	–	–	–	–	–	3	–	2	1	8/2	1
WR Davies (1972)	–	–	15/1	4	1	–	–	–	–	–	16/1	4
AD Dawson (1956/71)	–	–	80	45	10	8	3	1	–	–	93	54
H Dean (1931)	–	–	2	–	–	–	–	–	–	–	2	–
J Delaney (1946/50)	–	–	164	25	19	3	–	–	–	–	183	28
MJ Dempsey (1983/86)	–	–	1	–	–	–	–	–	–/1	–	1/1	–
J Denman (1891)	–	–	6	–	1	–	–	–	–	–	7	–
W Dennis (1923)	–	–	3	–	–	–	–	–	–	–	3	–
N Dewar (1932/33)	–	–	36	14	–	–	–	–	–	–	36	14
J Doherty (1952/57)	–	–	25	7	1	–	–	–	–	–	26	7
B Donaghy (1905)	–	–	3	–	–	–	–	–	–	–	3	–
MM Donaghy (1988/92)	–	–	76/13	–	10	–	10/4	–	2/3	–	98/20	–
IR Donald (1972)	–	–	4	–	–	–	2	–	–	–	6	–
R Donaldson (1892/97)	–	–	153	76	16	10	–	–	8*	–	177	86
J Donnelly (1890)	–	–	1	–	–	–	–	–	–	–	1	–
A Donnelly (1908/12)	–	–	34	–	3	–	–	–	–	–	37	–
T Dougan (1938)	–	–	4	–	–	–	–	–	–	–	4	–
J Doughty (1886/91)	–	–	26	11	3	3	–	–	–	–	29	14
R Doughty (1891/96)	–	–	56	3	5	1	–	–	3*	–	64	4
W Douglas (1893/95)	–	–	55	–	1	–	–	–	1*	–	57	–
JM Dow (1893/95)	–	–	48	6	1	–	–	–	1*	–	50	6
ALB Downie (1902/09)	–	–	172	12	19	2	–	–	–	–	191	14
JD Downie (1948/52)	–	–	110	35	5	1	–	–	–	–	115	36
WL Draycott (1896/98)	–	–	81	6	10	–	–	–	4*	–	95	6
D Dublin (1992/94)	4/8	2	–	–	1/1	–	1/1	1	–/1	–	6/11	3

Player	FAPL		League		FACup		LgeCup		Europe		Totals	
	App	Goals	App	Goals	App	Goals	App	Goals	App	Goals	App	Goals
R Duckworth (1903/12)	–	–	225	11	26	–	–	–	–	–	251	11
W Dunn (1897)	–	–	10	–	2	–	–	–	–	–	12	–
AP Dunne (1960/72)	–	–	414	2	54/1	2	21	–	40	–	529/1	2
PAJ Dunne (1964/65)	–	–	45	–	7	–	1	–	13	–	66	–
M Duxbury (1980/90)	–	–	274/25	6	20/5	1	32/2	–	17/1	–	343/33	7
JA Dyer (1905)	–	–	1	–	–	–	–	–	–	–	1	–
J Earp (1886)	–	–	–	–	1	–	–	–	–	–	1	–
A Edge (1891)	–	–	19	6	3	3	–	–	–	–	22	9
H Edmonds (1910/11)	–	–	43	–	7	–	–	–	–	–	50	–
D Edwards (1952/57)	–	–	151	20	12	–	–	–	12	1	175	21
PF Edwards (1969/72)	–	–	52/2	–	10	–	4	1	–	–	66/2	1
D Ellis (1923)	–	–	11	–	–	–	–	–	–	–	11	–
FC Erentz (1892/1901)	–	–	280	9	23	–	–	–	7*	–	310	9
H Erentz (1897)	–	–	6	–	3	–	–	–	–	–	9	–
G Evans (1890)	–	–	12	5	1	–	–	–	–	–	13	6
S Evans (1923)	–	–	6	2	–	–	–	–	–	–	6	2
JW Fall (1893)	–	–	23	–	3	–	–	–	–	–	27	–
AH Farman (1889/94)	–	–	111	43	7	6	–	–	3*	4	121	53
I Feeman (1949)	–	–	12	–	2	–	–	–	–	–	14	–
G Felton (1890)	–	–	8	–	1	–	–	–	–	–	9	–
D Ferguson (1927)	–	–	4	–	–	–	–	–	–	–	4	–
D Ferguson (1990/94)	16/2	–	4/5	–	1	–	1/1	–	1*	–	22/8	–
J Ferguson (1931)	–	–	8	–	–	–	–	–	–	–	8	1
RJ Ferrier (1935/37)	–	–	18	4	1	–	–	–	–	–	19	4
WJ Fielding (1946)	–	–	6	–	1	–	–	–	–	–	7	–

Player	FAPL App	FAPL Goals	League App	League Goals	FACup App	FACup Goals	LgeCup App	LgeCup Goals	Europe App	Europe Goals	Totals App	Totals Goals
J Fisher (1900/01)	-	-	42	2	4	1	-	-	-	-	46	3
J Fichett (1902/04)	-	-	16	1	2	-	-	-	-	-	18	1
GA Fitton (1931/32)	-	-	12	2	-	-	-	-	-	-	12	2
JH Fitzpatrick (1964/72)	-	-	111/6	8	11	-	12	1	7	-	141/6	10
D Fitzsimmons (1895/99)	-	-	28	-	3	-	-	-	-	-	31	-
T Fitzsimmons (1892/93)	-	-	27	6	1	-	-	-	2*	-	30	6
P Fletcher (1972/73)	-	-	2/5	-	-	-	-	-	-	-	2/5	-
A Foggan (1976)	-	-	-/3	-	-	-	-	-	-	-	-/3	-
G Foley (1899)	-	-	7	1	-	-	-	-	-	-	7	1
JB Ford (1908/09)	-	-	5	-	-	-	-	-	-	-	5	-
T Forster (1919/21)	-	-	35	1	1	-	-	-	-	-	36	1
A Forsyth (1972/77)	-	-	99/2	4	10	1	7	-	-/1	-	116/3	5
WA Foulkes (1952/69)	-	-	563/3	7	61	-	3	-	52	2	679/3	9
W Fox (1914)	-	-	-	-	1	-	-	-	-	-	1	-
T Frame (1932/33)	-	-	51	4	1	-	-	-	-	-	52	4
SH Gallimore (1930/33)	-	-	72	19	4	1	-	-	-	-	76	20
CR Gardner (1935/36)	-	-	16	1	2	-	-	-	-	-	18	1
WF Garton (1984/88)	-	-	39/2	-	3	-	5/1	-	-/1	-	47/4	-
J Garvey (1900)	-	-	6	-	-	-	-	-	-	-	6	-
JD Gaskell (1957/66)	-	-	96	-	16	-	1	-	5	-	118	-
R Gaudie (1903)	-	-	7	-	1	-	-	-	-	-	8	-
CJ Gibson (1985/91)	-	-	74/5	9	8/1	-	7	-	-	-	89/6	9
R Gibson (1921)	-	-	11	-	1	-	-	-	-	-	12	-
TB Gibson (1985/87)	-	-	14/9	1	1/1	-	-	-	-/2	-	15/12	1
TRD Gibson (1950/54)	-	-	108	-	6	-	-	-	-	-	114	-

Player	FAPL App	FAPL Goals	League App	League Goals	FACup App	FACup Goals	LgeCup App	LgeCup Goals	Europe App	Europe Goals	Totals App	Totals Goals
J Gidman (1981/86)	–	–	94/1	4	9	–	5	–	7/2	–	115/3	4
R Giggs (1990/)	102/7	23	33/7	5	17/2	5	13/5	6	9	–	174/21	41
MJ Giles (1959/62)	–	–	99	10	13	2	2	1	–	–	114	13
AGD Gill (1986/88)	–	–	5/5	1	2/2	–	2	–	–	–	7/7	2
K Gillespie (1992/1995)	3/6	–	–	–	1	–	3	–	–	–	7/6	2
M Gillespie (1896/90)	–	–	74	17	11	4	–	–	4*	–	89	21
T Gipps (1912/14)	–	–	23	–	–	–	–	–	–	–	23	–
DJ Givens (1969)	–	–	4/4	1	1	–	–	–	–	–	5/4	1
GWE Gladwin (1936/38)	–	–	27	1	1	–	–	–	–	–	28	1
G Godsmark (1899)	–	–	9	4	–	–	–	–	–	–	9	4
EH Goldthorpe (1922/24)	–	–	27	15	3	1	–	–	–	–	30	16
FJ Goodwin (1954/59)	–	–	95	7	8	1	–	–	3	–	106	8
W Goodwin (1920/21)	–	–	7	1	1	–	–	–	–	–	7	1
J Gotheridge (1886)	–	–	5	–	1	–	–	–	–	–	6	–
J Gourlay (1898)	–	–	1	–	–	–	–	–	–	–	1	–
AE Gowling (1967/71)	–	–	64/7	18	6/2	2	7/1	1	–	–	77/10	21
A Graham (1983/84)	–	–	33/4	5	1	–	6	1	6/1	–	46/5	7
DWT Graham (1987)	–	–	1/1	–	0/1	–	0/1	–	–	–	1/3	–
G Graham (1972/74)	–	–	41/2	2	2	–	1	–	–	–	44/2	2
J Graham (1893)	–	–	4	–	–	–	–	–	–	–	4	–
W Grassam (1903/04)	–	–	29	13	8	1	–	–	–	–	37	14
ID Greaves (1954/59)	–	–	67	–	6	–	–	–	2	–	75	–
RE Green (1933)	–	–	9	4	–	–	–	–	–	–	9	4
B Greenhoff (1973/79)	–	–	218/3	13	24	2	19	2	6	–	267/3	17
J Greenhoff (1976/80)	–	–	94/3	26	18/1	9	4	1	2	–	118/4	36

Player	FAPL		League		FACup		LgeCup		Europe		Totals	
	App	Goals	App	Goals	App	Goals	App	Goals	App	Goals	App	Goals
W Greenwood (1900)	–	–	3	–	–	–	–	–	–	–	3	–
H Gregg (1957/66)	–	–	210	–	24	–	2	–	11	–	247	–
CL Griffiths (1973)	–	–	7	–	–	–	–	–	–	–	7	–
J Griffiths (1933/39)	–	–	168	1	8	–	–	–	–	–	176	1
W Griffiths (1898/1904)	–	–	157	27	18	3	–	–	–	–	175	30
AA Grimes (1977/82)	–	–	62/28	10	5	1	6	–	4/2	–	77/30	11
A Grimshaw (1975)	–	–	–/1	–	–	–	–/1	–	–	–	–/2	–
JB Grimwood (1919/26)	–	–	196	8	9	–	–	–	–	–	205	8
J Grundy (1899/1900)	–	–	11	3	–	–	–	–	–	–	11	3
H Gyves (1890)	–	–	–	–	1	–	–	–	–	–	1	–
J Hacking (1933/34)	–	–	32	–	2	–	–	–	–	–	34	–
J Hall (1933/35)	–	–	67	–	6	–	–	–	–	–	73	–
J Hall (1925)	–	–	3	–	–	–	–	–	–	–	3	–
P Hall (1903)	–	–	8	2	–	–	–	–	–	–	8	2
HJ Halse (1907/11)	–	–	109	41	15	9	–	–	–	–	124	50
RL Halton (1936)	–	–	4	1	–	–	–	–	–	–	4	1
M Hamill (1911/13)	–	–	57	2	2	–	–	–	–	–	59	2
JJ Hanlon (1938/48)	–	–	64	20	6	2	–	–	–	–	70	22
C Hannaford (1925/26)	–	–	11	–	1	–	–	–	–	–	12	–
J Hanson (1924/29)	–	–	138	47	9	5	–	–	–	–	147	52
HP Hardman (1908)	–	–	4	–	–	–	–	–	–	–	4	–
FE Harris (1919/21)	–	–	46	2	3	–	–	–	–	–	49	2
T Harris (1926)	–	–	4	1	–	–	–	–	–	–	4	1
C Harrison (1889)	–	–	9	–	1	–	–	–	–	–	10	–
WE Harrison (1920/21)	–	–	44	5	2	–	–	–	–	–	46	5

Player	FAPL		League		FACup		LgeCup		Europe		Totals	
	App	Goals	App	Goals	App	Goals	App	Goals	App	Goals	App	Goals
RW Harrop (1957/58)	–	–	10	–	1	–	–	–	–	–	11	–
W Hartwell (1903/04)	–	–	3	–	1	–	–	–	–	–	4	–
G Haslam (1921/27)	–	–	25	–	2	–	–	–	–	–	27	–
R Haworth (1926)	–	–	2	–	–	–	–	–	–	–	2	–
A Hawksworth (1956)	–	–	1	–	–	–	–	–	–	–	1	–
T Hay (1889)	–	–	15	–	1	–	–	–	–	–	16	–
F Haydock (1960/62)	–	–	6	–	–	–	–	–	–	–	6	–
JV Hayes (1900/10)	–	–	115	2	13	–	–	–	–	–	128	2
H Haywood (1932/33)	–	–	4	2	–	–	–	–	–	–	4	2
JF Haywood (1913/14)	–	–	26	–	–	–	–	–	–	–	26	–
J Heathcote (1899/1900)	–	–	7	–	1	–	–	–	–	–	8	–
W Henderson (1921/24)	–	–	34	17	2	–	–	–	–	–	36	17
J Hendry (1892)	–	–	2	1	–	–	–	–	–	–	2	1
A Henrys (1891/92)	–	–	23	–	3	–	–	–	–	–	26	–
DG Herd (1961/67)	–	–	201/1	114	35	15	1	1	25	14	262/1	144
FTR Heron (1957/60)	–	–	3	–	–	–	–	–	–	–	3	–
W Higgins (1901)	–	–	10	–	–	–	–	–	–	–	10	–
MN Higgins (1985/87)	–	–	6	–	2	–	–	–	–	–	8	–
J Higson (1901)	–	–	5	1	–	–	–	–	–	–	5	1
CG Hilditch (1919/31)	–	–	301	7	21	–	–	–	–	–	322	7
GA Hill (1975/77)	–	–	100/1	39	17	6	7	4	8	2	132/1	51
CE Hillam (1933)	–	–	8	–	–	–	–	–	–	–	8	–
EW Hine (1932/34)	–	–	51	12	2	–	–	–	–	–	53	12
J Hodge (1910/19)	–	–	79	2	7	–	–	–	–	–	86	2
J Hodge (1913/14)	–	–	30	–	–	–	–	–	–	–	30	–

Player	FAPL App	FAPL Goals	League App	League Goals	FACup App	FACup Goals	LgeCup App	LgeCup Goals	Europe App	Europe Goals	Totals App	Totals Goals
FC Hodges (1919/20)	–	–	20	4	–	–	–	–	–	–	20	4
L. Hofton (1910/20)	–	–	17	–	1	–	–	–	–	–	18	1
GJ Hogg (1983/87)	–	–	82/1	1	–	–	7/1	–	10	–	107/2	1
RH Holdren (1904/12)	–	–	106	–	11	–	–	–	–	–	117	–
J Holt (1899)	–	–	1	1	–	–	–	–	–	–	1	1
JA Holton (1972/74)	–	–	63	5	2	–	4	–	–	–	69	5
TP Homer (1909/11)	–	–	25	14	–	–	–	–	–	–	25	14
W Hood (1892/93)	–	–	48	11	3	–	–	–	2*	–	53	11
AH Hooper (1909/13)	–	–	7	1	–	–	–	–	–	–	7	1
F Hopkin (1919/20)	–	–	70	8	4	–	–	–	–	–	74	8
J Hopkins (1898)	–	–	1	–	–	–	–	–	–	–	1	–
S Hopkinson (1930/33)	–	–	51	10	2	2	–	–	–	–	53	12
SM Houston (1973/79)	–	–	204/1	13	22	1	16	2	6/1	–	248/2	16
JT Howarth (1921)	–	–	4	–	1	–	–	–	–	–	4	–
E Howells (1886)	–	–	–	–	1	–	–	–	–	–	–	–
EK Hudson (1913/14)	–	–	11	–	–	–	–	–	–	–	11	–
M Hughes (1983/1995)	110/1	35	227/8	85	45/1	17	37/1	16	30/3	9	449/14	162
A Hulme (1907/08)	–	–	4	–	–	–	–	–	–	–	4	–
GH Hunter (1913/14)	–	–	22	2	1	–	–	–	–	–	23	2
RJ Hunter (1958)	–	–	1	–	–	–	–	–	–	–	1	–
W Hunter (1912)	–	–	3	2	–	–	–	–	–	–	3	2
DJ Hurst (1902)	–	–	16	4	5	–	–	–	–	–	21	4
R Iddon (1925/26)	–	–	2	–	–	–	–	–	–	–	2	–
PEC Ince (1989/1995)	116	19	87/2	6	25/1	1	24/1	2	19	–	271/4	28
WW Inglis (1925/28)	–	–	14	1	–	–	–	–	–	–	14	1

Player	FAPL App	FAPL Goals	League App	League Goals	FACup App	FACup Goals	LgeCup App	LgeCup Goals	Europe App	Europe Goals	Totals App	Totals Goals
D Irwin (1990/	122	9	70/2	4	23	6	27/2	–	12	–	254/4	19
TA Jackson (1975/76)	–	–	18/1	–	4	–	4	–	–	–	22/1	–
W Jackson (1899/1900)	–	–	61	12	3	2	–	–	–	–	64	14
SR James (1968/74)	–	–	129	4	12	–	17/1	–	2	–	160/1	4
CAL Jenkyns (1896/97)	–	–	35	5	8	–	–	–	4*	1	47	6
WR John (1936)	–	–	15	–	–	–	–	–	–	–	15	–
SC Johnson (1900)	–	–	1	–	–	–	–	–	–	–	1	–
WG Johnston (1927/31)	–	–	71	24	6	3	–	–	–	–	77	27
D Jones (1937)	–	–	1	–	–	–	–	–	–	–	1	–
EP Jones (1957)	–	–	1	–	–	–	–	–	–	–	1	–
M Jones (1950/57)	–	–	103	1	7	–	–	–	10	–	120	1
OJ Jones (1898)	–	–	2	–	–	–	–	–	–	–	2	–
T Jones (1924/36)	–	–	189	4	11	–	–	–	–	–	200	4
TJ Jones (1934)	–	–	20	4	2	–	–	–	–	–	22	4
J Jordan (1977/80)	–	–	109	37	11/1	2	4	2	1	–	125/1	41
N Jovanovich (1979/80)	–	–	20/1	4	1	–	2	–	2	–	25/1	4
A Kanchelskis (1990/	67/20	23	29/6	5	14/1	5	12	2	7	1	129/27	36
R Keane (1993/	57/4	7	–	–	12/1	1	7/1	–	7	3	83/6	11
JW Kelly (1975)	–	–	–/1	–	–	–	–	–	–	–	–/1	–
F Kennedy (1923/24)	–	–	17	4	1	–	–	–	–	–	18	4
PA Kennedy (1954)	–	–	1	–	–	–	–	–	–	–	1	–
WJ Kennedy (1895/96)	–	–	30	11	3	1	–	–	–	–	33	12
H Kerr (1903)	–	–	2	–	–	–	–	–	–	–	2	–
B Kidd (1967/73)	–	–	195/8	52	24/1	8	20	7	16	3	255/9	70
J Kinloch (1892)	–	–	1	–	–	–	–	–	–	–	1	–

Player	FAPL App	FAPL Goals	League App	League Goals	FACup App	FACup Goals	LgeCup App	LgeCup Goals	Europe App	Europe Goals	Totals App	Totals Goals
AJ Kinsey (1964)	–	–	–	–	1	1	–	–	–	–	1	1
F Knowles (1911/14)	–	–	46	1	1	–	–	–	–	–	47	1
F Kopel (1967/68)	–	–	8/2	–	1	–	–	–	1	–	10/2	–
JG Lancaster (1949)	–	–	2	–	2	–	–	–	–	–	4	–
T Lang (1935/36)	–	–	12	1	1	–	–	–	–	–	13	1
L Langford (1934/35)	–	–	15	–	–	–	–	–	–	–	15	–
HH Lappin (1900/02)	–	–	27	4	–	–	–	–	–	–	27	4
D Law (1961/72)	–	–	305/4	171	44/2	34	11	3	33	28	393/6	236
RR Lawson (1900)	–	–	3	–	–	–	–	–	–	–	3	–
N Lawton (1959/62)	–	–	36	6	7	–	1	–	–	–	44	6
E Lee (1898/99)	–	–	11	5	–	–	–	–	–	–	11	5
T Leigh (1899/1900)	–	–	43	15	3	–	–	–	–	–	46	15
J Leighton (1988/91)	–	–	73	–	14	–	7	–	–	–	94	–
HD Leonard (1920)	–	–	10	5	–	–	–	–	–	–	10	5
E Lewis (1952/55)	–	–	20	9	4	2	–	–	–	–	24	11
L Lievesley (1931)	–	–	2	–	–	–	–	–	–	–	2	–
W Lievesley (1922)	–	–	2	–	1	–	–	–	–	–	3	–
OHS Linkson (1908/12)	–	–	55	–	4	–	–	–	–	–	59	–
GT Livingstone (1908/13)	–	–	43	4	3	–	–	–	–	–	46	4
AW Lochhead (1921/25)	–	–	147	50	6	–	–	–	–	–	153	50
W Longair (1894)	–	–	1	–	–	–	–	–	–	–	1	–
W Longton (1886)	–	–	–	–	1	–	–	–	–	–	1	–
T Lowrie (1947/49)	–	–	13	–	1	–	–	–	–	–	14	–
G Lydon (1930/31)	–	–	3	–	–	–	–	–	–	–	3	–
D Lyner (1922)	–	–	3	–	–	–	–	–	–	–	3	–

Player	FAPL		League		FACup		LgeCup		Europe		Totals	
	App	Goals	App	Goals	App	Goals	App	Goals	App	Goals	App	Goals
S Lynn (1947/49)	–	–	–	–	–	–	–	–	–	–	13	–
G Lyons (1903/05)	–	–	4	–	1	–	–	–	–	–	5	–
L Macari (1972/83)	–	–	311/18	78	31/3	8	22/5	10	9/1	1	373/27	97
N McBain (1921/22)	–	–	42	2	1	–	–	–	–	–	43	2
J McCalliog (1973/74)	–	–	31	7	1	–	5/1	–	–	–	37/1	7
P McCarthy (1911)	–	–	1	–	–	–	–	–	–	–	1	–
W McCartney (1903)	–	–	13	–	–	–	–	–	–	–	13	–
WJ McCartney (1894)	–	–	18	1	1	–	–	–	1*	–	20	1
BJ McClair (1987/)	87/20	15	190/3	70	34/5	14	40/1	19	17	5	368/29	123
J McClelland (1936)	–	–	5	1	–	–	–	–	–	–	5	1
JJ McCrae (1925)	–	–	9	–	4	–	–	–	–	–	13	–
D McCreery (1974/78)	–	–	48/39	7	1/6	–	4/4	1	4/3	–	57/52	8
K MacDonald (1922/23)	–	–	9	2	–	–	–	–	–	–	9	2
W McDonald (1931/33)	–	–	27	4	–	–	–	–	–	–	27	4
EJ MacDougall (1972)	–	–	18	5	–	–	–	–	–	–	18	5
NW McFarlane (1953)	–	–	1	–	–	–	–	–	–	–	1	–
R McFarlane (1891)	–	–	18	1	3	–	–	–	–	–	21	1
D McFetteridge (1894)	–	–	1	–	–	–	–	–	–	–	1	–
ST McGarvey (1891/92)	–	–	13/12	3	–	–	–	–	–	–	13/12	3
C McGillivray (1933)	–	–	8	1	1	–	–	–	–	–	9	–
J McGillivray (1907/08)	–	–	3	–	1	–	–	–	–	–	4	–
W McGlen (1946/51)	–	–	110	2	12	–	–	–	–	–	122	2
P McGrath (1982/89)	–	–	159/4	12	15/3	2	13	2	4	–	191/7	16
W McGuinness (1955/59)	–	–	81	2	2	–	–	–	2	–	85	2
SB McIlroy (1971/81)	–	–	320/22	57	35/3	6	25/3	6	10	2	390/28	71

Player	FAPL App	FAPL Goals	League App	League Goals	FACup App	FACup Goals	LgeCup App	LgeCup Goals	Europe App	Europe Goals	Totals App	Totals Goals
E McIlvenny (1950)	–	–	2	–	–	–	–	–	–	–	2	–
W McKay (1933/39)	–	–	171	15	13	–	–	–	–	–	184	15
C McKee (1994)	1	–	–	–	–	–	–	–	–	–	1	–
C Mackie (1904)	–	–	5	3	2	1	–	–	–	–	7	4
GH McLachlan (1929/32)	–	–	110	4	6	–	–	–	–	–	116	4
H McLenahan (1929/32)	–	–	112	11	4	1	–	–	–	–	116	12
A Macmillan (1890)	–	–	2	–	–	–	–	–	–	–	2	–
ST McMillan (1961/62)	–	–	15	6	–	–	–	–	–	–	15	6
WS McMillen (1933/34)	–	–	27	2	2	–	–	–	–	–	29	2
JR McNaught (1893/97)	–	–	140	12	17	–	–	–	5*	–	162	12
T McNulty (1949/53)	–	–	57	–	2	–	–	–	–	–	59	–
FC McPherson (1923/27)	–	–	159	45	16	7	–	–	–	–	175	52
G McQueen (1977/84)	–	–	184	20	21	2	16	4	7	–	228	26
H McShane (1950/53)	–	–	56	8	1	–	–	–	–	–	57	8
G Maiorana (1988/	–	–	2/5	–	–	–	–/1	–	–	–	2/6	–
T Manley (1931/38)	–	–	188	40	7	1	–	–	–	–	195	41
FD Mann (1922/29)	–	–	180	5	17	–	–	–	–	–	197	5
H Mann (1931)	–	–	13	2	–	–	–	–	–	–	13	2
T Manns (1933)	–	–	2	–	–	–	–	–	–	–	2	–
AE Marshall (1902)	–	–	6	–	–	–	–	–	–	–	6	–
LA Martin (1987/1993)	1	–	55/17	1	13/1	1	8/2	1	6/5	–	83/25	2
MP Martin (1972/74)	–	–	33/7	2	2	–	1	–	–	–	36/7	2
D May (1994/	15/4	2	–	–	–	–	2	1	4	–	22/4	3
W Mathieson (1892/93)	–	–	13	3	–	–	–	–	–	–	13	3
T Meehan (1919/20)	–	–	51	6	2	–	–	–	–	–	53	6

Player	FAPL App	FAPL Goals	League App	League Goals	FACup App	FACup Goals	LgeCup App	LgeCup Goals	Europe App	Europe Goals	Totals App	Totals Goals
J Mellor (1930/36)	–	–	116	–	6	–	–	–	–	–	122	–
AW Menzies (1906/07)	–	–	23	4	2	–	–	–	–	–	25	4
WH Meredith (1906/20)	–	–	303	35	29	–	–	–	–	–	332	35
JW Mew (1912/25)	–	–	186	–	13	–	–	–	–	–	199	–
R Milarvie (1890)	–	–	22	4	1	–	–	–	–	–	23	4
G Millar (1894)	–	–	6	5	1	–	–	–	–	–	7	5
J Miller (1923)	–	–	4	1	–	–	–	–	–	–	4	1
T Miller (1920)	–	–	25	7	2	1	–	–	–	–	27	8
R Milne (1988/91)	–	–	19/4	3	7	–	–	–	–	–	26/4	3
A Mitchell (1886/93)	–	–	90	3	–	–	–	–	3*	–	90	3
A Mitchell (1932)	–	–	1	–	–	–	–	–	–	–	1	–
C Mitten (1946/49)	–	–	142	50	19	11	–	–	–	–	161	61
HH Moger (1903/11)	–	–	242	–	22	–	–	–	–	–	264	–
I Moir (1960/64)	–	–	45	5	–	–	–	–	–	–	45	5
A Montgomery (1905)	–	–	3	–	–	–	–	–	–	–	3	–
J Montgomery (1914/20)	–	–	27	1	–	–	–	–	–	–	27	1
J Moody (1931/32)	–	–	50	–	1	–	–	–	–	–	51	–
CW Moore (1919/29)	–	–	309	4	19	1	–	–	–	–	328	5
G Moore (1963)	–	–	18	4	1	1	–	–	–	–	19	5
KR Moran (1978/88)	–	–	228/3	21	18	1	24/1	2	13/1	–	283/5	24
H Morgan (1900)	–	–	20	4	3	–	–	–	–	–	23	4
W Morgan (1896/1902)	–	–	143	6	9	1	–	–	–	–	152	7
W Morgan (1968/75)	–	–	236/2	25	27	4	24/1	3	4	1	291/3	33
KG Morgans (1957/60)	–	–	17	–	2	–	–	–	4	–	23	–
J Morris (1946/48)	–	–	83	32	9	3	–	–	–	–	92	35

252

Player	FAPL App	FAPL Goals	League App	League Goals	FACup App	FACup Goals	LgeCup App	LgeCup Goals	Europe App	Europe Goals	Totals App	Totals Goals
T Morrison (1902/03)	–	–	29	7	7	1	–	–	–	–	36	8
BW Morton (1935)	–	–	1	–	–	–	–	–	–	–	1	–
RM Moses (1981/88)	–	–	143/7	7	11	1	22/2	4	12/1	–	188/10	12
AJH Muhren (1982/84)	–	–	65/5	13	8	–	11	1	8	3	92/5	18
RD Murray (1937)	–	–	4	–	–	–	–	–	–	–	4	–
G Mutch (1934/37)	–	–	112	46	8	3	–	–	–	–	120	49
J Myerscough (1920/22)	–	–	33	8	1	–	–	–	–	–	34	8
G Neville (1992/	16/3	–	–	–	4	–	2/1	–	1/4	–	24/7	–
P Neville (1995/	1/1	–	–	–	1	–	–	–	–	–	2/1	–
GW Nevin (1933)	–	–	4	–	1	–	–	–	–	–	5	–
P Newton (1933)	–	–	2	–	–	–	–	–	–	–	2	–
JM Nicholl (1974/81)	–	–	188/9	3	22/4	1	14	–	10	1	234/13	6
JJ Nicholson (1960/65)	–	–	58	5	7	–	3	–	–	–	68	6
G Nichol (1927/28)	–	–	6	2	1	–	–	–	–	–	7	2
R Noble (1965/66)	–	–	31	–	2	–	–	–	–	–	33	–
JP Norton (1913/14)	–	–	37	3	–	–	–	–	–	–	37	3
TA Nuttall (1911/12)	–	–	16	4	–	–	–	–	–	–	16	4
LF O'Brien (1986/88)	–	–	16/15	2	–/2	–	1/2	–	–	–	17/19	2
W O'Brien (1901)	–	–	1	–	–	–	–	–	–	–	1	–
P O'Connell (1914)	–	–	34	2	1	–	–	–	–	–	35	2
J O'Kane (1994/	–	–	–	–	1	–	1/1	–	–	–	2/1	–
RL Olive (1952)	–	–	2	–	–	–	–	–	–	–	2	–
J Olsen (1984/89)	–	–	119/20	21	13/3	2	10/3	–	6/1	–	148/27	24
TP O'Neil (1970/72)	–	–	54	–	7	–	7	–	–	–	68	–
W O'Shaughnessey (1890)	–	–	–	–	1	–	–	–	–	–	1	–

Player	FAPL		League		FACup		LgeCup		Europe		Totals	
	App	Goals	App	Goals	App	Goals	App	Goals	App	Goals	App	Goals
A Owen (1898)	–	–	1	–	–	–	–	–	–	–	1	–
G Owen (1889)	–	–	12	2	1	–	–	–	–	–	13	2
J Owen (1889/91)	–	–	52	3	6	–	–	–	–	–	58	3
W Owen (1934/35)	–	–	17	1	–	–	–	–	–	–	17	1
LA Page (1931/32)	–	–	12	–	–	–	–	–	–	–	12	–
GA Pallister (1989/	124	4	108/3	4	31	2	34	–	23/1	1	321/4	11
AA Pape (1924/25)	–	–	18	5	–	–	–	–	–	–	18	5
B Parker (1893)	–	–	11	–	1	–	–	–	–	–	12	–
P Parker (1991/	71/3	1	24/2	–	13	–	14	–	16/4	–	128/21	1
TA Parker (1930/31)	–	–	17	–	–	–	–	–	–	–	17	–
R Parkinson (1899)	–	–	15	7	–	–	–	–	–	–	15	7
AE Partridge (1920/28)	–	–	148	16	12	2	–	–	–	–	160	18
SW Paterson (1976/79)	–	–	3/3	1	2	–	–	–	–/2	–	5/5	1
E Payne (1908)	–	–	2	–	–	–	–	–	–	–	2	–
S Pears (1984)	–	–	4	–	–	–	1	–	–	–	5	–
M Pearson (1957/62)	–	–	68	12	7	1	3	1	2	–	80	14
SC Pearson (1937/53)	–	–	315	128	30	21	–	–	–	–	345	149
JS Pearson (1974/77)	–	–	138/1	55	22	5	12	5	6	1	178/1	66
JH Peddie (1902/06)	–	–	112	52	9	6	–	–	1*	–	121	58
J Peden (1893)	–	–	28	7	4	1	–	–	–	–	32	8
J Pedley (1889)	–	–	1	–	–	–	–	–	–	–	1	–
D Pegg (1952/57)	–	–	127	24	9	–	–	–	12	4	148	28
E Pegg (1902/03)	–	–	41	13	10	7	–	–	–	–	51	20
JK Pegg (1947)	–	–	2	–	–	–	–	–	–	–	2	–
F Pepper (1898)	–	–	7	–	1	–	–	–	–	–	8	–

Player	FAPL		League		FACup		LgeCup		Europe		Totals	
	App	Goals	App	Goals	App	Goals	App	Goals	App	Goals	App	Goals
G Perrins (1892/95)	–	–	92	–	6	–	–	–	4*	–	102	–
J Peters (1894/95)	–	–	46	13	4	1	–	–	1*	–	51	14
M Phasey (1891)	–	–	1	–	–	–	–	–	–	–	1	–
MC Phelan (1989/1994)	5/7	1	82/7	2	10	–	14/2	–	14/3	–	125/19	4
JB Picken (1905/10)	–	–	113	39	8	7	–	–	–	–	121	46
K Pilkington (1994/)	–/1	–	–	–	–	–	–	–	–	–	–/1	–
MJ Pinner (1960)	–	–	4	–	–	–	–	–	–	–	4	–
W Potter (1934/37)	–	–	61	–	4	–	–	–	–	–	65	–
AA Potts (1913/19)	–	–	27	5	1	–	–	–	–	–	28	5
J Powell (1886/90)	–	–	21	–	4	–	–	–	–	–	25	–
JH Prentice (1919)	–	–	1	–	–	–	–	–	–	–	1	–
S Preston (1901/02)	–	–	33	14	1	–	–	–	–	–	34	14
AJ Prince (1914)	–	–	1	–	–	–	–	–	–	–	1	–
D Prince (1893)	–	–	2	–	–	–	–	–	–	–	2	–
J Pugh (1921/22)	–	–	2	–	–	–	–	–	–	–	2	–
JJ Quinn (1908/09)	–	–	2	–	–	–	–	–	–	–	2	–
A Quixall (1958/63)	–	–	165	50	14	4	1	2	3	–	183	56
G Radcliffe (1898)	–	–	1	–	–	–	–	–	–	–	1	–
C Radford (1920/23)	–	–	91	1	5	–	–	–	–	–	96	1
CW Ramsden (1927/30)	–	–	14	3	2	–	–	–	–	–	16	3
R Ramsey (1890)	–	–	22	5	1	–	–	–	–	–	23	5
P Rattigan (1890)	–	–	–	–	1	–	–	–	–	–	1	–
WE Rawlings (1927/29)	–	–	35	19	1	–	–	–	–	–	36	19
TH Read (1902/03)	–	–	35	–	7	–	–	–	–	–	42	–
W Redman (1950/53)	–	–	36	–	2	–	–	–	–	–	38	–

255

Player	FAPL		League		FACup		LgeCup		Europe		Totals	
	App	Goals	App	Goals	App	Goals	App	Goals	App	Goals	App	Goals
H Redwood (1935/39)	–	–	89	3	7	–	–	–	–	–	96	4
T Reid (1928/32)	–	–	96	63	5	4	–	–	–	–	101	67
C Rennox (1924/26)	–	–	60	24	8	–	–	–	–	–	68	25
CH Richards (1902)	–	–	8	1	3	1	–	–	–	–	11	2
W Richards (1901)	–	–	9	–	3	–	–	–	–	–	9	1
LH Richardson (1925/28)	–	–	38	–	4	–	–	–	–	–	42	–
W Ridding (1931/33)	–	–	42	14	2	–	–	–	–	–	44	14
JA Ridgway (1895/97)	–	–	14	–	3	–	–	–	–	–	17	–
JJ Rimmer (1967/72)	–	–	34	–	3	–	6	–	2/1	–	45/1	–
AT Ritchie (1977/80)	–	–	26/7	13	3/1	–	3/2	–	–	–	32/10	13
J Roach (1945)	–	–	–	–	2	–	–	–	–	–	2	–
DM Robbie (1935)	–	–	1	–	–	–	–	–	–	–	1	–
B Roberts (1898/99)	–	–	9	2	1	–	–	–	–	–	10	2
C Roberts (1903/12)	–	–	271	22	28	1	–	–	–	–	299	23
RHA Roberts (1913)	–	–	2	–	–	–	–	–	–	–	2	–
A Robertson (1903/05)	–	–	33	1	2	–	–	–	–	–	35	1
A Robertson (1903/04)	–	–	28	10	6	–	–	–	–	–	34	10
T Robertson (1903)	–	–	3	–	–	–	–	–	–	–	3	–
WS Robertson (1933/35)	–	–	47	–	3	–	–	–	–	–	50	–
MG Robins (1988/91)	–	–	19/29	11	4/4	3	–/7	2	4/2	1	27/42	17
JW Robinson (1919/21)	–	–	21	3	–	–	–	–	–	–	21	3
M Robinson (1931)	–	–	10	–	–	–	–	–	–	–	10	–
B Robson (1981/94)	15/14	2	310/5	72	33/1	10	50/2	5	26/1	8	434/23	97
PJ Roche (1974/81)	–	–	46	–	4	–	3	–	–	–	53	–
M Rogers (1977)	–	–	1	–	–	–	–	–	–	–	1	–

Player	FAPL App	FAPL Goals	League App	League Goals	FACup App	FACup Goals	LgeCup App	LgeCup Goals	Europe App	Europe Goals	Totals App	Totals Goals
C Rothwell (1893/96)	-	-	2	1	1	2	-	-	-	-	3	3
H Rothwell (1902)	-	-	22	-	6	-	-	-	-	-	28	-
WG Roughton (1936/38)	-	-	86	-	6	-	-	-	-	-	92	-
E Round (1909)	-	-	2	-	-	-	-	-	-	-	2	-
J Rowe (1913)	-	-	1	-	-	-	-	-	-	-	1	-
HB Rowley (1928/36)	-	-	173	55	7	-	-	-	-	-	180	55
JF Rowley (1937/54)	-	-	380	182	42	26	-	-	-	-	422	208
EJ Royals (1912/13)	-	-	7	-	-	-	-	-	-	-	7	-
J Ryan (1965/69)	-	-	21/3	4	1	-	-	-	2	-	24/3	4
D Sadler (1963/73)	-	-	266/6	22	22/1	1	22	-	16	3	326/7	27
T Sadler (1890)	-	-	-	-	1	-	-	-	-	-	1	-
C Sagar (1905/06)	-	-	30	20	3	4	-	-	-	-	33	24
GD Sapsford (1919/21)	-	-	52	16	1	1	-	-	-	-	53	17
C Sartori (1968/71)	-	-	26/13	4	9	1	3/2	-	2	1	40/15	6
W Sarvis (1922)	-	-	1	-	-	-	-	-	-	-	1	-
J Saunders (1901/02)	-	-	12	-	1	-	-	-	-	-	13	-
RE Savage (1937)	-	-	4	-	1	-	-	-	-	-	5	-
F Sawyer (1899/1900)	-	-	6	-	-	-	-	-	-	-	6	-
AJ Scanlon (1954/60)	-	-	115	34	6	-	3	-	3	1	127	35
P Schmeichel (1991/	114	-	40	-	20	-	16	-	11	-	201	-
A Schofield (1900/06)	-	-	157	30	22	5	-	-	-	-	179	35
GW Schofield (1920)	-	-	1	-	-	-	-	-	-	-	1	-
J Schofield (1903)	-	-	2	-	-	-	-	-	-	-	2	-
P Schofield (1921)	-	-	1	-	-	-	-	-	-	-	1	-
P Scholes (1994/	6/11	5	-	-	1/2	-	3	2	-/2	-	10/15	7

Player	FAPL		League		FACup		LgeCup		Europe		Totals	
	App	Goals	App	Goals	App	Goals	App	Goals	App	Goals	App	Goals
J Scott (1921)	–	–	23	–	1	–	–	–	–	–	24	–
J Scott (1952/56)	–	–	3	–	–	–	–	–	–	–	3	–
LJ Sealey (1989/94)	–	–	33	–	4/1	–	9	–	8	–	54/1	–
ME Setters (1959/64)	–	–	159	12	25	1	2	–	7	1	193	14
LS Sharpe (1988)	79/6	13	59/17	4	18/5	1	13/8	9	13/2	3	182/38	30
WH Sharpe (1890/91)	–	–	25	6	–	–	–	–	–	–	25	6
J Sheldon (1910/12)	–	–	26	1	–	–	–	–	–	–	26	1
A Sidebottom (1972/73)	–	–	16	–	2	–	2	–	–	–	20	–
J Silcock (1919/33)	–	–	423	2	26	–	–	–	–	–	449	2
J Sivebaek (1985/87)	–	–	29/2	1	2	–	1	–	–	–	32/2	1
JF Slater (1890/91)	–	–	41	–	4	–	–	–	–	–	45	–
T Sloan (1978/80)	–	–	4/7	–	–	–	–/1	–	–	–	4/8	–
AC Smith (1926)	–	–	5	1	–	–	–	–	–	–	5	1
J Smith (1937/45)	–	–	37	14	5	1	–	–	–	–	42	15
L Smith (1902)	–	–	8	–	2	1	–	–	–	–	10	1
R Smith (1894/1900)	–	–	93	35	7	2	–	–	1*	–	101	37
TG Smith (1923/26)	–	–	83	12	7	4	–	–	–	–	90	16
W Smith (1901)	–	–	16	–	1	–	–	–	–	–	17	–
J Sneddon (1891)	–	–	21	6	3	1	–	–	–	–	24	7
JW Spence (1919/32)	–	–	481	158	29	10	–	–	–	–	510	168
CW Spencer (1928/29)	–	–	46	–	2	–	–	–	–	–	48	–
W Spratt (1914/19)	–	–	13	–	–	–	–	–	–	–	13	–
G Stacey (1907/14)	–	–	241	9	26	1	–	–	–	–	267	9
H Stafford (1895/1902)	–	–	183	–	17	1	–	–	–	–	200	1
FA Stapleton (1981/87)	–	–	204/19	60	21	7	26/1	6	14/1	5	265/21	78

Player	FAPL App	FAPL Goals	League App	League Goals	FACup App	FACup Goals	LgeCup App	LgeCup Goals	Europe App	Europe Goals	Totals App	Totals Goals
R Stephenson (1895)	–	–	1	1	–	–	–	–	–	–	1	1
AC Stepney (1966/77)	–	–	433	2	44	–	35	–	23	–	535	2
A Steward (1920/31)	–	–	309	–	17	–	–	–	–	–	326	–
W Stewart (1932/33)	–	–	46	7	3	–	–	–	–	–	49	7
WS Stewart (1890/94)	–	–	138	23	9	–	–	–	2*	–	149	23
NP Stiles (1960/70)	–	–	311	17	38	–	7	–	36	2	392	19
H Stone (1893/94)	–	–	6	–	1	–	–	–	–	–	7	–
I Storey-Moore (1971/73)	–	–	39	11	–	–	4	1	1*	–	43	12
GD Strachan (1984/89)	–	–	155/5	33	22	2	12/1	1	6	2	195/6	38
E Street (1902)	–	–	1	–	2	–	–	–	–	–	3	–
JW Sutcliffe (1903)	–	–	21	–	7	–	–	–	–	–	28	–
EE Sweeney (1925/29)	–	–	27	6	5	1	–	–	–	–	32	7
T Tait (1889/90)	–	–	7	1	–	–	–	–	–	–	7	1
NH Tapken (1938)	–	–	14	–	2	–	–	–	–	–	16	–
C Taylor (1924/29)	–	–	28	6	2	1	–	–	–	–	30	7
E Taylor (1957/58)	–	–	22	2	6	–	–	–	2	1	30	4
T Taylor (1952/57)	–	–	166	112	9	5	–	–	14	11	189	128
W Taylor (1921)	–	–	1	–	–	–	–	–	–	–	1	–
H Thomas (1921/29)	–	–	128	12	7	1	–	–	–	–	135	13
MR Thomas (1978/80)	–	–	90	11	13	2	5	2	2	–	110	15
A Thomson (1929/30)	–	–	3	1	2	–	–	–	–	–	5	1
E Thomson (1907/08)	–	–	4	–	–	–	–	–	–	–	4	–
J Thompson (1913)	–	–	6	1	–	–	–	–	–	–	6	1
JE Thompson (1936/37)	–	–	3	1	–	–	–	–	–	–	3	1
W Thompson (1893)	–	–	3	–	–	–	–	–	–	–	3	–

Player	FAPL		League		FACup		LgeCup		Europe		Totals	
	App	Goals	App	Goals	App	Goals	App	Goals	App	Goals	App	Goals
B Thornley (1994/	-/1	–	–	–	–	–	–	–	–	–	-/1	–
G Tomlinson (1994/	–	–	–	–	–	–	-/2	–	–	–	-/2	–
WE Toms (1919/20)	–	–	13	3	1	1	–	–	–	–	14	4
HW Topping (1932/34)	–	–	12	1	–	–	–	–	–	–	12	1
WJ Tranter (1963)	–	–	–	–	–	–	–	–	–	–	–	–
GE Travers (1913/14)	–	–	21	4	–	–	–	–	–	–	21	4
A Turnbull (1906/14)	–	–	220	90	25	10	–	–	–	–	245	100
JM Turnbull (1907/09)	–	–	67	36	9	6	–	–	–	–	76	42
B Turner (1890)	–	–	1	–	–	–	–	–	–	–	1	–
CR Turner (1985/88)	–	–	64	1	8	–	7	–	–	–	79	1
J Turner (1898/1902)	–	–	3	–	1	–	–	–	–	–	4	–
R Turner (1898)	–	–	2	–	–	–	–	–	–	–	2	–
S Tyler (1923)	–	–	-/1	–	–	–	–	–	–	–	-/1	–
JF Ure (1969/70)	–	–	47	1	8	–	10	–	–	–	65	1
R Valentine (1904/05)	–	–	10	–	–	–	–	–	–	–	10	–
J Vance (1895/96)	–	–	11	1	–	–	–	–	–	–	11	1
E Vincent (1931/33)	–	–	64	1	1	–	–	–	–	–	65	1
DS Viollet (1952/61)	–	–	259	159	18	5	2	1	12	13	291	178
G Vose (1933/39)	–	–	197	1	14	–	–	–	–	–	211	1
C Waldron (1976)	–	–	3	–	–	–	1	–	–	–	4	–
DA Walker (1962)	–	–	1	–	–	–	–	–	–	–	1	–
R Walker (1898)	–	–	2	–	–	–	–	–	–	–	2	–
G Wall (1905/14)	–	–	287	89	29	9	–	–	–	–	316	98
DL Wallace (1989/93)	/2	–	36/9	6	7/2	2	4/3	3	5/2	–	52/18	11
G Walsh (1986/	12/1	–	37	–	–	–	7	–	6	–	62/1	–

Player	FAPL App	FAPL Goals	League App	League Goals	FACup App	FACup Goals	LgeCup App	LgeCup Goals	Europe App	Europe Goals	Totals App	Totals Goals
JA Walton (1951)	–	–	2	–	–	–	–	–	–	–	2	–
JW Walton (1945/47)	–	–	21	–	2	–	–	–	–	–	23	–
A Warburton (1929/33)	–	–	35	10	4	–	–	–	–	–	39	10
J Warner (1892)	–	–	22	–	–	–	–	–	–	–	22	–
J Warner (1938/47)	–	–	105	1	13	1	–	–	–	–	118	2
JV Wassall (1935/39)	–	–	46	6	2	–	–	–	–	–	48	6
W Watson (1970/72)	–	–	11	–	–	–	3	–	–	–	14	–
JA Wealands (1982/83)	–	–	7	–	–	–	1	–	–	–	8	–
NJ Webb (1989/92)	/1	–	70/4	8	9	1	14	1	11	1	104/5	11
C Webster (1953/58)	–	–	65	26	9	4	–	–	5	1	79	31
FE Wedge (1897)	–	–	2	2	–	–	–	–	–	–	2	2
EJ West (1910/14)	–	–	166	72	15	8	–	–	–	–	181	80
J Wetherell (1896)	–	–	2	–	–	–	–	–	–	–	2	–
A Whalley (1909/19)	–	–	97	6	9	–	–	–	–	–	106	6
H Whalley (1935/46)	–	–	33	–	6	–	–	–	–	–	39	–
AG Whelan (1980)	–	–	-/1	–	–	–	–	–	–	–	-/1	–
LA Whelan (1954/57)	–	–	79	43	6	4	–	–	11	5	96	52
J Whitefoot (1949/55)	–	–	93	–	2	–	–	–	–	–	95	–
J Whitehouse (1900/02)	–	–	59	–	5	–	–	–	–	–	64	–
W Whitehurst (1955)	–	–	1	–	–	–	–	–	–	–	1	–
KD Whiteside (1907)	–	–	–	–	1	–	–	–	–	–	1	–
N Whiteside (1981/89)	–	–	193/13	47	24	10	26/3	9	11/2	1	254/18	67
J Whitney (1895/1900)	–	–	3	–	–	–	–	–	–	–	3	–
W Whittaker (1895)	–	–	3	–	–	–	–	–	–	–	3	–
J Whitle (1931)	–	–	1	–	–	–	–	–	–	–	1	–

Player	FAPL		League		FACup		LgeCup		Europe		Totals	
	App	Goals	App	Goals	App	Goals	App	Goals	App	Goals	App	Goals
N Whitworth (1990/94)	–	–	1	–	–	–	–	–	–	–	1	–
TWJ Wilcox (1908)	–	–	2	–	–	–	–	–	–	–	2	–
RC Wilkins (1979/83)	–	–	158/2	7	10	1	14/1	1	8	1	190/3	10
H Wilkinson (1903)	–	–	8	–	1	–	–	–	–	–	9	–
IM Wilkinson (1991)	–	–	–	–	–	–	1	–	–	–	1	–
DR Williams (1927/28)	–	–	31	2	4	–	–	–	–	–	35	2
F Williams (1902)	–	–	8	–	2	4	–	–	–	–	10	4
F Williams (1930)	–	–	3	–	–	–	–	–	–	–	3	–
H Williams (1922)	–	–	5	2	–	–	–	–	–	–	5	2
H Williams (1904/05)	–	–	33	7	4	1	–	–	–	–	37	8
J Williams (1906)	–	–	3	1	–	–	–	–	–	–	3	1
W Williams (1901)	–	–	4	–	–	–	–	–	–	–	4	–
J Williamson (1919)	–	–	2	–	–	–	–	–	–	–	2	–
DG Wilson (1988)	–	–	–/4	–	–/2	–	–	–	–	–	–/6	–
E Wilson (1889)	–	–	19	6	1	–	–	–	–	–	20	6
JT Wilson (1926/31)	–	–	130	3	10	–	–	–	–	–	140	3
T Wilson (1907)	–	–	1	–	–	–	–	–	–	–	1	–
W Winterbottom (1936/37)	–	–	25	–	2	–	–	–	–	–	27	3
R Wombwell (1904/06)	–	–	47	3	4	–	–	–	–	–	51	3
J Wood (1922)	–	–	15	1	1	–	–	–	–	–	16	1
NA Wood (1985/86)	–	–	2/1	–	–	–	–/1	–	–	–	2/2	–
RE Wood (1949/58)	–	–	178	–	15	–	–	–	12	–	205	–

262

Name															
W Woodcock (1913/19)	–	–	–	58	20	3	1	–	–	–	–	–	61	21
H Worrall (1946/47)	–	–	–	6	–	–	–	–	–	–	–	–	6	–
P Wratten (1990/91)	–	–	–	-/2	–	–	–	–	–	–	–	–	-/2	–
W Wrigglesworth (1936/46)	–	–	–	30	8	7	2	–	–	–	–	–	37	10
W Yates (1906)	–	–	–	3	–	–	–	–	–	–	–	–	3	–
J Young (1906)	–	–	–	2	–	–	–	–	–	–	–	–	2	–
TA Young (1970/75)	–	–	–	69/14	1	5	–	–	5/4	–	–	–	79/18	1

Players' International Appearances Whilst with United

VA Anderson	– 1987 W Germany, 1988 Hungary, Columbia (3)
J Aston	– 1948 Denmark, Wales, Switzerland; 1949 Scotland, Sweden, Norway, France, Rep of Ireland, Wales, N Ireland, Italy; 1950 Scotland, Portugal, Belgium, Chile, USA, N Ireland(17)
GR Bailey	– 1985 Rep of Ireland, Mexico (2)
JJ Berry	– 1953 Argentina, Chile, Uruguay; 1956 Sweden (4)
W Bradley	– 1959 Italy, Mexico, USA, (3)
RW Byrne	– 1954 Scotland, Yugoslavia, Hungary, Belgium, Switzerland, Uruguay, N Ireland, Wales, West Germany; 1955 Scotland, France, Spain, Portugal, Denmark, Wales, N Ireland, Spain; 1956 Scotland, Sweden, Brazil, Finland, West Germany, N Ireland, Wales, Yugoslavia, Denmark; 1957 Scotland, Rep of Ireland, Denmark, Rep of Ireland, Wales, N Ireland, France(33)
R Charlton	– 1958 Scotland, Portugal, Yugoslavia, N Ireland, USSR, Wales; 1959 Scotland, Italy, Brazil, Peru, Mexico, USA, Wales, Sweden; 1960 Scotland, Yugoslavia, Spain, Hungary, N Ireland, Luxembourg, Spain, Wales; 1961 Scotland, Mexico, Portugal, Italy, Austria, Luxembourg, Wales, Portugal, N Ireland; 1962 Austria, Scotland, Switzerland, Peru, Hungary, Argentina, Bulgaria, Brazil; 1963 France, Scotland, Brazil, Czechoslovakia, East Germany, Switzerland, Wales, Rest of World, N Ireland; 1964 Scotland, Uruguay, Portugal, Rep of Ireland, USA, Brazil, Argentina, N Ireland, Holland; 1965 Scotland, Wales, Austria, N Ireland, Spain; 1966 West Germany, Scotland, Yugoslavia, Finland, Norway, Poland, Uruguay, Mexico, France, Argentina, Portugal, West Germany, N Ireland, Czechoslovakia, Wales; 1967 Scotland, Wales, N Ireland, USSR; 1968 Scotland, Spain, Spain, Sweden, Yugoslavia, USSR, Romania, Bulgaria; 1969 Romania, N Ireland, Wales, Scotland, Mexico, Brazil, Holland, Portugal; 1970 Holland, Wales, N Ireland, Colombia, Ecuador, Romania, Brazil, Czechoslovakia, West Germany (106)
AC Chilton	– 1950 N Ireland; 1951 France (2)
H Cockburn	– 1946 N Ireland, Rep of Ireland, Wales; 1948 Scotland, Italy, Denmark, N Ireland, Switzerland; 1949 Scotland, Sweden; 1951 Argentina, Portugal, France (13)
A Cole	– 1995 Uruguay (1)
JM Connelly	– 1965 Hungary, Yugoslavia, Sweden, Wales, Austria, N Ireland; 1966 Scotland, Norway, Denmark, Uruguay (10)
SJ Coppell	– 1977 Italy; 1978 West Germany, Brazil, Wales, N Ireland,

	Scotland, Hungary, Denmark, Rep of Ireland, Czechoslovakia; 1979 N Ireland (twice), Wales, Scotland, Bulgaria, Austria, Denmark, N Ireland; 1980 Rep of Ireland, Spain, Argentina, Wales, Scotland, Belgium, Italy, Romania, Switzerland; 1981 Romania, Brazil, Wales, Scotland, Switzerland, Hungary (twice); 1982 Scotland, Finland, Spain, Czechoslovakia, Kuwait, West Germany, Luxembourg; 1983 Greece (42)
M Duxbury	– 1983 Luxembourg; 1984, France, Wales, Scotland, USSR, Brazil, Uruguay, Chile, East Germany, Finland (10)
D Edwards	– 1955 Scotland, France, Spain, Portugal; 1956 Scotland, Brazil, Sweden, Finland, West Germany, N Ireland, Denmark; 1957 Scotland, Rep of Ireland, Denmark, Rep of Ireland, Wales, N Ireland, France (18)
WA Foulkes	– 1954 N Ireland (1)
B Greenhoff	– 1976 Wales, N Ireland, Rep of Ireland, Finland, Italy; 1977 Holland, N Ireland, Wales, Scotland, Brazil, Argentina, Uruguay; 1978 Brazil, Wales, N Ireland, Scotland, Hungary (17)
HJ Halse	– 1909 Austria (1)
GA Hill	– 1976 Italy, Rep of Ireland, Finland; 1977 Luxembourg, Switzerland, Luxembourg (6)
P Ince	– 1992 Spain, Norway, Turkey; 1993 Turkey, Holland, Poland, USA, Brazil, Germany; 1994 Poland, Holland, San Marino, Norway, Romania; 1995 Eire (16)
B Kidd	– 1970 N Ireland, Ecuador (2)
W McGuinness	– 1958 N Ireland; 1959 Mexico (2)
JW Mew	– 1920 Ireland (1)
GA Pallister	– 1991 Cameroon, Turkey, Germany; 1993 Norway, USA, Brazil, Germany; 1994 Poland, Holland, San Marino, Denmark, USA, Romania; 1995 Eire, Uruguay (15)
P Parker	– 1991 Germany; 1994 Holland, Denmark (3)
JS Pearson	– 1976 Wales, N Ireland, Scotland, Brazil, Finland, Rep of Ireland; 1977 Holland, Wales, Scotland, Brazil, Argentina, Uruguay, Italy; 1978 West Germany, N Ireland (15)
SC Pearson	– 1948 Scotland, N Ireland; 1949 Scotland, N Ireland, Italy; 1951 Portugal; 1952 Scotland, Italy (8)
D Pegg	– 1957 Rep of Ireland (1)
MC Phelan	– 1989 Italy (1)
C Roberts	– 1905 Ireland, Wales, Scotland (3)
B Robson	– 1981 Hungary; 1982 N Ireland, Wales, Holland, Scotland, Finland, France, Czechoslovakia, West Germany, Spain, Denmark, Greece, Luxembourg; 1983 Scotland, Hungary,

	Luxembourg; 1984 France, N Ireland, Scotland, USSR, Brazil, Uruguay, Chile, East Germany, Finland, Turkey; 1985 Rep of Ireland, Romania, Finland, Scotland, Italy, Mexico, West Germany, USA, Romania, Turkey; 1986 Israel, Mexico, Portugal, Morocco, N Ireland; 1987 Spain, N Ireland, Turkey, Brazil, Scotland, Turkey, Yugoslavia; 1988 Holland, Hungary, Scotland, Columbia, Switzerland, Rep of Ireland, Holland, USSR, Denmark, Sweden, Saudi Arabia; 1989 Greece, Albania, Albania, Chile, Scotland, Poland, Denmark, Poland, Italy, Yugoslavia; 1990 Czechoslovakia, Uruguay, Tunisia, Rep of Ireland, Holland; 1991 Cameroon, Rep of Ireland, Turkey (77)
JF Rowley	– 1948 Switzerland; 1949 Sweden, France, N Ireland, Italy; 1952 Scotland (6)
D Sadler	– 1967 N Ireland, USSR; 1970 Ecuador, East Germany (4)
LS Sharpe	– 1991 Rep of Ireland; 1993 Turkey, Norway, USA, Brazil, Germany; 1994 Poland (7)
J Silcock	– 1921 Wales, Scotland; 1923 Sweden (3)
JW Spence	– 1926 Belgium, N Ireland (2)
AC Stepney	– 1968 Sweden
NP Stiles	– 1965 Scotland, Hungary, Yugoslavia, Sweden, Wales, Austria, N Ireland, Spain; 1966 Poland, West Germany, Scotland, Norway, Denmark, Poland, Uruguay, Mexico, France, Argentina, Portugal, West Germany, N Ireland, Czechoslovakia, Wales; 1967 Scotland; 1968 USSR; 1969 Romania; 1970 N Ireland, Scotland (28)
T Taylor	– 1953 Argentina, Chile, Uruguay; 1954 Belgium, Switzerland; 1956 Scotland, Brazil, Sweden, Finland, West Germany, N Ireland, Yugoslavia, Denmark; 1957 Rep of Ireland, Denmark, Rep of Ireland, Wales, N Ireland, France (19)
DS Viollet	– 1960 Hungary; 1961 Luxembourg (2)
G Wall	– 1907 Wales; 1908 Ireland; 1909 Scotland; 1910 Wales, Scotland; 1912 Scotland; 1913 Ireland (7)
NJ Webb	– 1989 Sweden; 1990 Italy; 1992 France, Hungary, Brazil (5)
RG Wilkins	– 1979 Denmark, N Ireland, Bulgaria; 1980 Spain, Argentina, Wales, N Ireland, Scotland, Belgium, Italy, Spain; 1981 Spain, Romania, Brazil, Wales, Scotland, Switzerland, Hungary; 1982 N Ireland, Wales, Holland, Scotland, Finland, France, Czechoslovakia, Kuwait, West Germany, Spain, Denmark, West Germany; 1983 Denmark; 1984 N Ireland, Wales, Scotland, USSR, Brazil, Uruguay, Chile (38)
RE Wood	– 1954 N Ireland, Wales; 1956 Finland (3)

T Anderson – 1973 Cyprus, England, Scotland, Wales, Bulgaria, Portugal (6)

G Best – 1964 Wales, Uruguay, England, Switzerland, Switzerland, Scotland; 1965 Holland, Holland, Albania, Scotland, England, Albania; 1966 England; 1967 Scotland; 1968 Turkey; 1969 England, Scotland, Wales, USSR; 1970 Scotland, England, Wales, Spain; 1971 Cyprus, Cyprus, England, Scotland, Wales, USSR; 1972 Spain, Bulgaria; 1973 Portugal (32)

J Blanchflower – 1954 Wales, England, Scotland; 1955 Scotland; 1956 Wales, England, Scotland; 1957 Portugal, Scotland, England, Italy; 1958 Italy (12)

T Breen – 1937 Wales, England, Scotland; 1938 Scotland; 1939 Wales (5)

WR Briggs – Wales (1)

JJ Carey – 1946 England, Scotland; 1947 Wales, England; 1948 England, Scotland; 1949 Wales (7)

W Crooks – 1922 Wales (1)

MM Donaghy – 1988 Spain; 1989 Spain, Malta, Chile, Rep of Ireland; 1990 Norway, Yugoslavia, Denmark, Austria; 1991 Poland, Yugoslavia, Faroe Islands, Faroe Islands, Austria, Denmark; 1992 Scotland, Lithuania (18)

K. Gillespie – Portugal, Austria, Rep of Ireland (3)

H Gregg – 1958 Wales, Czechoslovakia, Argentina, West Germany, France, England; 1959 Wales, Scotland, England; 1960 Wales, England, Scotland; 1961 Scotland, Greece; 1963 Scotland, England (16)

M Hamill – 1912 England; 1914 England, Scotland (3)

TA Jackson – 1975 Sweden, Norway, Yugoslavia; 1976 Holland, Belgium; 1977 West Germany, England, Scotland, Wales, Iceland (10)

D Lyner – 1922 England (1)

D McCreery – 1976 Scotland, England, Wales, Holland, Belgium; 1977 West Germany, England, Scotland, Wales, Iceland, Iceland, Holland, Belgium; 1978 Scotland, England, Wales, Rep of Ireland, Denmark, Bulgaria; 1979 England, Bulgaria, Wales, Denmark (23)

RC McGrath – 1976 Belgium; 1977 West Germany, England, Scotland, Wales, Iceland, Iceland, Holland, Belgium; 1978 Scotland, England, Wales, Bulgaria; 1979 England (15)

SB McIlroy – 1972 Spain, Scotland; 1974 Scotland, England, Wales, Norway, Sweden; 1975 Yugoslavia, England, Scotland, Wales, Sweden, Norway, Yugoslavia; 1976 Scotland, England, Wales, Holland, Belgium; 1977 England, Scotland, Wales, Iceland, Iceland, Holland, Belgium; 1978 Scotland, England, Wales, Rep of

	Ireland, Denmark, Bulgaria; 1979 England, Bulgaria, England, Scotland, Wales, Denmark, England, Rep of Ireland; 1980 Israel, Scotland, England, Wales, Australia, Australia, Australia, Sweden, Portugal; 1981 Scotland, Portugal, Scotland, Sweden, Scotland, Israel (52)
ST McMillan	– 1962 England, Scotland (2)
WS McMillen	– 1933 England; 1934 Scotland; 1936 Scotland (3)
JM Nicholl	– 1976 Israel, Wales, Holland, Belgium; 1977 England, Scotland, Wales, Iceland, Iceland, Holland, Belgium; 1978 Scotland, England, Wales, Rep of Ireland, Denmark, Bulgaria; 1979 England, Bulgaria, England, Scotland, Wales, Denmark, England, Rep of Ireland; 1980 Israel, Scotland, England, Wales, Sweden, Australia, Australia, Australia, Sweden, Portugal; 1981 Scotland, Portugal, Scotland, Sweden, Scotland, Israel; 1982 England (41)
JJ Nicholson	– 1960 Scotland; 1961 Wales, Greece, England; 1962 Wales, Holland, Poland, England, Scotland, Poland (10)
T Sloan	– 1979 Scotland, Wales, Denmark (3)
N Whiteside	– 1982 Yugoslavia, Honduras, Spain, Austria, France, West Germany, Albania; 1983 Turkey, Austria, Turkey, West Germany, Scotland; 1984 England, Wales, Finland, Romania, Israel, Finland; 1985 England, Spain, Turkey, Romania, England; 1986 France, Denmark, Morocco, Algeria, Spain,Brazil, England; 1987 Israel, England, Yugoslavia, Turkey; 1988 Poland, France (36)

Scotland

A Albiston	– 1982 N Ireland; 1983 Uruguay, Belgium, East Germany; 1984 Wales, England, Yugoslavia, Iceland, Spain; 1985 Spain, Wales, East Germany; 1986 Holland, Uruguay (14)
A Bell	– 1912 Ireland (1)
MM Buchan	– 1972 Wales, Yugoslavia, Czechoslovakia, Brazil, Denmark, Denmark; 1973 England; 1974 West Germany, N Ireland, Wales, Norway, Brazil, Yugoslavia, East Germany; 1975 Spain, Portugal, Denmark, Romania; 1976 Finland, Czechoslovakia; 1977 Chile, Argentina, Brazil, East Germany, Wales; 1978 N Ireland, Peru, Iran, Holland, Austria, Norway, Portugal(32)
FS Burns	– 1969 Austria (1)
PT Crerand	– 1963 N Ireland; 1965 England, Poland, Finland, Poland (5)
J Delaney	– 1947 England, N Ireland, Wales; 1948 England (4)
A Forsyth	– 1973 England; 1974 East Germany, Spain; 1975 N Ireland, Romania, Denmark (6)
G Graham	– 1973 England, Wales, N Ireland, Switzerland, Brazil (5)

JA Holton	– 1973 Wales, N Ireland, England, Switzerland, Brazil, Czechoslovakia, West Germany; 1974 N Ireland, Wales, England, Norway, Zaire, Brazil, Yugoslavia, East Germany (15)
SM Houston	– 1975 Denmark (1)
J Jordan	– 1978 Bulgaria, N Ireland, England, Peru, Iran, Holland, Austria, Portugal; 1979 Wales, N Ireland, England, Norway, Belgium; 1980 N Ireland, Wales, England, Poland; 1981 Israel, Wales, England (20)
D Law	– 1962 Wales, N Ireland; 1963 England, Austria, Norway, Rep of Ireland, Spain, Norway, Wales; 1964 England, West Germany, Wales, Finland, N Ireland; 1965 England, Spain, Poland, Finland, N Ireland, Poland; 1966 England, Wales; 1967 England, USSR, N Ireland; 1968 Austria; 1969 West Germany, N Ireland; 1972 Peru, N Ireland, Wales, England, Yugoslavia, Czechoslovakia, Brazil (35)
J Leighton	– 1988 Colombia, England, Norway; 1989 Cyprus, France, Cyprus, England, Chile, Yugoslavia, France, Norway; 1990 Argentina, Malta, Costa Rica, Sweden, Brazil (16)
N McBain	– 1922 England (1)
BJ McClair	– 1987 Bulgaria; 1988 Malta, Spain, Norway, Yugoslavia, Italy; 1989 Cyprus, France, Norway; 1990 Argentina, Bulgaria; 1991 Bulgaria, San Marino, Switzerland, Romania; 1992 Northern Ireland, USA, Canada (18)
G McQueen	– 1978 Bulgaria, N Ireland, Wales, Austria, Norway, Portugal; 1979 N Ireland, England, Norway, Peru, Austria, Belgium; 1981 Wales (13)
L Macari	– 1973 England, Wales, N Ireland, England; 1975 Sweden, Portugal, Wales, England, Romania; 1977 N Ireland, England, Chile, Argentina, East Germany, Wales; 1978 Bulgaria, Peru, Iran (18)
T Miller	– 1921 Ireland, England (2)
W Morgan	– 1972 Peru, Yugoslavia, Czechoslovakia, Brazil, Denmark, Denmark; 1973 England, Wales, N Ireland, England, Switzerland, Brazil, Czechoslovakia, Czechoslovakia, West Germany; 1974 West Germany, N Ireland, Belgium, Brazil, Yugoslavia (20)
GD Strachan	– 1985 Spain, England, Iceland, Wales, Australia; 1986 Romania, Denmark, West Germany, Uruguay, Bulgaria, Rep of Ireland; 1987 Rep of Ireland, Hungary; 1989 France (14)

Wales

SR Bennison	– 1925 Scotland; 1926 Scotland; 1927 Scotland, England; 1928 N Ireland, Scotland, England; 1929 N Ireland, Scotland; 1931 N Ireland (10)

CG Blackmore	– 1985 Norway, Scotland, Hungary; 1986 Saudi Arabia, Rep of Ireland, Uruguay, Finland; 1987 USSR, Finland, Czechoslovakia, Denmark, Denmark, Czechoslovakia; 1988 Yugoslavia, Sweden, Malta, Italy, Holland, Finland; 1989 Israel, West Germany, Finland, Holland, West Germany; 1990 Costa Rica, Belgium, Luxembourg; 1992 Rep of Ireland, Austria, Romania, Holland, Argentina, Japan; 1993 Faroe Islands, Cyprus, Belgium, Czechoslovakia; 1994 Sweden (38)
T Burke	– 1887 England, Scotland, 1888 Scotland (3)
A Davies	– 1983 N Ireland, Brazil; 1984 England, N Ireland, Iceland, Iceland; 1985 Norway (7)
J Davies	– 1888 England, Ireland, Scotland; 1889 Scotland; 1890 England (5)
R W Davies	– 1972 England; 1973 Scotland, N Ireland (3)
J Doughty	– 1887 Ireland, Scotland; 1888 England, Ireland, Scotland; 1889 Scotland; 1890 England (7)
R Doughty	– 1888 Ireland, Scotland (2)
RJ Giggs	– 1991 Germany, Luxembourg; 1992 Romania, Faroe Islands, Belgium; 1993 Czechoslovakia, Belgium, Faroe Islands; 1994 Czechoslovakia, Cyprus, Romania, Albania; 1995 Bulgaria (13)
LM Hughes	– 1984 England, N Ireland, Iceland, Spain, Iceland; 1985 Norway, Scotland, Spain, Norway, Scotland, Hungary; 1986 Uruguay; 1988 Holland, Finland; 1989 Israel, Sweden, West Germany, Finland, West Germany; 1990 Costa Rica, Denmark, Belgium, Luxembourg; 1991 Belgium, Iceland, Poland, Germany, Brazil, Germany, Luxembourg; 1992 Rep of Ireland, Romania, Holland, Argentina, Japan; 1993 Faroe Islands, Belgium, Czechoslovakia. Cyprus, Eire, Belgium, Faroe Islands; 1994 Norway; 1994 Czechoslovakia, Cyprus, Georgia, Bulgaria, Germany (48)
CAL Jenkyns	– 1897 Ireland (1)
T Jones	– 1926 N Ireland; 1927 England, N Ireland; 1930 N Ireland (4)
WH Meredith	– 1907 Ireland, Scotland, England; 1908 England, Ireland; 1909 Scotland, England, Ireland; 1910 Scotland, England, Ireland; 1911 Ireland, Scotland, England; 1912 Scotland, England, Ireland; 1913 Ireland, Scotland, England; 1914 Ireland, Scotland, England; 1920 Ireland, Scotland, England (26)
G Moore	– 1963 Scotland; 1964 N Ireland (2)
G Owen	– 1889 Scotland, Ireland (2)
J Owen	– 1892 England (1)
W Owen	– 1888 England; 1889 England, Scotland, Ireland (4)
J Powell	– 1887 England, Scotland; 1888 England, Ireland, Scotland (5)
H Thomas	– 1927 England

MR Thomas	– 1978 Turkey; 1979 West Germany, Malta, Rep of Ireland, West Germany, Turkey; 1980 England, Scotland, N Ireland, Czechoslovakia; 1981 Scotland, England, USSR (13)
J Warner	– 1939 France (1)
C Webster	– 1957 Czechoslovakia; 1958 Hungary, Mexico, Brazil (4)
DR Williams	– 1928 Scotland, England (2)

Republic of Ireland

T Breen	– 1937 Switzerland, France (2)
SA Brennan	– 1965 Spain, Spain; 1966 Austria, Belgium, Spain, Turkey, Spain; 1969 Czechoslovakia, Denmark, Hungary, Scotland, Czechoslovakia, Denmark, Hungary; 1970 Poland, West Germany (16)
N Cantwell	– 1961 Scotland, Scotland, Czechoslovakia, Czechoslovakia; 1962 Austria, Iceland, Iceland; 1963 Scotland, Austria; 1964 Spain, England, Poland; 1965 Spain, Spain, Spain; 1966 Austria, Belgium, Spain; 1967 Turkey (19)
B Carey	– 1992 USA, 1993 Wales (2)
JJ Carey	– 1937 Norway; 1938 Czechoslovakia, Poland, Switzerland, Poland; 1939 Hungary, Hungary, Germany; 1946 Portugal, Spain, England; 1947 Spain, Portugal; 1948 Portugal, Spain, Switzerland; 1949 Belgium, Portugal, Sweden, Spain, Finland, England, Finland, Sweden; 1950 Norway; 1951 Argentina, Norway; 1952 France; 1953 Austria (29)
JE Carolan	– 1959 Sweden; 1960 Chile (2)
GA Daly	– 1973 Poland, Norway; 1974 Brazil, Uruguay; 1975 West Germany, Switzerland; 1976 England, Turkey, France (9)
AP Dunne	– 1962 Austria, Iceland; 1963 Scotland, Austria; 1964 Spain, Norway, England, Norway, England, Poland; 1965 Spain, Spain, Spain; 1966 Austria, Belgium, Spain, Turkey, Spain; 1968 Poland, Denmark; 1969 Hungary, Hungary; 1970 Sweden; 1971 Italy, Austria (24)
PAJ Dunne	– 1965 Spain, Spain, Spain; 1966 West Germany, Turkey (5)
MJ Giles	– 1959 Sweden; 1960 Chile, Wales, Norway; 1961 Scotland, Scotland, Czechoslovakia, Czechoslovakia; 1962 Austria, Iceland; 1963 Scotland (11)
DJ Givens	– 1969 Denmark, Hungary, Scotland, Czechoslovakia, Denmark, Hungary (6)
AA Grimes	– 1978 Turkey, Poland, Norway, England; 1979 Bulgaria, USA, N Ireland; 1980 England, Cyprus; 1981 Czechoslovakia, West Germany, Poland; 1982 Algeria, Spain; 1983 Spain (15)
DJ Irwin	– 1990 Morocco, Turkey; 1991 Wales, England, Poland, USA,

		Hungary, Poland; 1992 Wales, USA, Albania, USA, Italy; 1993 Latvia, Denmark, Spain, N. Ireland, Denmark, Albania, Latvia, Lithuania; 1994 Lithuania, Spain, N. Ireland, Bolivia, Germany, Italy, Mexico, Latvia, N. Ireland; 1995 England, N.Ireland, Portugal (33)
R Keane	–	1994 Lithuania, Spain, N.Ireland, Bolivia, Germany, Czechoslovakia, Italy, Mexico, Norway, Holland, N.Ireland; 1995 N. Ireland (13)
P McGrath	–	1985 Italy, Israel, England, Norway, Switzerland, Switzerland, Denmark; 1986 Wales, Iceland, Czechoslovakia, Belgium, Scotland, Poland; 1987 Scotland, Bulgaria, Belgium, Brazil, Luxembourg, Luxembourg, Bulgaria; 1988 Yugoslavia, Poland, Norway, England, Holland, N Ireland; 1989 France, Hungary, Spain, Malta, Hungary (31)
MP Martin	–	1973 USSR, Poland, France, Norway, Poland; 1974 Brazil, Uruguay, Chile, USSR, Turkey; 1975 West Germany, Switzerland, USSR, Switzerland (14)
KR Moran	–	1980 Switzerland, Argentina, Belgium, France, Cyprus; 1981 Wales, Belgium, Czechoslovakia, West Germany, Poland, France; 1982 Algeria, Iceland, Holland, Malta; 1984 Israel, Mexico; 1985 Denmark, Iceland, Czechoslovakia, Belgium, Scotland, Poland; 1987 Scotland, Bulgaria, Belgium, Brazil, Luxembourg, Luxembourg, Bulgaria, Israel; 1988 Romania, Yugoslavia, Poland, Norway, England, USSR, Holland (38)
LF O'Brien	–	1987 Brazil, Israel; 1988 Romania, Yugoslavia, Poland, Tunisia (6)
PJ Roche	–	1974 USSR, Turkey; 1975 West Germany, Switzerland, USSR, Switzerland, Turkey (7)
FA Stapleton	–	1981 Holland, France; 1982 Algeria, Holland, Iceland, Spain; 1983 Malta, Spain, Iceland, Holland, Malta; 1984 Israel, Poland, China, Norway, Denmark; 1985 Italy, Israel, England, Norway, Switzerland, Switzerland, USSR, Denmark; 1986 Uruguay, Iceland, Czechoslovakia, Belgium, Scotland, Poland; 1987 Scotland, Bulgaria, Belgium, Luxembourg (34)
L A Whelan	–	1956 Holland, Denmark; 1957 England, England (4)
France		
E Cantona	–	1994 Italy; 1993 Finland; 1993 Israel, Sweden, Sweden, Finland, Israel, Bulgaria; 1994 Slovakia, Romania, Poland, Azerbajan, Holland (13)

Denmark

J Olsen — 1984 Austria, Norway, Switzerland; 1985 East Germany, USSR, Rep of Ireland; 1986 N Ireland, Bulgaria, Poland, Paraguay, Scotland, Uruguay, West Germany, Spain, East Germany, West Germany, Czechoslovakia; 1987 Czechoslovakia, Sweden, West Germany, Wales; 1988 Austria, Hungary, Czechoslovakia, Belgium (25)

P Schmeichel — 1991 Italy, Sweden, Faroe Islands, Austria, N Ireland; 1992 England, Sweden, France, Holland, Germany; 1994 England, 1992 Latvia, Lithuania, Eire, N. Ireland; 1993 Spain, Latvia, Eire, Albania, Lithuania, Albania, N.Ireland, Spain; 1994 Macedonia, Belgium, Spain 1995 Cyprus, Macedonia (22)

J Sivebaek — 1986 N Ireland, Bulgaria, Norway, Poland, Scotland, West Germany, East Germany, Finland, West Germany; 1987 Finland, Czechoslovakia (11)

USSR/Russia

A Kanchelskis — 1991 Hungary, England, Argentina, Cyprus, Sweden, Italy, Norway, Hungary, Italy, Cyprus; 1992 Spain, England; 1994 Germany, San Marino, Scotland; 1995 Slovakia, Scotland (22)

Yugoslavia

N Jovanovic — 1980 Luxembourg, Denmark; 1982 N Ireland, Spain, Honduras (5)

Rest of the World

D Law — 1963 England (1)

Rest of Europe

JJ Carey — 1947 Great Britain (1)
R Charlton — 1964 Scandinavia (1)
D Law — 1964 Scandinavia (1)

Full Record in Domestic Cup Competitions – *FA Cup*

1886/87

1st Round	v Fleetwood Rangers	(a)	2-2	Doughty 2

(tie awarded to Fleetwood as Newton Heath refused to play extra-time)

1889/90

1st Round	v Preston North End	(a)	1-6	Craig

1890/91

1st Qual Round	v Higher Walton	(h)	2-0	Farman, Evans
2nd Qual Round	v Bootle Reserves	(a)	0-1	

(both teams fielded virtual Reserve teams)

1891/92

1st Qual Round	v Ardwick	(h)	5-1	Farman 2, Doughty, Sneddon, Edge
2nd Qual Round	v Heywood			*(Heywood withdrew)*
3rd Qual Round	v South Shore	(a)	2-0	Farman, Doughty,
4th Qual Round	v Blackpool	(h)	3-4	Farman, Edge 2

1892/93

1st Round	v Blackburn Rovers	(a)	0-4	

1893/94

1st Round	v Middlesbrough	(h)	4-0	Farman, Pedden Donaldson 2,
2nd Round	v Blackburn Rovers	(h)	0-0†	
Replay	v Blackburn Rovers	(a)	1-5	Donaldson

1894/95

1st Round	v Stoke City	(h)	2-3	Smith, Peters

1895/96

1st Round	v Kettering Town	(h)	2-1	Donaldson, Smith
2nd Round	v Derby County	(h)	1-1	Kennedy
Replay	v Derby County	(a)	1-5	Donaldson

1896/97

3rd Qual Round	v West Manchester	(h)	7-0	Cassidy 2, Gillespie 2, Rothwell 2, Bryant
4th Qual Round	v Nelson	(a)	3-0	Cassidy, Donaldson, Gillespie
5th Qual Round	v Blackpool	(h)	2-2	Gillespie, Donaldson
Replay	v Blackpool	(a)	2-1	Boyd, Cassidy
1st Round	v Kettering Town	(h)	5-1	Cassidy, Donaldson
2nd Round	v Southampton	(a)	1-1	Donaldson
Replay	v Southampton	(h)	3-1	Bryant 2, Cassidy
3rd Round	v Derby County	(a)	0-2	

† Extra time

274

1897/98

1st Round	v Walsall	(h)	1-0	Own Goal
2nd Round	v Liverpool	(h)	0-0	
Replay	v Liverpool	(a)	1-2	Collinson

1898/99

1st Round	v Tottenham Hotspur	(a)	1-1	Cassidy
Replay	v Tottenham Hotspur	(h)	3-5	Bryant 3

1899/00

3rd Qual Round	v South Shore	(a)	1-3	Jackson

1900/01

Prelim Round	v Portsmouth	(h)	3-0	Griffiths, Jackson, Stafford
1st Round	v Burnley	(h)	0-0	
Replay	v Burnley	(a)	1-7	Schofield

1901/02

Prelim Round	v Lincoln City	(h)	1-2	Fisher

1902/03

3rd Qual Round	v Accrington Stanley	(h)	7-0	Williams 3, Peddie, Richards, Pegg, Morgan
4th Qual Round	v Oswaldtwistle Rovers	(h)	3-2	Pegg, Beardsworth, Williams
5th Qual Round	v Southport Central	(h)	4-1	Pegg 3, Banks
6th Qual Round	v Burton United	(h)	1-1	Griffiths
Replay	v Burton United	(h)	3-1	Schofield, Pegg, Peddie
1st Round	v Liverpool	(h)	2-1	Peddie 2
2nd Round	v Everton	(a)	1-3	Griffiths

1903/04

Prelim Round	v Small Heath	(h)	1-1	Schofield
Replay	v Small Heath	(a)	1-1†	Arkesden
2nd Replay	v Small Heath	(n)	1-1†	Schofield
3rd Replay	v Small Heath	(n)	3-1	Arkesden 2, Grassam
1st Round	v Notts County	(a)	3-3	Downie, Schofield, Arkesden
Replay	v Notts County	(h)	2-1	Morrison, Pegg
2nd Round	v Sheffield Wednesday	(a)	0-6	

1904/05

Prelim Round	v Fulham	(h)	2-2	Mackie, Arkesden
Replay	v Fulham	(a)	0-0†	
2nd Replay	v Fulham	(n)	0-1	

1905/06

1st Round	v Staple Hill	(h)	7-2	Beddow 3, Picken 2, Allen, Williams

2nd Round	v Norwich City	(h)	3-0	Downie, Peddie, Sagar
3rd Round	v Aston Villa	(h)	5-1	Picken 3, Sagar 2
4th Round	v Woolwich Arsenal	(h)	2-3	Peddie, Sagar

1906/07

1st Round	v Portsmouth	(a)	2-2	Picken, Wall
Replay	v Portsmouth	(h)	1-2	Wall

1907/08

1st Round	v Blackpool	(h)	3-1	Wall 2, Bannister
2nd Round	v Chelsea	(h)	1-0	A.Turnbull
3rd Round	v Aston Villa	(a)	2-0	A.Turnbull, Wall
4th Round	v Fulham	(a)	1-2	J.Turnbull

1908/09

1st Round	v Brighton & H.A	(h)	1-0	Halse
2nd Round	v Everton	(h)	1-0	Halse
3rd Round	v Blackburn Rovers	(h)	6-1	A.Turnbull 3, J.Turnbull 3
4th Round	v Burnley	(a)	3-2	J Turnbull 2, Halse
Semi Final	v Newcastle United	(n)	1-0	Halse
Final	v Bristol City	(n)	1-0	A.Turnbull

1909/10

1st Round	v Burnley	(a)	0-2	

1910/11

1st Round	v Blackpool	(a)	2-1	Picken, West
2nd Round	v Aston Villa	(h)	2-1	Halse, Wall
3rd Round	v West Ham United	(a)	1-2	A.Turnbull

1911/12

1st Round	v Huddersfield Town	(h)	3-1	West 2, Halse
2nd Round	v Coventry City	(a)	5-1	Halse 2, West, Turnbull, Wall
3rd Round	v Reading	(a)	1-1	West
Replay	v Reading	(h)	3-0	A.Turnbull 2, Halse
4th Round	v Blackburn Rovers	(h)	1-1	Own Goal
Replay	v Blackburn Rovers	(a)	2-4†	West 2

1912/13

1st Round	v Coventry City	(h)	1-1	Wall
Replay	v Coventry City	(a)	2-1	Anderson, Roberts
2nd Round	v Plymouth Argyle	(a)	2-0	Anderson, Wall
3rd Round	v Oldham Athletic	(a)	0-0	
Replay	v Oldham Athletic	(h)	1-2	West

1913/14

1st Round	v Swindon Town	(a)	0-1	

1914/15

1st Round	v Sheffield Wednesday	(a)	0-1	

1919/20
1st Round	v Port Vale	(a)	1-0	Toms
2nd Round	v Aston Villa	(h)	1-2	Woodcock

1920/21
1st Round	v Liverpool	(a)	1-1	Miller
Replay	v Liverpool	(h)	1-2	Partridge

1921/22
1st Round	v Cardiff City	(h)	1-4	Sapsford

1922/23
1st Round	v Bradford City	(a)	1-1	Partridge
Replay	v Bradford City	(h)	2-0	Barber, Goldthorpe
2nd Round	v Tottenham Hotspurs	(a)	0-4	

1923/24
1st Round	v Plymouth Argyle	(h)	1-0	McPherson
2nd Round	v Huddersfield Town	(h)	0-3	

1925/25
1st Round	v Sheffield Wednesday	(a)	0-2	

1925/26
3rd Round	v Port Vale	(a)	3-2	Spence 2, McPherson
4th Round	v Tottenham Hotspurs	(a)	2-2	Spence, Thomas
Replay	v Tottenham Hotspurs	(h)	2-0	Spence, Rennox
5th Round	v Sunderland	(a)	3-3	Smith 2, McPherson
Replay	v Sunderland	(h)	2-1	Smith, McPherson
6th Round	v Fulham	(a)	2-1	Smith, McPherson
Semi Final	v Manchester City	(n)	0-3	

1926/27
3rd Round	v Reading	(a)	1-1	Bennion
Replay	v Reading	(h)	2-2	Spence, Sweeney
2nd Replay	v Reading	(n)	1-2	McPherson

1927/28
3rd Round	v Brentford	(h)	7-1	Hanson 4, Spence, McPherson, Johnston
4th Round	v Bury	(a)	1-1	Johnston
Replay	v Bury	(h)	1-0	Johnston
5th Round	v Birmingham	(h)	1-0	Spence
6th Round	v Blackburn Rovers	(a)	0-2	Johnston

1928/29
3rd Round	v Port Vale	(a)	3-0	Spence, Hanson, Taylor
4th Round	v Bury	(h)	0-1	

1929/30
3rd Round	v Swindon Town	(h)	0-2	

1930/31

3rd Round	v Stoke City	(a)	3-3	Reid 3
Replay	v Stoke City	(h)	0-0†	
2nd Replay	v Stoke City	(n)	4-2	Hopkinson 2, Spence, Gallimore
4th Round	v Grimsby Town	(a)	0-1	

1931/32

3rd Round	v Plymouth Argyle	(a)	1-4	Reid

1932/33

3rd Round	v Middlesbrough	(h)	1-4	Spence

1933/34

3rd Round	v Portsmouth	(h)	1-1	McLenahan
Replay	v Portsmouth	(a)	1-4	Ball

1934/35

3rd Round	v Bristol Rovers	(a)	3-1	Bamford 2, Mutch
4th Round	v Nottingham Forest	(a)	0-0	
Replay	v Nottingham Forest	(h)	0-3	

1935/36

3rd Round	v Reading	(a)	3-1	Mutch 2, Manley
4th Round	v Stoke City	(a)	0-0	
Replay	v Stoke City	(h)	0-2	

1936/37

3rd Round	v Reading	(h)	1-0	Bamford
4th Round	v Arsenal	(a)	0-5	

1937/38

3rd Round	v Yeovil Town	(h)	3-0	Baird, Bamford, Pearson
4th Round	v Barnsley	(a)	2-2	Baird, Carey
Replay	v Barnsley	(h)	1-0	Baird
5th Round	v Brentford	(a)	0-2	

1938/39

3rd Round	v West Bromwich Alb	(a)	0-0	
Replay	v West Bromwich Alb	(h)	1-5	Redwood

1945/46

3rd Round(leg1)	v Accrington Stanley	(a)	2-2	Smith, Wrigglesworth
3rd Round(leg2)	v Accrington Stanley	(h)	5-1(7-3)	Rowley 2, Bainbridge, Wrigglesworth, Own goal
4th Round(leg1)	v Preston North End	(h)	1-0	Hanlon
4th Round(leg2)	v Preston North End	(a)	1-3(2-3)	Hanlon

1946/47

3rd Round	*v* Bradford	(a)	3-0	Rowley 2, Buckle
4th Round	*v* Nottingham Forest	(h)	0-2	

1947/48

3rd Round	*v* Aston Villa	(a)	6-4	Pearson 2, Morris 2, Delaney, Rowley
4th Round	*v* Liverpool	(h)	3-0	Morris, Rowley, Mitten
5th Round	*v* Charlton Athletic	(h)	2-0	Warner, Mitten
6th Round	*v* Preston North End	(h)	4-1	Pearson 2, Rowley, Mitten
Semi Final	*v* Derby County	(n)	3-1	Pearson 3
Final	*v* Blackpool	(n)	4-2	Rowley 2, Pearson, Anderson

1948/49

3rd Round	*v* Bournemouth	(h)	6-0	Burke 2, Rowley 2, Pearson, Mitten
4th Round	*v* Bradford	(h)	1-1	Mitten
Replay	*v* Bradford	(a)	1-1†	Mitten
2nd Replay	*v* Bradford	(h)	5-0	Burke 2, Rowley 2, Pearson
5th Round	*v* Yeovil Town	(h)	8-0	Rowley 5, Burke 2, Mitten
6th Round	*v* Hull City	(a)	1-0	Pearson
Semi Final	*v* Wolves	(n)	1-1†	Mitten
Replay	*v* Wolves	(n)	0-1	

1949/50

3rd Round	*v* Weymouth	(h)	4-0	Rowley 2, Pearson, Delaney
4th Round	*v* Watford	(a)	1-0	Rowley
5th Round	*v* Portsmouth	(h)	3-3	Mitten 2, Pearson
Replay	*v* Portsmouth	(a)	3-1	Delaney, Downie, Mitten
Round 6	*v* Chelsea	(a)	0-2	

1950/51

3rd Round	*v* Oldham Athletic	(h)	4-1	Pearson, Aston, Birch, Whyte og
4th Round	*v* Leeds United	(h)	4-0	Pearson 3, Rowley
5th Round	*v* Arsenal	(h)	1-0	Pearson
6th Round	*v* Birmingham City	(a)	0-1	

1951/52

3rd Round	*v* Hull City	(h)	0-2	

1952/53

3rd Round	*v* Millwall	(a)	1-0	Pearson
4th Round	*v* Walthamstow Avenue	(h)	1-1	Lewis

Replay	v Walthamstow Avenue	(n)	5-2	Rowley, Byrne, Lewis, Pearson
5th Round	v Everton	(a)	1-2	Rowley

1953/54

3rd Round	v Burnley	(a)	3-5	Blanchflower, Taylor, Viollet

1954/55

3rd Round	v Reading	(a)	1-1	Webster
Replay	v Reading	(h)	4-1	Webster 2, Viollet, Rowley
4th Round	v Manchester City	(a)	0-2	

1955/56

3rd Round	v Bristol Rovers	(a)	0-4	

1956/57

3rd Round	v Hartlepool United	(a)	4-3	Whelan 2, Berry, Taylor
4th Round	v Wrexham	(a)	5-0	Whelan 2, Taylor 2, Byrne
5th Round	v Everton	(h)	1-0	Edwards
6th Round	v Bournemouth	(a)	2-1	Berry 2
Semi Final	v Birmingham City	(n)	2-0	Berry, Charlton
Final	v Aston Villa	(n)	1-2	Taylor

1957/58

3rd Round	v Workington	(a)	3-1	Viollet 3
4th Round	v Ipswich Town	(h)	2-0	Charlton 2
5th Round	v Sheffield Wednesday	(h)	3-0	Brennan 2, Dawson
6th Round	v West Bromwich Alb	(a)	2-2	E.Taylor, Dawson
Replay	v West Bromwich Alb	(h)	1-0	Webster
Semi Final	v Fulham	(n)	2-2	Charlton 2
Replay	v Fulham	(n)	5-3	Dawson 3, Charlton, Brennan
Final	v Bolton Wanderers	(n)	0-2	

1958/59

3rd Round	v Norwich City	(a)	0-3	

1959/60

3rd Round	v Derby County	(a)	4-2	Goodwin, Charlton, Scanlon, Own goal
4th Round	v Liverpool	(a)	3-1	Charlton 2, Bradley
5th Round	v Sheffield Wednesday	(h)	0-1	

1960/61

3rd Round	v Middlesbrough	(h)	3-0	Dawson 2, Cantwell
4th Round	v Sheffield Wednesday	(a)	1-1	Cantwell
Replay	v Sheffield Wednesday	(h)	2-7	Dawson, Pearson

1961/62

3rd Round	v Bolton Wanderers	(h)	2-1	Nicholson, Herd
4th Round	v Arsenal	(h)	1-0	Setters
5th Round	v Sheffield Wednesday	(h)	0-0	
Replay	v Sheffield Wednesday	(a)	2-0	Charlton, Giles
6th Round	v Preston North End	(a)	0-0	
Replay	v Preston North End	(h)	2-1	Herd, Charlton
Semi Final	v Tottenham Hotspurs	(n)	1-3	Herd

1962/63

3rd Round	v Huddersfield Town	(h)	5-0	Law 3, Giles, Quixall
4th Round	v Aston Villa	(h)	1-0	Quixall
5th Round	v Chelsea	(h)	2-1	Quixall, Law
6th Round	v Coventry City	(a)	3-1	Charlton 2, Quixall
Semi Final	v Southampton	(n)	1-0	Law
Final	v Leicester City	(n)	3-1	Herd 2, Law

1963/64

3rd Round	v Southampton	(a)	3-2	Crerand, Moore, Herd
4th Round	v Bristol City	(h)	4-1	Law 3, Herd
5th Round	v Barnsley	(a)	4-0	Law 2, Best, Herd
6th Round	v Sunderland	(h)	3-3	Charlton, Best, Own goal
Replay	v Sunderland	(a)	2-2†	Charlton, Law
2nd Replay	v Sunderland	(n)	5-1	Law 3, Chisnall, Herd
Semi Final	v West Ham United	(n)	1-3	Law

1964/65

3rd Round	v Chester	(h)	2-1	Kinsey, Best
4th Round	v Stoke City	(a)	0-0	
Replay	v Stoke City	(h)	1-0	Herd
5th Round	v Burnley	(h)	2-1	Crerand, Law
6th Round	v Wolves	(a)	5-3	Law 2, Crerand, Herd, Best
Semi-Final	v Leeds United	(n)	0-0	
Replay	v Leeds United	(n)	0-1	

1965/66

3rd Round	v Derby County	(a)	5-2	Best 2, Law 2, Herd
4th Round	v Rotherham United	(h)	0-0	
Replay	v Rotherham United	(a)	1-0†	Connelly
5th Round	v Wolves	(a)	4-2	Law 2, Herd, Best
6th Round	v Preston North End	(a)	1-1	Herd
Replay	v Preston North End	(h)	3-1	Law 2, Connelly
Semi Final	v Everton	(n)	0-1	

1966/67

3rd Round	v Stoke City	(h)	2-0	Law, Herd

4th Round	v Norwich City	(h)	1-2	Law

1967/68

3rd Round	v Tottenham Hotspurs	(h)	2-2	Best, Charlton
Replay	v Tottenham Hotspurs	(a)	0-1†	

1968/69

3rd Round	v Exeter City	(a)	3-1	Fitzpatrick, Kidd, Own goal
4th Round	v Watford	(h)	1-1	Law
Replay	v Watford	(a)	2-0	Law 2
5th Round	v Birmingham City	(a)	2-2	Law, Best
Replay	v Birmingham City	(h)	6-2	Law 3, Kidd, Morgan, Crerand
6th Round	v Everton	(h)	0-1	

1969/70

3rd Round	v Ipswich Town	(a)	1-0	Own goal
4th Round	v Manchester City	(h)	3-0	Kidd 2, Morgan
5th Round	v Northampton Town	(a)	8-2	Best 6, Kidd 2
6th Round	v Middlesbrough	(a)	1-1	Sartori
Replay	v Middlesbrough	(h)	2-1	Charlton, Morgan
Semi Final	v Leeds United	(n)	0-0	
Replay	v Leeds United	(n)	0-0†	
2nd Replay	v Leeds United	(n)	0-1	
3rd Place p/o	v Watford	(n)	2-0	Kidd 2

1970/71

3rd Round	v Middlesbrough	(h)	0-0	
Replay	v Middlesbrough	(a)	1-2	Best

1971/72

3rd Round	v Southampton	(a)	1-1	Charlton
Replay	v Southampton	(h)	4-1†	Best 2, Sadler, Aston
4th Round	v Preston North End	(a)	2-0	Gowling 2
5th Round	v Middlesbrough	(h)	0-0	
Replay	v Middlesbrough	(a)	3-0	Morgan, Charlton, Best
6th Round	v Stoke City	(h)	1-1	Best
Replay	v Stoke City	(a)	1-2†	Best

1972/73

3rd Round	v Wolves	(a)	0-1	

1973/74

3rd Round	v Plymouth Argyle	(h)	1-0	Macari
4th Round	v Ipswich Town	(h)	0-1	

1974/75

3rd Round	v Walsall	(h)	0-0	
Replay	v Walsall	(a)	2-3†	McIlroy, Daly

1975/76

3rd Round	v Oxford United	(h)	2-1	Daly 2
4th Round	v Peterborough United	(h)	3-1	Forsyth, McIlroy, Hill
5th Round	v Leicester City	(a)	2-1	Daly, Macari
6th Round	v Wolves	(h)	1-1	Daly
Replay	v Wolves	(a)	3-2†	B.Greenhoff, McIlroy, Pearson
Semi Final	v Derby County	(n)	2-0	Hill 2
Final	v Southampton	(n)	0-1	

1976/77

3rd Round	v Walsall	(h)	1-0	Hill
4th Round	v Queens Park Rangers	(h)	1-0	Macari
5th Round	v Southampton	(a)	2-2	Macari, Hill
Replay	v Southampton	(h)	2-1	J.Greenhoff 2
6th Round	v Aston Villa	(h)	2-1	Houston, Macari
Semi Final	v Leeds United	(n)	2-1	Coppell, J.Greenhoff
Final	v Liverpool	(n)	2-1	Pearson, J.Greenhoff

1977/78

3rd Round	v Carlisle United	(a)	1-1	Macari
Replay	v Carlisle United	(h)	4-2	Pearson 2, Macari 2
4th Round	v West Bromwich Alb	(h)	1-1	Coppell
Replay	v West Bromwich Alb	(a)	2-3	Pearson, Hill

1978/79

3rd Round	v Chelsea	(h)	3-0	Coppell, J.Greenhoff, Grimes
4th Round	v Fulham	(a)	1-1	J.Greenhoff
Replay	v Fulham	(h)	1-0	J.Greenhoff
5th Round	v Colchester United	(a)	1-0	J.Greenhoff
6th Round	v Tottenham Hotspurs	(a)	1-1	Thomas
Replay	v Tottenham Hotspurs	(h)	2-0	McIlroy, Jordan
Semi Final	v Liverpool	(n)	2-2	Jordan, B.Greenhoff
Replay	v Liverpool	(n)	1-0	J.Greenhoff
Final	v Arsenal	(n)	2-3	McQueen, McIlroy

1979/80

3rd Round	v Tottenham Hotspurs	(a)	1-1	McIlroy
Replay	v Tottenham Hotspurs	(h)	0-1†	

1980/81

3rd Round	v Brighton & Hove Alb	(h)	2-2	Duxbury, Thomas
Replay	v Brighton & Hove Alb	(a)	2-0	Nicholl, Birtles
4th Round	v Nottingham Forest	(a)	0-1	

1981/82

3rd Round	v Watford	(a)	0-1	

1982/83

3rd Round	v West Ham United	(h)	2-0	Stapleton, Coppell
4th Round	v Luton Town	(a)	2-0	Moses, Moran
5th Round	v Derby County	(a)	1-0	Whiteside
6th Round	v Everton	(h)	1-0	Stapleton
Semi Final	v Arsenal	(n)	2-1	Robson, Whiteside
Final	v Brighton & Hove Alb	(n)	2-2†	Stapleton, Wilkins
Replay	v Brighton & Hove Alb	(n)	4-0	Robson 2, Muhren, Whiteside

1983/84

3rd Round	v AFC Bournemouth	(a)	0-2	

1984/85

3rd Round	v AFC Bournemouth	(h)	3-0	Strachan, McQueen, Stapleton
4th Round	v Coventry City	(h)	2-1	Hughes, McGrath
5th Round	v Blackburn Rovers	(a)	2-0	Strachan, McGrath
6th Round	v West Ham United	(h)	4-2	Whiteside 3, Hughes
Semi Final	v Liverpool	(n)	2-2†	Robson, Stapleton
Replay	v Liverpool	(n)	2-1	Robson, Hughes
Final	v Everton	(n)	1-0†	Whiteside

1985/86

3rd Round	v Rochdale	(h)	2-0	Stapleton, Hughes
4th Round	v Sunderland	(a)	0-0	
Replay	v Sunderland	(h)	3-0	Olsen 2, Whiteside
5th Round	v West Ham United	(a)	1-1	Stapleton
Replay	v West Ham United	(h)	0-2	

1986/87

3rd Round	v Manchester City	(h)	1-0	Whiteside
4th Round	v Coventry City	(h)	0-1	

1987/88

3rd Round	v Ipswich Town	(a)	2-1	Own goal, Anderson
4th Round	v Chelsea	(h)	2-0	Whiteside, McClair
5th Round	v Arsenal	(a)	1-2	McClair

1988/89

3rd Round	v Queens Park Rangers	(h)	0-0	
Replay	v Queens Park Rangers	(a)	2-2†	Gill, Graham
2nd Replay	v Queens Park Rangers	(h)	3-0	McClair 2(1pen), Robson
4th Round	v Oxford United	(h)	4-0	Hughes, Bruce, Own goal, Robson
5th Round	v AFC Bournemouth	(a)	1-1	Hughes
Replay	v AFC Bournemouth	(h)	1-0	McClair
6th Round	v Nottingham Forest	(h)	0-1	

1989/90

3rd Round	v Nottingham Forest	(a)	1-0	Robins
4th Round	v Hereford United	(a)	1-0	Blackmore
5th Round	v Newcastle United	(a)	3-2	Robins, Wallace, McClair
6th Round	v Sheffield United	(a)	1-0	McClair
Semi Final	v Oldham Athletic	(n)	3-3aet	Robson, Webb, Wallace
Replay	v Oldham Athletic	(n)	2-1aet	McClair, Robins
Final	v Crystal Palace	(n)	3-3aet	Hughes 2, Robson
Replay	v Crystal Palace	(n)	1-0	Martin

1990/91

3rd Round	v Queens Park Rangers	(h)	2-1	Hughes, McClair
4th Round	v Bolton Wanderers	(h)	1-0	Hughes
5th Round	v Norwich City	(a)	1-2	McClair

1991/92

3rd Round	v Leeds United	(a)	1-0	Hughes
4th Round	v Southampton	(a)	0-0	
Replay	v Southampton	(h)	2-2	Kanchelskis, McClair

(Southampton won 4-2 on penalties)

1992/93

3rd Round	v Bury	(h)	2-0	Gillespie, Phelan
4th Round	v Brighton & Hove Alb	(h)	1-0	Giggs
5th Round	v Sheffield United	(a)	1-3	Giggs

1993/94

3rd Round	v Sheffield United	(a)	1-0	Hughes
4th Round	v Norwich City	(a)	2-0	Keane, Cantona
5th Round	v Wimbledon	(a)	3-0	Cantona, Bruce, Irwin
6th Round	v Charlton Athletic	(h)	3-1	Hughes, Kanchelskis 2
S/F	v Oldham Athletic	(n)	1-1	Hughes
S/F	v Oldham Athletic	(n)	4-1	Ince, Kanchelskis, Robson, Giggs
Final	v Chelsea	(n)	4-0	Cantona 2pen Hughes, McClair

1994/95

3rd Round	v Sheffield United	(a)	2-0	Hughes, Cantona
4th Round	v Wrexham	(h)	5-2	Irwin 2, Giggs, McClair, og
5th Round	v Leeds United	(h)	3-1	Bruce, McClair, Hughes
6th Round	v Queens Park Rangers	(h)	2-0	Sharpe, Irwin

S/F	v Crystal Palace	(n)	2-2	Irwin, Pallister
Replay	v Crystal Palace	(n)	2-0	Bruce, Pallister
Final	v Everton	(n)	0-1	

Full record in Domestic Cup Competitions – *League Cup*

1960/61

1st Round	v Exeter City	(a)	1-1	Dawson
Replay	v Exeter City	(h)	4-1	Quixall 2(1pen), Giles, Pearson
2nd Round	v Bradford City	(a)	1-2	Viollet

1966/67

2nd Round	v Blackpool	(a)	1-5	Herd

1969/70

2nd Round	v Middlesbrough	(h)	1-0	Sadler
3rd Round	v Wrexham	(h)	2-0	Kidd, Best
4th Round	v Burnley	(a)	0-0	
Replay	v Burnley	(h)	1-0	Best
5th Round	v Derby County	(a)	0-0	
Replay	v Derby County	(h)	1-0	Kidd
Semi Final(leg1)	v Manchester City	(a)	1-2	Charlton
Semi Final(leg2)	v Manchester City	(h)	2-2 (3-4)	Edwards, Law

1970/71

2nd Round	v Aldershot	(a)	3-1	Law, Kidd, Best
3rd Round	v Portsmouth	(h)	1-0	Charlton
4th Round	v Chelsea	(h)	2-1	Best, Charlton
5th Round	v Crystal Palace	(h)	4-2	Kidd 2, Charlton, Fitzpatrick
Semi Final(leg1)	v Aston Villa	(h)	1-1	Kidd
Semi Final(leg2)	v Aston Villa	(a)	1-2 (2-3)	Kidd

1971/72

2nd Round	v Ipswich Town	(a)	3-1	Best 2, Morgan
3rd Round	v Burnley	(h)	1-1	Charlton
Replay	v Burnley	(a)	1-0	Charlton
4th Round	v Stoke City	(h)	1-1	Gowling
Replay	v Stoke City	(a)	0-0†	
2nd Replay	v Stoke City	(a)	1-2	Best

1972/73

2nd Round	v Oxford United	(a)	2-2	Charlton, Law
Replay	v Oxford United	(h)	3-1	Best 2, Storey-Moore
3rd Round	v Bristol Rovers	(a)	1-1	Morgan
Replay	v Bristol Rovers	(h)	1-2	McIlroy

1973/74

2nd Round	v Middlesbrough	(h)	0-1	

1974/75

2nd Round	v Charlton Athletic	(h)	5-1	Macari 2, Houston, McIlroy, Own goal
3rd Round	v Manchester City	(h)	1-0	Daly
4th Round	v Burnley	(h)	3-2	Macari 2, Morgan
5th Round	v Middlesbrough	(a)	0-0	
Replay	v Middlesbrough	(h)	3-0	McIlroy, Pearson, Macari
Semi Final(leg1)	v Norwich City	(h)	2-2	Macari 2
Semi Final(leg2)	v Norwich City	(a)	0-1(2-3)	

1975/76

2nd Round	v Brentford	(h)	2-1	McIlroy, Macari
3rd Round	v Aston Villa	(a)	2-1	Coppell, Macari
4th Round	v Manchester City	(a)	0-4	

1976/77

2nd Round	v Tranmere Rovers	(h)	5-0	Daly 2, Pearson, Macari, Hill
3rd Round	v Sunderland	(h)	2-2	Pearson, Own goal
Replay	v Sunderland	(a)	2-2†	Daly, B.Greenhoff
2nd Replay	v Sunderland	(h)	1-0	B.Greenhoff
4th Round	v Newcastle United	(h)	7-2	Hill 3, Nicholl, Houston, Coppell, Pearson
5th Round	v Everton	(h)	0-3	

1977/78

2nd Round	v Arsenal	(a)	2-3	McCreery, Pearson

1978/79

2nd Round	v Stockport County	(a)	3-2	McIlroy, J.Greenhoff, Jordan
3rd Round	v Watford	(h)	1-2	Jordan

1979/80

2nd Round(leg1)	v Tottenham Hotspurs	(a)	1-2	Thomas
2nd Round (leg2)	v Tottenham Hotspurs	(h)	3-1(4-3)	Coppell, Thomas, Miller
3rd Round	v Norwich City	(a)	1-4	McIlroy

1980/81

2nd Round (leg1)	v Coventry City	(h)	0-1	
2nd Round (leg2)	v Coventry City	(a)	0-1(0-2)	

1981/82

2nd Round (leg1)	v Tottenham Hotspurs	(a)	0-1	
2nd Round (leg2)	v Tottenham Hotspurs	(h)	0-1(0-2)	

1982/83

2nd Round (leg1)	v AFC Bournemouth	(h)	2-0	Own goal, Stapleton
2nd Round (leg2)	v AFC Bournemouth	(a)	2-2	Muhren, Coppell

3rd Round	v Bradford City	(a)	0-0	
Replay	v Bradford City	(h)	4-1	Moses, Albiston, Moran, Coppell
4th Round	v Southampton	(h)	2-0	McQueen, Whiteside
5th Round	v Nottingham Forest	(h)	4-0	McQueen 2, Coppell, Robson
Semi Final (leg1)	v Arsenal	(a)	4-2	Coppell 2, Whiteside, Stapleton
Semi Final (leg2)	v Arsenal	(h)	2-1(6-3)	Coppell, Moran
Final	v Liverpool	(n)	1-2†	Whiteside

1983/84

2nd Round (leg1)	v Port Vale	(a)	1-0	Stapleton
2nd Round (leg2)	v Port Vale	(h)	2-0(3-0)	Whiteside, Wilkins
3rd Round	v Colchester United	(a)	2-0	McQueen, Moses
4th Round	v Oxford United	(a)	1-1	Hughes
Replay	v Oxford United	(h)	1-1†	Stapleton
2nd Replay	v Oxford United	(a)	1-2aet	Graham

1984/85

2nd Round (leg1)	v Burnley	(h)	4-0	Hughes 3, Robson
2nd Round (leg2)	v Burnley	(a)	3-0 (7-0)	Brazil 2, Olsen
3rd Round	v Everton	(h)	1-2	Brazil

1985/86

2nd Round (leg1)	v Crystal Palace	(a)	1-0	Barnes
2nd Round (leg2)	v Crystal Palace	(h)	1-0 (2-0)	Whiteside
3rd Round	v West Ham United	(h)	1-0	Whiteside
4th Round	v Liverpool	(a)	1-2	McGrath

1986/87

2nd Round (leg1)	v Port Vale	(h)	2-0	Stapleton, Whiteside
2nd Round (leg2)	v Port Vale	(a)	5-2 (7-2)	Moses 2, Stapleton, Barnes, Davenport
3rd Round	v Southampton	(h)	0-0	
Replay	v Southampton	(a)	1-4	Davenport

1987/88

2nd Round (leg1)	v Hull City	(h)	5-0	McGrath, Davenport, Whiteside, Strachan, McClair
2nd Round (leg2)	v Hull City	(a)	1-0 (6-0)	McClair
3rd Round	v Crystal Palace	(h)	2-1	McClair 2
4th Round	v Bury	(a)	2-1	Whiteside, McClair
5th Round	v Oxford United	(a)	0-2	

1988/89

2nd Round (leg1)	v Rotherham United	(a)	1-0	Davenport

2nd Round (leg2)	v Rotherham United	(h)	5-0 (6-0)	McClair 3, Robson, Bruce
3rd Round	v Wimbledon	(a)	1-2	Robson

1989/90

2nd Round (leg1)	v Portsmouth	(a)	3-2	Ince 2, Wallace
2nd Round (leg2)	v Portsmouth	(h)	0-0 (3-2)	
3rd Round	v Tottenham Hotspurs	(h)	0-3	

1990/91

2nd Round (leg1)	v Halifax Town	(a)	3-1	Blackmore, McClair, Webb
2nd Round (leg2)	v Halifax Town	(h)	2-1 (5-2)	Bruce, Anderson
3rd Round	v Liverpool	(h)	3-1	Bruce, Hughes, Sharpe
4th Round	v Arsenal	(a)	6-2	Sharpe 3, Blackmore, Hughes, Wallace
5th Round	v Southampton	(a)	1-1	Hughes
Replay	v Southampton	(h)	3-2	Hughes 3
Semi Final (leg1)	v Leeds United	(h)	2-1	Sharpe, McClair
Semi Final (leg2)	v Leeds United	(a)	1-0 (3-1)	Sharpe
Final	v Sheffield Wednesday	(n)	0-1	

1991/92

2nd Round (leg1)	v Cambridge United	(h)	3-0	Giggs, McClair, Bruce
2nd Round (leg2)	v Cambridge United	(a)	1-1 (4-1)	McClair
3rd Round	v Portsmouth	(h)	3-1	Robins 2, Robson
4th Round	v Oldham Athletic	(h)	2-0	McClair, Kanchelskis
5th Round	v Leeds United	(a)	3-1	Blackmore, Kanchelskis, Giggs
Semi Final (leg1)	v Middlesbrough	(a)	0-0	
Semi Final (leg2)	v Middlesbrough	(h)	2-1 (2-1)	Sharpe, Giggs
Final	v Nottingham Forest	(n)	1-0	McClair

1992/93

2nd Round (leg1)	v Brighton & Hove Alb	(h)	1-1	Hughes
2nd Round (leg2)	v Brighton & Hove Alb	(a)	1-0	Wallace
3rd Round	v Aston Villa	(h)	0-1	

1993/94

2nd Round (leg1)	v Stoke City	(a)	1-2	Dublin
2nd Round (leg2)	v Stoke City	(h)	2-0	Sharpe, McClair
3rd Round	v Leicester City	(h)	5-1	Bruce 2, McClair, Sharpe, Hughes
4th Round	v Everton	(a)	2-0	Hughes, Giggs
5th Round	v Portsmouth	(h)	2-2	Giggs, Cantona
Replay	v Portsmouth	(a)	1-0	McClair

Semi Final (leg1)	v Sheffield Wednesday	(h)	1-0	Giggs	
Semi Final (leg2)	v Sheffield Wednesday	(a)	4-1	Hughes 2, McClair, Kanchelskis	
Final	v Aston Villa	(n)	1-3	Hughes	

1994/95

2nd Round (leg 1)	v Port Vale	(a)	2-1	Giggs 2, Kanchelskis, Sharpe McClair, May
2nd Round (leg2)	v Port Vale	(h)	2-0	
3rd Round	v Newcastle Utd	(a)	0-2	

Cup Final Squads – *FA Cup*

Date	Opponents	Venue	Score	Att.
24/4/09	v Bristol City	The Crystal Palace	Won 1-0	71,401

Team: Moger, Stacey, Hayes, Duckworth, Roberts, Bell, Meredith, Halse, Turnbull, **A Turnbull**, Wall   J

24/4/48	v Blackpool	Wembley	Won 4-2	100,000

Team: Crompton, Carey, Aston, **Anderson**, Chilton, Cockburn, Delaney, Morris, **Rowley** (2), **Pearson**, Mitten

5/5/57	v Aston Villa	Wembley	Lost 1-2	100,000

Team: Wood, Foulkes, Byrne, Colman, Blanchflower, Edwards, Berry, Whelan, T **Taylor**, Charlton, Pegg

3/5/58	v Bolton Wanderers	Wembley	Lost 0-2	100,000

Team: Gregg, Foulkes, Greaves, Goodwin, Cope, Crowther, Webster, E Taylor, Dawson, Charlton, Brennan

Stan Crowther having played for Aston Villa twelve months earlier thus played against and for United in consecutive FA Cup Finals.

25/5/63	v Leicester City	Wembley	Won 3-1	100,000

Team: Gaskell, Dunne, Cantwell, Crerand, Foulkes, Setters, Giles, Stiles, Quixall, **Herd** (2), **Law**, Charlton

1/5/75	v Southampton	Wembley	Lost 0-1	100,000

Team: Stepney, Forsyth, Houston, Daly, B Greenhoff, Buchan, Coppell, McIlroy, Pearson, Macari, Hill (McCreery)

21/5/76	v Liverpool	Wembley	Won 2-1	100,000

Team: Stepney, Nicholl, Albiston, McIlroy, B Greenhoff, Buchan, Coppell, **J Greenhoff**, **Pearson**, Macari, Hill (McCreery)

This was Arthur Albiston's FA Cup debut. Martin Buchan became the first player ever to captain both an English and a Scottish Cup winning side.

12/5/79	v Arsenal	Wembley	Lost 2-3	100,000

Team: Bailey, Nicholl, Albiston, **McIlroy**, **McQueen**, Buchan, Coppell, J.Greenhoff, Jordan, Macari, Thomas

21/5/83   v Brighton & Hove Albion   Wembley   Drew 2-2 aet 100,000
Team: Bailey, Duxbury, Albiston, **Wilkins**, Moran, McQueen, Robson, Muhren, **Stapleton**, Whiteside, Davies
Like Albiston seven years earlier, this was Alan Davies' FA Cup debut.

26/5/83   v Brighton & Hove Albion   Wembley   Won 4-0   92,000
Team: Bailey, Duxbury, Albiston, Wilkins, Moran, McQueen, **Robson (2)**, **Muhren**, Stapleton, **Whiteside**, Davies
In this game Davies created the unusual career record of only ever playing two FA Cup ties for United, both of which were FA Cup Finals. He compounded this record further 12 months later when he made his only European appearance. He certainly knew how to pick his games for he came on as substitute against Juventus in the semi-final of the Cup-winners Cup and scored United's equaliser in a 1-1 draw! Norman Whiteside also set the record in this game of becoming the youngest ever player to score in the Finals of both League Cup and FA Cup.

18/5/85   v Everton   Wembley   Won 1-0 aet 100,000
Team: Bailey, Gidman, Albiston (Duxbury), **Whiteside**, McGrath, Moran, Robson, Strachan, Hughes, Stapleton, Olsen
Kevin Moran was the first player ever to be dismissed in a FA Cup Final.

12/5/90   v Crystal Palace   Wembley   Drew 3-3 aet 80,000
Team: Leighton, Ince, Martin (Blackmore), Bruce, Phelan, Pallister (Robins), **Robson**, Webb, McClair, **Hughes (2)**, Wallace

17/5/90   v Crystal Palace   Wembley   Won 1-0   80,000
Team: Sealey, Ince, **Martin**, Bruce, Phelan, Pallister, Robson, Webb, McClair, Hughes, Wallace
This FA Cup winning goal was the only goal Martin ever scored in the competition.

14/5/94   v Chelsea   Wembley   Won 4-0   80,000
Team: Schmeichel, Parker, Irwin (Sharpe), Bruce, Pallister, Ince, Keane, **Cantona (2)**, Kanchelskis (**McClair**), **Hughes**, Giggs

20/05/95   v Everton   Wembley   Lost 0-1   79,592
Team: Schmeichel, G. Neville, Bruce (Giggs), Pallister, Irwin, Butt, Keane, Ince, Sharpe (Scholes), Hughes, McClair. Sub Walsh (G)

Cup Final Squads – *League Cup*

Date	Opponents	Venue	Score	Att.
26/3/83	v Liverpool	Wembley	Lost 1-2 aet 100,000	

Team: Bailey, Duxbury, Albiston, Moses (Macari), McQueen, Wilkins, Muhren, Stapleton, **Whiteside**, Coppell

| 21/4/91 | v Sheffield Wednesday | Wembley | Lost 0-1 | 80,000 |

Team: Sealey, Irwin, Blackmore, Bruce, Webb (Phelan), Pallister, Robson, Ince, McClair, Hughes, Sharpe

Note: Scorers in **bold** text.

12/4/92   *v* Nottingham Forest   Wembley   Won 1-0   76,810
Team: Schmeichel, Parker, Irwin, Bruce, Phelan, Pallister, Kanchelskis (Sharpe), Ince, **McClair**, Hughes, Giggs

27/3/94   *v* Aston Villa   Wembley   Lost 1-3   77,231
Team: Sealey, Parker, Irwin, Bruce (McClair), Pallister, Cantona, Ince, **Hughes**, Giggs (Sharpe), Kanchelskis, Keane

Cup Final Squads – *European Champions' Cup*

Date	Opponents	Venue	Score	Att.
29/5/68	*v* Benfica	Wembley	Won 4-1 aet	100,000

Team: Stepney, Dunne, Burns, Crerand, Foulkes, Stiles, **Best**, **Kidd**, Charlton (2), Sadler, Aston

Cup Final Squads – *European Cup-Winners' Cup*

Date	Opponents	Venue	Score	Att.
15/5/91	*v* Barcelona	Rotterdam	Won 2-1	45,000

Team: Schmeichel, Irwin, Blackmore, Bruce, Phelan, Pallister, Robson, Ince, McClair, **Hughes (2)**, Sharpe

United in Europe – *European Champions' Cup*

1956/57

Prelim (1)	*v* Anderlecht	(a)	2-0	Viollet, Taylor
Prelim (2)	*v* Anderlecht	(h)	10-0	Viollet 4, Taylor 3, Whelan 2, Berry
Round 1(1)	*v* Borussia Dortmund	(h)	3-2	Viollet 2, Pegg
Round 1(2)	*v* Borussia Dortmund	(a)	0-0	
Q Final(1)	*v* Athletic Bilbao	(a)	3-5	Taylor, Viollet, Whelan
Q Final(2)	*v* Athletic Bilbao	(h)	3-0	Viollet, Taylor, Berry
S Final(1)	*v* Real Madrid	(a)	1-3	Taylor
S Final(2)	*v* Real Madrid	(h)	2-2	Taylor, Charlton

1957/58

Prelim (1)	*v* Shamrock Rovers	(a)	6-0	Taylor 2, Whelan 2, Pegg, Berry
Prelim (2)	*v* Shamrock Rovers	(h)	3-2	Viollet 2, Pegg
Round 1(1)	*v* Dukla Prague	(h)	3-0	Webster, Taylor, Pegg
Round 1(2)	*v* Dukla Prague	(a)	0-1	
Q Final(1)	*v* Red Star Belgrade	(h)	2-1	Colman, Charlton
Q Final(2)	*v* Red Star Belgrade	(a)	3-3	Charlton 2, Viollet

S Final(1)	v AC Milan	(h)	2-1	Taylor(pen), Viollet
S Final(2)	v AC Milan	(a)	0-4	

1965/66

Prelim (1)	v HJK Helsinki	(a)	3-2	Connelly, Herd, Law
Prelim (2)	v HJK Helsinki	(h)	6-0	Connelly 3, Best 2, Charlton
Round 1(1)	v ASK Vorwaerts	(a)	2-0	Law, Connelly
Round 1(2)	v ASK Vorwaerts	(h)	3-1	Herd 3
Q Final(1)	v Benfica	(h)	3-2	Herd, Law, Foulkes
Q Final(2)	v Benfica	(a)	5-1	Best 2, Charlton, Connelly, Crerand.
S Final(1)	v FK Partizan Belgrade	(a)	0-2	
S Final(2)	v FK Partizan Belgrade	(h)	1-0	Stiles

1967/68

Round 1(1)	v Hibernians (Malta)	(h)	4-0	Sadler 2, Law 2
Round 1(2)	v Hibernians (Malta)	(a)	0-0	
Round 2(1)	v FK Sarajevo	(a)	0-0	
Round 2(2)	v FK Sarajevo	(h)	2-1	Best, Aston
Q Final(1)	v Gornik Zabre	(h)	2-0	Kidd, own goal
Q Final(2)	v Gornik Zabre	(a)	0-1	
S Final(1)	v Real Madrid	(h)	1-0	Best
S Final(2)	v Real Madrid	(a)	3-3	Foulkes, Sadler, Own goal
Final	v Benfica	(n)	4-1	Charlton 2, Best, Kidd

1968/69

Round 1(1)	v Waterford	(a)	3-1	Law 3
Round 1(2)	v Waterford	(h)	7-1	Law 4, Stiles, Burns, Charlton
Round 2(1)	v RSC Anderlecht	(h)	3-0	Law 2, Kidd
Round 2(2)	v RSC Anderlecht	(a)	1-3	Sartori
Q Final(1)	v Rapid Vienna	(h)	3-0	Best 2, Morgan
Q Final(2)	v Rapid Vienna	(a)	0-0	
S Final(1)	v AC Milan	(a)	0-2	
S Final(2)	v AC Milan	(h)	1-0	Charlton

1993/94

Round 1(1)	v Honved	(a)	3-2	Keane 2, Cantona
Round 1(2)	v Honved	(h)	2-1	Bruce 2
Round 2(1)	v Galatasary	(h)	3-3	Robson, own goal, Cantona
Round 2(2)	v Galatasary	(a)	0-0	

1994/95

Group A	v IFK Gothenburg	(h)	4-2	Giggs 2, Kanchelskis, Sharpe

Group A	v Galatasary	(a)	0-0	
Group A	v Barcelona	(a)	2-2	Hughes, Sharpe
Group A	v Barcelona	(a)	0-4	
Group A	v IFK Gothenburg	(a)	1-3	Hughes
Group A	v Galatasary	(h)	4-0	Davies, Beckham, Keane, OG

United in Europe – *European Cup-Winners' Cup*

1963/64

Round 1(1)	v Willem II	(a)	1-1	Herd
Round 1(2)	v Willem II	(h)	6-1	Law 3, Charlton, Chisnall, Setters
Round 2(1)	v Tottenham Hotspurs	(a)	0-2	
Round 2(2)	v Tottenham Hotspurs	(h)	4-1	Charlton 2, Herd 2
Q Final(1)	v Sporting Club Lisbon	(h)	4-1	Law 3, Charlton
Q Final(2)	v Sporting Club Lisbon	(a)	0-5	

1977/78

Round 1(1)	v AS Saint-Etienne	(a)	1-1	Hill
Round 1(2)	v AS Saint-Etienne	(h)	2-0	Coppell, Pearson
Round 2(1)	v FC Porto	(a)	0-4	
Round 2(2)	v FC Porto	(h)	5-2	Coppell 2, Nicholl, 2 own goals

1983/84

Round 1(1)	v Dukla Prague	(h)	1-1	Wilkins
Round 1(2)	v Dukla Prague	(a)	2-2	Robson, Stapleton
Round 2(1)	v Spartak Varna	(a)	2-1	Robson, Graham
Round 2(2)	v Spartak Varna	(h)	2-0	Stapleton 2
Q Final(1)	v FC Barcelona	(a)	0-2	
Q Final(2)	v FC Barcelona	(h)	3-0	Robson 2, Stapleton
S Final(1)	v Juventus	(h)	1-1	Davies
S Final(2)	v Juventus	(a)	1-2	Whiteside

1990/91

Round 1(1)	v Pecsi Munkas	(h)	2-0	Blackmore, Webb
Round 1(2)	v Pecsi Munkas	(a)	1-0	McClair
Round 2(1)	v Wrexham	(h)	3-0	McClair, Bruce, Pallister
Round 2(2)	v Wrexham	(a)	2-0	Robins, Bruce
Q Final(1)	v Montpellier	(h)	1-1	McClair
Q Final(2)	v Montpellier	(a)	2-0	Blackmore, Bruce
S Final(1)	v Legia Warsaw	(a)	3-1	McClair, Hughes, Bruce
S Final(2)	v Legia Warsaw	(h)	1-1	Sharpe
Final	v Barcelona	(n)	2-1	Hughes 2

1991/92

Round 1(1)	v Panathinaikos	(a)	0-0	

Round 1(2)	v Panathinaikos	(h)	2-0	Hughes, McClair
Round 2(1)	v Athletico Madrid	(a)	0-3	
Round 2(2)	v Athletico Madrid	(h)	1-1	Hughes

United in Europe – *Inter-Cities Fairs Cup*

1964/65

Round 1(1)	v Djurgardens IF	(a)	1-1	Herd
Round 1(2)	v Djurgardens IF	(h)	6-1	Law 3, Charlton 2, Best
Round 2(1)	v Borussia Dortmund	(a)	6-1	Charlton 3, Herd, Law, Best
Round 2(2)	v Borussia Dortmund	(h)	4-0	Charlton 2, Connelly, Law
Round 3(1)	v Everton	(h)	1-1	Connelly
Round 3(2)	v Everton	(a)	2-1	Connelly, Herd
Q Final(1)	v RC Strasbourg	(a)	5-0	Law 2, Connelly, Charlton, Herd.
Q Final(2)	v RC Strasbourg	(h)	0-0	
S Final(1)	v Ferencvaros	(h)	3-2	Herd 2, Law
S Final(2)	v Ferencvaros	(a)	0-1	
Play Off	v Ferencvaros	(a)	1-2	Connelly

United in Europe – *UEFA Cup*

1976/77

Round 1(1)	v Ajax Amsterdam	(a)	0-1	
Round 1(2)	v Ajax Amsterdam	(h)	2-0	McIlroy, Macari
Round 2(1)	v Juventus	(h)	1-0	Hill
Round 2(2)	v Juventus	(a)	0-3	

1980/81

Round 1(1)	v Widzew Lodz	(h)	1-1	McIlroy
Round 1(2)	v Widzew Lodz	(a)	0-0	

1982/83

Round 1(1)	v Valencia CF	(h)	0-0	
Round 1(2)	v Valencia CF	(a)	1-2	Robson

1984/85

Round 1(1)	v Raba Vasas ETO	(h)	3-0	Robson, Muhren, Hughes
Round 1(2)	v Raba Vasas ETO	(a)	2-2	Brazil, Muhren
Round 2(1)	v PSV Eindhoven	(a)	0-0	
Round 2(2)	v PSV Eindhoven	(h)	1-0	Strachan
Round 3(1)	v Dundee United	(h)	2-2	Strachan, Robson
Round 3(2)	v Dundee United	(a)	3-2	Hughes, Muhren, Own goal

Q Final(1)	v Videoton	(h)	1-0	Stapleton
Q Final(2)	v Videoton	(a)	0-1	
				Lost 5-4 on penalties

1992/93
Round 1(1)	v Moscow Torpedo	(h)	0-0	
Round 1(2)	v Moscow Torpedo	(a)	0-0	
				Lost 4-3 on penalties

United in Europe – *European Super Cup*

1991
| Final | v Red Star Belgrade | (h) | 1-0 | McClair |

United in Europe – *World Club Championship*

1968
| 1st Leg | v Estudiantes de la Plata | (a) | 0-1 | |
| 2nd Leg | v Estudiantes de la Plata | (h) | 1-1 | Morgan |

Other Competitions – *World Club Championships*

Date	Round/Leg	Opponents	Venue	Score	Att.
25/9/68	First Leg	v Estudiantes	(a)	lost 0-1	55,000

Team: Stepney, Dunne, Burns, Crerand, Foulkes, Stiles, Morgan, Sadler, Charlton, Law, Best.

| 16/10/68 | Second Leg | v Estudiantes | (h) | drew 1-1 | 63,500 |

Team: Stepney, Brennan, Dunne, Crerand, Foulkes, Sadler, Morgan, Kidd, Charlton, Law (Sartori), Best.

Other Competitions – *European Super Cup*

Date	Round/Leg	Opponents	Venue	Score	Att.
19/11/91		v Red Star Belgrade		won 1-0	22,110

Team; Schmeichel, Irwin, Martin (Giggs), Bruce, Webb, Pallister, Kanchelskis, Ince, **McClair,** Hughes, Blackmore.

Other Competitions – *Anglo-Italian Cup*

Group 1
21st February 1973	v Fiorentina (h)	drew 1-1	Att: 23,951
21st March 1973	v Lazio (a)	drew 0-0	Att: 52,834
4th April 1973	v Bari (h)	won 3-1	Att: 14,303
2nd May 1973	v Verona (a)	won 4-1	Att: 8,168

Despite remaining unbeaten United failed to qualify for the semi-final stages.

Other Competitions – *Watney Cup*

Date	Round/Leg	Opponents	Venue	Score	Att.
1970/71	1st Round	*v* Reading	(a)	Won 3-2	
	Semi-Final	*v* Hull City	(a)	1-1aet	

Won 4-3 on penalties. This is thought to be the first occasion any first class game in England was decided by penalties.

| | Final | *v* Derby County | (a) | Lost 1-4 | |
| 1971/72 | 1st Round | *v* Halifax Town | (a) | Lost 1-2 | |

Of the thirteen United players to take part in this game, eleven – Stepney, Dunne, Crerand, Burns, Sadler, Morgan, Kidd, Charlton, Law and Best – were full internationals whilst Gowling was an Under 23 International.

United in the FA Charity Shield

27/4/08   *v* Queen's Park Rangers   Stamford Bridge 1-1   6,000
Scorer: Meredith
Team: Moger, Stacey, Burgess, Duckworth, Roberts, Bell, **Meredith,** Bannister, J Turnbull, A Turnbull, Wall

29t/8/08   *v* Queen's Park Rangers   Stamford Bridge 4-0   6,000
Team: Moger, Stacey, Burgess, Duckworth, Roberts, Bell, Meredith, Bannister, J **Turnbull (3),** Picken, **Wall**

25t/9/11   *v* Swindon Town   Stamford Bridge 8-4   10,000
Team: Edmonds, Hofton, Stacey, Duckworth, Roberts, Bell, Meredith, Hamill, **Halse (6), Turnbull, Wall**

6/10/48   *v* Arsenal   Highbury   3-4   31,000
Team: Crompton, Carey, Aston, Anderson, Chilton, Warner, Delaney, Morris, **Burke, Rowley,** Mitten – Smith (o.g)

24/9/52   *v* Newcastle United   Old Trafford   4-2   11,381
Team: Wood, McNulty, Aston, Carey, Chilton, Gibson, Berry, **Downie, Rowley (2),** Pearson, **Byrne**

24/10/56   *v* Manchester City   Maine Road   1-0   30,495
Team: Wood (Gaskell), Foulkes, Byrne, Colman, Jones, Edwards, Berry, Whelan, Taylor, **Viollet,** Peg

22/10/57   *v* Aston Villa   Old Trafford   4-0   27,923
Team: Wood, Foulkes, Byrne, Goodwin, Blanchflower, Edwards, **Berry,** Whelan, **Taylor (3),** Viollet, Pegg

17/8/63   *v* Everton   Goodison Park   0-4   54,840
Team: Gaskell, A Dunne, Cantwell, Crerand, Foulkes, Setters, Giles, Quixall, Herd, Law, Charlton

14/8/65   *v* Liverpool   Old Trafford   2-2   48,502

Team: P Dunne, Brennan, A Dunne, Crerand, Cantwell, Stiles, **Best** (Anderson), Charlton, **Herd**, Law, Aston

12/8/67   *v* Tottenham Hotspurs   Old Trafford   3-3   54,106
Team: Stepney, Brennan, A Dunne, Crerand, Foulkes, Stiles, Best, Kidd, **Charlton (2), Law,** Aston

13/8/77   *v* Liverpool   Wembley   0-0   82,000
Team: Stepney, Nicholl, Albiston, McIlroy, B Greenhoff, Buchan, Coppell, J Greenhoff (McCreery), Pearson, Macari, Hill

20/8/83   *v* Liverpool   Wembley   2-0   92,000
Team: Bailey, Duxbury, Albiston, Wilkins, Moran, McQueen, **Robson (2),** Muhren (Gidman), Stapleton, Whiteside, Graham

10/8/85   *v* Everton   Wembley   0-2   82,000
Bailey, Gidman, Albiston, Whiteside, McGrath, Hogg, Robson, Duxbury (Moses), Hughes, Stapleton, Olsen

19/8/90   *v* Liverpool   Wembley   1-1   66,558
Team: Sealey, Irwin, Donaghy, Bruce, Phelan, Pallister, **Blackmore,** Ince, McClair, Hughes, Wallace (Robins)

7/8/93   *v* Arsenal   Wembley   1-1   60,000
United won 5-4 on penalties
Team: Schmeichel, Parker, Irwin, Bruce, Kanchelskis, Pallister, Cantona, Ince, Keane, **Hughes** (Robson)

14/08/94   *v* Blackburn Rovers   Wembley   2-0   60,402
Team: Schmeichel, May, Bruce, Pallister, Sharpe, Kanchelskis, McClair, **Ince,** Giggs, **Cantona** (pen), Hughes

United in FA Youth Cup Finals

4/5/53   1st Leg   *v* Wolves   Old Trafford   7-1   20,934
Team: Clayton, Fulton, Kennedy, Colman, Cope, Edwards, **McFarlane (2), Whelan, Lewis (2), Pegg, Scanlon**

9/5/53   2nd Leg   *v* Wolves   Molineux   2-2   14,290
Team: Clayton, Fulton, Kennedy, Colman, Cope, Edwards, McFarlane, **Whelan, Lewis,** Pegg, Scanlon   *Aggregate: 9-3*

23/4/54   1st Leg   *v* Wolves   Old Trafford   4-4   18,246
Team: Hawksworth, Beswick, Rhodes, Colman, Harrop, McGuinness, Littler, **Edwards (2),** Charlton, **Pegg (2-1 via penalty),** Scanlon

26/4/54   2nd Leg   *v* Wolves   Molineux   1-0   28,651
Team: Hawksworth, Beswick, Rhodes, Colman, Harrop, McGuinness, Littler, Edwards, Charlton, **Pegg (penalty),** Scanlon   *Aggregate: 5-4*

27/4/55   1st Leg   *v* West Brom   Old Trafford   4-1   16,696
Team: Hawksworth, Queenan, Rhodes, **Colman (2),** Jones, McGuinness, **Beckett,** Brennan, Edwards, **Charlton,** Fidler

30/4/55   2nd Leg   v West Brom   The Hawthorns   3-0   8,335
Team: Hawksworth, Queenan, Rhodes, Colman, Jones, McGuinness, Beckett, Brennan, **Edwards, Charlton**, Fidler – **Cooke (og)**   *Aggregate: 7-1*

30/4/56   1st Leg   v Chesterfield   Old Trafford   3-2   25,544
Team: Hawksworth, Queenan, Jones, **Carolan**, Holland, McGuinness, Morgans, **Pearson**, Dawson, **Charlton**, Fidler

7/5/56   2nd Leg   v Chesterfield   Recreation Grnd   1-1   15,838
Team: Hawksworth, Queenan, Jones, Carolan, Holland, McGuinness, Morgans, Pearson, Dawson, Charlton, **Fidler**   *Aggregate: 4-3*
Gordon Banks kept goal for Chesterfield in both games

2/5/57   1st Leg   v West Ham Utd   Upton Park   3-2   14,000
Team: Gaskell, Smith, Madison, English, Holland, Bratt, Morgans, **Lawton, Dawson,** Pearson, **Hunter**

7/5/57   2nd Leg   v West Ham Utd   Old Trafford   5-0   23,349
Team: Gaskell, Smith, Madison, English, Holland, Bratt, **Morgans,** Lawton, Dawson, **Pearson (3), Hunter**   *Aggregate: 8-2*

27/5/64   1st Leg   v Swindon Town   County Ground   1   17,000
Team: Rimmer, Duff, Noble, McBride, Farrar, Fitzpatrick, Anderson, **Best,** Sadler, Kinsey, Aston.

30t/4/64   2nd Leg   v Swindon Town   Old Trafford)   4-1   25,563
Team: Rimmer, Duff, Noble, McBride, Farrar, Fitzpatrick, Anderson, Best, **Sadler (3)**, Kinsey, **Aston**   *Aggregate: 5-2*

26/4/82   1st Leg   v Watford   Old Trafford   2-3   7,280
Team: P Hughes, Hill, Scott, Hogg, Garton, **Blackmore,** Pearson, **Dempsey,** Whiteside, M Hughes, Docherty (Woods)

6/5/82   2nd Leg   v Watford   Vicarage Road   4-4†   8,000
Team: P Hughes, Hill, Scott, Hogg, Garton, Williams (Wood), Blackmore, **Dempsey, Whiteside, M Hughes (2),** Docherty   *Aggregate: 6-7*

24/4/86   1st Leg   v Manchester City   Old Trafford   1-1   7,602
Team: Walsh, Gill, Martin, Scott, Gardner, Bottomley, Murphy, Todd, Cronin, Wilson (Hopley), **Harvey**

29/5/86   2nd Leg   v Manchester City   Maine Road   0-2   18,158
Team: Walsh, Gill, Martin, Scott, Gardner, Harvey, Murphy, Todd, Cronin, Bottomley (Hopley), Goddard   *Aggregate: 1-3*

14/4/92   1st Leg   v Crystal Palace   Selhurst Park   3-1   7,825
Team: Pilkington, O'Kane, Switzer, Casper, G Neville, **Beckham, Butt (2),** Davies, McKee, Savage (Roberts), Thornley

15/5/92   2nd Leg   v Crystal Palace   Old Trafford   3-2   14,681
Team: Pilkington, O'Kane, Switzer, Casper, G Neville, Beckham, Butt, Davies (Gillespie), McKee, Giggs, Thornley (Savage)   *Aggregate: 6-3*

N.B - of the starting line up for this second leg tie, only George Switzer never made a first team appearance. he subsequently went on to play in the Football League for Darlington.

10/4/93   1st Leg   *v* Leeds Utd   Old Trafford   0-2   30,562
Team: Whitmarsh, O'Kane, Riley, Casper, G Neville, Gillespie, Butt, Beckham (Savage), Irving (Murdock), Scholes, Thornley

13/5/93   2nd Leg   *v* Leeds Utd   Elland Road   1-2   31,037
Team: Whitmarsh, P.Neville, Riley, Casper, G Neville, Gillespie, **Scholes** (pen), Beckham, Irving (Murdock), Savage, Thornley   *Aggregate: 1-4*

11/05/95 1st Leg   *v* Tottenham Hotspur White Hart Lane 1-2   3,000
Team: Gibson, P Neville, Westwood, Clegg, Wallwork, Mulryne (Gordon), Mustoe, Hall, Baker (Crutis), Johnson, **Cooke**, Sub: Maxon (G)

15/05/95 2nd Leg   *v* Tottenham Hotspur Old Trafford   1-0   20,190
Team: Gibson, Curtis, Westwood, Wallwork, P Neville, Mustoe, Hall (Gardner), Brebner, Mulryne (Hilton), **Cooke**, Baker, Sub: Maxon (G)
(After Extra-Time – Aggregate Score 2-2 , United won 4-3 on penalties)

Miscellaneous

Managers

Ernest Mangnall (1903-1912)
Football League champions	1907/8, 1910/11
Division Two runners-up	1905/06
FA Cup winners	1909

John Robson (1914-1921)
The first person to assume the title of Manager – Mangnall's official title had been Secretary.

John Chapman (1921-1926)
Division Two runners-up	1924/25

Although full details were never made known, the FA suspended Chapman from football in 1926.

Clarence Hilditch (1926-1927)
The only player–manager in United's history.

Herbert Bamlett (1927-1931)
Made history by being the youngest man ever to referee an FA Cup Final – in 1914 aged 32. As a manager he guided United into their worst ever spell.

Walter Crickmer (1931-1932)
Another never to assume the title of manager although he was responsible for team selection. Crickmer was one of the victims of the Munich Air Crash.

Scott Duncan (1932-1937)
Division Two champions	1935/36

Walter Crickmer (1937-1945)

Sir Matt Busby (1945-1969)
Football League champions	1951/52, 1955/56, 1956/57, 1964/65, 1966/67
Division One runners–up	1946/47, 1947/48, 1948/49, 1950/51, 1958/59, 1963/64, 1967/68
FA Cup winners	1948, 1963
FA Cup runners–up	1957
European champions	1967/68

Jimmy Murphy (1958)
In the absence of Matt Busby, seriously injured in the Munich Air Crash, Jimmy Murphy took over for six months from February to August 1958. During that time he led the makeshift team to an FA Cup Final appearance.
FA Cup runners–up	1958

Wilf McGuinness (1969-70)

United's only attempt to promote from within. Two League Cup semi–finals and one FA Cup semi–final were not sufficient to keep him in the job.

Frank O'Farrell (1971-72)

At Christmas of his first season in charge, United were five points clear at the top of the league when there were only two points for a win but they slumped to finish eighth. He soon paid the penalty.

Tommy Docherty (1972-77)

Division Two champions	1974/75
FA Cup winners	1977
FA Cup runners–up	1976

Dave Sexton (1977-1981)

FA Cup runners–up	1979
First Division runners–up	1979/80

Tommy Docherty was the first manager to offer Dave Sexton a chance in management when he appointed Sexton as his coach at Stamford Bridge. Sexton was later to replace Docherty at both Chelsea and Manchester United.

Ron Atkinson (1981-1986)

FA Cup winners	1983, 1985
League Cup runners–up	1983

Looked likely to succeed in bringing the Holy Grail back to Old Trafford when his side began the 1985/86 campaign with ten straight league victories but it wasn't to be.

Alex Ferguson (1986-)

FA Premier League champions	1992/93, 1993/94
FA Premier League runners–up	1994/95
Division One runners–up	1987/88, 1991/92
FA Cup winners	1990, 1994
FA Cup finalists	1995
League Cup winners	1992
League Cup runners–up	1991, 1994
European Cup Winners' Cup winners	1991

Post War Average Attendances

Season	Home	Away	Season	Home	Away
46/47	43,615	31,364	71/72	45,999	44,085
47/48	53,660	40,493	72/73	48,623	41,171
48/49	46,023	44,720	73/74	42,721	35,337
49/50	41,455	46,172	74/75	48,388	25,556
50/51	37,159	38,091	75/76	54,750	37,037
51/52	41,870	40,945	76/77	53,710	35,357
52/53	35,737	37,068	77/78	51,938	30,424
53/54	33,637	37,096	78/79	46,687	30,498
54/55	34,077	35,865	79/80	51,562	34,101
55/56	38,880	32,872	80/81	45,055	29,849
56/57	45,192	39,772	81/82	44,685	27,214
57/58	45,583	45,352	82/83	41,583	25,294
58/59	53,258	44,028	83/84	42,534	24,936
59/60	47,288	41,026	84/85	43,010	27,884
60/61	37,807	34,139	85/86	44,422	28,204
61/62	33,490	33,964	86/87	40,625	25,221
62/63	40,317	34,894	87/88	39,155	23,041
63/64	43,753	38,697	88/89	36,488	23,713
64/65	45,990	41,377	89/90	39,078	26,666
65/66	38,456	38,171	90/91	43,241	25,020
66/67	53,984	45,577	91/92	44,985	27,893
67/68	57,759	45,802	92/93	35,132	28,254
68/69	51,121	44,295	93/94	44,240	28,868
69/70	51,115	43,997	94/95	43,692	27,331
70/71	44,754	41,695			

The Cost of Post War Championship Sides

These costs are not necessarily exact as they depend on newspaper reports which may not have been 100% accurate. Also it has to borne in mind that some of the cost will have been offset by outgoing transfers.

1951/52   *Total Cost £61,000*

Reg Allen (QPR) £6,000, John Downie (Bradford PA) £20,000,   Johnny Berry (Birmingham City) £25,000, Harry McShane £5,000.
NB Johnny Carey and Jack Rowley had been signed before the Second World War for nominal fees.

1955/56 and 1956/57   *Total Cost £60,999*

Ray Wood (Darlington) £6,000, Tommy Taylor (Barnsley) £29,999,
Johnny Berry (Birmingham City) £25,000.

1964/65   *Total Cost £283,000*

Tony Dunne (Shelbourne) £6,000, David Herd (Arsenal) £40,000,
Denis Law (Torino) £115,000, Pat Crerand (Celtic) £56,000,
John Connolly (Burnley) £56,000, Pat Dunne £10,000 (Shamrock Rovers).

1966/67   *Total Cost £269,750*

Tony Dunne (Shelbourne) £6,000, Denis Law (Torino) £115,000,
David Herd £40,000, Pat Crerand (Celtic) £56,000, David Sadler (Maidstone) £750,
Alex Stepney (Millwall) £52,000.

1992/93   *Total Cost £21,800,000*

Peter Schmeichel (Brondby) £850,000, Paul Parker (QPR) £2,000,000,
Denis Irwin (Oldham Athletic) £625,000, Steve Bruce (Norwich City) £800,000,
Gary Pallister (Middlesbrough) £2,300,000, Lee Sharpe (Torquay United)
£185,000, Paul Ince (West Ham United) £1,250,000 plus £5,000 a game,
Mark Hughes (Barcelona) £1,500,000, Eric Cantona (Leeds United) £1,000,000,
Bryan Robson (West Bromwich Albion) £1,500,000, Mike Phelan (Norwich City)
£750,000, Brian McClair (Celtic) £850,000, Dion Dublin (Cambridge Utd)
£1,000,000

1993/94   *Total Cost £25,800,000*

As above plus Roy Keane (Notts Forest) £3,750,000, Ince played approx 50 games.

Alex Stepney (Millwall) £52,000, Tony Dunne (Shelbourne) £6,000,
Pat Crerand (Celtic) £56,000, David Sadler (Maidstone) £750.

Important Dates in the History of Old Trafford

1909	–	After winning the FA Cup, United are given the then huge sum of £60,000 to purchase a new site and build a modern (for the times) stadium.
19/02/1910	–	United leave their old ground in Clayton and play their first ever game at Old Trafford. The visitors are Liverpool and 45,000 fans turn up but go home disappointed as United lose 4-3 after twice leading by two goals.
29/04/1911	–	United beat Sunderland 5-1 on the final day of the season at Old Trafford to take the First Division title by one point. Two World Wars would be waged before it landed back at Old Trafford again.
1911	–	The new stadium is quickly rewarded as the Football Association choose it for the FA Cup replay between Bradford City and Newcastle United. The Yorkshire club win their one and only FA Cup, beating the Geordies 1-0.
1915	–	Old Trafford hosts the FA Cup Final to end a 19 year association with Crystal Palace as the venue. With war clouds over Europe, the Final became known as "The Khaki Final" as the terraces were packed with soldiers at home on leave for the weekend. Sheffield United beat Chelsea 3-0.
27/12/1920	–	The record attendance for a League game is set at 70,504 for the visit of Aston Villa who win 3-1.
1922	–	Old Trafford stages the FA Charity Shield match between Huddersfield Town and Liverpool which goes to the Yorkshire side 1-0.
17/04/1926	–	The last England v. Scotland full International to be played in England outside of Wembley Stadium takes place at Old Trafford. The Scots win with the only goal of the game from Jackson.
Sept 1930	–	United concede thirteen goals in successive home games four days apart when Huddersfield hit them for six and Newcastle United knock in seven. In the worst ever start by any Football League club, United's first point of the campaign does not come until November when Birmingham City are beaten 2-0 at Old

		Trafford after twelve straight defeats.
16/11/1938	–	The ground witnesses the fastest ever hat–trick in International football as Willie Hall (Spurs) nets a treble inside three and a half minutes against Ireland. He goes on to score five times in succession thus equalling the England record in a 7-0 rout.
25/03/1939	–	The ground's record attendance of 76,962 is set when Old Trafford stages the FA Cup semi–final between Portsmouth and Grimsby Town. The 'Mariners' lose their 'keeper very early in the match and Portsmouth take full advantage to win 5-0.
11/03/1941	–	The ground, situated on the perimeter of Manchester's vast Trafford Park industrial complex, is virtually demolished as Hitler's bombs target the area to halt engineering production for Britain's war effort.
8/01/1949	–	United play their first FA Cup tie at Old Trafford for ten years when they hammer Bournemouth 6-0. Their last tie at Old Trafford had been a Third Round replay on 11th January 1939 when West Bromwich Albion had beaten the Reds 5-1.
1951	–	The first foreign team to play United at Old Trafford are Red Star Belgrade in a fixture organised to celebrate the Festival of Britain. The match finishes 1-1 with Jack Rowley equalising from the penalty spot late in the game.
26/04/1952	–	United swamp Arsenal, the only team who can catch them, 6-1 in the final game of the season to capture the title for the first time since 1911. Rowley nets a hat–trick.
24/01/1955	–	The longest ever FA Cup tie is finally resolved at Old Trafford when Stoke City eventually beat Bury 3-2 after nine hours twenty–two minutes.
07/04/1956	–	United clinch their third ever First Division title by beating Blackpool 2-1 at Old Trafford in front of their biggest crowd of the season, 62,277.
30/04/1956	–	The programme for the First Leg of the FA Youth Cup Final at Old Trafford against Chesterfield contains the following pen picture of a Chesterfield youngster. *"Gordon Banks (Goalkeeper), a Sheffield boy in his second year at the club. Has played several games in the Reserves recently and acquitted himself well".*
6/10/1956	–	In a strange coincidence, Bobby Charlton makes his debut at Old Trafford against his namesake team, Charlton Athletic. He scores twice and in the return game hits a hat–trick!
20/10/1956	–	United lose 5-2 to Everton at Old Trafford where they had been unbeaten for eighteen months. The last team to beat them at

		home had also been Everton in March 1955.
25/03/1957	–	United play their first ever game at Old Trafford under floodlights but fail to celebrate as they go down 2-0 in a league match to Bolton Wanderers.
08/04/1957	–	United's Youth team lose 3-2 to Southampton at Old Trafford in the semi–final of the FA Youth Cup. It is their first ever defeat in the competition since it was formed in 1952 but they still go on to win it again as they had won the first leg at the Dell 5-1.
25/04/1957	–	Old Trafford stages its first ever European cup tie as Real Madrid provide stiff resistance in a 2-2 draw which sees them through to the Final having beaten United 3-1 in Spain. All United's previous home games in the European Cup had been played at Maine Road.
2/10/1957	–	Shamrock Rovers become United's first ever Old Trafford European victims when they are beaten 3-2 in the European Cup.
30/10/1957	–	Brian Clough becomes the second player to score five goals in a Representative game at Old Trafford when he goes 'nap' for an FA XI against the Army.
30/11/1957	–	Having never been beaten by a London club at Old Trafford since October 1938 when Charlton Athletic won 2-0, United finally lose 4-3 to Spurs. United then proceeded to lose their very next home game to another London outfit, Chelsea!
19/02/1958	–	United's first game after the Munich Air Crash takes place in an emotional atmosphere at Old Trafford. The FA Cup Fifth Round tie is won 3-0 with a make shift team of youngsters. Shay Brennan's opening goal was in fact United's first ever FA Cup goal against Wednesday as the Yorkshire side had been victorious in all the previous encounters by scores of 6-0, 1-0 and 2-0.
14/01/1961	–	United beat Spurs 2-0 at Old Trafford – the only occasion that the famous Tottenham 'double' side failed to score all season.
1961	–	Old Trafford stages the first ever League Cup semi–final replay when Aston Villa beat Burnley 2-1.
1966	–	Old Trafford is selected to host three of the Group games in the World Cup. Portugal, who beat England on to defeat in the semi–final score their first ever goal in World Cup Finals stages when Augusto nets in a 3-1 win over Hungary at Old Trafford.
26/11/1966	–	David Herd scores one of the most unusual hat–tricks ever when Sunderland visit Old Trafford. Each of his three goals was put past a different 'keeper! He scored first of all against Jim

		Montgomery who was injured and then against his replacement, central defender Charlie Hurley. The Sunderland management then decided the team pattern was better served by Hurley reverting to his outfield position and he was replaced by John Parke against whom Herd completed his treble!
1967/68	–	United, with Best, Law and Charlton in the side set an average attendance record for the season at Old Trafford (and the Football League) of 57,758.
17/12/1969	–	Old Trafford sets a record attendance for the League Cup when United draw 2-2 with neighbours Manchester City in the second leg of a semi–final tie. A crowd of 63,418 see City reach the Final, having won the first leg 2-1.
1970	–	Old Trafford stages its third FA Cup Final when Leeds United and Chelsea replay there after a 2-2 draw at Wembley. The game finishes 2-1 to Chelsea after extra–time.
1972	–	Bobby Moore saves a penalty at Old Trafford in the League Cup 2nd Replay between West Ham United and Stoke City. He had to go in net when the 'Hammers' 'keeper Ferguson was taken off injured but although Moore saved the spot kick, Bernard followed up to convert. When Conroy scored the winner for Stoke, the tie had been under way for seven hours.
1977	–	Old Trafford sees League Cup history made when Aston Villa beat Everton in a League Cup Final 2nd Replay by 3-2. They become the first club to win the trophy three times.
1978	–	The League Cup Final is back again at Old Trafford with Nottingham Forest defeating Liverpool 1-0 via a hotly disputed John Robertson penalty.
22/03/1980	–	The 100th 'Derby' match with Manchester City takes place at Old Trafford. A Micky Thomas goal gives the Reds victory.
14/10/1980	–	Old Trafford hosts the England 'B' international with the United States. The home side win 1-0.
12/12/1984	–	Celtic are ordered to replay their European tie with Rapid Vienna at Old Trafford after crowd trouble on their own ground and are well beaten by the Austrians.
22/04/1989	–	The Women's FA Cup Final takes place at Old Trafford and is televised for the first time. Leasowe Pacific beat Fulham 3-2.
21/10/1989	–	Rugby League history is made at Old Trafford when Paul Newlove becomes the youngest Great Britain international at the age of 18 years and 72 days in the 24-16 reverse at the hands of New Zealand.

The History of Manchester United

Although now a household name in most countries of the world where football is played, Manchester United's beginnings were, extremely humble and on at least two occasions they were nearly forced out of business. The origins of the club can be traced back to 1878 and a railway carriage making department at the Newton Heath works of the Lancashire and Yorkshire Railway Company. Not surprisingly, the workmen who formed the first side called themselves Newton Heath Lancashire and Yorkshire Railway.

The first ground was by the side of a clay pit in North Road, Newton Heath but there was no running straight out on to the pitch in those days. The players changed in a pub called the Three Crowns about eight hundred yards up the road from the ground but, nevertheless, the side were easily the best railway side in the area at that time and other works teams failed to give the Newton Heath side a decent game on most occasions. Soon, Newton Heath were looking further afield for matches. By the time professionalism was legalised in 1885, Newton Heath were on the fringe of the better class of sides in the area such as Bootle and Bolton Wanderers. In order to progress, Newton Heath decided to begin recruiting professionals who could also be offered work in the carriage department to boost their soccer earnings. This double–barrelled bargaining point enabled Newton Heath to attract some quite decent players including several Welsh internationals.

Indeed, no fewer than five Newton Heath players appeared for Wales in an international against Scotland in 1888. No matter that the Welsh side were beaten 5-1 in that game, the fact was that Newton Heath were growing in stature. Jack and Roger Doughty had been recruited from the top Welsh side of the day, Druids, whilst Jack Powell, who signed in 1886, became captain. Many is the player these days who says he would *"walk to Old Trafford for the privilege of playing for United"*. In the late 1880's a Scot by the name of Patrick O'Donnell did just that (except of course it was then Newton Heath). The distance from Glasgow to Manchester, however, was the same those days as a century later and he was rewarded for his epic walk with a job at the railway as well as playing football.

It may seem nonsensical now but, on the first occasion United (Newton Heath) applied for membership of the Football League in 1891, they received just one vote. They therefore turned their attentions in the direction of the Football Alliance and were promptly accepted. They won their first game against Sunderland Albion 4-1 and beat Small Heath 9-1 in their first campaign but struggled away, winning just twice on their travels, a feat they were to repeat in their second season. The third term of Alliance soccer got under way with yet another away beating but this disguised the course of events that lay ahead. When a second application to join the Football League was made, they could hardly have fared worse than on the first occasion but they did with Newton Heath not receiving a single vote of support. After this set back and an opening day defeat at Burton, few could have forecast the success that was to arrive in the 1891/92 season. After the loss at Burton, Newton

Heath remained unbeaten in their next fifteen outings and lost only twice more all season to secure runners–up spot behind Notts Forest who drew a crowd of 16,000 to North Road on New Year's Day 1892. At the end of that season, the Football League decided to enlarge and the Football Alliance were virtually encompassed en bloc. Newton Heath and Forest, as the Alliance's top two teams, went straight into the First Division and, now in the big time, the LYR was dropped from the club's title and the first full time Secretary, A.H.Albut appointed.

Thus, United began their Football League life under the name Newton Heath with a 4-3 defeat at Blackburn Rovers and, a week later, First Division football came to Manchester for the first time when Burnley visited North Road and went home with a 1-1 draw under their belts. It took Newton Heath seven games to notch their first ever Football League victory but it was done in some style. Strangely, their first ever win, 10-1 against Wolves remains today, well over 3,600 games later, their record score in the Football League! The big victory, however, was just a flash in the pan and Newton Heath finished rock bottom to be saved from relegation only by a 'Test Match' defeat of Small Heath. Newton Heath were, however, out of their depth in the First Division and finished bottom yet again the following campaign. They were relegated after losing their 'Test Match' to a side that were going to become, a century later, one of United's chief protagonists, Liverpool.

By now, Newton Heath had moved to pastures new at Bank Street but crowds were disappointing and, starved of cash, Newton Heath remained by and large a struggling Second Division outfit. There were highlights, however, including what almost was a record Football League scoreline of 14-0 over Walsall. The Midlanders, though, were obviously gluttons for punishment as they put in a protest, which was upheld, and when the game was replayed, Newton Heath could only find the net nine times!

Although nowadays a fashionable shirt to wear, the green and gold halves were dropped and the team kitted out in white but the side still languished in the lower reaches. By the turn of the century, the club were in serious financial trouble but were saved in bizarre fashion at a Bazaar by a St Bernard dog. The Bazaar had been organised to raise much needed money for the club and the captain of the side, Harry Stafford, tied a collection box to the neck of his St Bernard and allowed it to roam freely about the hall. Unfortunately, or, as it turned out, very fortunately, the dog wandered off out of the building and was eventually found by a wealthy businessman, John Davies. He became the club's first saviour.

On hearing of Newton Heath's plight, Davies paid off the club's debts of £2,500 (an astronomical sum in those days) and put in a further £500 to get some new players. He immediately became Chairman, decreed a change of name to Manchester United and bought a new kit – the famous red and white!

The first game under the new name was at Gainsborough Trinity in September 1902 and ended in a 1-0 victory. The season was to see another, much more, significant development, however, with the appointment of James Mangall as Secretary. Although his official title was Secretary, Mangnall is accepted as the first manager of the club as he was responsible for team selection and policy. It is a sign of how significant this move was, that Mangnall ranks with Sir Matt Busby and, latterly, Alex Ferguson in the top three managers the club has ever had.

In modern day parlance, Mangnall quite simply *"turned the club round"*. After finishing fifth in the Second Division in his first season (Manchester City, unfortunately for United supporters, won it) a crowd of over 40,000 turned out for the opening game of the 1903/04 campaign. For the next two seasons United were to just miss out on promotion but in 1905/06, after twice finishing third, United returned to the top flight after an absence of twelve years. They were about to embark on their most successful era and one that would not be repeated until another forty years had elapsed.

The strength of the team lay in the midfield, or half back line as it was then known, with Duckworth, Bell and Roberts acknowledged as the finest to be seen in English football until the 1940s. Mangnall also recruited the unrelated Sandy and James Turnbull along with Harold Halse and the legendary Billy Meredith. Halse was to play in FA Cup Finals for three different clubs in a seven year period (United, Villa and Chelsea) and it was his goal that brought United an FA Cup Final appearance for the first time in 1909. Meredith and Sandy Turnbull were part of a deal that saw United sign five players from Manchester City in 1906 with suspensions still to be served until 1907 over an illegal payments row. It wasn't, therefore, until the start of the 1907/08 season that Mangnall could at last get the team he wanted out on to the field but when he did, it was to prove a resounding success.

They won 14 of their first 15 league games in 1907/08, the only set back being a 2-1 reverse at Middlesbrough in the third game of the campaign. In those 15 games, Sandy Turnbull found the net 19 times, Meredith 8 and Jack Turnbull scored six after missing the opening five matches through injury. United dominated the Championship, finishing nine points (when there were only two points awarded for a win) clear of second placed Aston Villa who themselves were only thirteen points off bottom spot! Given that domination, United surprisingly didn't figure at all in the following season's Championship but they did put their appaling FA Cup record behind them by lifting the famous trophy for the first time.

United had never been beyond the quarter–final stage, indeed they had only reached the last eight on three occasions, and they needed an inordinate slice of luck to get past that stage on their way to capturing the Cup. They were losing 1-0 at Burnley with only eighteen minutes play left when a blizzard put paid to the game. When the replay took place, United won 3-2 and were then fortunate to tackle in the semi–final the most successful FA Cup side of that era, Newcastle United, when the Geordies were reduced to ten men with Halse scoring the only goal. Halse also had a big role to play in the final, for it was his shot that hit the Bristol City crossbar before bouncing down for Sandy Turnbull to score the only goal.

Satisfied with the success that his money had brought, John Davies now put in a further £60,000, a colossal amount in that period, to build a new stadium that would match the brilliance of the team his money had enabled Mangnall to establish.

United played their last game at Clayton, ending with a 5-0 victory against Spurs and in February 1910, Old Trafford was born. The last game at Clayton was witnessed by a crowd of only 7,000 but in true Old Trafford tradition the opening of the new stadium attracted 45,000!

The first game was a hard pill to swallow as arch enemies Liverpool spoiled the party with a 4-3 success after United had led 3-1. The first full campaign in the stadium, which matched the best anywhere in the country, saw the crowds flock to Old Trafford to watch United take their second Championship, but whereas their first title had been all over bar the winning from home, this one went right to the finishing line. Again, Villa were the nearest challengers and going into the penultimate game of the season United had a two point lead. They lost at Villa Park which put Villa level on 50 points and a game in hand, a game which they proceeded to draw. The final day saw United at home to Sunderland whilst Villa, with a superior goal average, played Liverpool who were languishing in the bottom half of the table and with nothing to play for. United had to win or alternatively, United win by a large score whilst Villa drew. The public showed what they thought of United's chances when only 10,000 turned up but United did their bit by winning 5-1 and then, with communications not as good as they are today, it was a case of sit and wait. For once, probably to their eternal sorrow, Liverpool did United a favour by beating Villa 3-1 and the title came to Old Trafford. But two World Wars were to pass before Old Trafford saw success again.

Mangnall left in 1912 as he saw his great team beginning to age and United were not to appoint a successor until John Robson in December 1914. The First World War, however, then intervened but when the country opened for football again in 1919, Old Trafford was inundated with crowds and the record league gate, 70,504 was set in 1920 for the visit of Aston Villa who won 3-1. United, however, were only a shadow of their former selves and Robson resigned after two seasons of mid–table mediocrity. His replacement, John Chapman, would doubtless have settled for a mid-table position as his first season in charge saw United relegated to the Second Division!

The relegation brought one of football's most famous names of the time, Frank Barson, to Old Trafford in an effort to regain a place in the top flight and a change of colours all to white with a red 'V'. But success was not achieved overnight and United had to wait until 1925 before gaining promotion behind Leicester City setting, in the process, a defensive record of just 23 goals conceded, a total never beaten before or since in the Second Division. Once again, however, the issue was not settled until the very last game of the campaign with United needing a point from their game with Barnsley to secure promotion in front of Derby County. They got the necessary point in a goalless draw at Barnsley but, in the event, County failed to win so United would have gone up anyway.

Back in the First Division, United had a reasonable season finishing ninth but they also had some bitter disappointments. There was a 5-0 hiding at Huddersfield and an even bigger 7-0 trouncing (then a record, later equalled but never surpassed) at Blackburn. Manager Chapman was quickly dismissed when the FA suspended him over a charge of "improper conduct", the exact details of which were never made known but, perhaps, the biggest blow of all was the FA Cup semi–final defeat at Bramall Lane against Manchester City. Another little piece of Old Trafford history was made with the appointment of Clarrie Hilditch as player/manager to replace Chapman, the only occasion the club have ever had such a position. No sooner was 1926 out of the way than the death of John Davies, who had done so much to first of all save, then resurrect, United was announced. The appointment of Hilditch had never been intended as anything other than temporary and 1927 saw the appointment of Herbert Bartlett along with a return to the familiar red shirts.

All these changes put United firmly on a downward road and the club headed towards oblivion. After four terms of being bottom half material, United had probably their worst ever season, being relegated back to the Second Division with a paltry 22 points and also set a Football League record that still exists when they lost all their first twelve games of 1930/31 season. In consecutive home games against Huddersfield Town and Newcastle United, the Reds conceded thirteen goals whilst in an away game at Stamford Bridge immediately prior to those two home disasters, Chelsea had also breached the United defence, if one could call it that, six times. Later in the season, Huddersfield Town and Derby County were also to find the net six times against United who, altogether, conceded 115 goals. Bamlett resigned but with the poor form, allied to the recession, attendances plummeted and the club was again financially crippled. With no John Davies to turn to, United were now saved by another local businessman, James Gibson, whose son Alan is still a Vice–President of the club.

He cleared the more pressing debts, paid the outstanding wages, injected a reported £20,000 to buy players and hired a new manager, Scott Duncan at a salary rumoured to be almost £1,000 a year. Duncan quickly spent the £20,000 recruiting his players mainly from his homeland, Scotland. Despite the vast expenditure he incurred, Duncan's early stewardship was a disaster and in 1933/34 they reached an all time low when they were just one game away from relegation to the Third Division North. United travelled to play Millwall in their final match of the season knowing they had to win in order to avert relegation. Lincoln City were already down but the Reds were in 21st spot with 32 points. Immediately above United were Millwall with 33 points but their problem had been picking up points away from home. At the Den they had a good home record, better in fact than the Champions, Grimsby Town and, as United travelled to London, the unthinkable was very much on the cards. Despite, or because of, using no fewer than 38 players (no substitutes in those days) during the campaign United looked doomed. In the event, United surprised everybody, including most probably themselves, and won 2-0 with goals from Cape and Manley. The Reds had, in fact, gone five games unbeaten at the end of the campaign to save themselves.

Immediately after this escape, Duncan made probably his best buy, capturing George Mutch from Arbroath for £800. He was leading scorer in his first term and when, twelve months later, United won the Second Division title thanks to an unbeaten run of 19 games stretching from 4th January, when Bradford City beat them 1-0, until the end of the season, it was Mutch's 21 goals that led the way. Mutch went on to be transferred for £5,000 to Preston North End and is still shown on television scoring the only goal of the 1938 FA Cup Final from the penalty spot in the last minute. Duncan was rewarded with a new five year contract for gaining promotion but the directors should have waited – twelve months later the Reds were back in the Second Division! Almost as bad was the fact that Manchester City had won the First Division title! Duncan resigned and moved to Ipswich Town whom he immediately proceeded to take into the Football League.

As the saying goes, football is a funny old game. The following season United won promotion back to the First whilst, almost unbelievably, Manchester City created history by being the first, and to date, only Champions to be immediately relegated. The boot was very firmly on the other foot! But, once again, it was a nail-biting climax that went to the last day. Aston Villa were up as Champions and Sheffield United were second with 53 points having finished their programme. United and Coventry City were level in third place, two points behind Sheffield, with United's goal average just the better. A crowd of over 50,000 saw United clinch promotion with a 2-0 victory whilst Coventry finished fourth when they only drew their last fixture. In this new look United were several unknowns who were not to remain unknown after World War Two – the era of Johnny Carey, Stan Pearson and Jack Rowley was beginning to unfold.

By the end of the war, Matt Busby had been named as manager but United had no ground. Old Trafford, situated in the heart of Manchester's main industrial complex, Trafford Park, had been destroyed as the Germans targeted factories in the area for almost daily bombings. Whilst in the Army, Busby had been in charge of an army side in Italy and had been helped out by Jimmy Murphy. Busby immediately turned to his war–time colleague and invited him to become his assistant. The partnership was to take United to great heights.

United had arguably the best team in the land but couldn't prove it with a title as they finished runners–up five times in the first five post–war championships. They did, however, lift the FA Cup for the second time nearly forty years after their first success in 1909. The 1948 Wembley victory came without playing anybody outside of the top flight. The Third Round tie against Aston Villa was a classic as the home side went in front in under 20 seconds only for United to lead 5-1 at half-time. Anybody who thought the game was over had another think coming. The Reds scraped home 6-4 in one of the classic FA Cup confrontations of all time. By the time they reached the Twin Towers, the Reds had scored eighteen goals but so had their opponents, Blackpool. With just over twenty minutes left it looked like United were going to be bridesmaids as Blackpool led 2-1 but Rowley equalised and goals from Pearson and Anderson secured the coveted trophy.

The crowds were returning in dramatic fashion and United, with their ground rebuilt, left their temporary home at Maine Road to return to Old Trafford in the knowledge that they had repaid all debts. The way was clear for progress. Despite being invited to take over the Italian National side, Busby remained at Old Trafford and by 1952 had landed his first Championship. It then seemed as if United could follow City in to the record books by getting relegated immediately after winning the title when, at the end of October they were bottom – not that City fans were laughing – they were next to bottom! To halt the rot, Busby introduced many of his young reserve team, Whitefoot, Pegg, Edwards, Viollett, Foulkes, Jones and Blanchflower. In addition he bought Tommy Taylor from Barnsley for £29,999, the missing £1 being because Busby didn't want the youngster being burdened with the tag of becoming the first £30,000 player. Another youngster, Roger Byrne, who had played in the Championship side as a left winger was switched to left back on the retirement of Carey and was to become one of the most astute captains ever to lead United.

The youngsters learned their trade under Busby and Murphy for two years, finishing fourth and fifth, before becoming the most dominant team of their era. The 1955/56 title was a one horse race when they took the title by eleven points (in the days of two points for a win) from Blackpool. There was no nail biting finish this time with the Championship nicely wrapped up as early as 7th April when the Reds beat their nearest rivals 2-1 at Old Trafford in front of almost 63,000 adoring fans. Only winger Johnny Berry and Roger Byrne, still a youngster himself, remained from the team that won the title just four years earlier and the average age was an incredible 22. Just Berry and Taylor had cost sizeable fees with almost the entire squad having come through the Youth ranks. Indeed, it was not uncommon for crowds of over 25,000 to turn out to watch the Youth team as it won the FA Youth Cup in each of the first five occasions it was competed for. The aggregate scores of 9-3, 7-1 and 8-2 in three of the Finals demonstrated how outclassed the opposition were in this competition whilst it took great goalkeeping by an unknown youngster, Gordon Banks, to keep United down to four in the 1956 Final against Chesterfield. Indeed, although the 25,000 plus crowd at that Final didn't realise it at the time, they were watching two players who were to become household names throughout the world, let alone England, in Banks and Bobby Charlton.

United ignored an FA request not to enter the newly instituted European Cup (Chelsea had obliged the FA the previous season) and, without floodlights, they played their home games at Maine Road. Having won the First Leg against Belgian champions, Anderlecht, barely 40,000 turned up to see one of most polished performances given by any team in the world. Anderlecht were not a bad team but they had no answer to United on that evening as the Reds ran riot scoring ten which would have been significantly more had several players refused to score, preferring instead to try to give a goal to Pegg, who didn't get on the scoresheet despite setting up many chances for his colleagues. In the league, United took their unbeaten run of fourteen games at the end of the previous campaign to 26 before Everton surprisingly put five past the Reds at Old Trafford. The title was wrapped up by eight points and there were high hopes of a treble as United reached the FA Cup Final and the semi-finals of the European Cup thanks to a momentous night at Maine Road. United were trailing by two goals to Spanish champions, Atletico Bilbao, from the first leg but overcame the deficit in an electric atmosphere.

United were now to embark on nine months that was nothing but grief. A truly great Real Madrid side containing players such as Di Stefano, Gento, Santamaria and Kopa drew 2-2 in Old Trafford's first European competitive game to knock United out 5-3 on aggregate. In the FA Cup Final, United's hopes were dashed by what today would have been an automatic sending off but McParland, after breaking 'keeper Wood's jaw stayed on to score both Aston Villa's goals against stand in custodian, Jackie Blanchflower. United were left with just the Championship in a season which marked the two goal debut of Bobby Charlton against, strangely, Charlton Athletic, whom he scored a hat-trick against in the return fixture!

United didn't quite dominate the 1957/58 title race as they had in the previous two seasons but, after winning a classic 5-4 encounter at Arsenal on 1st February, after putting seven past Bolton Wanderers in the previous match, everything seemed on course for a third successive championship. The Reds left Arsenal in good spirits to travel to Red Star Belgrade confident of protecting a 2-1 First Leg lead to reach the semi-finals of the European Cup for a second successive time. The game finished 3-3 but, as the whole football world knows, tragedy was to wipe out most of the team at a stroke. Attempting to take off for a third time following a refuelling stop at Munich, an iced up wing caused the plane to veer off the runway and crash. Roger Byrne, Eddie Colman, Mark Jones, David Pegg, Billy Whelan, Tommy Taylor and a reserve player, Geoff Bent were amongst those killed instantly. Duncan Edwards, as one would expect from such a giant, fought for life against overwhelming odds for almost two weeks before losing the one sided battle. When he died in his 21st year, he already held 18 full caps, two championship medals and an FA Cup Final medal.

Miraculously, United beat AC Milan 2-1 in the first leg of the European Cup semi-final and reached the FA Cup Final, but won only one more league match (against Sunderland 2-1, away) as not surprisingly they fell down the table to finish ninth. As Matt Busby fought successfully for his life, Jimmy Murphy, who had not been on the ill fated trip due to his commitments with the Welsh national side, took charge and produced a team for the first match after Munich, a 5th Round FA Cup-tie against Sheffield Wednesday, containing only two players, Harry Gregg and Billy Foulkes, who had played in the previous round, three weeks earlier against Ipswich Town. Ian Greaves, Ronnie Cope, Mark 'Pancho'' Pearson, Shay Brennan and Alex Dawson were boys who became men overnight. Two reserve players who had played in the first team previously, Colin Webster and Freddie Goodwin made up the side along with two signings, Ernie Taylor and Stan Crowther, who were given special dispensation by the FA to play as they had already appeared for Blackpool and Aston Villa in that season's competition. Carried along on a wave of emotion, the cobbled together side won 3-0 with two goals from Brennan and one from Dawson. The Sixth Round saw a Colin Webster goal dispose of West Bromwich Albion on another emotional night after a 2-2 draw at the Hawthorns in a match that saw the arrival back of Bobby Charlton – little could he have known then what responsibility he was going to have thrust on him over the next few years. Fulham (and a young Jimmy Hill) almost put United out in the semi-final but two Charlton goals saved the day and a Dawson treble in the Highbury replay did the rest. Incredibly, the ravaged United were in the FA Cup Final.

Unbelievably, United were to have their 'keeper injured for the second Final in succession when Lofthouse quite blatantly bundled both Gregg and the ball into the net for Bolton's second and decisive goal. Charlton had hit the post for United and had had another fine effort saved by England 'keeper Eddie Hopkinson but the Reds became the first side in the 20th century to lose two successive FA Cup Finals. Eleven days later, their European dreams also crashed when they lost 4-0 in Milan.

Amazingly, the following season United finished runners–up to Wolverhampton Wanderers as Denis Viollet broke the club scoring record for a campaign with 32 strikes. But the momentum began to wane and United had some average seasons finishing seventh twice and then 15th as well as being humiliated 7-2 at home in the FA Cup by Sheffield Wednesday. In 1963 it looked for much of the time as if they would be relegated but a draw in the third last game of the season at Maine Road virtually kept the Reds up and City down. The FA Cup, however, redeemed an otherwise forgettable year with United completely outclassing Leicester City who had finished fifteen places above them in the First Division. Goals from David Herd (two) and Denis Law brought the Cup back to Old Trafford.

Just as almost thirty years earlier when the near drop into the Third Division galvanised United, so did the threat of relegation in 1963. The following year saw the introduction of a youngster from Northern Ireland, George Best, who became an instant hit with the fans. United finished runners–up to Liverpool and reached the semi–final of the FA Cup only to be beaten by a Bobby Moore inspired West Ham on a quagmire at Hillsborough just days after finally overcoming Sunderland at the third attempt on another bog at Leeds Road, Huddersfield. But the biggest disappointment was reserved for the Cup–winners Cup where everyone went home after a 4-1 first–leg victory over Sporting Lisbon thinking all United had to do was to turn up in Portugal. Apparently, the players also thought along those lines for they crashed 5-0 in one of the biggest ever turn rounds in European history.

The crowds flocked back to Old Trafford as United boasted three of the world's best players, Law, Best and Charlton on display every Saturday afternoon. United won the 1964/65 title on goal difference from Leeds United although it wasn't quite as close as that as they already had the title sewn up when they lost their last game at Aston Villa. Leeds had the last laugh, however, when they beat United in the semi–final of the FA Cup after two games. United were also destined to lose in the semi–final of the Inter–Cities Fairs Cup over three matches to the Hungarian outfit, Ferencvaros.

United were now back on the big stage of the European Cup itself and the dream was shortly to become reality but not before more disappointment. Best became christened 'El Beatle' after demolishing Benfica 5-1 in the Stadium of Light. After such a performance United were considered very serious contenders for the European crown but the soldiers of Partisan Belgrade surprised everybody with a 2-

0 home win that United could not overcome in the return. Busby presumably thought his dream had vanished for ever. But his side bounced back to grab the title once more in 1966/67 with a relentless run of twenty games unbeaten to the end of the season culminating in a 6-1 celebration at Upton Park. The boys were back!

The following season they lost their title of Champions but the fact that it was Manchester City who deprived them of top spot made it hurt just that little bit more. However, there was a glittering prize that was more than ample consolation. Comparatively easy wins over Hibernians of Malta, Sarajevo, and Gornik saw United up against Real Madrid in the semi-final. A George Best goal gave United a slender advantage to take to the Bernabeau Stadium but surely it wasn't enough. And so it looked with a quarter of an hour left as United trailed 3-1 but then, as in all fairy stories, came the unlikeliest of heroes. Billy Foulkes had started down the European road in United's first ever tie in 1956. Twelve years later he was to inspire United from adversity to their golden goal. In a career spanning almost 700 games, Foulkes rarely ventured over the half way line and scored just nine goals in a 17 year career. Suddenly, he rose above the Madrid defence to head a Crerand free-kick on for Sadler to convert and, then, three minutes later appeared from nowhere to stab home the equaliser on the night and the winner on aggregate.

On a nostalgic night that nobody who was present will ever forget, United finally overcame Benfica 4-1 in extra time at Wembley. Even that game, however, could have gone the other way had Stepney not made a great save from Eusebio in normal time. Best was a wizard, Charlton scored a rare goal with his head, and Kidd celebrated his 19th birthday with a goal but the lad who played the game of his life that night was the one who was the target of the boo boys for much of the campaign, John Aston, whose pace tore the Portuguese side apart.

United were unable to retain their new title the following year when they lost 2-1 to AC Milan and Busby handed over the reins to Wilf McGuinness. It heralded an era of managerial change at Old Trafford and with McGuinness soon departed, Busby took over again temporarily before Frank O'Farrell experienced an even worse time than McGuinness. In 1972, with relegation once more a very real prospect, Tommy Docherty was brought in. He saved them from the immediate threat but couldn't keep them up the following season which had a sting in the tail, for it was former United hero Denis Law, now returned to Manchester City, who back heeled the goal at Old Trafford that confirmed the relegation. Law took no pleasure from the act and did not join in the City celebrations. The following day he announced his retirement – his last league goal had put United down. At least the Board kept faith with Docherty and he rewarded them with probably the best 'flair' team to play between Busby's 1967 championship side and Ferguson's 1992 Champions. Gordon Hill and Steve Coppell patrolled the wings and scored goals at the same time, Martin Buchan had developed into a fine defender as well as a fine leader and there were talents such as Macari and McIlroy. They were lucky with injuries and, by the end of the season, no fewer than ten players had played over 30 games. They won their first game at Orient and were never headed.

Back in the First Division, Docherty saw his young side more than hold their own and they also reached Wembley where they were hot favourites to dispose of Southampton, then a mid–table Division Two side. On the day, United never performed and a good strike by Bobby Stokes sealed victory for the 'Saints'. The following year they were back at the Twin Towers but very much in the role that Southampton had adopted twelve months previously. Liverpool had won the League and Wembley was merely a stopping off point on the way to a unique treble as they were also to take the European crown. Unfortunately for the Anfield club, nobody had given United a copy of the script and two goals in a five minute second half spell gave United a victory as unexpected as their defeat in the previous final. Two months after this success, Docherty was dismissed for undertaking a relationship with the wife of the United 'physio, Laurie Brown.

After flirting in more ways than one with the outgoing personality of Docherty, United turned back to the quiet and unassuming type in Dave Sexton even though their experience with O'Farrell should have been sufficient to let the Board know it was not what the fans wanted. Sexton, to an extent, was unlucky for he saw his team come second in one of the best modern FA Cup Finals. United fought back from 2-0 down to level against Arsenal in the last four minutes of the 1979 Wembley spectacular only to immediately concede a third goal themselves. The following campaign saw United level with Liverpool at the top of the First Division on the final Saturday of the season but Liverpool beat Villa whilst United lost at Elland Road. 1980/81 saw the end of Sexton's reign and he must look back and think it was a case of so near, yet so far. Sadly, for a man of immense integrity, he left with the millstone of his £1 million plus signing, striker Gary Birtles, around his neck – Birtles had failed to find the net in the 25 league games he played under Sexton.

United's hierarchy realised they had to give the fans someone with charisma and in those stakes they didn't come much bigger than Ron Atkinson. Where Sexton and O'Farrell had struggled in communication with the fans, Atkinson, like Docherty, loved the publicity and banter. He also had a flair for producing attractive sides and United looked good again. He took twelve months to settle in and then gave the Reds their first ever League Cup Final but it ended in defeat against Liverpool after extra–time. Just weeks later the Red hordes were back at Wembley for the FA Cup Final against Brighton. That, too, almost finished in disaster as Bailey made a great reflex save to deny Brighton the winner with virtually the last kick of the match. Brighton had had their opportunity and paid heavily in the replay, losing to a 4-0 scoreline that flattered them. In these games Alan Davies created what will surely be a record that stands for all time. He only played two FA Cup ties for United, both of which were FA Cup Finals! Two years later United made FA Cup history again when Kevin Moran became the first player to be sent off in a FA Cup Final as United beat Everton with a Norman Whiteside goal in extra–time.

The coveted title still eluded United but, in 1985, it looked to be on its way as United won their first ten matches. It all went sadly wrong, however, and a bad start to the next campaign left Atkinson to rue that two Cup wins in three seasons was no compensation for not winning the Championship. United appointed Alex Ferguson, destined to become the first man since Busby to land the title, but it took him six years to end the obsession. In November 1986, just weeks after Ferguson's arrival, United were in 21st position but had recovered to finish 11th by the end of the season. In 1987/88 they improved to finish second but near misses were no good to United followers and 1988/89 brought only disappointment. Indeed, many United fans were beginning to see Ferguson in the mould of Sexton and O'Farrell and there were distant rumblings. The league performance in 89/90 was tantamount to disillusionment for many Old Trafford faithful and the rumblings were getting very much closer to home and almost reached a crescendo when a United side that had cost Ferguson £11m were crushed like schoolboys 5-1 by Manchester City. Off the field, United were almost becoming a laughing stock with Robert Maxwell expressing interest in buying the club and then a ball juggling Michael Knighton appearing out of the blue in a bid to become Chairman. United finished 13th but Ferguson was probably saved by an incredible cup run. United were drawn away in every round, drew 3-3 with Oldham Athletic in the semi-final and, amazingly, drew by the same scoreline in the Final itself with Crystal Palace. In the replay, the only FA Cup goal ever scored by Lee Martin brought Ferguson his first trophy.

Having broken his duck at last, Ferguson collected prizes for fun. Although they slipped up badly against Sheffield Wednesday (and Ron Atkinson) in the Final of the Rumbelows' League Cup, United lifted their second European honour when they beat Barcelona 2-1 in Rotterdam in the Cup–Winners Cup. The next year it was the League Cup with Nottingham Forest the victims but the Reds let the league title slip away to Leeds. Still the ultimate prize eluded them but then in the late autumn of 1992 with his side again failing to set the world alight, Ferguson, quite out of character, took an immense gamble. He purchased from Leeds United the volatile Frenchman, Eric Cantona. Most pundits agreed that Ferguson had flipped his lid but, in fact, the last piece of the jigsaw had just been slotted into place. On a stage fit for world class acts, Cantona became one. The bald statistics show just what a bargain Ferguson landed for £1m. In the Frenchman's first fifty games, United lost just twice! The title was won at last, and by ten points, but it was never that easy. Indeed, at 4.45 on 10th April 1993, United appeared to have lost the lead to Aston Villa for they trailed Sheffield Wednesday by 1-0 at Old Trafford whilst title rivals Villa (and Ron Atkinson) were winning. In the next minute Villa dropped two valuable points and United gained three as Steve Bruce scored twice in time added on for injury to the referee! The five point turn around in that decisive moment proved vital and United went on to win their last seven games as Villa fell away. Strangely, just twenty four hours earlier, central defender Bruce had said on TV that it was about time he started scoring again following a run of over 30 games without finding the net! The Holy Grail came back to Old Trafford in a carnival atmosphere as United entertained Blackburn Rovers on 3rd May but nobody mentioned Harry Stafford and his dog!

The return of the Holy Grail, however, was only the prelude to the most successful season ever in the club's history. Never in with a realistic hope of European Cup success due to the 'foreign players' rule, it was still a major surprise to see the Reds go out to little known Turkish side Galatasary after holding a 3-1 lead at one stage in the first leg at Old Trafford. But this proved to be almost a blessing in disguise as the dismissal enabled United to concentrate their minds on the domestic scene. And how they concentrated! A massive lead by Christmas in the League gave the Old Trafford outfit the opportunity to pour everything into the the two home Cup competitions. The Coca Cola League Cup that did not figure on their hit list whilst they were still in Europe now assumed more importance and progress was made in the FA Cup. The club were rocked in January by the death of Sir Matt Busby and it seemed with his passing that the team were blown off course. By the end of March, Hughes, Cantona (in successive games), Schmeichel, and Kanchelskis were all sent off, United's once substantial lead in the League was whittled away to nothing by Blackburn and former Red boss Ron Atkinson tactically outmanoeuvred United in the Coca Cola League Cup Final.

United's campaign seemed to be doomed to insignificant failure with just one minute of extra time in the FA Cup semi–final against Oldham Athletic left. The hoardes that United had taken to Wembley were silent, almost unbelieving, as they pondered how so much could have gone wrong so quickly. Then came the one moment in time that saved United's season as Mark Hughes volleyed a last gasp equaliser out of nothing. Had they lost that game, many fervently believe they would have ended up with nothing.

As it was, their season resumed what had been assumed for many months to be its destiny. Having stared the precipice in the face, the Reds somehow became revitalised, thrashing Oldham in the replay and gaining the League title as Blackburn faltered. A 4-0 victory over Chelsea in FA Cup Final was not as easy as the scoreline suggests but it was good enough to give Alex Ferguson the double, the first United team to accomplish the feat – and how near they had come to a treble after becoming the first club in English Football history to win the Championship and appear in both major domestic Cup Finals. A fitting memory to Sir Matt.

Awards

European Footballer of the Year

| 1964 | Denis Law | 1966 | Bobby Charlton | 1968 | George Best |

NB – The only other British club to have had a player voted European Footballer of the Year are Blackpool whose Stanley Matthews won the first award in 1956.

Footballer of the Year

| 1949 | Johnnie Carey | 1966 | Bobby Charlton | 1968 | George Best |

PFA Player of the Year

| 1989 | Mark Hughes | 1991 | Mark Hughes | 1992 | Gary Pallister |
| 1994 | Eric Cantona | | | | |

NB – Mark Hughes is the only player to have won this award on more than one occasion.

PFA Young Player of the Year

| 1985 | Mark Hughes | 1991 | Lee Sharpe | 1992 | Ryan Giggs |
| 1993 | Ryan Giggs | | | | |

(NB – Ryan Giggs is the only player to have won this award in successive seasons. United are the only club to have had three successive winners)

PFA Merit Awards

| 1974 | Bobby Charlton | 1975 | Denis Law | 1980 | Sir Matt Busby |
| 1993 | 1968 Manchester United team | | | | |

Manager of the Year

| 1968 | Sir Matt Busby | 1993 | Alex Ferguson | 1994 | Alex Ferguson |

Barclay's Young Eagle of the Year

| 1992 | Ryan Giggs |

Squad Performances 1994-95

Reserves

Pontins League Division One

Date		Opponent		Score	Scorers
17/08/94	v	Leeds United	(a)	1-2	O'Kane
24/08/94	v	Aston Villa	(h)	2-0	Scholes (2)
1/09/94	v	Wolves	(a)	1-0	Davies
3/09/94	v	Blackburn Rovers	(h)	3-0	Gillespie. Tomlinson, Butt (pen)
7/09/94	v	Liverpool	(h)	1-3	Butt
22/09/94	v	Nottingham Forest (a) 0-2			
11/10/94	v	Notts County	(a)	3-1	Scholes 2, Tomlinson
17/10/94	v	Coventry City	(a)	3-0	Irving 2, Cooke
26/10/94	v	Derby County	(a)	2-3	Tomlinson, Irving
3/11/94	v	Rotherham United	(h)	0-1	
8/11/94	v	Bolton Wanderers	(a)	1-3	Irving
16/11/94	v	Sunderland	(h)	2-1	Johnson, Rawlinson
24/11/94	v	Tranmere Rovers	(a)	1-1	Butt
30/11/94	v	Coventry City	(h)	1-0	Davies
8/12/94	v	Leeds United	(h)	0-1	
11/01/95	v	Everton	(a)	0-3	
18/01/95	v	Stoke City	(h)	2-1	Ince, Kirovski
24/01/95	v	Derby County	(h)	2-2	Irving, G.Neville
1/02/95	v	Bolton Wanderers	(h)	2-4	Butt 2
8/02/95	v	Sunderland	(a)	2-3	Davies 2
16/02/95	v	Tranmere Rovers	(h)	2-1	Hughes, Beckham
20/02/95	v	Aston Villa	(a)	0-2	
15/03/95	v	Blackburn Rovers	(a)	2-2	Cooke, Irving
17/03/95	v	Sheffield United	(h)	1-1	Irving
21/03/95	v	Wolves	(h)	0-0	
4/04/95	v	Sheffield United	(a)	1-1	Kirovski
10/04/95	v	Nottingham Forest	(h)	1-1	McGibbon
12/04/95	v	West Bromwich Albion	(h)	0-0	
20/04/95	v	Stoke City	(a)	0-1	
22/04/95	v	Everton	(h)	1-0	Tomlinson
29/04/95	v	Liverpool	(a)	1-0	Tomlinson
2/05/95	v	Rotherham United	(a)	3-0	Irving, Rawlinson, Beckham
5/05/95	v	West Bromwich Albion	(a)	2-3	Tomlinson, McGibbon
11/05/95	v	Notts County	(h)	2-2	Scholes, Kirovski

'A' Team

Lancashire League Division One

20/08/94	v	Crewe Alexandra Res	(h)	0-1
27/08/94	v	Everton 'A'	(h)	4-3
3/09/94	v	Morecambe Res	(a)	2-0
10/09/94	v	Bury 'A'	(h)	5-0
17/09/94	v	Blackpool 'A'	(a)	0-0
24/09/94	v	Morecambe Res	(h)	9-0
1/10/94	v	Tranmere Rovers 'A'	(h)	5-1
8/10/94	v	Blackburn Rovers 'A'	(a)	7-2
15/10/94	v	Liverpool 'A'	(a)	2-2
22/10/94	v	Marine Reserves	(h)	3-0
29/10/94	v	Blackburn Rovs 'A'	(h)	0-3
5/11/94	v	Liverpool 'A'	(h)	1-1
12/11/94	v	Bury 'A'	(a)	3-0
19/11/94	v	Oldham Athletic 'A'	(h)	1-1
26/11/94	v	Blackpool 'A'	(h)	2-1
3/12/94	v	Burnley 'A'	(a)	3-2
17/12/94	v	Everton 'A'	(a)	4-1
7/01/95	v	Burnley 'A'	(h)	1-0
14/01/95	v	Marine Reserves	(a)	3-1
21/01/95	v	Tranmere Rovers 'A'	(a)	2-2
4/02/95	v	Oldham Athletic 'A'	(a)	4-1
11/02/95	v	Crewe Alexandra Res	(a)	4-2

'B' Team

Lancashire League Division Two

13/08/94	v	Liverpool 'B'	(a)	4-1
20/08/94	v	Man City 'A'	(a)	6-1
23/08/94	v	Stockport County 'A'	(a)	3-0
27/08/94	v	Blackpool 'B'	(a)	3-1
3/09/94	v	Marine Youth	(h)	2-2
10/09/94	v	Everton 'B'	(a)	2-2
17/09/94	v	Oldham Athletic 'B'	(h)	2-0
24/09/94	v	Burnley 'B'	(h)	6-1
1/10/94	v	Tranmere Rovers 'B'	(h)	2-1
8/10/94	v	Blackburn Rovers 'B'	(a)	0-1
15/10/94	v	Preston North End 'A'	(h)	2-2
22/10/94	v	Rochdale 'A'	(a)	1-2
29/10/94	v	Stockport County 'A'	(h)	3-0
5/11/94	v	Bury 'B'	(a)	4-1
12/11/94	v	Crewe Alexandra 'A'	(h)	5-0
19/11/94	v	Bolton Wanderers 'A'	(a)	1-0

26/11/94	v	Bury 'B'	(h)	5-0
17/12/94	v	Man City 'A'	(h)	1-5
7/01/95	v	Marine Youth	(a)	7-0
14/01/95	v	Blackpool 'B'	(h)	2-0
21/01/95	v	Bolton Wanderers 'A'	(h)	6-0
28/01/95	v	Everton 'B'	(h)	3-3
4/02/95	v	Tranmere Rovers 'B'	(a)	1-2
11/02/95	v	Burnley 'B'	(a)	0-2
18/02/95	v	Preston North End 'A'	(a)	2-3
25/02/95	v	Blackburn Rovs 'B'	(h)	1-2
11/03/95	v	Rochdale 'A'	(h)	3-3
18/03/95	v	Chester 'A'	(h)	4-0
25/03/95	v	Wigan Athletic 'A'	(h)	0-4
1/04/95	v	Chester 'A'	(a)	4-1
15/04/95	v	Wigan Athletic 'A'	(a)	1-1
22/04/95	v	Oldham Athletic 'B'	(a)	1-0
26/04/95	v	Crewe Alexandra 'A'	(a)	0-4
29/04/95	v	Carlisle Utd 'A'	(a)	2-0
6/05/95	v	Carlisle Utd 'A'	(h)	2-1
9/05/95	v	Liverpool 'B'	(h)	2-1

Pontins Central League Table

Division One

Club	P	W	D	L	F	A	Pts
Bolton Wanderers	34	22	5	7	69	46	71
Everton	34	17	10	7	63	32	61
Leeds United	34	19	4	11	53	37	61
Sheffield United	34	17	8	9	49	36	59
Tranmere Rovers	34	16	9	9	65	53	57
Derby County	34	15	7	12	51	52	52
Notts County	34	15	6	13	46	48	51
West Bromwich Albion	34	13	8	13	53	54	47
Wolverhampton Wanderers	34	12	11	11	40	52	47
MANCHESTER UNITED	34	12	9	13	45	45	45
Stoke City	34	12	7	15	46	44	43
Blackburn Rovers	34	10	12	12	31	37	42
Liverpool	34	11	9	14	41	48	42
Nottingham Forest	34	9	11	14	45	46	38
Sunderland	34	10	8	16	49	56	38
Aston Villa	34	11	4	19	41	53	37
Coventry City	34	8	7	19	30	45	31
Rotherham United	34	7	5	22	34	67	26

Division One

Club	P	W	D	L	F	A	Pts
MANCHESTER UNITED 'A'	22	15	5	2	65	24	50
Crewe Alexandra Res	22	13	5	4	65	40	44
Burnley 'A'	22	14	2	6	52	33	44
Everton 'A'	22	12	0	10	49	34	36
Blackburn Rovers 'A'	22	11	3	8	38	35	36
Tranmere Rovers 'A'	22	10	5	7	46	33	35
Liverpool 'A'	22	10	4	8	41	28	34
Oldham Athletic 'A'	22	8	4	10	34	40	28
Bury 'A'	22	7	5	10	28	44	26
Blackpool 'A'	22	6	3	13	36	50	21
Marine Res	22	4	1	17	29	64	13
Morecambe Res	22	2	3	17	14	72	9

Lancashire League

Division Two

Club	P	W	D	L	F	A	Pts
Manchester City 'A'	36	25	5	6	89	34	80
Blackburn Rovers 'B'	36	24	6	6	84	33	78
MANCHESTER UNITED 'B'	36	21	6	9	93	47	69
Preston North End 'B'	36	20	7	9	90	54	67
Liverpool 'B'	36	21	4	11	80	52	67
Crewe Alexandra 'A'	36	17	5	14	73	62	56
Tranmere Rovers 'B'	36	16	7	13	64	49	55
Everton 'B'	36	15	9	12	67	61	54
Burnley 'B'	36	16	6	14	61	66	54
Wigan Athletic 'A'	36	16	6	14	65	73	54
Oldham Athletic 'B'	36	15	5	16	54	54	50
Bolton Wanderers 'A'	36	13	10	13	43	45	49
Blackpool 'B'	36	15	3	18	70	66	48
Carlisle United 'A'	36	12	8	16	61	63	44
Stockport County 'A'	36	10	6	20	66	94	36
Chester City 'A'	36	9	6	21	49	95	33
Rochdale 'A'	36	8	6	22	44	94	30
Bury 'B'	36	7	6	23	47	92	27
Marine Youth	36	4	5	27	25	91	17

Youth Team

Lancashire FA Youth Cup

8/02/95	v	Oldham Athletic	(h)	2-1
1/05/95	v	Manchester City	(a)	0-2

FA Youth Cup

30/11/94	v	Wrexham	(h)	4-1
21/12/94	v	Charlton Athletic	(h)	1-1
12/01/95	v	Charlton Athletic	(a)	5-2
1/02/95	v	Arsenal	(h)	2-1
28/02/95	v	Aston Villa	(a)	3-2
25/03/95 (SF1)	v	Wimbledon	(h)	2-1
8/04/95 (SF2)	v	Wimbledon	(a)	3-0

(United won 5-1 on aggregate)

FA Youth Final

11/05/95 (F1)	v	Tottenham Hotspur	(a)	1-2
15/05/95 (F2)	v	Tottenham Hotspur	(h)	1-0

(United won 4-3 on penalties)

55th Swiss International Youth Tournament

(Played over Easter 1995)

	v	AC Belinzona	3-1	Kirovski 2, Cooke
	v	Napoli	0-0	
	v	Benfica	1-0	Kirovski
Final	v	Lugano	2-1	Kirovski, Thornley

Lugano had topped their Group which included Barcelona, Kaiserslautern and PSV Eindhoven.

'Ton Up Boys'

A select band of just fourteen players have scored a century or more goals for United. They are:

J	Cassidy	(1892-99)	D	Herd	(1961-67)
A	Turnbull	(1906-14)	D	Law	(1961-72)
J	Spence	(1919-32)	G	Best	(1963-73)
S	Pearson	(1937-53)	B	Robson	(1981-1994)
T	Taylor	(1952-57)	M	Hughes	(1983-1995)
D	Viollet	(1952-61)	B	McClair	(1987-
R	Charlton	(1956-72)			

There is a long list of 'one goal wonders' but since the Second World War, the following players have scored on just one occasion for United:

W Bainbridge	9/01/46	v Accrington Stanley (FA Cup)	(h)	Won 5-1
P Coyne	24/04/76	v Leicester City	(a)	Lost 1-2
L Cunningham	23/04/83	v Watford	(h)	Won 2-0
A Davies	11/04/83	v Juventus	(h)	Drew 1-1
P Edwards	17/12/69	v Man City (League Cup)	(h)	Drew 2-2
T Gibson	24/01/87	v Arsenal	(h)	Won 2-0
D Givens	30/08/69	v Sunderland	(h)	Won 3-1
D Graham	11/01/87	v QPR (FA Cup)	(a)	Drew 2-2 aet
G Hogg	7/02/84	v Birmingham City	(a)	Drew 2-2
M Jones	17/12/55	v Birmingham City	(h)	Won 2-1
A Kinsey	9/01/65	v Chester (FA Cup)	(h)	Won 2-1
R McGrath	10/12/77	v West Ham Utd	(a)	Lost 1-2
J Sivebaek	22/11/86	v QPR	(h)	Won 1-0
I Ure	13/12/69	v Liverpool	(a)	Won 4-1
T Young	3/11/73	v Chelsea	(h)	Drew 2-2

Strangely, Bainbridge, Graham, and Kinsey all scored their only goals for United in the only FA Cup–ties they ever played. Davies scored his goal in the only European match he played in, and Coyne scored his solitary goal in his only full appearance.

Manchester United

Old Trafford, Manchester, M16 0RA

Nickname: Red Devils   **Colours:** Red Shirts, White Shorts
Change: All Black or Yellow/Green Halves
Capacity: 44,622   **Pitch:** 116yds x 76yds

Officials

Chairman/Chief Executive:	Martin Edwards
Directors:	J M.Edelson, R Charlton, E M Watkins,
	A M Midani, L Olive, R P Launders.
Manager:	Alex Ferguson
Assistant Manager:	Brian Kidd
Physio:	David Feavor
Secretary:	Ken Merrett

Honours

FA Premier League Champions:	1992-93, 1993-94
FA Premier League Runners–up:	1994-95
Division 1 Champions:	1907-8, 1910-11, 1951-52, 1955-56,
	1956-57, 1964-65, 1966-67
Division 1 Runners–up:	1946-47, 1947-48, 1948-49, 1950-51,
	1958-59, 1963-64, 1967-68, 1979-80,
	1987-88, 1991-92
Division 2 Champions:	1935-36, 1974-75
Division 2 Runners–up:	1896-97, 1905-06, 1924-25, 1937-38.
FA Cup Winners:	1909, 1948, 1963, 1977, 1983, 1985, 1990
FA Cup Runners–up:	1957, 1958, 1976, 1979, 1995
Football League Cup Winners:	1991-92
Football League Cup Runners–up:	1982-83, 1990-91, 1993-94

European Honours

European Cup Winners:	1968
European Cup Winners' Cup:	1991
European Super Cup Winners:	1991

Miscellaneous Records

Record Attendance:	76,962 for FA Cup Semi-Final
	Wolves v Grimsby Town, 25th March 1939
Record League Attendance:	70,504 v Aston Villa, 27th December 1920

League History

1892	Elected to Division 1	1936-1937	Division 1
1894-1906	Division 2	1937-1938	Division 2
1906-1922	Division 1	1938-1974	Division 1
1922-1925	Division 2	1974-1975	Division 2
1925-1931	Division 1	1975-1992	Division 1
1931-1936	Division 2	1992 -	FA Premier League

Managers and Secretary-Managers

1900-12	Ernest Magnall	1944-45	Walter Crickmer
1914-21	John Robson	1945-69	Matt Busby*
1921-26	John Chapman	1969-70	Wilf McGuinness
1926-27	Clarence Hildrith	1971-72	Frank O'Farrell
1927-31	Herbert Bamlett	1972-77	Tommy Docherty
1931-32	Walter Crickmer	1977-81	Dave Sexton
1932-37	Scott Duncan	1981-86	Ron Atkinson
1938-44	Jimmy Porter	1986-	Alex Ferguson

continued as GM then Director

Birth of the Red Devils

Came into being in 1902 changing name from Newton Heath. Predecessors appear to have been formed in 1878 as Newton Heath (LYR) when workers at the Carriage and Wagon Department at the Lancashire and Yorkshire Railway formed a club. This soon outgrew railway competition.

Turned professional in 1885 and founder member of Football Alliance in 1889. In 1892 Alliance Runners–up Newton Heath was elected to an enlarged Division One of the Football League. In 1902 the club became Manchester United and, in February 1910, moved from Bank Street, Clayton, to Old Trafford. Premier League founder member 1992.

Directions:

From North:
From the M63 Junction 4 follow the signs for Manchester (A5081). Turn right after 2½ miles into Warwick Road.

From South:
From the M6 Junction 19 follow the A556 then the A56 (Altrincham). From Altrincham follow the signs for Manchester turning left into Warwick Road after six miles.

From East:
From the M62 Junction 17 take the A56 to Manchester. Follow the signs South and then to Chester. Turn right into Warwick Road after two miles.

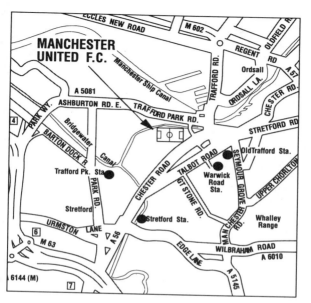

Telephone Numbers

Main Switchboard:	0161 872 1661
Ticket and Match Information:	0161 872 0199
Commercial Enquiries:	0161 872 3488
Development Association:	0161 872 4676
Membership and Supporters Office:	0161 872 5208
Club Call:	0891 121161
Museum:	0161 877 4002
Membership & Travel Info:	0161 873 8303
Executive Suite:	0161 872 3331
Superstore:	0161 872 3398

3-Year Form & Fixture Guide

Here's your guide to the 1995-96 season. It includes details of previous premiership encounters plus a few pointers as to what you can expect from the match. Dates are subject to change what with Cup matches, TV requirements and bad weather – so always double check along with kick-off times. Enjoy the games!

No	Date	Opponents	92/3	93/4	94/5	95/6
1	19/08/95	**Aston Villa (a)**	0-1	2-1	2-1	

A far from easy opener for the Reds. Although they have never lost a semi–final at Villa Park they have only won there 16 times in 62 league visits.

| 2 | 23/08/95 | **WEST HAM UNITED (h)** | – | 3-0 | 1-0 | |

United have not failed to beat West Ham at Old Trafford since August 1986 whilst the Hammers have not scored there in the FAPL. United will be expecting three points.

| 3 | 26/08/95 | **WIMBLEDON (h)** | 0-1 | 3-1 | 3-0 | |

After their shock victory over United in 1992/93 the Dons have not caused the Reds a great deal of trouble at Old Trafford and it should be another comfortable three points.

| 4 | 29/08/95 | **Blackburn Rovers (a)** | 0-0 | 0-2 | 4-2 | |

Don't expect another four goal blast from the Reds that they enjoyed last season. It could be back to the wall stuff as in 92/93 and 93/94.

| 5 | 9/09/95 | **Everton (a)** | 2-0 | 1-0 | 0-1 | |

Joe Royle has stiffened up the Toffees since his arrival and they hold two 1-0 victories over the Reds under his stewardship. A difficult one for United to negotiate.

| 6 | 16/09/95 | **BOLTON WANDERERS (h)** | – | – | – | |

Bolton have a good record against United but having lost manager Bruce Rioch they could find it difficult to come away from Old Trafford with anything.

| 7 | 23/09/95 | **Sheffield Wednesday (a)** | 3-3 | 3-2 | 0-1 | |

United have only won twelve times in over fifty league visits to Hillsborough but could improve on that this time round.

| 8 | 30/09/95 | **LIVERPOOL (h)** | 2-2 | 1-0 | 2-0 | |

Liverpool have a poor record visiting United with only eleven wins in over sixty trips but they seem to be on an upward curve again and will run the Reds close.

| 9 | 14/10/95 | **MANCHESTER CITY (h)** | 2-1 | 2-0 | 5-0 | |

Three points from this one!

No	Date	Opponents	92/3	93/4	94/5	95/6

10 21/10/95 Chelsea (a)   1-1   0-1   3-2
Chelsea have the best FAPL record of any club against United and it will be another difficult trip for the Reds especially if Mark Hughes is waiting for them!

11 28/10/95 MIDDLESBROUGH (h)   3-0   –   –
Bryan Robson will be out to prove a point but history is on United's side as they have only lost eight times at home to the North East team in 38 meetings. A ninth is not in prospect.

12 4/11/95 Arsenal (a)   1-0   2-2   0-0
Always a dour game at Highbury and things are unlikely to change as the Gunners look to defeat United for the first time in the FAPL.

13 18/11/95 SOUTHAMPTON (h)   2-1   2-0   2-1
The Saints have made things tough for United at Old Trafford in recent seasons and another close game can be expected.

14 22/11/95 Coventry City (a)   1-0   1-0   3-2
Usually one of the most boring fixtures in United's calender but last season's game was a classic. Perhaps it was no coincidence that Ron Atkinson had just taken over at Highfield Road and this could be a more entertaining trip than normal trip to Highfield Rd where the Reds hold a 100% record in the FAPL.

15 25/11/95 Nottingham Forest (a)   2-0   –   1-1
Forest could struggle without Collymore but the Reds have won only 14 times in 45 trips to the City Ground.

16 2/12/95 CHELSEA (h)   3-0   0-1   0-0
Chelsea have a good record at Old Trafford and not only in recent years. United have won only 22 times when playing hosts to the London side in over fifty league meetings and the homecoming of 'Sparky' Hughes could ignite Chelsea again.

17 9/12/95 SHEFFIELD WEDNESDAY (h)   2-1   5-0   1-0
Wednesday inflicted United's biggest ever home FA Cup defeat when putting seven past the Reds in 1961. But that's about all the success they have had when visiting the Reds as they have won only six times in over fifty league trips. Not likely to improve that record.

18 16/12/95 Liverpool (a)   2-1   3-3   0-2
Since taking a 3-0 lead at Anfield in 93/94 United have conceded five goals without reply at the home of their great rivals. They could find it tough.

19 23/12/95 Leeds United (a)   0-0   2-0   1-2
Leeds finally laid their United hoodoo to rest last season and the Reds could find it difficult to get all three points.

20 26/12/95 NEWCASTLE UNITED (h)   –   1-1   2-0
The third tricky game of an uncompromising Christmas programme but the Magpies have only won nine times in almost sixty league visits to Old Trafford.

No	Date	Opponents	92/3	93/4	94/5	95/6

21 30/12/95 QUEENS PARK RANGERS (h)   3-1   2-1   2-0
United were stunned by QPR at New Year 1992 when the London side blasted four
past the Reds at Old Trafford. But since then things have gone very much in
United's favour and should do so again.

22 1/01/96 Tottenham Hotspur (a)   1-1   1-0   1-0
United have only lost once in their last eight league visits to White Hart Lane but
the scoreline is always close.

23 13/01/96 ASTON VILLA (h)   1-1   3-1   1-0
Usually one of the best games of the season. Make it if you can.

24 20/01/96 West Ham United (a)   —   2-2   1-1
It was hardly a surprise to followers of statistics that the Reds failed to win at Upton
Park last season as United have won only seven times there in 42 league meetings.

25 3/02/96 Wimbledon (a)   2-1   0-1   1-0
United have a very average away record in the league against the Dons with just
four wins in nine visits.

26 10/02/96 BLACKBURN ROVERS (h)   3-1   1-1   1-0
Rovers have left Old Trafford on their last two visits feeling very hard done by and
will be well wound up for this fixture.

27 17/02/96 EVERTON (h)   0-3   1-0   2-0
Everton were the first team to win at Old Trafford in the FAPL but haven't scored
there since.

28 24/02/96 Bolton Wanderers (a)   —   —   —
Burnden Park is definitely one of United's least favourite grounds with only eleven
wins in almost fifty visits. Even the Busby Babes were soundly thrashed there 4-0
after winning the title in the previous two seasons!

29 2/03/96 Newcastle United (a)   —   1-1   1-1
The last two season's results at St James Park indicate absolutely nothing between
the two teams and another close encounter can be expected.

30 9/03/96 LEEDS UNITED (h)   2-0   0-0   0-0
Forget last season's 3-1 FA Cup victory over the Yorkshire side. They regularly
come to Old Trafford under Howard Wilkinson with the sole intention of
containing the Reds and are likely to do so again. No league win for Leeds at Old
Trafford since Feb 1981.

31 16/03/96 Queens Park Rangers (a)   3-1   3-2   3-2
United had a poor record at Loftus Road in the Football League with just four wins
and 18 goals in 15 trips but things have looked up for the Reds in the FAPL with a
100% record and nine goals in three visits.

32 23/03/96 TOTTENHAM HOTSPUR (h)   4-1   2-1   0-0

Always one of the season's most attractive fixtures with Spurs usually on the wrong end of the result as they have won only once on their last seventeen league visits to Old Trafford.

33 30/03/96 ARSENAL (h)   0-0   1-0   3-0

A repeat of last season's scoreline would see United clock up their 150th home league goal against the Gunners who have won only 12 of their 76 visits. Arsenal not yet scored against United at Old Trafford in the FAPL.

34 6/04/96 Manchester City (a)   1-1   3-2   3-0

City's big day of the season. Three points for United.

35 8/04/96 COVENTRY CITY (h)   5-0   0-0   2-0

Coventry have not found the net on their last six league visits to Old Trafford but will have a better chance of doing so under Big Ron than any of their previous managers.

36 13/04/96 Southampton (a)   1-0   3-1   2-2

No defeat for United in their last six league trips to the Dell.

37 27/04/96 NOTTINGHAM FOREST (h)   2-0   –   1-2

United had their impressive home record dented last season by Forest and will be looking for a return to their earlier form against the Midlands side who had won only eight of 44 visits prior to last season.

38 4/05/96 Middlesbrough (a)   1-1   –   –

Could be a dilemma for Bryan Robson if United need to win to capture the title and his own side's future is already decided!